⤳ CATO ⤴
SUPREME COURT
REVIEW

2020 — 2021

CATO
SUPREME COURT
REVIEW

2020—2021

ILYA SHAPIRO
Publisher

ROGER PILON
Founder

TREVOR BURRUS
Editor in Chief

ROBERT A. LEVY
Associate Editor

CLARK NEILY
Associate Editor

WALTER OLSON
Associate Editor

THOMAS A. BERRY
Managing Editor

WILL YEATMAN
Associate Editor

Board of Advisors

ROBERT A. LEVY
CENTER FOR CONSTITUTIONAL STUDIES

INSTITUTE
Washington, D.C.

THE CATO SUPREME COURT REVIEW (ISBN 978-1-952223-24-2) is published annually at the close of each Supreme Court term by the Cato Institute, 1000 Massachusetts Ave., N.W.,Washington, D.C. 20001-5403.

CORRESPONDENCE. Correspondence regarding subscriptions, changes of address, procurement of back issues, advertising and marketing matters, and so forth, should be addressed to:

Publications Department
The Cato Institute
1000 Massachusetts Ave., N.W.
Washington, D.C. 20001

All other correspondence, including requests to quote or reproduce material, should be addressed to the editor.

CITATIONS: Citation to this volume of the Review should conform to the following style: 2020-2021 Cato Sup. Ct. Rev. (2021).

DISCLAIMER. The views expressed by the authors of the articles are their own and are not attributable to the editor, the editorial board, or the Cato Institute.

INTERNET ADDRESS. Articles from past editions are available to the general public, free of charge, at www.cato.org/pubs/scr.

978-1-952223-24-2 (print)
978-1-952223-25-9 (digital)

Printed in the United States of America.

Cato Institute
1000 Massachusetts Ave., N.W.
Washington, D.C. 20001
www.cato.org

Published through the generosity of George M. Yeager

Contents

Contents

A Court in Flux That Doesn't Need "Reform"

Ilya Shapiro*

The Cato Institute's Robert A. Levy Center for Constitutional Studies is pleased to publish this 20th volume of the *Cato Supreme Court Review*, an annual critique of the Court's most important decisions from the term just ended plus a look at the term ahead. We are the first such journal to be released, and the only one that approaches its task from a classical liberal, Madisonian perspective, grounded in the nation's first principles, liberty through constitutionally limited government. We release this volume each year at Cato's annual Constitution Day symposium on September 17, a day that really ought to be celebrated as much as July 4 and, belatedly, June 19 (Juneteenth, our newest federal holiday).

Of course, the fact that we can even have an in-person symposium again marks a bit of a return to normal, or perhaps a new normal as the COVID-19 pandemic wanes—or becomes an endemic part of our lives like the common cold (which actually covers many different viral strains, including coronaviruses). We may still be dealing with lingering mask mandates and other restrictions of dubious constitutionality—let alone policy wisdom—but at least vaccines and therapeutics allow most of us to live our lives essentially as in the "before times."

The same could also be said about the Supreme Court, not in terms of scientific developments, but that the addition of three new

* Vice president and director, Robert A. Levy Center for Constitutional Studies, Cato Institute; publisher, *Cato Supreme Court Review*. This foreword in part adapts my July 20, 2021 testimony before the Presidential Commission on the Supreme Court, which in turn adapted part of my book, *Supreme Disorder: Judicial Nominations and the Politics of America's Highest Court* (Regnery Gateway 2020).

justices in the last four years hasn't yet transformed the body as it returns to in-person arguments. This past term was supposed to be the coming-out party for a new, 6-3 hyper-conservative Court, but—despite the last day's high-profile cases that broke on such "partisan" lines, correctly resolving issues of election regulation and donor disclosure—was marked largely by surprising unanimity and never-before-seen splits. There just weren't too many ideological-looking decisions, though that's partly because the more pragmatic justices forged grand compromises.

More savvy observers are calling it the 3-3-3 Court, with Stephen Breyer, Sonia Sotomayor, and Elena Kagan on the left; Clarence Thomas, Samuel Alito, and Neil Gorsuch on the right; and John Roberts, Brett Kavanaugh, and Amy Coney Barrett in the middle (or center-right). I'm not yet convinced of that, even if that's a correct general description of how the justices align relative to each other. And recall that the biggest recent conservative "betrayal" was Justice Gorsuch's authorship last year of *Bostock v. Clayton County*—but that's only if conservatives don't consider Chief Justice Roberts worth counting on at all anymore.

Perhaps most notably, Justice Barrett shocked doomsayers (but nobody else) by ruling according to her own brand of jurisprudence more than any political agenda. She joined her Democratic-appointed colleagues when the law, as she saw it, demanded it, including in the 7-2 majority that rejected the latest (and last) existential challenge to Obamacare. Those senators, activists, and pundits who acted during her confirmation process as if she were nominated to take health care away from millions were either misinformed or disingenuous (or both).

Interestingly, the "shadow" docket—a range of orders and summary decisions other than in cases that enjoy full briefing and argument—showed Barrett's impact more than the regular one. Before Justice Ruth Bader Ginsburg died, the Court sustained pandemic-related restrictions on religious services, 5-4 with Roberts joining the liberals. After "ACB" joined the Court, it started blocking similar restrictions, with the chief in dissent.

Justice Barrett wasn't alone in defying expectations. When you look at the numbers, the justices were all over the place—except Justice Kavanaugh, who was in the majority in all but two cases and is the definitive man in the middle. This mish-mash is the ultimate vindication for Justice Breyer, who at a Harvard lecture in April repeated that the Court is a *legal* rather than political institution. The Court's politics-avoidance tamped down calls for court-packing and other radical changes—though we'll see what the presidential commission on the Supreme Court comes up with when it issues its report (due November 15, right in time for Thanksgiving).

And speaking of Breyer, court-watchers waited with bated breath for word of whether he'd retire. The oldest justice, having just turned 83, is well aware of the Democrats' razor-thin Senate margin, but he's enjoying finally becoming the leader of the liberal bloc (having initially been the junior justice for 11 years, the longest of anyone since the Court was fixed at nine seats). It also could be that pressure from progressive activists marginally pushed him to stay another year ahead of the 2022 midterms. In any case, even as Democrats fear a repeat of the late Justice Ginsburg's refusal to retire when their party last held both the White House and Senate, that concern won't truly ripen until next year.

Interestingly, this term had the second-lowest number of opinions after argument (57) since the Civil War, topping only the previous term, when the pandemic forced the postponement of oral arguments and bumped some cases into this term. So the Court is being stingy with its cert. grants, which frustrates advocates who see many worthy petitions inexplicably denied—or sometimes with one, two, or even three dissents from denial (which shows that, however they rule on the merits, Justices Kavanaugh and Barrett are more cautious on this aspect of the shadow docket).

But note that 27 of those 57 opinions were decided unanimously. When you add in the cases with one dissent, you're already at 60 percent of the docket—so the narrative of a starkly divided Court is false. There were only a dozen 6-3 opinions and half a dozen 5-4 ones. Notably, Chief Justice Roberts issued his first-ever solo dissent, in the nominal-damages student speech case of *Uzuegbunam v. Preczewski.*

But back to Kavanaugh: the only other justices in the last half-century who were in the majority as much as he was this term (97 percent of the time) are Roberts last year and Anthony Kennedy three times. Kavanaugh isn't exactly a "swing" vote—there were six different alignments in the 6-3 cases and five in the 5-4 cases—but he's definitely at the Court's center. Not surprisingly, Justice

Sotomayor was least in the majority, being on the winning side in fewer than half the nonunanimous cases. Also not surprisingly, Kavanaugh and Roberts continue to be the justices most likely to agree, while Sotomayor and Alito are least likely to be on the same side.

The Ninth Circuit attained a magnificent 1-15 record—the one affirmance was in the NCAA antitrust case—keeping its crown as the biggest loser (unless you count courts with few reviewed cases). It may not maintain that dubious distinction for long, however, because President Trump's ten appointments to that court mean that there are now five circuits with a higher ratio of Democratic to Republican-appointed judges (and thus presumably, but not automatically, less in sync with the Supreme Court). But really, wherever your appeal originates, getting the justices to take your case is most of the battle; this term, an amazing 80 percent of lower court rulings on the regular (sunshine?) docket were reversed or vacated.

Finally, getting back to my original theme, the liberal bloc was in the majority in 13 of the 29 nonunanimous decisions, and there were only six "partisan" 6-3 decisions. So while the Court certainly leans right in conventional shorthand, it's very much in flux.

Still, the last few years have shown that the Supreme Court is now covered by the same toxic cloud that has enveloped all the nation's public discourse. Although it's still respected more than most institutions, it's increasingly viewed through a political lens. What most concerns people is how judicial politics affect the Court's "legitimacy"—a broader subject that I've written about elsewhere—but given the controversy over the confirmation of the previous administration's three justices, what lessons can we draw from the history of confirmation battles? I came up with seven, and they show that, to the extent we need institutional reform, it has nothing to do with process or structural issues.

1. Politics Has Always Been Part of the Process

Politics has always been part of the process of selecting and confirming judicial nominees. From the early republic, presidents have picked justices for reasons that include balancing regional interests, supporting policy priorities, and providing representation to key constituencies. They've tried to find people in line with their own political thinking, and that of their party and supporters. Look at the judicial battles of John Adams and Thomas Jefferson, with the Midnight Judges Act: the original court-packing. There's never been a golden age when "merit" as an objective measure of legal acumen was the sole consideration for judicial selection.

And control of the Senate is key. Historically, the Senate has confirmed fewer than 60 percent of Supreme Court nominees under divided government, as compared to just under 90 percent when the president's party controlled the Senate. Timing matters too: over 80 percent of nominees in the first three years of a presidential term have been confirmed, but barely more than half in the fourth year. Combining these disparities shows that only 20 percent of election-year nominees have been confirmed under divided government but 90 percent under united.

Nearly half the presidents have had at least one unsuccessful nomination, starting with George Washington and running all the way through Barack Obama. In all, of 164 nominations formally sent to the Senate, only 127 were confirmed, a success rate of 77 percent. Of those 127, one died before taking office and seven declined to serve, the last one in 1882—an occurrence unlikely ever to happen again. Of the rest, 12 were rejected, 12 were withdrawn, ten expired without the Senate's taking any action, and three were "postponed indefinitely" or tabled. So the 2016 blockade of Merrick Garland was hardball politics, but hardly unprecedented.

2. Confirmation Fights Are Now Driven by Judicial Philosophy

To a certain extent, the politicization of Supreme Court appointments has tracked political divisions nationally. But couching opposition in terms of judicial philosophy is a relatively new phenomenon.

Earlier controversies tended to revolve around either the president's relationship with the Senate or deviations from shared understandings of the factors that go into nominations for particular seats—especially geography and patronage. That dynamic is markedly different from the ideological considerations we see now for at least two reasons. With the culmination of several trends whereby divergent interpretive theories map onto partisan preferences at a time when the parties are ideologically sorted and polarized, it's impossible for a president to find an "uncontroversial" nominee.

The conservative legal movement, meanwhile, has learned its lesson; "no more Souters" means there must be a proven record, not simply center-right views and affiliations, showing not telling a commitment to originalism and textualism. The entire reason candidate Trump released his list was to convince Republicans, as well as cultural conservatives who may otherwise have stayed home or voted Democrat, that he could be trusted to appoint the right kind of judges. This was a real innovation, and we could see lists become standard practice, even if candidates from the two parties might use different criteria for shaping those lists, with more concern for demographic representation among the Democrats, who have a broader swath of lawyers to choose from.

3. Modern Confirmations Are Different Because the Political Culture Is Different

The inflection point for our legal culture, as for our social and political culture, was 1968, which ended that 70-year near-perfect run of nominations. Until that point, most justices were confirmed by voice vote, without having to take a roll call. Since then, there hasn't been a single voice vote, not even for the five justices confirmed unanimously or the four whose no votes were in the single digits. And despite those "easy" confirmations, we've seen an upswing in no votes; five of the closest eight confirmation margins have come in the last 30 years. Not surprisingly, the increased opposition and scrutiny has also signaled an increase in the time it takes to confirm a justice; six of the eight longest confirmations have come since 1986.

There are many factors going into the contentiousness of the last half-century: the Warren Court's activism and then *Roe v. Wade* spawned a conservative reaction; the growth of presidential power to the point where the Senate felt the need to reassert itself; the culture of scandal since Watergate; a desire for transparency when technology allows not just a 24-hour media cycle but a constant *and instant* delivery of information and opinion; and, fundamentally, more divided government. As the Senate has grown less deferential, and presidential picks more ideological, the clashes have grown.

To put a finer point on it, all but one failed nomination since Abe Fortas in 1968 have come when the opposite party controlled the Senate. The one exception is Harriet Miers, who withdrew because she was the first nominee since Harrold Carswell in 1969 to be seen as not up to the task. For that matter, this turbulent modern period has seen few outright rejections—just three in 53 years—with prenomination vetting and Senate consultation obviating most problematic picks. At the same time, the inability to object to qualifications has led to manufactured outrage and scandal-mongering.

4. Hearings Have Become Kabuki Theater

Public hearings have only been around for a century, starting with the contested Louis Brandeis nomination in 1916. But Brandeis didn't testify himself; it simply wasn't regular practice until the 1950s, when Dixiecrats used hearings to rail against *Brown v. Board of Education*. Otherwise, hearings became perfunctory discussions of personal biography. John Paul Stevens, the first nominee after *Roe v. Wade*, wasn't even asked about that case—which was already controversial, have no doubt.

Things changed in the 1980s, not coincidentally when the hearings began to be televised. Now all senators ask questions but nominees largely refuse to answer, creating what Elena Kagan 25 years ago called a "vapid and hollow charade." But even with this conventional narrative, there has been a subtle shift; from Robert Bork in 1987 through Stephen Breyer in 1994, nominees went into some detail about doctrine. Clarence Thomas discussed natural law and the role that the Declaration of Independence plays in constitutional interpretation. Ruth Bader Ginsburg talked about gender equality and the relationship between liberty and privacy.

Beginning with John Roberts in 2005, however, the nominees still covered the holdings of cases and what lawyers call "black letter law"—what you need to know to get a good grade in law school—but there's been little revelation of personal opinions. These days, senators try to get nominees to admit that certain controversial cases are "settled law," whether *Roe* when coming from a Democrat or *District of Columbia v. Heller* from a Republican. Of course, when you're dealing with the Supreme Court, law is settled until it isn't, so nominees have come to say that every ruling is "due all the respect of a precedent of the Supreme Court," or some such. And that's before we even get to last-minute accusations of sexual impropriety.

5. Every Nomination Can Have a Significant Impact

The confirmation process has little to do with being a judge or justice. Once that spectacle is over, the new justice takes his or her seat among new colleagues—a lifetime "team of nine," as Justice Kavanaugh called it at his hearing—to begin reading briefs and considering technical legal issues. As former White House Counsel Don McGahn has described, "it's a Hollywood audition to join a monastery."

Regardless, as the late Justice Byron White was fond of saying, every justice creates a new Court, so each change shakes up the previous balance. Not all historically significant cases would've turned out differently if one justice were replaced, but some would have. And not simply by changing the party of the president making the appointment. The *Slaughterhouse Cases*, which eviscerated the Fourteenth Amendment's protections against state action, was a 5-4 ruling with Lincoln appointees split 2-3, Grant appointees split 2-1, and a Buchanan appointee breaking the tie. *Lochner v. New York* was another 5-4, with Republican appointees split 3-3 and Democratic appointees split 2-1.

And all that's before we get to the modern era, when we got used to having certain justices as the swing votes on issues ranging from affirmative action and redistricting to religion in the public square and gay rights. So many cases would've been decided differently had the conservative Bork been confirmed instead of the moderate Kennedy, and differently still had the libertarian Douglas Ginsburg—President Reagan's next nominee after Bork, who withdrew after revelations of marijuana use—occupied that seat. For that matter, had Edith Jones been nominated in 1990 instead of David Souter, Kennedy wouldn't have been the median vote from 2005 to 2018; John Roberts would've been. And if Michael Luttig had been picked instead of Roberts in 2005, it would've been a *very* different Court these last 16 years.

In part because they've been burned so many times, Republicans focus on the Court as an election issue much more than Democrats. *Bush v. Gore*, *Citizens United*, and *Shelby County*, the three biggest progressive losses of the last 25 years, have riled activists and elites, and ratcheted up confirmation battles, but haven't translated into campaigns regarding judges as such. Democrats may now be catching up, even though *during* the Garland experience, they didn't make much of the vacancy.

Moreover, vacancies have become more important in the last half-century because justices now serve longer. Before 1970, the average tenure of a Supreme Court justice was less than 15 years. Since then, it's been more than 25. Justices appointed at or before age 50, like Roberts, Kagan, Gorsuch, and Barrett, are likely to serve 35 years, or about nine presidential terms. Justice Thomas, who was 43 when he joined the Court and has already served 30 years, could stay on another decade!

6. The Hardest Confirmations Come When There's a Potential for a Big Shift

Replacing liberal lion Thurgood Marshall with counterculture conservative Clarence Thomas was a fight, but appointing Antonin Scalia to William Rehnquist's seat when Rehnquist was elevated was a cakewalk. Would Kavanaugh have faced such strong opposition if he had been nominated for Thomas's seat? Would there have been as big a ruckus last fall if President Trump were replacing Justice Thomas rather than Justice Ginsburg? Will the fight to replace Justice Breyer be fiercer under President Biden or a Republican president?

Of course, presidents aren't always successful in moving the Court in their preferred direction. Thomas Jefferson tried valiantly to dislodge the powerful Federalist judicial impulse, only to see his nominees fall under John Marshall's sway. Abraham Lincoln named Treasury Secretary Salmon P. Chase as chief justice, partly to get him out of his hair, but more importantly to uphold the legislation by which the federal government had financed the Civil War. Instead, Chief Justice Chase wrote the opinion finding the Legal Tender Act unconstitutional. Teddy Roosevelt should've been pleased with the great progressive Oliver Wendell Holmes, but after a major antitrust case, TR inveighed that "I could carve out of a banana a judge with more backbone than that."

Woodrow Wilson, a renowned scholar of jurisprudence and thus in theory more sensitive to these concerns than most other presidents, named another storied progressive, Brandeis, but also the most retrograde justice of that or possibly any time, James Clark McReynolds, who didn't seem to share any of Wilson's views other than with regard to antitrust (and bigotry). Calvin Coolidge's sole nominee, Harlan F. Stone, would end up betraying his benefactor's laissez-faire proclivities by joining with Holmes and Brandeis in taking the Court in a judicially restrained, and therefore progressive, direction. Harry Truman called putting Tom Clark on the Supreme Court his "biggest mistake" after Justice Clark ruled against his 1952 seizure of steel mills. Dwight Eisenhower was disappointed with both Earl Warren and William Brennan, although the latter was more of a political calculation ahead of the 1956 election, intended to help with the Catholic (and crossover Democrat) vote. Nixon's appointment of Harry Blackmun similarly mitigated the reversal of the Warren Court that he had hoped to achieve. I could go on.

Moreover, a nominee picked for his views on the issues of the day might act contrary to type when the issue mix changes. The judicial restraint of Felix Frankfurter, a New Deal progressive who co-founded the ACLU, made him a conservative in the postwar era, while John Roberts's similar restraint led him to defer both to a wartime president and a peacetime Congress.

7. The Court Rules on So Many Controversies That Political Battles Are Unavoidable

Under the Framers' Constitution, by which the country more-or-less lived for its first 150 years, the Supreme Court hardly ever had to curtail a federal law. If you read the Congressional Record of the 18th and 19th centuries, Congress debated whether particular legislation was constitutional much more than whether something was a good idea. In 1887, Grover Cleveland vetoed an appropriation of $10,000 for seeds to Texas farmers who were suffering from a terrible drought because he could find no warrant for such appropriation in the Constitution.

Judges play bigger roles today; as the Court has allowed the government to grow, so has its own power to police the federal programs its own jurisprudence enabled. For example, the idea that the General Welfare Clause justifies any legislation that gains a majority in Congress—as opposed to *limiting* federal reach to national issues—emerged in the Progressive Era. In the 1930s and '40s, we thus had the perverse expansion of the Commerce Clause with cases like *NLRB v. Jones & Laughlin* and *Wickard v. Filburn*, which gained renewed prominence in the constitutional debate over Obamacare.

We've also had the flipside of the expansion of powers: the warping of rights. In 1938, the infamous Footnote Four in the *Carolene Products* case bifurcated our rights such that certain rights are more equal than others in a kind of *Animal Farm* approach to the Constitution. So it's the New Deal Court that politicized the Constitution, and thus also the confirmation process, by laying the foundation for judicial mischief of every stripe.

In that light, modern confirmation battles are all part of, and a logical response to, political incentives, to which senators are merely responding. As my predecessor Roger Pilon wrote presciently nearly 20 years ago, "Because constitutional principles limiting federal power to enumerated ends have been ignored, the scope of federal power and the subjects open to federal concern are determined now by politics alone. Because the rights that would limit the exercise of that power are grounded increasingly not in the Constitution's first principles but in the subjective understandings of judges about evolving social values, they too increasingly reflect the politics of the day."[1]

The ever-expanding size and scope of the federal government has increased the number of issues brought under Washington's control, while the collection of those new federal powers in the administrative state has transferred ultimate decision-making authority to the courts. The imbalance between the executive branch and Congress has made the Supreme Court into the decider both of controversial social issues and complex policy disputes.

Possible Changes to the Confirmation Process

But will any reforms to the confirmation process change the toxic dynamic people complain about? Should we have rules for how many days after a nomination there must be a hearing and then a vote? Maybe we should consider restoring the filibuster for nominees— although Gorsuch was the first and only Supreme Court nominee subjected to a partisan filibuster. Of course, if we had the political alignment for these kinds of changes, we wouldn't have the toxic atmosphere we're in, so it's a chicken-and-egg problem.

Henry Saad, a former Michigan Court of Appeals judge whose nomination to the Sixth Circuit was filibustered under George W. Bush, has proposed a number of reforms to the nomination and confirmation process, most of which are relevant only to the

[1] Roger Pilon, "How Constitutional Corruption Has Led to Ideological Litmus Tests for Judicial Nominees," Cato Inst. Pol'y Analysis No. 446, at 11, Aug. 6, 2002.

lower courts.[2] With respect to reforms that would apply equally to Supreme Court nominees, Saad would make it a violation of judicial ethics for nominees to give their opinions about a case, while making hearings untelevised, with questions submitted in writing, restricted to professional qualifications, and asked by the chief counsel for each party's judiciary committee members. Some committees allow this in other contexts, and while it didn't seem to work very well for Republicans in the supplemental Kavanaugh hearing, that was largely a function of the five-minute increments the counsel questioning was forced into. Any personal information or ethical concerns could be handled in the confidential session that the judiciary committee already holds to discuss the FBI background investigation and other sensitive matters.

These sort of post-nomination proposals are healthy because they target the spectacle that confirmations have become, with senators either not equipped to handle the required lines of questioning or grandstanding to produce a gotcha moment, or at least B-roll for campaign videos. "It's like testifying in a restaurant," quipped Don McGahn, with photographers clicking away in front and protestors haranguing in the back. And it's not like we learn anything about nominees, who are now coached to avoid saying anything newsworthy.

I've come to the conclusion that we should get rid of hearings altogether, that they've served their purpose for a century but now inflict greater cost on the Court, Senate, and rule of law than any informational or educational benefit. Nominees have instantly searchable records these days—going back to collegiate writings and other digitized archives—so is there any need to subject them, and the country, to a public inquisition? At the very least, the Senate could hold nomination hearings entirely in closed session.

Outside-the-box thinking should be commended and proposals to improve confirmation processes shouldn't be discounted lightly, especially if cosmetic or easy changes would enhance public confidence in the Court's integrity. I'm willing to consider anything that would show that there's a difference between interpreting the law and making it, between judging and legislating.

---

[2] Henry Saad, remarks at conference on "The Politics of Judicial Nominations in an Age of Mistrust," Princeton Univ., Mar. 6, 2020.

But I'm not sure any of these formalistic changes would do anything given that it's not a breakdown in the rules that caused the poisonous atmosphere surrounding nominations, but the other way around. All of this "reform" discussion boils down to re-arranging the deck chairs on a sinking ship. And this Titanic is not the appointment process, but the ship of state. The fundamental problem we face, and that the Supreme Court faces, is the politicization not of the *process* but of the *product*. The only way judicial confirmations will be detoxified, and the only way we reverse the trend whereby people increasingly see judges as "Trump judges" and "Obama judges," is for the Supreme Court to restore our constitutional order by returning improperly amassed federal power to the states, while forcing Congress to legislate on the remaining truly national issues rather than letting bureaucratic rules govern us.

*   *   *

As one Court watcher wrote a quarter-century ago, "Today's confirmation battles are no longer government affairs between the President and the Senate; they are public affairs open to a broad range of players. Thus, overt lobbying, public opinion polls, advertising campaigns, focus groups, and public appeals have all become a routine part of the process."[3] Those trends have only accelerated in the intervening 25 years, such that Supreme Court nominations are perhaps the highest-profile set-pieces in the American political system. Not even set-pieces but months-long slogs. Once the inside game of picking the nominee ends, the outside game begins, culminating in the literally made-for-TV hearing and then a vote that can be just as dramatic.

It's not good, but we've gotten here because Congress and the presidency have gradually taken more power for themselves, and the Supreme Court has allowed them to get away with it, aggrandizing itself in the process. As we've gone down that warped jurisprudential track, the judiciary now affects the direction of public policy more than ever—so of course judicial confirmations are going to be fraught.

There are two big buckets of cases where that dynamic has contributed to the ratcheting up of tensions that has both crumbled

[3] John A. Maltese, The Selling of the Supreme Court Nominees 143 (1995).

Senate norms and filtered down into lower-court nominations: (1) cultural issues, ranging from abortion and LGBTQ issues to the Second Amendment and death penalty, and (2) what I'll call "size of government" issues, which encompasses everything from environmental regulations to Obamacare, guidance documents to enforcement practices. And then there's an overlay of "structural" cases on election regulation whose legal issues in the abstract shouldn't have partisan valence, but in the real world of American politics obviously do.

As the response of the conservative legal movement to various judicial provocations has shifted, the debate over that constellation of issues has crystallized. From calls for restraint in the face of the Warren Court's making up social policy out of whole cloth—which ultimately led to too much deference to the political branches, and thus a long-term loss for constitutional governance—the focus now is on engaging the law instead of exercising what Alexander Bickel called the "passive virtues." Indeed, "activism" has become a vacuous term that conveys only disagreement with the judge or opinion being criticized. The battle has been joined over the legal theory rather than judicial process.

That is, so long as we accept that judicial review is constitutional and appropriate in the first place—how a judiciary is supposed to ensure that the government secures and protects our liberties without it is beyond me—then we should only be concerned that a court "gets it right," regardless of whether that correct interpretation leads to the challenged law being upheld or overturned. To paraphrase John Roberts at his confirmation hearings, the "little guy" should win when he's in the right, and the big corporation should win when it's in the right. The dividing line, then, is not between judicial activism (or passivism) and judicial restraint, but between legitimate and vigorous judicial engagement and illegitimate judicial imperialism.

The judicial debates we've seen the last few decades were never really about the nominees themselves—just like proposals for court-packing and the like aren't about "good government." They're about the Court's direction. The left in particular needs its social and regulatory agendas, as promulgated by the executive branch, to get through the judiciary, because they would never pass as legislation at the national level. That's why progressive forces pull out all the stops against originalist nominees who would enforce limits on federal power. Indeed, all the big nominee blowups in modern times have come with Republican appointments. The one quasi-exception didn't involve any attacks on the nominee, but the rare case of an election-year vacancy arising under divided government.

If nominations were depoliticized, whether through term limits or any other reforms, or some unpredictable shock that recalibrated norms, that would likewise depoliticize the exercise of judicial power, both in perception and reality. But term limits would take a constitutional amendment and everything else is either completely unworkable or doesn't actually solve the identified problem. We can't just wave a magic wand and go back to some halcyon age where the issues we faced as a country, the development of the law, and the political dynamic, were all different. "If they could truly, truly go back, I hear from most senators that they would prefer a return to the pre-nuclear-option days," Ron Klain observed to me, drawing on his experience with judicial nominations in the Clinton and Obama administrations. The man who's now President Biden's chief of staff (some say "prime minister") continued, "in many ways, it's easier for them now, because there's very little constituency for voting for the other party's nominees."

The only lasting solution to what ails our body juridic is to return to the Founders' Constitution by rebalancing and devolving power, so Washington isn't making so many big decisions for the whole country. Depoliticizing the judiciary and toning down our confirmation process is a laudable goal, but that'll happen only when judges go back to judging rather than bending over backwards to ratify the constitutional abuses of the other branches.

The judiciary needs to once again hold politicians'—and bureaucrats'—feet to the constitutional fire by rejecting overly broad legislation of dubious constitutional warrant, thus curbing executive-agency overreach and putting the ball back in Congress's court. And by returning power to the people, while ensuring that local majorities don't invade individual constitutional rights. After all, the separation of powers and federalism exist not as a dry exercise in Madisonian political theory but as a means to that singular end of protecting our freedom.

Ultimately, judicial power is not a means to an end, but an enforcement mechanism for the strictures of a founding document intended just as much to curtail the excesses of democracy as to empower its exercise. In a country ruled by law, and not men, the proper response to an unpopular legal decision is to change the law or amend the Constitution. Any other method leads to a sort of judicial abdication and the loss of those very rights and liberties that can only be vindicated through the judicial process. Or to government by black-robed philosopher kings—and as Justice Scalia liked to say, why would we choose nine lawyers for that job?

The reason we have these heated court battles is that the federal government is simply making too many decisions at a national level for such a large, diverse, and pluralistic country. There's no more reason that there needs to be a one-size-fits-all health care system, for example, than that zoning laws must be uniform in every city. Let federal legislators make the hard calls about truly national issues like defense or (actually) interstate (actual) commerce, but let states and localities make most of the decisions that affect our daily lives. Let Texas be Texas and California be California. That's the only way we're going to defuse tensions in Washington, whether in the halls of Congress or in the marble palace of the highest court in the land.

Introduction

*Trevor Burrus**

This is the 20th volume of the *Cato Supreme Court Review*, the nation's first in-depth critique of the Supreme Court term just ended, plus a look at the term ahead. Things changed last year, my second year as editor in chief, as the COVID-19 pandemic shut down Cato's offices and the *Review* had to be put together while working remotely. We then had a virtual version of our annual Constitution Day symposium, which came together nicely, all things considered. Now, as the pandemic continues to persist in many ways, Cato's employees are still working mostly remotely, and the future remains distressingly uncertain. That also applies to the Supreme Court, which hasn't yet announced whether oral arguments will continue to be conducted telephonically for the October 2021 term.

While the pandemic continues, it can't stop the *Cato Supreme Court Review*. We release the *Review* every year in conjunction with our annual Constitution Day symposium (which this year will be both online and in person), less than three months after the previous term ends and two weeks before the next term begins. It would be difficult to produce a law journal faster, even under normal conditions. The Court typically likes to hold big decisions until the end of June—rarely going into July—but in 2020 the last decision was issued July 9. In 2021, it was a little better, with the last major decisions coming down July 1. Our authors work hard to produce quality work in a short time. I thank them for that. Some even submitted early, which allowed us to get a welcomed head start on our furious editing process.

We're proud that this isn't a typical law review, filled with long, esoteric articles on, say, the influence of Immanuel Kant on evidentiary

---

* Research fellow, Robert A. Levy Center for Constitutional Studies, Cato Institute, and editor in chief, *Cato Supreme Court Review*.

approaches in 18th-century Bulgaria.[1] Instead, this is a book of essays on law intended for everyone from lawyers and judges to educated laymen and interested citizens. This year, we asked our authors to adhere to even shorter word counts. I think the result is a tighter and more readable edition.

Despite some authors' attachment to them, we try to keep footnotes relatively low in number and length, and we don't make our authors provide cites for sentences like "the Internet exploded in the late 90s" (as once happened to me). There's more than enough esoteric legal scholarship out there, and the workings of the Supreme Court should be, as much as possible, accessible and understandable to average citizens. In the end, the Constitution is sustained by Americans' belief in it, and every year the justices write several thousand words explaining and expounding on our founding document. This review provides a deeper look into a few of the most important decisions.

And we're happy to confess our bias: It's the same bias that infected Thomas Jefferson when he drafted the Declaration of Independence and James Madison as he contemplated a new plan for the government of the United States. After discarding ideas like the divine right of kings and other theories by which governments are said to be imbued with a monopoly on the legitimate use of force in a geographic area, Enlightenment thinkers, most prominently John Locke, properly concluded that governments don't inherently have any power whatsoever. Like a pile of stones found in the woods, a government, by itself, is not a moral agent or an object of moral concern. Yet if someone takes those stones and turns them into a house, that pile of stones becomes an object of moral concern—a piece of property—via the actions of

---

[1] Chief Justice John Roberts once opined on the uselessness of law reviews: "Pick up a copy of any law review that you see and the first article is likely to be, you know, the influence of Immanuel Kant on evidentiary approaches in 18th-century Bulgaria, or something, which I'm sure was of great interest to the academic that wrote it, but isn't of much help to the bar." Remarks at the Annual Fourth Circuit Court of Appeals Jud. Conf. 28:45–32:05 (June 25, 2011), https://cs.pn/30QsLpx. See also Orin S. Kerr, The Influence of Immanuel Kant on Evidentiary Approaches in 18th-Century Bulgaria, 18 Green Bag 2d 251, 251 (2015) ("Chief Justice Roberts has drawn attention to the influence of Immanuel Kant on evidentiary approaches in 18th-century Bulgaria. No scholarship has analyzed Kant's influence in that context. This Article fills the gap in the literature by exploring Kant's influence on evidentiary approaches in 18th-century Bulgaria. It concludes that Kant's influence, in all likelihood, was none.").

the primary moral agent: a rights-holding person. Governments don't have rights, they have powers. People have rights and they can sometimes delegate to a government the power to secure those rights. Or, as was once said by a much wiser person: "That to secure these rights, Governments are instituted among Men, deriving their just powers from the consent of the governed."

Individual liberty is protected and secured by a government of delegated, enumerated, separated, and thus limited powers. Through the ratification process, the People created a federal government bound by the strictures of the Constitution. A government that acts beyond those powers is not just unconstitutional, it is fundamentally immoral and illegitimate. It is pure force without reason or justification.

The delicate balance of powers within the government is partially maintained by a judiciary that enforces the Constitution according to its original public meaning, which sometimes means going against the "will of the people" and striking down popularly enacted legislation. The Constitution is not an authorization for "good ideas." Everyone who cares about the Constitution should be able to think of something that they believe is a good idea but is unconstitutional, as well as something that is a bad idea but is constitutionally authorized. If you can't think of such examples, then you don't really believe in the Constitution, you just believe in your good ideas. That's fine if you're a member of Congress—although they also take an oath to support and defend the Constitution—but judges are supposed to think beyond their preferences and to enforce the law.

* * *

On September 18, 2020, a few weeks before the October 2020 term was to begin, we saw the death of Justice Ruth Bader Ginsburg. Although I had many disagreements with her, I respected her as someone rightly revered as a liberal lion on the Court. And she was an old-school liberal who didn't regard those who disagree with her as somehow evil or stupid. Her long-time friendship with Justice Antonin Scalia was ample evidence of that. Few jurists in history have ever had more diametrically opposed judicial philosophies while being such great friends.

Ginsburg's death set up a political clash that, while bad, could have been much worse. After the contentious confirmation of Justice

Brett Kavanaugh to replace Justice Anthony Kennedy, there was little doubt in most Court-watchers' minds that Justice Ginsburg's replacement would be a woman, and that it was likely to be Seventh Circuit Judge Amy Coney Barrett. As a practicing Catholic and a mother of seven (two adopted from Haiti), Barrett's character was seemingly unimpeachable—that is, of course, except for those who attacked her for being a Catholic, as had happened during her first confirmation process.

In the end, the Democrats did not have the votes to stop her, and she was approved 52-48. It was the first time since 1870 that a justice was confirmed without a single minority party vote.

There were, of course, many dire predictions about how Justice Barrett would bring about a *Handmaid's Tale* vision of America. While those fears are obviously overblown, replacing Ginsburg with the decidedly conservative Barrett promises to be one of the most consequential nominations in generations.

As Justice Byron White liked to say, "every justice makes a new Court." And while that is true, it might be truer with the arrival of Justice Barrett. In July 2020, before Justice Ginsburg's death, CNN's Joan Biskupic published a major story shedding light on some of the behind-the-scenes action among the justices. The story was surprising in that it clearly resulted from leaks from within the Court, something that is extremely rare (and concerning). Biskupic reported how Chief Justice John Roberts had "maneuvered on controversial cases in the justices' private sessions, at times defying expectations as he sided with liberal justices."[2] The chief also "exerted unprecedented control over cases and the court's internal operations," particularly the cert. docket. In one of the more surprising revelations, Biskupic wrote that "Roberts also sent enough signals during internal deliberations on firearms restrictions, sources said, to convince fellow conservatives he would not provide a critical fifth vote anytime soon to overturn gun control regulations." This was particularly shocking because Roberts voted with the majority in both landmark gun-rights cases: *District of Columbia v. Heller* and *McDonald v. City of Chicago*. In the 11 years since *McDonald*, many lower courts have been in almost open resistance to the implications of those rulings, a classic situation

---

[2] Joan Biskupic, "Behind Closed Doors During One of John Roberts' Most Surprising Years on the Supreme Court," CNN, July 27, 2020, https://cnn.it/3iG0laI.

demanding Supreme Court review. That Roberts had apparently tele-
graphed that he was no longer a reliable vote for the Second Amendment is concerning and raises the question: what is he thinking?

Conservatives have been asking that question at least since
Roberts saved the Affordable Care Act in 2012. That decision continues to haunt Roberts's public image among conservatives. Whatever
he was thinking, it seems clear that it was more political than jurisprudential. His fears of the Court's becoming politicized overrode
his jurisprudential sensibilities.

And that seems to be what's been happening in recent years. In my
estimation, what keeps John Roberts up at night is a fear of presiding
over a Court that comes to be regarded as illegitimate by a substantial number of Americans. That is an understandable concern, but
acting on it by, say, not voting to take any Second Amendment cases
when there is a clear reason for the Court to take them is, paradoxi-
cally, what turns Roberts into a political rather than judicial actor.

But those trained to be on the Supreme Court aren't (usually) very
good at politics. Being a judge is a singular skill, and judges often
lose their way when they try to bring nonjudicial considerations to
decision-making. Sometimes that makes more sense, such as when
Chief Justice Earl Warren (himself a former politician) exhorted his
colleagues to reach a unanimous decision in *Brown v. Board of Education*. While the legal reasoning in that case is suspect—there were
better ways the Court could have decided school segregation was
unconstitutional—Warren wasn't wrong to be concerned with the
consequences of even a single dissenting vote.

Yet, whatever the state of John Roberts's political sensibilities, it is
a very different Court after Justice Barrett joined. Roberts's vote—
whether for cert. or on the merits—is now less necessary. The six
Republican-appointed justices can achieve the four votes for cert. or
the five votes for a majority without the chief. And that was likely
made clear by the Court granting cert. to both a Second Amendment
case and an abortion case for next term. For more about those cases,
see Amy Howe's excellent "Looking Ahead" article in this volume.

*   *   *

Turning to the *Review* and the Supreme Court term itself, the Court
continued its recent trend of deciding fewer cases—a trend that has
increased during the pandemic. The Court issued 57 total opinions,

with 43 percent of the cases being decided unanimously. That's a bit lower than the 47 percent rate of unanimity over the past decade, but it still shows that, much of the time, the justices are not deciding cases along purely partisan lines. Twelve of the decisions were 6-3, but only six of those were along the expected "partisan" line.

Justice Brett Kavanaugh and Chief Justice Roberts continue to occupy the Court's "middle," but this term Kavanaugh replaced Roberts as the justice most often in the majority—97 percent of the time. The chief justice tied with Justice Barrett for second—91 percent in the majority. Justice Sonia Sotomayor was most often on the losing side, voting with the majority 69 percent of the time. Sotomayor also wrote half (four of eight) of the solo dissents in the term, but Justice Clarence Thomas continued his trend of writing the most total opinions, mostly due to his penchant for writing solo concurrences.

All in all, the justices continue to demonstrate that they are *judges* who decide cases on judicial rather than political grounds. Nevertheless, many Americans believe that the Court is a pure political institution, not too different from our dysfunctional Congress. Yet, fundamentally, the justices are trying their best to expound on a constitution—*the* Constitution—a fact which is increasingly forgotten by American citizens.

That point is highlighted in Judge Don Willett's excellent 2020 Simon Lecture, which leads off this volume. Judge Willett took to the difficult task of remotely delivering the keynote address at our 2020 Constitution Day with characteristic gusto. Wearing a coat and tie—while strategically concealing the shorts from the camera—Judge Willett reminded us that a well-functioning republic requires not just an informed citizenry, but an engaged citizenry. Americans are woefully uninformed about even the most basic facts of our constitutional system. The Framers knew that "American citizenship is not a spectator sport," but Judge Willett fears it is becoming one. His Simon Lecture is a good reminder of the responsibility that comes with being an American.

Next, Douglas Laycock of the University of Virginia School of Law and Thomas Berg of the University of St. Thomas School of Law discuss *Fulton v. City of Philadelphia*, which may end up being seen as one of the most consequential religious liberty decisions in recent history. *Fulton* was a challenge to the city of Philadelphia's decision to terminate the foster-services contract of Catholic Social Services (CSS) on the ground that CSS does not certify same-sex couples as foster parents. The Court was asked to overturn the 30-year-old precedent of *Employment Division v. Smith*, a decision that has long troubled many religious-liberty scholars. In *Smith*, the Court held that the Free Exercise Clause does not exempt religious practitioners from generally applicable and neutral laws. While the Court's decision in *Fulton* did not overturn *Smith*, at least five justices indicated that the *Smith* precedent is on shaky ground. Justice Barrett wrote separately to say she is skeptical of *Smith* but does not know what can replace it. Laycock and Berg try to assuage Barrett's doubts by arguing for a heightened scrutiny approach that "balances the burden on religion against government interests, with the thumb on the scale for religious exercise." Ultimately, "the logic and purpose of free exercise can generate a protective but workable doctrine for challenges to generally applicable laws."

Next, Bradley A. Smith of Capital University Law School, and former chairman of the Federal Election Commission, writes on the important decision in *Americans for Prosperity Foundation v. Bonta* (*AFPF*). In *AFPF*, the Court reaffirmed what has been true since the Founding: Americans have a right to anonymously support charitable causes. The case arose almost a decade ago when the then-attorney general of California, Kamala Harris, decided that all nonprofits that raised money in the state would have to file with the state a special IRS form called a Schedule B. Schedule Bs disclose the top donors to a charitable organization. In this time of "cancel culture," when people have lost their jobs when their political giving was publicized, AFPF and Thomas More Law Center, the co-plaintiff, understandably feared for the disclosure of their top donors. They fought all the way to the Supreme Court to vindicate the right to anonymously support charities, and they won by a 6-3 vote. Smith argues that the Republican-appointed justices in the majority were well-aware of the current climate of shaming and "cancelling" people because of their political activities. "At a minimum," he writes, "the government should neither be harassing citizens for their beliefs, nor forcing citizens to provide the information for their own undoing, without a darn good reason." Thankfully, most of the Court agrees.

In the third article covering a First Amendment issue, David Hudson of Belmont University College of Law comments on *Mahanoy Area School District v. B.L.*, the "cussing cheerleader" case. After "B.L."— a minor when the case arose but later revealed herself to be Brandi

Levy—failed to make the varsity cheerleading squad, she posted to Snapchat a profanity-laden rant about her feelings on the matter. The school disciplined her by suspending her from cheerleading for a year. She and her parents sued, arguing that the school's action violated her free-speech rights. The Court agreed and weighed in on an increasingly common issue: How much does the First Amendment protect online student-speech outside of school grounds and activities? While it was a welcome victory for the free-speech rights of students, it unfortunately "leaves many unanswered questions." "For one," writes Hudson, "the Court never really defined off-campus speech or explained precisely the boundaries between on-campus and off-campus speech." Justice Stephen Breyer's majority opinion, while leaving "much to be desired," is still an important "victory for student rights" and a "victory for parental rights." For off-campus speech, it's better to let parents discipline their children, not government officials.

Turning to questions of constitutional structure, Josh Blackman of the South Texas College of Law Houston returns to the pages of the *Review* to discuss the third part of the "epic" trilogy of cases reviewing the Affordable Care Act (ACA, a.k.a. "Obamacare"). First, in 2012's *National Federation of Independent Business v. Sebelius* (*NFIB*), there was the question of whether Congress could constitutionally impose a fine on those who failed to purchase health insurance. Chief Justice Roberts saved the ACA by rewriting the statute to turn a penalty into a "tax." Then in 2015's *King v. Burwell*, the chief justice again saved the ACA by ruling that subsidies are available to those who buy health insurance on federally created exchanges, even though the statutory words "established by the state" seemed to preclude that possibility. This term, in *California v. Texas*, it was Justice Breyer, joined by six justices, who saved the ACA by dismissing the challenge for lack of standing. The case arose after Congress in 2017 reduced to $0 the "tax" for not purchasing health insurance, thus calling into question the continued viability of Chief Justice Roberts's decision in *NFIB*. Justice Breyer ruled that the lack of any enforceable penalty meant that the plaintiffs were not being sufficiently harmed by the individual mandate to challenge it. Blackman disagrees, arguing that "the individual mandate—working in conjunction with the ACA's insurance-reform provisions—force the plaintiffs to buy unwanted, overpriced products." The ACA's interrelated provisions—namely the mandate and the "guaranteed issue" and "community rating" provisions—function together to create "standing-through-inseverability." And although the Court managed to dodge the ACA bullet this year, Blackman argues that the ACA "trilogy will become a quadrilogy" when someone "who is subject to an ACA enforcement action can raise the mandate's unconstitutionality as a defense."

Aaron Nielson of the J. Reuben Clark Law School at Brigham Young University writes about a case that he argued before the Court: *Collins v. Yellen*. After the federal government changed its position, Nielson was appointed by the Court to argue that the structure of the Federal Housing Finance Agency (FHFA) was constitutionally permissible after last term's decision in *Seila Law*. In that case, covered by Professor Ilan Wurman in last year's *Review*, the Court held unconstitutional the removal restrictions on the director of the Consumer Financial Protection Bureau. Plaintiffs challenging several actions by the FHFA raised the same issue about the removal protections on that agency's director—limiting the president's power to remove the director only "for cause." The Court decided that *Seila Law* also applies to the FHFA, and the then-director of FHFA, Mark Calabria, formerly Cato's director of financial regulatory studies, was removed by the president the same day the decision came down. Nielson writes about his experience with the case and the Court's broad ruling, which he says "may be the most pro-'unitary executive' decision in history." At bottom, however, *Collins* is "three cases in one"—a statutory debate, the constitutional question, and the remedy—and to understand it one needs to "view all three parts at the same time."

My colleague Sam Spiegelman joins Gregory C. Sisk of the University of St. Thomas School of Law to comment on one of the term's under-the-radar blockbusters. In *Cedar Point Nursery v. Hassid*, the Court ruled 6-3 that it was a per se taking under the Fifth Amendment for California to allow union organizers access to the grounds of agricultural businesses for up to three hours a day, 120 days per year. What made the Court's decision particularly important was that Chief Justice Roberts's majority opinion eschewed the complex and unpredictable *Penn Central* test in favor of a clearer rule. *Penn Central* has long been rightly criticized both for being confusing and for allowing judges substantial leeway in "balancing" their way to a result. Spiegelman and Sisk argue that *Cedar Point*, while imperfect, "moves regulatory takings in a direction that accords far better with the history of Anglo-American property law."

Christopher Slobogin of Vanderbilt Law School contributes what is likely the article on the shortest Court opinion in *Cato Supreme Court Review* history. In *Caniglia v. Strom*, Justice Thomas took four pages to decide that the "community caretaking exception" to the Fourth Amendment did not justify the police entering Edward Caniglia's house to take his guns after Mr. Caniglia had been voluntarily taken for a psychiatric evaluation. Chief Justice Roberts, Justice Samuel Alito, and Justice Kavanaugh all wrote concurring opinions expressing their views on when the "community caretaking exception" should be allowed. Slobogin's commentary is timely because it looks to current questions over the use—and misuse—of police in America. Should we be resorting to police in so many situations where it might be better to use other types of government officials, like mental-health experts? Thomas's *Caniglia* opinion rejects a broad reading of the caretaker exception, so "the argument is strong that, when a nonexigent search or seizure is carried out by police, the assertion that it is not aimed at 'ordinary crime control' should be irrelevant to Fourth Amendment analysis, regardless of whether it occurs inside or outside the home." *Caniglia* can "provide doctrinal support for the fledgling movement to de-police those government services that, whatever might be the tradition, do not require the intervention of armed individuals trained to fight crime."

Derek Muller of the University of Iowa College of Law comments on the voting-rights decision in *Brnovich v. Democratic National Committee*, in which the Court by a 6-3 "partisan" vote upheld two Arizona voting provisions that the DNC had challenged under Section 2 of the Voting Rights Act (VRA) as disproportionately burdening minority voters. One provision, the "out-of-precinct" policy, requires election officials to discard ballots cast in the wrong precinct. The other prohibits "ballot harvesting," that is, collecting and delivering another person's ballot. Justice Alito's opinion looks to the "totality of circumstances" when a change in voting laws might violate the Voting Rights Act. It's important, argues Muller, that the Court looked to the "usual burdens of voting" and declined to say that the VRA applies to "mere inconvenience." *Brnovich* "continues the Court's path away from federal judicial involvement in election rules and toward greater deference to state power." As with all "totality of circumstances" tests handed down by the Court, we will have to wait and see how lower courts apply it. In the end, *Brnovich* is unlikely to "stem the tide of litigation in the politically polarized years ahead."

The final article covering a decision from the 2020 term is by Adam Mossoff of George Mason University's Antonin Scalia Law School. Adam is expert in intellectual property, so the *Review* is lucky to have a contribution from him on the significant copyright dispute decided in *Google v. Oracle*. It's a little technical, but the gist is this: Google copied from Oracle about 11,500 lines of "declaring code" (a type of a back-end interface) and didn't want to pay for it. Years of litigation ensued, culminating in the Court's opinion by Justice Breyer, holding that Google's use of the code was protected under the fair use doctrine. Oddly, Mossoff argues, Justice Breyer brushed aside many of the core legal issues in the case. The result is an opinion focused on a novel view of the fair use doctrine that ignores some of the problems that will inevitably result. As Mossoff writes, "There are early indications of lawyers and judges being as creative with *Google* as *Google* itself was with the fair use doctrine that preexisted it."

Finally, we have the annual "Looking Ahead" article, this year by Amy Howe of "Howe on the Court." Amy focuses on three hot-button issues that the Court will hear next year: guns, abortion, and school choice/religious liberty. Those cases alone mean that next term will be contentious. The possibility that *Roe v. Wade* could be overturned will be discussed extensively, as well as the possibility that the Court will extend the protections of the Second Amendment to carrying a gun outside the home. And in the school-choice case, *Carson v. Makin*, the Court will decide whether a state violates the Constitution if it "prohibits students participating in an otherwise generally available student-aid program from choosing to use their aid to attend schools that provide religious, or 'sectarian,' instruction." It'll be a big term.

*   *   *

This is the third volume of the *Cato Supreme Court Review* I've edited, and I could not have done so without help. I'd like to thank Ilya Shapiro for being an excellent vice president and director of the Robert A. Levy Center for Constitutional Studies, and Roger Pilon for supplying the vision for the department and leadership for so many years. I'd also like to thank the authors, without whom there would be nothing to edit or read. They are often given a difficult task—to write a 10,000-word article in about five weeks. This year the authors were all on time, and a surprising number were even early. Thank you.

Thanks also goes to Thomas Berry, the new managing editor. Tommy was a superstar intern, then a superstar legal associate, and now he's a superstar research fellow and managing editor. I look forward to many years of collaboration. Also, my colleagues Walter Olson, Will Yeatman, and (again) Ilya and Roger helped edit the articles, while legal associates Spencer Davenport, Stacy Hanson, Nived Rajendran, Mallory Reader, and Christian Townsend performed the thankless but essential tasks of cite checking and proofreading. Legal interns Madalyn Brooks and Richard Friedl were also essential in these tasks, despite the unfortunate fact that their entire internship was remote. Special thanks goes again to Sam Spiegelman, who stepped up and did an exceptional job with all the nuts and bolts of putting out the *Review*, as well as a significant amount of editing. Sam again proved indispensable.

I hope that this collection of essays will secure and advance the Madisonian first principles of our Constitution, giving renewed voice to the Framers' fervent wish that we have a government of laws and not of men. Our Constitution was written in secret but ratified by the people in one of the most extraordinary acts of popular governance ever undertaken. During that ratification process, ordinary people debated the pros and cons of the document, and, in so doing, helped turn the Constitution into a type of American DNA, belonging to no one but part of all of us. Those of the Founding generation shared many of our concerns today. They fretted over the possibility of rule by elites. They wished to ensure prosperity throughout the country. They worried that self-interested rulers would ignore the law and collect power in themselves. The Constitution is their best attempt at creating an energetic yet restrained government. It reflects and protects the natural rights of life, liberty, and property, and serves as a bulwark against government abuses. In this schismatic time, it's more important than ever to remember our proud roots in the Enlightenment tradition.

We hope that you enjoy this 20th volume of the *Cato Supreme Court Review*.

Flunking the Founding: Civic Illiteracy and the Rule of Law

*Judge Don R. Willett**

Ilya, thank you so much for that generous introduction. And thanks to the Cato Institute for having me—or, more accurately, *streaming* me from Austin, Texas. But even from afar, I'm honored to find myself among the distinguished jurists and scholars who've delivered this lecture. I grew up in a tiny Texas town of 32 people. It was so small, our town square had only three sides. (The beauty of Zoom is that you can't hear the groaning.) But for a kid who grew up in a trailer surrounded by cotton and cattle, this is high cotton. So thank you.

2020 has been a wild ride, and I say that as a former rodeo cowboy. A confluence of overlapping crises: pandemic, recession, impeachment, social unrest. So far, the most normal part of 2020 has been *Tiger King.*

But we look for silver linings where we can. And the turmoil has perhaps sharpened our focus on first principles. According to the 2020 Constitution Day Civics Survey, 51 percent of American adults can now name all three branches of government—up from 39 percent last year (which was the all-time high).[1] But truth be told, our nation still has an abysmal civic IQ. We inhabit an age of miracles and wonders, with access to mankind's accumulated knowledge at our fingertips. Yet it's also an age of staggering civic illiteracy. Our civic *temperature* may be high, but our civic *knowledge* is not. There is much to indict. But through commendable events like today's symposium, perhaps we can move from indicting to informing—and better still, inspiring and invigorating.

---

*Judge, U.S. Court of Appeals for the Fifth Circuit. This is a slightly revised version of the 19th annual B. Kenneth Simon Lecture in Constitutional Thought, delivered at the Cato Institute's annual Constitution Day symposium on September 17, 2020.

1 "Amid Pandemic and Protests, Civics Survey Finds Americans Know More of Their Rights," Annenberg Pub. Pol'y Ctr., Sept. 14, 2020, https://bit.ly/3tjCbVw.

Doctor's Orders

Two hundred thirty-three years ago today, the Rolling Stones cut their first album. No—though Mick Jagger's bunch is a combined 306 years old—on this date, a throng of Philadelphians waited outside Independence Hall. And like most Philly crowds, it was tense. Our infant nation was floundering. The *United* States were anything but. The Articles of Confederation had created a loose "league of friendship," but the former colonies had yet to coalesce into a country.

For four sweltering months, delegates to the Constitutional Convention huddled in secret behind closed doors. And those outside were wary of those inside.

Presiding was the "venerated Virginian veteran,"[2] George Washington: the indispensable man. No Washington, no Republic. But Benjamin Franklin was the nation's renaissance man. His achievements—in science, diplomacy, letters—were unrivaled. Franklin was the first embodiment of the American Dream. From penniless runaway to protean polymath, he was the most illustrious figure in early America. He truly was "the incarnation of the true American character."[3]

On the convention's final day, Franklin delivered the last great speech of his life, urging adoption of the new Constitution "with all its faults."[4] And Franklin found plenty of faults. He wanted federal judges to be elected, for example. But Franklin, 81 years old, the oldest delegate and the most renowned American in the world, flexed his considerable diplomatic skills and implored his fellow delegates to "doubt a little of his own infallibility."[5] "[T]he older I grow," said Franklin, "the more apt I am to doubt my own judgment, and to pay more respect to the judgment of others."[6] We could all use a refreshing dose of that intellectual modesty today; more humility and less superiority. Franklin was actually too frail to deliver his rousing

[2] Lin-Manuel Miranda, "Right Hand Man," on Hamilton, at 1:27 (Atlantic Recording Co. 2015).

[3] "The Inauguration of the Franklin Statue," N.Y. Times, Sept. 19, 1856, at 1.

[4] Benjamin Franklin, Final Speech at the Constitutional Convention (Sept. 17, 1787), in James Madison, 2 The Records of the Federal Convention of 1787, 642–43 (Max Farrand ed., 1911), https://bit.ly/2QInsq9.

[5] *Id.*

[6] *Id.*

speech himself. A fellow Pennsylvanian, James Wilson, read it for him. But it was extraordinary. And it worked. There was unity, if not unanimity. And as James Madison scribbled in his notes—rather understatedly, if you ask me—"The members then proceeded to sign the instrument."[7]

We all know what happened next. A triumphant Franklin was approached by Mrs. Powel, who blurted out, "Well Doctor, what have we got, a republic or a monarchy?" And Franklin delivered his sharp-witted rejoinder: "A republic," "if you can keep it."[8]

Franklin's zinger was heartening—"A republic"—no more royal absolutism! But it was also frightening—"if you can keep it"—because it suggested that the survival of freedom depends on people, not parchment.

The duty of preserving our rich civic inheritance falls on us. *We* must ensure our Republic doesn't descend into anarchy or monarchy. This is a job for everyday Americans, like Mrs. Powel, who posed a question for the ages, one that echoes today—"What have *we* got?" This Republic is ours. Ours to keep. And ours to lose.

---

[7] Madison, *supra* note 4, at 648.

[8] James McHenry, 3 The Records of the Federal Convention of 1787, 85 (Max Farrand ed., 1911) (punctuation added), https://bit.ly/2So0ll3. In one retelling of the story, James McHenry added that, after Franklin's quip, Ms. Powel responded, "And why not keep it?" To which Franklin allegedly retorted, "Because the people, on tasting the dish, are always disposed to eat more of it than does them good." This extended version was first published by McHenry in a newspaper in 1803, 16 years after the exchange between Franklin and Ms. Powel occurred, but it is not included in McHenry's original diary entry. See Gillian Brockell, "'A Republic, if You Can Keep It': Did Ben Franklin Really Say Impeachment Day's Favorite Quote?," Wash. Post, Dec. 18, 2019, https://wapo.st/3xHPNxe. Perhaps the often-prescient Franklin feared apathy, abdication to "blissful" ignorance. See, e.g., Letter from Benjamin Franklin to Samuel Johnson (Aug. 23, 1750), https://bit.ly/3iE9OhJ ("[N]othing is of more importance for the public weal, than to form and train up youth in wisdom and virtue. Wise and good men are, in my opinion, the *strength* of a state: much more so than riches or arms, which, under the management of Ignorance and Wickedness, often draw on destruction, instead of providing for the safety of a people."). He knew that the death of civic virtue would mean the death of our Republic. Education reformer Horace Mann put it this way: "It may be an easy thing to make a Republic; but it is a very laborious thing to make Republicans; and woe to the republic that rests upon no better foundations than ignorance, selfishness, and passion." Horace Mann, Report No. 12 of the Massachusetts School Board, in The Republic and the School: Horace Mann on the Education of Free Men 79, 92 (Lawrence A. Cremin ed., 1957), transcribed at https://bit.ly/3nR9f6k.

But Franklin was not the first to recognize whose job it is to build an enduring nation. Eleven years earlier, on the same politically sacred spot, the Declaration of Independence—our original birth announcement; the greatest breakup letter of all time—proclaimed that we wanted government, as Lincoln put it four score and seven years later, "of the people, by the people, for the people."[9]

This uniquely American Theory of Government[10] was a radical experiment, the first time in history that a nation came into being asserting the inborn, individual natural rights and equality of every human being.[11]

Listen to this word choice, from the Declaration:

- *"We* hold these truths to be self-evident."
- Governments "deriv[e] their just powers from the consent *of the governed."*
- When government becomes destructive, "it is the Right *of the People"* to change course.
- And when abuses and usurpations lead to despotism, "it is *their* right, it is *their* duty, to throw off such Government, and to provide new Guards for *their* future security."

Pre-Constitution, the Founders said the People wield supreme sovereignty over their government. To lay its foundation. To structure

---

[9] Abraham Lincoln, Gettysburg Address (Nov. 19, 1863), https://bit.ly/3riXKGt; see also Leon Kass, "Abraham Lincoln's Re-founding of the Nation," What So Proudly We Hail, https://bit.ly/3nKqJ4j (last visited Apr. 26, 2021).

[10] See Randy E. Barnett, The Declaration of Independence and the American Theory of Government: "First Come Rights, and then Comes Government," 42 Harv. J.L. & Pub. Pol'y 23, 25 (2019).

[11] President Reagan said the American Revolution was "the only true philosophical revolution in all history." Ronald Reagan, "What July Fourth Means to Me," Parade, June 28, 1981, https://bit.ly/3vvKMWK. "Oh, there have been revolutions before and since ours," he said. "But those revolutions simply exchanged one set of rules for another. Ours was a revolution that changed the very concept of government." *Id.* The reason that the Declaration is "regarded as one of the great charters," said President Coolidge on the Declaration's sesquicentennial, is "not because it was proposed to establish a new nation, but because it was proposed to establish a nation on new principles." Calvin Coolidge, The Inspiration of the Declaration of Independence (July 5, 1926), https://bit.ly/3eU48hq. And lest anyone think that Americans' civics know-nothingness is unique to the 21st century, President Coolidge lamented almost a century ago, "We do need . . . a better knowledge of the foundations of government." *Id.*

its powers. All according to what seems "to them" most likely to secure their safety and happiness.[12] This power of the People is a truth that provides great comfort . . . and grave discomfort.

Facts Are Stubborn Things

Fast-forward to Constitution Day 2020:

- 23 percent of American adults still cannot name a single branch of government.[13]
- 19 percent cannot name *one* right guaranteed by the First Amendment.[14]
- Only 19 percent of adults under age 45 can pass a rudimentary, 10-question, multiple-choice quiz about our Founding.[15]

Many Americans don't know the *how* of our Republic because they don't know the *why* of our Republic. Margaret Thatcher once noted that Europe, unlike the United States, is "the product of history and not of philosophy."[16] America is *sui generis*, she said, because it was "built upon an idea—the idea of liberty." She was echoing Churchill, who called the Declaration a "great title deed," praising "the love of liberty and justice on which the American nation was founded."[17] Madison agreed. The European vision, he said, was "charters of liberty . . . granted by power," as opposed to the American vision: "charters of power granted by liberty."[18]

Our Founders, imperfect yet inspired, aimed for something transcendent: not to enshrine a *process*—democracy—but to enshrine

---

[12] See Barnett, American Theory of Government, *supra* note 10, at 26–27.

[13] Amid Pandemic and Protests, *supra* note 1.

[14] *Id.*

[15] News Release, National Survey Finds Just 1 in 3 Americans Would Pass Citizenship Test, Woodrow Wilson Nat'l F'ship Found., Oct. 3, 2018, https://bit.ly /3ui3eBN.

[16] Margaret Thatcher, Speech at Hoover Inst. Lunch (Mar. 8, 1991), https://bit.ly /3nQyXHZ.

[17] Richard M. Langworth, "Churchill on July 4, 1918," July 4, 2015, https://bit.ly /3thTmH3 (quoting Winston S. Churchill, Speech at Liberty Day Meeting, Central Hall, Westminster (July 4, 1918), in Robert Rhodes James, 3 Winston S. Churchill: His Complete Speeches 1897–1963, at 2613–16 (1974)).

[18] James Madison, "Charters," Nat'l Gazette, Jan. 18, 1792, https://bit.ly/3efKnBX.

a *promise*—liberty. Individual freedom. The essential condition of human flourishing.

Our Founders gambled big, and they hit the trifecta:

- They had *hindsight*: They knew the history of kings and dictators, so they insisted on a government of laws and not of men.
- They had *insight*: They knew that government exists to "ensure the blessings of liberty"; that liberty is not *provided* by government but *preexists* government; that liberty is our natural birthright, not a gift from politicians.
- And they had *foresight*: They knew that to safeguard liberty, government must be structured to control its power.

Knowing that a bunch of guys dumped tea into Boston Harbor means nothing if we don't know *why* they dumped it, which was, of course, as the Beastie Boys taught us, because, "You gotta fight, for your right, to pour tea!" And if we don't grasp the *why* of our design, it'll never command affection and reverence.[19]

- Most Americans now say they do not trust any branch of government.[20]
- American national pride is at an all-time low.[21]
- Only 46 percent of high school and college students say they are patriotic.[22]

The Father of the Country would be dismayed. Washington made clear in his first inaugural address that this is on us: "[T]he preservation of the sacred fire of liberty, and the destiny of the Republican

---

[19] Thatcher made a similar point, explaining that "[p]olitical institutions cannot be imposed if they are to endure. They have to evolve and they have to command the affection, loyalty, and respect of populations living under them, and they have to be accountable to the people." Thatcher, *supra* note 16.

[20] David Byler, "Nobody Can Predict This Election. Here's Why," Wash. Post, Sept. 3, 2020, https://wapo.st/2Sncvuu.

[21] Megan Brenan, "U.S. National Pride Falls to Record Low," Gallup, June 15, 2020, https://bit.ly/3eU621w (42 percent "extremely," and 21 percent "very," proud to be an American).

[22] Spencer Brown, "Youth Patriotism Index Shows High School Students More Patriotic than College Peers," Young America's Found., July 1, 2020, https://bit.ly/3gX0TbP.

model of Government, are . . . staked[] on the experiment entrusted to the hands of the American people."[23] And frankly, Washington was pessimistic, confiding to another delegate, "I do not expect the Constitution to last for more than 20 years."[24] Thankfully, he was wrong.

Some nations number their years by millennia.[25] America is approaching its semiquincentennial: 250 years. And God willing, this Nation has a long life left. But how can we be expectant about our future if we're ignorant about our past?

It's a short trip from "ignorance" of our founding ideals to "erasure" of them. When he was 28 years old, Abraham Lincoln spoke of this rich "legacy bequeathed us," how we are "the legal inheritors of these fundamental blessings."[26] And he warned of how danger would spring from within, from "the increasing disregard for law," from what he called "this mobocratic spirit." The Founding generation had died, and Lincoln was worried about lawlessness and the perpetuation of our institutions. The antidote, he said: "the attachment of the People." And attachment includes "a reverence for the constitution and laws."[27]

But civic illiteracy—obliviousness to the what and why of America—accelerates *de*tachment. Because if we don't *know* our history, warts and all, we can never *understand* our history. We'll have nothing to hold onto. Nothing to ground us.

Just a few weeks ago, Ben Franklin—Mr. "if you can keep it"—who warned of the tendency of republics to implode, was himself targeted for cancellation, thus proving the wisdom of his insight.

---

[23] George Washington, First Inaugural Address (Apr. 30, 1789), https://bit.ly/33bzoDl.

[24] Herbert Mitgang, "New Light on 1787 and Washington's Doubts," N.Y. Times, July 4, 1987, https://nyti.ms/3egD112; see also Myron Magnet, The Founders' Grandson, Part II, City J. (Winter 2018), https://bit.ly/3xTX1hZ ("The Framers had hopes, but no illusions, that the Constitution would be eternal.").

[25] Frederick Douglass, What to the Slave Is the Fourth of July?, (July 5, 1852), https://bit.ly/2QWrGu2 ("Seventy-six years, though a good old age for a man, is but a mere speck in the life of a nation.").

[26] Abraham Lincoln, The Perpetuation of Our Political Institutions, Address before the Young Men's Lyceum of Springfield (Jan. 27, 1838), in 6 J. Abraham Lincoln Ass'n 6 (1984), https://bit.ly/33gfHdn.

[27] Id.

Franklin has gone from "The First American"[28] to "Person of Concern," according to a D.C. government committee.[29] Franklin's name should be scrubbed from a historic landmark, they claim, and his statue should be "removed, relocated, or contextualized."[30] And not just him. George Washington, the man after whom the city itself is named, is also a "Person of Concern." Thus, the Washington Monument—I guess all 81,000 tons of it—should also be removed, relocated, or contextualized.[31] Notably, the D.C. panel made no recommendation on renaming the city itself.

I suspect that many of those we saw on TV lassoing monuments want to topple more than statues.

The Aspirational Declaration: Our Golden Apple

Amid today's pandemic is something endemic: a deep misunderstanding of American self-government. Today is Constitution Day. But our confusion also runs to our *true* founding document: The Declaration of Independence.

Jefferson called the Declaration "an expression of the [A]merican mind."[32] Lincoln called the promise of the Declaration an "apple of gold" framed by the silver frame of the Constitution.[33] Lincoln ex-

---

[28] See generally, e.g., H.W. Brands, The First American: The Life and Times of Benjamin Franklin (2000).

[29] D.C. Facilities & Commemorative Expressions Working Group, DC Faces: Working Group Report 21 (Aug. 31, 2020), https://bit.ly/3b1okwP.

[30] *Id.* A revised report does not reference the Benjamin Franklin statute. See Laura Wainman, "Task Force Recommends Renaming 49 DC Schools, Parks and Government Buildings," WUSA9, Sept. 2, 2020, https://bit.ly/3xIXR0J (describing revision and relaying screenshots of initial version). The original report is no longer available.

[31] Associated Press, "Bowser Task Force Targets Washington Monument, Jefferson Memorial, Dozens More," NBC News, Sept. 2, 2020, https://nbcnews.to/2PLGc7o (describing recommendation as to the Washington Monument). The revised report does not reference the Washington Monument. See Wainman, *supra* note 30.

[32] Letter from Thomas Jefferson to Henry Lee (May 8, 1825), https://bit.ly/2QLjvRy.

[33] Abraham Lincoln, Fragment on the Constitution and Union (Jan. 1, 1861), https://bit.ly/3efJmty. Shortly before his inauguration, President-elect Lincoln, speaking at Independence Hall on George Washington's birthday, said, "I have never had a feeling politically that did not spring from the sentiments embodied in the Declaration of Independence." Abraham Lincoln, Address at Independence Hall (Feb. 22, 1861), transcribed at https://bit.ly/3eRTZC2 (citing Mark E. Neely, Jr., The Abraham Lincoln Encyclopedia (1982)).

plained that "[t]he picture" frame "was made, not to conceal, or destroy the apple, but to adorn, and preserve it. The picture was made for the apple—not the apple for the picture."[34] The Constitution exists to serve the Declaration's promise of "Liberty to all."[35] The Constitution provides the tools to build a government that secures the rights proclaimed in the Declaration.

The Declaration was high treason. It was a literal indictment of the Crown, in painstaking detail, that married disobedience with eloquence. Legend has it that one delegate who was afflicted with a palsy, said as he signed, "My hand trembles, but my heart does not!"[36]

Every spring, there's a Colonial Day at my kids' school. And I put on an itchy costume, unroll a scroll, and recite the Declaration of Independence, accompanied by tiny 5th grade voices.

The first two paragraphs are vacuum-packed.[37] There was no beating around the bush. No hemming or hawing or throat-clearing. No gauzy phrases like "irreconcilable differences." The Declaration is declarative. This was the Festivus of 1776, the airing of grievances, and the Founders dialed it up to 11.

The second sentence is the most famous—"We hold these truths to be self-evident . . ." This line does a lot of heavy lifting. It declares: (1) these rights belong to us as individuals; (2) they are fixed, innate, our natural birthright, unrelinquishable, unwaivable, unsurrenderable; and (3) they are God-given, so they may not be taken by man.

Next is where Jefferson drops the mic—or the quill: the ultimate end of government is to secure these preexisting inborn rights. Boom.

---

[34] *Id.*; see also Barnett, American Theory of Government, *supra* note 10, at 23 ("[T]he Constitution is not our founding document—the Declaration is."). As historian Allen Guelzo explains, Lincoln understood that our Constitution does not exist as a simple "set of procedural rules with no better goal than letting people do what they pleased *with* what they pleased." Allen C. Guelzo, Apple of Gold in a Picture of Silver: The Constitution and Liberty, in The Lincoln Enigma: The Changing Faces of an American Icon 86, 87 (2001).

[35] Guelzo, *supra* note 34, at 87.

[36] See, e.g., Denise Kiernan & Joseph D'Agnese, Signing Their Lives Away: The Fame and Misfortune of the Men Who Signed the Declaration of Independence 52 (2009).

[37] See Randy E. Barnett, "What the Declaration of Independence Said and Meant," Wash. Post: The Volokh Conspiracy, July 4, 2017, https://wapo.st/3h5mteb.

As Professor Randy Barnett famously puts it, "first come rights and then comes government."[38]

The Declaration unveiled the "American Theory of Government,"[39] and its bottom line is clear: Government exists to protect our individual, unalienable rights—rights that are ours by virtue of our very humanity.

But as the Founding generation passed away, so too did the Declaration's uniting principle. In 1838, long before he was president, Lincoln lamented the "mobocratic spirit" that was sweeping the country. He worried that "wild and furious passions" would destroy "the strongest bulwark of any Government . . . the attachment of the People."[40] Lincoln warned that when the People lose sight of that which binds us together—the ideal of liberty enshrined in the Declaration—"this Government cannot last."[41] Again, Lincoln was just 28 when he warned of America being torn asunder from within. Fort Sumter was still 23 years away.

It is undeniable that at the Founding, the *ideals* collided with the *reality*, America's original sin of slavery. One-third of the Declaration's signers were slave-owners.[42] We were flawed and stained at the start. Jefferson's initial draft included an anti-slavery passage, but it was cut. America is imperfect as all human things are.

Even so, the Declaration's underlying ideals are timeless, and they are winning out. Lincoln would not abandon them even to avoid civil war. At Independence Hall, just before he was inaugurated, Lincoln described equal liberty as a gift "not alone to the people of this country, but, I hope, to the world, for all future

---

[38] Randy E. Barnett, Our Republican Constitution: Securing the Liberty and Sovereignty of We the People 41 (2016). Next comes the bill of indictment against the Crown, and Jefferson lets loose. Many of these itemized "abuses and usurpations" are tackled head-on in our Bill of Rights and also, more fundamentally, in the very structure of our Constitution. Barnett, "What the Declaration of Independence Said and Meant," *supra* note 37.

[39] Barnett, American Theory of Government, *supra* note 10, at 24.

[40] Lincoln, Perpetuation of Our Political Institutions, *supra* note 26.

[41] *Id.*

[42] Yohuru Williams, "Why Thomas Jefferson's Anti-Slavery Passage Was Removed from the Declaration of Independence," History Channel, June 29, 2020, https://bit.ly/3b3f0bJ.

time."[43] The Declaration was a linchpin argument for abolitionists, and the Supreme Court feebly tried to explain it away in *Dred Scott*.

My favorite piece of art in my chambers is an oil painting of Frederick Douglass. In his iconic speech, "What to the Slave is the Fourth of July?," Douglass notes that the promises of liberty and equality in the Declaration are eternal, even if America broke those promises. There was a jarring disconnect between the commendable words of the Declaration and the condemnable deeds of those who adopted it. But those founding ideals still lay the foundation for righting wrongs, including the "new birth of freedom" wrought by our Second Founding and the Civil War Amendments that belong at the center of America's constitutional story.

The quest to live up to America's ideals is never-ending; it requires constant striving. Even the aspirational Fourteenth Amendment failed to fulfill its promise during its first 75 years.[44] But the central idea of the Declaration—that "all men are created equal"—set in motion an inexorable march.

Martin Luther King, perhaps the most renowned protestor in our nation's history, called on his fellow citizens not to tear down America's heritage but to live up to it.[45] After his own March on Washington, Dr. King demanded not that our Founding documents be changed to fit *new* ideals, but that our government change to fit the *enduring* ideals of our Founding documents, which he called "a promissory note to which every American was to fall heir."[46] Perfection is elusive in this life. But bit by bit, amendment by amendment,

---

[43] Abraham Lincoln, Address at Independence Hall, *supra* note 33.

[44] See Ernest A. Young, Dying Constitutionalism and the Fourteenth Amendment, 102 Marq. L. Rev. 949, 949 (2019).

[45] See Martin Luther King, Jr., I Have a Dream, Speech Delivered at the Lincoln Memorial, Washington, D.C. (Aug. 28, 1963), transcribed at https://bit.ly/3ejcPmg.

[46] See *id.* ("When the architects of our republic wrote the magnificent words of the Constitution and the Declaration of Independence, they were signing a promissory note to which every American was to fall heir. This note was a promise that all men, yes, Black men as well as white men, would be guaranteed the unalienable rights of life, liberty, and the pursuit of happiness. It is obvious today that America has defaulted on this promissory note insofar as her citizens of color are concerned. . . . We refuse to believe that there are insufficient funds in the great vaults of opportunity of this nation. So we have come to cash this check—a check that will give us upon demand the riches of freedom and the security of justice.").

we are drawing nearer to the first enumerated purpose of the Preamble: formation of that "more perfect Union."

The Architectural Constitution: Our Silver Frame

So far, I've focused on the Declaration, our golden apple, which lies at the heart of the American project. But it is preserved through its silver frame, the Constitution. The Declaration is aspirational; the Constitution is architectural. The Declaration declared the purpose of government: to secure our God-given rights. The Constitution erected an ingenious structure to achieve that purpose.

It is imperative that we understand *both* documents so that, as Lincoln cautioned, "neither picture, or apple shall ever be blurred, or bruised or broken."[47]

The Framers were not tinkerers. They didn't pledge their lives, fortunes, and sacred honors to fiddle around the edges. They upended things. Madisonian architecture infused with Newtonian genius: three co-equal branches locked in synchronous orbit by competing interests. "Ambition . . . counteract[ing] ambition," as Madison put it.[48] A radical structure that *divided* power to *control* power.

And the most extraordinary element? These three rival branches derive power from three unrivaled words, supersized on the page for all the world to see: "We the People." Not We the Government, We the Judges, or We the Subjects. In an era of kings and sultans, this was a script-flipping heresy. Nothing was more radical than the idea that sovereignty resides not in government but in the governed.

Popular sovereignty is a duty, not a mere theory. Shortly after the Constitution was signed, Jefferson wrote from Paris: "[W]herever the people are well informed they can be trusted with their own government."[49]

But how can we give informed say-so if we lack informed know-how? We the People are meant to be watchdogs, not lapdogs. Franklin's warning "if you can keep it" presumes "if you know it" . . . that everyday Americans will be well-informed and thus wield their sovereignty smartly.

---

[47] Lincoln, Fragment on the Constitution, *supra* note 33.

[48] The Federalist No. 51 (James Madison), https://bit.ly/3vFQGom.

[49] Letter from Thomas Jefferson to Richard Price (Jan. 8, 1789), https://bit.ly/3ejG60t.

But again, We the People's civic illiteracy is staggering:

- 71 percent of Americans can't identify the Constitution as the supreme law of the land.
- 63 percent can't name one of their state's U.S. senators.
- 62 percent can't identify the governor of their state.[50]

Heck, 10 percent of college graduates think Judith Sheindlin (aka "Judge Judy") sits on the Supreme Court.[51]

Madison warned of this expressly: "A popular Government, without popular information . . . is but a Prologue to a Farce or a Tragedy; or, perhaps both."[52] Get this: Most of America's elite universities no longer require history majors to take a single course in U.S. history.[53]

But there is a ray of hope: naturalized Americans, those who've risked everything to help write the next chapter of the American story. When it comes to the U.S. citizenship exam, immigrants "get the job done."[54] Do you know what percentage of immigrants pass the civics test their first try? 90 percent.[55] (Congratulations, Ilya, on having been one of those.) The same 100 multiple-choice questions were given to some American high schoolers. The passage rate: 5 percent.[56] The generation with the greatest access to information is also the least informed.

An *informed* citizenry is indispensable to *self*-government. But even that is no guarantee of *good* government. Beyond education, you need engagement. Franklin said "if you can keep it" because he knew the secret sauce: an *engaged* citizenry.

American civic-spiritedness, Tocqueville explained, is rooted in our three-dimensional sense of participation: (1) we participate in

---

[50] Michael F. Ford, "Civic Illiteracy: A Threat to the American Dream," Xavier Univ.: Ctr. for the Study of the Am. Dream, Apr. 26, 2012, https://bit.ly/3xOwUsr.

[51] Am. Council of Trs. & Alumni, A Crisis in Civic Education 5 (Jan. 2016), https://bit.ly/3tfiePD.

[52] Letter from James Madison to W.T. Barry (Aug. 4, 1822), https://bit.ly/3eU5eK1.

[53] Am. Council of Trs. & Alumni, No U.S. History?: How College History Departments Leave the United States out of the Major 2 (July 2016), https://bit.ly/2PMGif4.

[54] Miranda, "Yorktown," *supra* note 2, at 0:18.

[55] Applicant Performance on the Naturalization Test – June 2020, U.S. C'ship & Immigr. Servs., https://bit.ly/33hkUBT (last updated Aug. 25, 2020).

[56] James Marshall Crotty, "Less Than 5% of Arizona Students Can Pass State's Super Simple Civics Exam. Can You?," Forbes, Jan. 16, 2015, https://bit.ly/3eU6H2Z.

creating our own, and thus our nation's, prosperity; (2) we participate in the administration of local government and voluntary associations (what Edmund Burke called the "little platoon[s]"[57] of family, church, and local community that incline us to civic virtue); and (3) through electing our representatives, we participate in the making of laws that advance our freedom and prosperity. American patriotism is anchored in that Tocquevillian vision of pro-active citizens, sleeves rolled up, who take charge of their own economic, social, and political happiness.[58]

American citizenship is not a spectator sport. Justice Louis Brandeis put it well: "The only title in our democracy superior to that of president is the title of citizen."[59] Our Constitution is an exquisite charter of freedom, but freedom requires patriots, not passersby. It demands fierce defenders, not feeble bystanders.

Take Lincoln. In 1858, he was "a financially insecure, failing politician with no administrative experience."[60] But the Supreme Court's *Dred Scott* decision galvanized Lincoln. That June, he delivered his "House Divided" speech. It was poetic and prophetic. Lincoln lost that election, but it was that legal analysis of a judicial decision that catapulted him to Mount Rushmore. Lincoln was no mere bystander. His civic participation educated voters, who liked what they heard and leveraged that knowledge into sending that "failing politician" to the White House two years later.

[57] See Edmund Burke, 24 Reflections on the French Revolution, paras. 75–99 (1790), in The Harvard Classics (Charles W. Eliot ed., 1909–14), https://bit.ly/3b1IrLk.

[58] Said Tocqueville: "A man understands the influence that the well-being of the country has on his own; he knows that the law permits him to contribute to producing this well-being, and he interests himself in the prosperity of his country at first as a thing that is useful to him, and afterwards as his own work." Alexis de Tocqueville, Democracy in America 225 (Harvey C. Mansfield & Debra Winthrop trans., 2000) (1835). As a result, every American "understands the influence that general prosperity exerts on his happiness" and "is accustomed to regarding this prosperity as his own work"; therefore, he "sees in the public fortune his own, and he works for the good of the state not only out of duty or out of pride. . . ." *Id.* at 226. "In our day," he observed, the civic spirit "seems to me inseparable from the exercise of political rights." *Id.*

[59] "Quotations about Democracy, Politics and Government, and Related Matters," Ctr. for Civic Educ. (cleaned up), https://bit.ly/3gXjiFq (last visited Apr. 27, 2021).

[60] Walter Dellinger, Speech Delivered to Duke Law School's 2020 Graduates (May 9, 2020), transcribed at https://bit.ly/3ti0FP1.

Putting the "C" in Constitution

Indeed, civic engagement can ripple across centuries. Let me tell you about a tenacious Texan with a Mensa-level civics IQ.

In 1982, Gregory Watson was a 19-year-old sophomore at the University of Texas. He wrote a research paper arguing that one of James Madison's proposed constitutional amendments was still eligible for ratification.[61] The dormant proposal would've barred Congress from giving itself a mid-term pay raise. It was part of the batch of amendments that eventually became the Bill of Rights.

The teaching assistant was thoroughly unimpressed. She awarded Watson a big fat C. So Watson, fueled by righteous indignation, spent the next 10 years lobbying state capitols from sea to shining sea. Until, in 1992, the Twenty-seventh Amendment was finally ratified—203 years after it was first proposed.

Gregory Watson got a bad grade. So he amended the Constitution, almost singlehandedly. All it took was aptitude and attitude. The cherry on top came in 2017, 25 years after ratification, when the university officially changed his grade. The official form states, "In light of the student's heroic efforts to prove the professor . . . wrong . . . Mr. Watson deserves A+."[62]

From Flunking to Dunking

Last year, the federal judiciary convened its first-ever national civics conference. Article III judges, including three Supreme Court justices, joined with law school deans, bar leaders, and others from Maine to Guam to discuss how the judiciary could help boost civics literacy.

A few weeks later, Chief Justice John Roberts wrote in his Year-End Report on the Federal Judiciary, "Each generation has an obligation to pass on to the next, not only a fully functioning government

---

[61] See Matt Largey, "The Bad Grade That Changed The U.S. Constitution," NPR, May 5, 2017, https://n.pr/33erzg6. See also Scott Bomboy, "Can a dormant proposed constitutional amendment come back to life?," Nat'l Const. Ctr.: Constitution Daily, May 31, 2018, https://bit.ly/3vEN6uz (discussing ratification deadlines).

[62] Ken Herman, "35 years later, A+ for Austinite who got Constitution Amended?," Austin Am.-Statesman, Sept. 25, 2018, https://bit.ly/3tdwA2V. In explaining why she changed a grade 35 years later, Professor Waite said Mr. Watson "certainly proved he knew how to work the Constitution and what it meant and how to be politically active," and for that effort, an A+ was deserved. Largey, *supra* note 61.

responsive to the needs of the people, but the tools to understand and improve it."[63] The chief justice was echoing Justice Sandra Day O'Connor, who's devoted her post-Court life to civics education: "Knowledge about our government isn't handed down through the gene pool."[64] And she was echoing President Ronald Reagan, who warned, "Freedom is never more than one generation away from extinction."[65] We didn't pass it to our children in the bloodstream.

They're right. This isn't something hardwired into our DNA. The habits of citizenship must be taught and learned anew by each generation.[66]

And schoolchildren are often center stage in transforming our Nation. Take Linda Brown, the schoolgirl at the center of *Brown v. Board of Education*. When the Supreme Court rejected racial segregation, it stressed the importance of education as a crucible for good citizenship. And for many students, schools may be the *only* place they might be exposed to the American political tradition.[67]

---

[63] John G. Roberts, Jr., 2019 Year-End Report on the Federal Judiciary, at 4 (Dec. 31, 2019), https://bit.ly/3edKCNP.

[64] Sandra Day O'Connor, Speech at Games for Change 5th Annual Festival (June 4, 2008) quoted in Seth Schiesel, "Former Justice Promotes Web-Based Civics Lessons," N.Y. Times, June 9, 2008, at 7.

[65] Ronald Reagan, Remarks at the Annual Convention of Kiwanis International (July 6, 1987), https://bit.ly/3vFvP4n (borrowing from Ronald Reagan, A Time for Choosing (Oct. 27, 1964), https://bit.ly/2SrsWWH); see also Ronald Reagan, Remarks at the Dedication of the James Madison Memorial Building of the Library of Congress (Nov. 20, 1981), https://bit.ly/3xLIt3K.

[66] Franklin urged us to focus on young people, as "general virtue is more probably to be expected and obtained from the *education* of youth, than from the *exhortation* of adult persons" since "bad habits and vices of the mind . . . like diseases of the body," are "more easily prevented than cured." Letter from Benjamin Franklin to Samuel Johnson (Aug. 23, 1750), https://bit.ly/3tn5xSN.

[67] Research confirms an undeniable link between civics classes in school and civics knowledge (and participation) after graduation. See "Americans' Civics Knowledge Increases but Still has a Long Way to Go," Annenberg Pub. Pol'y Ctr. (Sept. 12, 2019), https://bit.ly/3h1F0YI; cf. Katharine Cornell Gorka, "Why We Need to Reemphasize America's Founding Principles in Civics Education," Heritage Found., May 27, 2020, https://herit.ag/3vIS7Cy ("We must teach the next generations a deeper understanding of why our Founders risked their lives for the right to govern themselves, why they believed a Constitution and the Bill of Rights were necessary, and why they committed to equality for all, but then failed to codify that in the Constitution.").

But it won't be easy. A recent study examined the mission and vision statements of America's hundred largest school districts.[68] The study asked, "What exactly is our purpose?" I always thought the chief purpose of education was to prepare the next generation for thoughtful self-government. To know math, yes, but to also know how to take the measure of leaders. To know history, yes, but to also know what it means to be an American—to cherish our stunning political heritage and its vision of liberty and equality and justice for all. To help children be not just college-ready or career-ready, but civic-ready.

As Jefferson put it, "if a nation expects to be ignorant & free . . . it expects what never was & never will be."[69] Education, he said, enables "every man to judge for himself what will secure or endanger his freedom."[70] For popular sovereignty to work, education must underscore, not undermine, our common civic identity. Education should instill in children a respect for American self-government and the tools to achieve it—to equip students not just academically but civically. But in the mission and vision statements of the 100 largest school districts in America, the word "America" appeared exactly zero times.

Schools, however, shouldn't bear the full burden. Judges play a role too. As Chief Justice Roberts put it, "Civic education, like all education, is a continuing enterprise and conversation," and judges, "[b]y virtue of their judicial responsibilities . . . are necessarily engaged in civics education."[71] We explain our reasoning in written opinions, lead naturalization ceremonies, oversee mock legal proceedings, etc. This past March, the Judicial Conference of the United States affirmed that civics education is a core component of judicial service. And the Administrative Office of the U.S. Courts has developed terrific online resources for judges, teachers, attorneys, and parents.[72]

---

[68] Robert Pondiscio & Kate Stringer, "On Constitution Day, in search of the public mission of schools," Thomas B. Fordham Inst., Sept. 16, 2015, https://bit.ly/3vMmOqt.

[69] Letter from Thomas Jefferson to Charles Yancey (Jan. 6, 1816), https://bit.ly/3nMYIZM.

[70] Letter from Thomas Jefferson to John Tyler (May 26, 1810), https://bit.ly/3thh0U9.

[71] Roberts, Report on the Federal Judiciary, *supra* note 63, at 2, 4.

[72] I provide all of this information both to plug the federal courts' civic education efforts and to emphasize that the opportunities to boost civic literacy are abundant. Certainly, as times change, approaches will need to change too, harnessing technology and experiential learning. I'm even willing to overlook the occasional F-bomb on the *Hamilton* soundtrack if it means more people know the ideals that animated our Founding.

And *lawyers*, which many of you are, are uniquely equipped to help. The public spiritedness of lawyers has *always* been a defining feature of America. Indeed, lawyers have played major roles in some of our most triumphant chapters:[73]

- 25 of 56 signers of the Declaration of Independence were lawyers;
- At least 34 of 55 delegates to the Constitutional Convention;
- 22 of 39 signers of the Constitution; and
- More than half our nation's presidents.[74]

The legal profession, as Justice Brandeis put it 116 years ago, affords "unusual opportunities for usefulness. . . . [that are] probably unequalled. There is a call upon the legal profession to do a great work for this country."[75] Lawyers are vital community connectors and civic switchboards.[76] The profession is different today, but the calling of lawyers to public spiritedness and robust citizenship endures.

[73] The number of lawyers in Congress has steadily declined even as the ranks of lawyers has grown, both in raw numbers and as a percentage of the population. The peak of Congress's lawyer population was around 1850: 80 percent. Ana Swanson, "How the Most Disliked—and Elected—Profession Is Disappearing from Politics," Wash. Post, Jan. 19, 2016, https://wapo.st/2N5nKRE. Today it's at an all-time low: just a third. Justin Fox, "Maybe Washington Does Need More Lawyers," Bloomberg, Mar. 8, 2019, https://bloom.bg/3eXh3iV.

[74] Nick Robinson, The Decline of the Lawyer-Politician, 65 Buff. L. Rev. 657, 667 (2017) (over half of presidents); *id.* at 669 (25 of 56 signers of Declaration of Independence); "Signers of the Constitution: Biographical Sketches," Nat'l Park Serv., July 29, 2004, https://bit.ly/2QSLYoq (22 of 39 signers of the Constitution); "Fascinating Facts about the U.S. Constitution," ConstitutionFacts.com, https://bit.ly/3xL66JA (last visited Apr. 27, 2021) (34 of 55 delegates to the Constitutional Convention); "Law Day: 10 famous people who were lawyers," Nat'l Const. Ctr.: Blog, May 1, 2021, https://bit.ly/3xL6mIy (35 of 55 delegates to the Constitutional Convention).

[75] Louis D. Brandeis, The Opportunity in the Law, in 5 The Professions 185, 194 (Melville Weston Fuller ed., 1911).

[76] Seventy years ago, Justice Robert Jackson penned a lyrical essay and described a lawyer who "understands the structure of society and how its groups interlock and interact," how the community "lives and works under the law." Robert H. Jackson, The County-Seat Lawyer, 36 A.B.A. J. 497, 497 (1950). Justice Jackson portrayed such lawyers as "unsung heroes of the Republic," whose monument is a "free and self-governing Republic." David F. Levi, Dana Remus & Abigail Frisch, Reclaiming the Role of Lawyers as Community Connectors, Judicature 32 (Fall 2019) (quoting Jackson, County-Seat Lawyer, *supra*, at 497), https://bit.ly/2Sm2c9T.

*   *   *

At Disney World a few years ago, my children were mortified in the Hall of Presidents when I yelled, "WHOO-HOO!" for animatronic Calvin Coolidge. But Silent Cal understood the ineffable genius of what happened 233 years ago today: "To live under the American Constitution is the greatest political privilege that was ever accorded to the human race."[77]

A republic comes with responsibility. Self-government is not self-perpetuating. It's tough sledding, and each generation must take its turn. This raucous Republic belongs to us all, and its preservation is up to us all. Franklin told Mrs. Powel, "if you *can* keep it." A quarter of a millennium later, with every tool laid at our feet, there is no longer a question of *capability*. There is only a question of *culpability*.

America boasts the oldest written national constitution on earth. What an extravagant blessing. But preserving that inheritance requires a culture that prizes liberty and public-spirited virtue. For now, We the People are—and through God's grace, will remain—the world's oldest constitutional republic.

If we can keep it.

---

[77] Calvin Coolidge, Speech, Dinner at the White House (Dec. 12, 1924), https://bit.ly/3d3TTqU.

Protecting Free Exercise under *Smith* and after *Smith*

*Douglas Laycock** and Thomas C. Berg***

Fulton v. City of Philadelphia[1] is an important win for religious liberty. The Supreme Court ruled that Philadelphia could not terminate its foster-care services contract with Catholic Social Services (CSS) on the ground that CSS declines, because of its religious beliefs, to certify same-sex couples as foster parents. Teachings about sex and marriage are central to many religions; so are works of service. If religions lose the ability to serve because they act on their central teachings, the harm to free exercise of religion is severe. The Court prevented that—and the result was unanimous.

Fulton protected CSS under the current free-exercise rules of *Employment Division v. Smith*.[2] It held that Philadelphia's nondiscrimination policy failed *Smith*'s requirement that a law burdening religion be generally applicable, because the policy allowed exceptions in the city's unconstrained discretion. The majority opinion thus avoided deciding the broader question, central to free-exercise issues in other cases: whether the unprotective half of *Smith* should be overruled, so that government should have to provide strong justification for substantially burdening religion even through a generally applicable, formally religion-neutral law. Three concurring justices, in an opinion by Justice Samuel Alito, argued at length for overruling *Smith*; two others, in an opinion by Justice Amy Coney Barrett,

---

* Robert E. Scott Distinguished Professor of Law and Professor of Religious Studies, University of Virginia, and Alice McKean Young Regents Chair in Law Emeritus, University of Texas.

** James L. Oberstar Professor of Law and Public Policy, University of St. Thomas (Minnesota).

[1] 141 S. Ct. 1868 (2021).

[2] 494 U.S. 872 (1990).

suggested that *Smith* was mistaken but that they were hesitant to overrule it without knowing what would replace it.

In this article, we first briefly examine free exercise under *Smith*, in light of *Fulton* and its effect on the current rules. Next, we briefly revisit the arguments for overruling aspects of *Smith* and reinstating strict or at least demanding scrutiny of the burdens on religion from generally applicable laws. But we give the most attention to describing, in the final part, how to replace *Smith* with a strong but workable doctrine protecting against generally applicable laws.

I. Free Exercise under *Smith*: What *Fulton* Does

Smith announced two rules. The better-known unprotective rule says that the Free Exercise Clause offers no protection against neutral and generally applicable laws.[3] No matter how severely such a law burdens the exercise of religion, it presents no free-exercise issue. Refusing religious exemptions requires no justification and need serve no government interest. But *Smith*'s protective rule says that if a law is not neutral, or not generally applicable, any burden it imposes on religion must be necessary to serve a compelling government interest.[4] *Fulton* clarifies *Smith*'s protective rule in ways that strengthen protection. It is the latest in a series of decisions protecting free exercise under *Smith*.[5]

First, *Fulton* confirms that neutrality and general applicability are distinct concepts, both of which must be satisfied. "Government fails to act neutrally," the Court said, "when it proceeds in a manner intolerant of religious beliefs or restricts practices because of their religious nature."[6] CSS had presented evidence of nonneutrality; for example, the relevant city agency head had asserted that CSS should

---

[3] *Id.* at 878–79.

[4] See *id.* at 877–78; Church of the Lukumi Babalu Aye v. City of Hialeah, 508 U.S. 520, 531–32 (1993) (following *Smith* and invalidating nonneutral ordinances under strict scrutiny).

[5] Tandon v. Newsom, 141 S. Ct. 1294 (2021) (per curiam) (finding that a COVID-related order restricting religious gatherings was not neutral or generally applicable); Roman Catholic Diocese of Brooklyn v. Cuomo, 141 S. Ct. 63 (2020) (same); Masterpiece Cakeshop, Ltd. v. Colo. Civil Rights Comm'n, 138 S. Ct. 1719 (2018) (holding that the civil rights commission acted nonneutrally in imposing nondiscrimination penalties on a wedding-cake baker).

[6] Fulton, 141 S. Ct. at 1877 (citing Masterpiece Cakeshop, 138 S. Ct. at 1730–32).

change its policy because that would be more consistent with Pope Francis's attitudes.[7] But the Court found it "more straightforward to resolve this case under the rubric of general applicability."[8]

A law or policy fails general applicability in at least two situations. One is when it "prohibits religious conduct while permitting secular conduct that undermines the government's asserted interests in a similar way."[9] A law can fail general applicability when it permits or exempts even a small number of secular activities; it need not target religion.[10] Earlier this term, the Court phrased the rule as applying whenever regulations exempt or permit even one comparable secular activity: that is, "whenever they treat *any* comparable secular activity more favorably than religious exercise."[11]

The other failure of general applicability occurred in *Fulton*. Philadelphia's standard foster-care contract allowed a city official to grant exceptions to the nondiscrimination policy "in his/her sole discretion."[12] It therefore fell within the principle, dating back to *Smith*, that "[a] law is not generally applicable if it 'invite[s]' the government to consider the particular reasons for a person's conduct by providing 'a mechanism for individualized exemptions.'"[13] *Smith* had announced that principle to explain *Sherbert v. Verner*[14] and other cases protecting the right to unemployment benefits for people who refused work for religious reasons. Unemployment-benefits laws allow benefits claimants to refuse available work for "'good cause,'" a standard that "permit[s] the government to grant exemptions based on the circumstances underlying each application."[15] When government has "[such] a system of individual exemptions, it may not refuse to extend that system to cases of 'religious hardship' without compelling reason."[16]

[7] *Id.* at 1875 (quoting App. to Pet. for Cert. 366).

[8] *Id.* at 1877.

[9] *Id.* (citing Lukumi, 508 U.S. at 542–46).

[10] See Douglas Laycock & Steven T. Collis, Generally Applicable Law and the Free Exercise of Religion, 95 Neb. L. Rev. 1, 19–23 (2016).

[11] Tandon, 141 S. Ct. at 1296 (emphasis in original).

[12] Fulton, 141 S. Ct. at 1878.

[13] *Id.* at 1877 (quoting Smith, 494 U.S. at 884).

[14] 374 U.S. 398 (1963).

[15] Fulton, 141 S. Ct. at 1877 (quoting Smith, 494 U.S. at 884).

[16] *Id.* (quoting Smith, 494 U.S. at 884).

This principle is protective, since many laws have provisions for discretionary exemptions or determinations.[17] And *Fulton* holds that the principle applies whenever a law "create[s] a formal mechanism" for discretionary exceptions, even if officials never grant any. The discretion is enough to enable discrimination against religion, "because it 'invite[s]' the government to decide which reasons for not complying with the policy are worthy of solicitude."[18] Discretion enables government to prohibit the religious practice without fear of later having to apply the same rule to some analogous secular practice it would prefer to permit.

Fulton also says that government cannot adopt a nonneutral or less-than-generally applicable policy just because it is setting rules for its contractors rather than regulating the general public.[19] Discrimination against religion is forbidden in whichever category covers public contracting, whether it is government "acting in its managerial role"[20] or government funding private entities for public purposes.[21]

Finally, *Fulton* holds that civil rights laws do not automatically, and in every context, serve a compelling government interest. Importantly, the liberals joined this holding. The specific holding depended on the finding that the city's policy was not generally applicable. The Court recognized that the interest in "the equal treatment of prospective foster parents and foster children" is "a weighty one"; "'gay persons and gay couples cannot be treated as social outcasts or as inferior in dignity and worth.'"[22] But that interest could not justify denying CSS a religious exception, given "[t]he creation of a system of exceptions under the contract"; the city offered "no compelling reason" for "denying an exception to CSS while making them available

---

[17] See, e.g., Richard F. Duncan, Free Exercise and Individualized Exemptions: Herein of Smith, Sherbert, Hogwarts, and Religious Liberty, 83 Neb. L. Rev. 1178 (2005) (collecting cases involving policies in public schools, state universities, government employment, and land-use regulation).

[18] 141 S. Ct. at 1879 (quoting Smith, 494 U.S. at 884).

[19] *Id.* at 1878.

[20] *Id.* (citation omitted); see Lyng v. Nw. Indian Cemetery Protective Ass'n, 485 U.S. 439, 453 (1988) ("The Constitution does not permit government to discriminate against religions" in managing public lands.).

[21] Espinoza v. Mont. Dep't of Revenue, 140 S. Ct. 2246 (2020); Trinity Lutheran Church v. Comer, 137 S. Ct. 2012 (2017).

[22] Fulton, 141 S. Ct. at 1882 (quoting Masterpiece Cakeshop, 138 S. Ct. at 1727).

to others."[23] Under this reasoning, a nondiscrimination law with no exceptions might still serve a compelling interest in ensuring equal treatment in every instance. Or it might not; that issue remains open.

But the Court also said something striking concerning this issue: "CSS seeks only an accommodation that will allow it to continue serving the children of Philadelphia in a manner consistent with its religious beliefs; it does not seek to impose those beliefs on anyone else."[24] This is the underlying issue in the clashes between nondiscrimination and religious liberty: are religious objectors imposing on LGBTQ claimants, or vice versa, or can each group have room to follow its own commitments? For all three liberal justices to join the statement that religious social services are not imposing their beliefs is a symbolically powerful point. And the point logically applies whether or not Philadelphia's policy was generally applicable. It may depend—or more precisely, the weight of the government's interest in regulating the church depends—on whether there are ample alternative providers and whether the religious agency will refer same-sex couples to them.

For these reasons, *Fulton* is significant. Even so, its general applicability holding turns on specific features of Philadelphia's rules. Cities can rewrite their rules to eliminate discretionary exceptions. And to reach its conclusion, the Court had to hold that Philadelphia's public-accommodations ordinance does not cover foster-care placement; the nondiscrimination laws in other jurisdictions may explicitly cover such services.[25] Pennsylvania's courts could even reject the Court's interpretation of Philadelphia's ordinance, as Justice Alito pointed out; state-court interpretation of local law would be binding.[26]

If cities take those steps, however, they might ultimately lose because the Court decides to strike down burdens on religion even from generally applicable laws. *Fulton* indicates that at least five justices believe *Smith*'s unprotective rule was wrongly decided. Alito's concurrence, joined by Justices Clarence Thomas and Neil Gorsuch, argued at length that the Court should overrule *Smith* and apply some form of heightened scrutiny to generally applicable laws. And Justice Barrett, joined by Justice Brett Kavanaugh, wrote separately that "it is

---

[23] *Id.*

[24] *Id.*

[25] 141 S. Ct. at 1879–81 (majority op.); *id.* at 1927–28 (Gorsuch, J., concurring in the judgment).

[26] *Id.* at 1887 n.21 (Alito, J., concurring in the judgment).

difficult to see why the Free Exercise Clause . . . offers nothing more than protection from discrimination."[27] They joined the majority opinion because overruling *Smith* was unnecessary and because they were unclear what would replace it. To these five we should probably add at least Justice Stephen Breyer; he did not join Barrett's criticism of *Smith*, but he previously called for reconsidering it.[28]

II. Overruling *Smith*

Our main goal in this article is to sketch how review should work if the Court overrules the unprotective part of *Smith* and reinstates demanding scrutiny of burdens from generally applicable laws. But it is worth saying a little to supplement Justice Alito's concurrence: why *Smith*'s unprotective part should be overruled.

Justice Barrett found the historical materials "more silent than supportive" in challenging *Smith*, but the textual and structural arguments against it "more compelling."[29] The textual and structural arguments are indeed convincing, and straightforward. A law that prohibits religious exercise in a particular application still prohibits religious exercise, even if it applies to other behavior as well. Religious individuals or entities still cannot practice their faith.

But the historical arguments, laid out by Justice Alito, are also persuasive. If the Free Exercise Clause does not apply to neutral and generally applicable laws, it cannot serve its original purposes. Those purposes include protecting individual conscience and preventing human suffering, social conflict, and persecution. In the 18th century, every colony found that free exercise required exempting dissenters from oaths, military service, and other requirements that burdened their religious practices.[30] Those laws, although neutral and generally

---

[27] *Id.* at 1883 (Barrett, J., concurring).

[28] City of Boerne v. Flores, 521 U.S. 507, 566 (1997) (Breyer, J., dissenting).

[29] Fulton, 141 S. Ct. at 1883 (Barrett, J., concurring).

[30] Scholarship setting forth this history includes Thomas J. Curry, The First Freedoms: Church and State in America to the Passage of the First Amendment (1986); Douglas Laycock, Regulatory Exemptions of Religious Behavior and the Original Understanding of the Establishment Clause, 81 Notre Dame L. Rev. 1793 (2006); Michael W. McConnell, The Origins and Historical Understanding of Free Exercise of Religion, 103 Harv. L. Rev. 1409 (1990). See also Brief of Christian Legal Society et al. as Amici Curiae in Support of Petitioners at 8–15, Fulton v. City of Philadelphia, 141 S. Ct. 1868 (2021) (No. 19-123) [hereinafter CLS Brief] (presenting concise historical account and collecting sources), https://bit.ly/3f6K7Fm.

applicable, overrode conscience, caused psychological suffering and loss of liberty or property, inflamed social conflict, and discouraged people from settling or remaining in the colony.

And free-exercise exemptions are still needed today. Generally applicable laws without exemptions coerce individuals and cause them to suffer for their faith. In today's atmosphere of cultural-political polarization, properly defined protections for religious commitments can reduce fear, resentment, and social conflict.[31]

Overruling *Smith*'s unprotective rule is important even though, in cases culminating in *Fulton*, the Court has strengthened *Smith*'s protective rule, finding various laws to be nonneutral or not generally applicable. Those protections are important, and the Court should not undo them in the course of undoing *Smith*'s unprotective rule. We return to that point below.

But a threshold requirement to show that a law is not generally applicable has multiple problems. First, it vastly complicates every litigation. Which secular exceptions are sufficiently analogous to count? What standard of review applies to that question? The series of lawsuits over COVID restrictions and religious gatherings dramatized the complications in such questions. Were restricted worship services analogous to permitted big-box retail shopping, or casinos and bowling alleys, or dining outdoors (or indoors)?[32]

The general-applicability threshold also prolongs litigation. Again, Philadelphia could eliminate its discretionary exception, enact a public-accommodations ordinance clearly covering foster care, and relitigate general applicability. But it might be deterred if it knew that heightened scrutiny would apply anyway because *Smith* was no more. And finally, some claimants lose under general applicability when they should not. Courts sometimes erroneously find a rule generally applicable. And rules that are truly generally applicable sometimes seriously burden religion. To illustrate such problems, Justice Alito cited to the COVID cases, while Justice Gorsuch cited baker Jack Phillips of Masterpiece Cakeshop, who won in the Supreme Court but now faces new civil penalties for continuing to

---

[31] See CLS Brief, *supra* note 30, at 16–19.

[32] See Fulton, 141 S. Ct. at 1930 (Gorsuch, J., concurring in the judgment) ("In the last nine months alone, this Court has had to intervene at least half a dozen times to clarify how *Smith* works.").

refuse to create cakes that celebrate events he cannot conscientiously participate in.[33]

Here is another case that highlights the consequences of complications and uncertainty in free-exercise law. Mary Stinemetz was a Jehovah's Witness who needed a liver transplant without a blood transfusion. Bloodless transplants were available in Omaha. But Kansas Medicaid wouldn't pay for medical care more than 50 miles beyond the Kansas state line—an arbitrary limit in any event, and more so because transplants were cheaper in Omaha than in Kansas. The rule wasn't even generally applicable, because Kansas officials had "absolute discretion" to grant exceptions.[34] But through multiple hearings and appeals, they refused any exception for Stinemetz. They failed, a court concluded, "to suggest any state interest, much less a compelling interest," that justified their refusal.[35] They understood *Smith* to mean that they didn't need a justification.

The court ultimately held that their refusal violated the federal Constitution, invoking *Smith*'s protective rule, and that it violated the Kansas constitution, rejecting *Smith*'s unprotective rule as a matter of state law.[36] But it was too late. During two years of administrative appeals and litigation, Stinemetz's condition had deteriorated, and she was no longer medically eligible for a transplant. She died of liver disease in the year after the court's decision.[37] She died for her faith while lawyers argued about general applicability.

After *Fulton*, the discretionary exception in Kansas's rules would clearly have entitled Stinemetz to relief. But governments have multiple ways to characterize their rules as neutral and generally applicable. If officials can argue over general applicability, they will. No matter how stringently general applicability is interpreted, free exercise under *Smith* will never protect in all the cases where it should.

---

[33] *Id.* at 1921–22 (Alito, J., concurring in the judgment); *id.* at 1930 (Gorsuch, J., concurring in the judgment) (citing AP, "Lakewood Baker Jack Phillips Sued for Refusing Gender Transition Cake," Mar. 22, 2021, https://cbsloc.al/3rPj0ny).

[34] Stinemetz v. Kan. Health Pol'y Auth., 252 P.3d 141, 155 (Kan. Ct. App. 2011).

[35] *Id.*

[36] *Id.* at 148–61.

[37] Brad Cooper, "Jehovah's Witness Who Needed Bloodless Transplant Dies," Kan. City Star, Oct. 25, 2012.

III. Free Exercise after *Smith*

Justices Barrett and Kavanaugh apparently believe that *Smith* is mistaken but want to know what should replace it. They did not need to overrule it in *Fulton*; the general-applicability holding was available. But some cases will rest primarily on challenging *Smith*. The Court denied certiorari in two such cases after *Fulton*,[38] but others are in the pipeline.

The Court can overrule *Smith* before it resolves every follow-on issue. But we want to lay out some considerations for a post-*Smith* approach and, in doing so, respond to the questions that Justice Barrett raised.

A. How Demanding Should Scrutiny Be, in General?

1. Compelling interest

We think the compelling-interest test of *Sherbert v. Verner*[39] and *Wisconsin v. Yoder*[40] should usually govern when a generally applicable law substantially burdens religious practice. That test properly holds that only the prevention of significant harm can justify prohibiting religiously motivated conduct. And it has a flexibility that allows it to apply to the wide range of circumstances in which religious exercise is prohibited.

The compelling-interest test is appropriate because the right to practice religion is a fundamental right. Substantial burdens on fundamental rights generally trigger the compelling-interest test. The test has applied to a variety of fundamental rights, from speech about public issues[41] or about labor organization[42] to decisions about procreation.[43] In particular, the test has frequently applied in cases of as-applied First Amendment challenges based on speech

---

[38] Ricks v. Idaho Contractors Bd., 435 P.3d 1 (Idaho Ct. App. 2018), cert. denied, (No. 19-66), 2021 WL 2637837 (U.S. June 28, 2021); Arlene's Flowers, Inc. v. Washington, 441 P.3d 1203 (Wash. 2019), cert. denied, (No. 19-333), 2021 WL 2742795 (U.S. July 2, 2021).

[39] 374 U.S. 398 (1963).

[40] 406 U.S. 205 (1972).

[41] Williams-Yulee v. Fla. Bar, 575 U.S. 433, 442–44 (2015) (citing, e.g., Eu v. S.F. Cty. Democratic Cent. Comm., 489 U.S. 214, 223 (1989)).

[42] Thomas v. Collins, 323 U.S. 516, 530 (1945) ("Only the gravest abuses, endangering paramount interests, give occasion for permissible limitation.").

[43] Carey v. Population Servs. Int'l, 431 U.S. 678, 686 (1977).

or association. As in free-exercise cases, these challenges seek exemption from facially neutral and generally applicable laws, often including laws regulating conduct. These cases support the idea of exemptions, but more specifically they support application of the compelling-interest test.

One set of cases involves laws compelling organizational disclosures. *Brown v. Socialist Workers '74 Campaign Committee*[44] held that a law requiring disclosure of political parties' campaign contributions and expenditures, valid on its face, "cannot be constitutionally applied" to a minor party whose members and contributors would face "threats, harassment or reprisals" if their identities were known.[45] Disclosure requirements mostly regulate conduct, not speech; disclosure serves an anti-corruption purpose unrelated to suppressing expression. But the Court required an exemption where the law would significantly deter political association.

Brown reaffirmed *NAACP v. Alabama ex rel. Patterson*,[46] which unanimously exempted the NAACP from an order, entered pursuant to a generally applicable corporation statute, requiring it to disclose its membership lists. Because those members would face public reprisals, the burden on association from disclosure had to serve a compelling interest, even if it was the incidental effect of a law that "appear[ed] to be totally unrelated to protected liberties."[47] The Court's new decision striking down mandatory charitable-donor disclosures muddies the analysis but remains consistent with the proposition that serious burdens on association require compelling justification.[48]

---

[44] 459 U.S. 87 (1982).

[45] *Id.* at 101–02.

[46] 357 U.S. 449 (1958).

[47] *Id.* at 461; see *id.* at 463 (The "'subordinating interest of the State must be compelling.'") (citation omitted).

[48] Ams. for Prosperity Found. v. Bonta, 141 S. Ct. 2373 (2021). The plurality in this case applied "exacting scrutiny" and struck down the disclosure law on its face, not just when it created severe burdens. *Id.* at 2383, 2387–89 (Roberts, C.J., for three justices). But Justices Alito and Gorsuch, who provided the decisive votes, noted that *NAACP v. Alabama* had required a "compelling" interest; they declined to embrace a lower standard than strict scrutiny. *Id.* at 2391–92 (Alito, J., concurring in part and concurring in the judgment). And the dissent reaffirmed the *NAACP* and *Boy Scouts of America v. Dale* holdings that significant burdens on association trigger demanding scrutiny. *Id.* at 2393–96 (Sotomayor, J., dissenting).

Another set of cases applying the compelling-interest test involves expressive associations' conflict with nondiscrimination laws. The Court ordered an exemption from a generally applicable nondiscrimination law in *Boy Scouts of America v. Dale*,[49] holding that the Scouts could not be penalized for dismissing a scoutmaster whose public statements and identity conflicted with the organization's message. *Dale* said that, while public-accommodation laws generally serve compelling interests, those interests did not justify applying the laws when they "would significantly burden the organization's right" to express its message.[50] The Court granted a similar exemption in *Hurley v. Irish-American Gay, Lesbian, and Bisexual Group of Boston*,[51] unanimously holding that parade organizers did not have to admit marchers with a message inconsistent with the organizers' message. *Hurley* applied at least demanding, and perhaps strict, scrutiny.[52] In cases involving business-related associations, the Court still applied the compelling-interest test but said the test was satisfied; the equality interest was strong, and the group's expressive interest was weaker because its membership was unrestricted apart from excluding women.[53]

A final example is *NAACP v. Button*,[54] which invalidated, as applied to the NAACP, a Virginia statute that prohibited any organization from retaining a lawyer in connection with litigation as to which it was not a party and had no pecuniary right or liability. The Court applied strict scrutiny even assuming that the law's purpose was "not to curtail free expression" but "merely to insure high professional standards" by preventing activity arguably analogous to barratry or champerty.[55] "However valid" those interests were concerning general civil litigation, and "however even-handed [the law's] terms appear," it unconstitutionally burdened the NAACP's litigation campaign.[56] That campaign was not a mere "technique of resolving private differences" but rather a form of "political

[49] 530 U.S. 640 (2000).

[50] *Id.* at 659.

[51] 515 U.S. 557 (1995).

[52] *Id.* at 577 (noting the requirement "that a challenged restriction on speech serve a compelling, or at least important, governmental object"); *id.* at 580.

[53] See Roberts v. U.S. Jaycees, 468 U.S. 609, 623–28 (1984).

[54] 371 U.S. 415 (1963).

[55] *Id.* at 438–39.

[56] *Id.* at 439, 436.

association," and likely "the most effective form" given the hostility of the white majority and elected officials.[57]

The compelling-interest test is demanding, but it will be satisfied more often in religious-exemption cases than in speech cases. Government has interests in regulating conduct that do not apply to belief or speech. "The [freedom to believe] is absolute but, in the nature of things, the [freedom to act] cannot be."[58] And conduct regulations that are neutral and generally applicable will be justified more often than those that are discriminatory or selective. A pattern of exceptions undercuts the government's asserted interest and causes it to fail strict scrutiny. "[A] law cannot be regarded as protecting an interest 'of the highest order' . . . when it leaves appreciable damage to that supposedly vital interest unprohibited."[59]

The compelling-interest test sets a strong but workable standard. When Congress reimposed the test in 1993 in the Religious Freedom Restoration Act (RFRA), it found that "compelling interest" was "a workable test for striking sensible balances between religious liberty and competing prior governmental interests."[60] Before *Smith*, the government had proved compelling interests in free-exercise cases involving racial equality in education,[61] tax collection,[62] and the military draft.[63] But the Court had always affirmed that the government had to show that the conduct "'posed some substantial threat to public safety, peace or order.'"[64]

The compelling-interest standard has not come close to producing the "anarchy" of which *Smith* warned.[65] One comparison of the

---

[57] *Id.* at 429, 431.

[58] Cantwell v. Connecticut, 310 U.S. 296, 303–04 (1940).

[59] Lukumi, 508 U.S. at 547 (quoting Fla. Star v. B.J.F., 491 U.S. 524, 541–42 (1989) (Scalia, J., concurring in part and concurring in the judgment)).

[60] 42 U.S.C. § 2000bb(a)(5).

[61] Bob Jones Univ. v. United States, 461 U.S. 574 (1983).

[62] United States v. Lee, 455 U.S. 252 (1982).

[63] Gillette v. United States, 401 U.S. 437 (1971).

[64] Yoder, 406 U.S. at 230 (quoting Sherbert, 374 U.S. at 403). For our fuller examinations of the pre-*Smith* case law, see Thomas C. Berg, What Hath Congress Wrought? An Interpretive Guide to the Religious Freedom Restoration Act, 39 Vill. L. Rev. 1, 9–12, 26–28 (1994); Douglas Laycock & Oliver S. Thomas, Interpreting the Religious Freedom Restoration Act, 73 Tex. L. Rev. 209, 224–28 (1994).

[65] 494 U.S. at 888.

results of strict scrutiny under various claims from 1990 through 2003 found that free-exercise claims, including RFRA claims, were the least likely to invalidate the government action: the government won 59 percent of the time, 74 percent if the category were limited to challenges to generally applicable laws (where strict scrutiny is triggered only by a RFRA claim).[66] Other studies show similar results.[67]

That is not a high success rate for religious claimants. RFRA has surely been underenforced—as one of us has concluded concerning its counterpart, the Religious Land Use and Institutionalized Persons Act (RLUIPA), which also applies the compelling-interest test.[68] But the success rates are also far from meaningless. Federal and state RFRAs have protected a number of minority religious practices.[69] Protection is important to those faiths, and to the larger faiths that have succeeded in important cases.

The compelling-interest test need not govern every situation. For example, interference with a religious organization's key internal governance decisions, like its selection of ministers, is absolutely barred under the *Hosanna-Tabor* decision, which Barrett mentions.[70] Indeed, the compelling-interest approach should not be all-or-nothing in nature. It is most workable and sensible, as one of us has long argued, when it balances the burdens on religion against the

[66] Adam Winkler, Fatal in Theory and Strict in Fact: An Empirical Analysis of Strict Scrutiny in the Federal Courts, 59 Vand. L. Rev. 793, 857–58, 861 (2006). By contrast, the government won only 22 percent of free-speech cases. *Id.* at 844.

[67] Stephanie H. Barclay & Mark L. Rienzi, Constitutional Anomalies or As-Applied Challenges? A Defense of Religious Exemptions, 59 B.C. L. Rev. 1595, 1640 (2018) (the government prevailed in 50 percent of RFRA appellate cases from 2014–2017, 71 percent if contraception-mandate cases are excluded); Luke W. Goodrich & Rachel N. Busick, Sex, Drugs, and Eagle Feathers: An Empirical Study of Federal Religious Freedom Cases, 48 Seton Hall L. Rev. 353, 379–80 (2018) (government prevailed in 56 percent of cases, 65 percent if contraception cases are excluded); Gregory C. Sisk, Michael Heise, & Andrew P. Morriss, Searching for the Soul of Judicial Decisionmaking: An Empirical Study of Religious Freedom Decisions, 65 Ohio St. L.J. 491, 544–45, 555 (2004) (finding 35.6 percent success rate for "free-exercise/accommodation" cases in federal appellate and trial courts from 1986 to 1995).

[68] Douglas Laycock & Luke W. Goodrich, RLUIPA: Necessary, Modest, and Under-Enforced, 39 Fordham Urb. L.J. 1021 (2012).

[69] Christopher C. Lund, RFRA, State RFRAs, and Religious Minorities, 53 San Diego L. Rev. 163, 165–71 (2016) (collecting cases).

[70] Fulton, 141 S. Ct. at 1883 (Barrett, J., concurring) (citing Hosanna-Tabor Evangelical Lutheran Church & Sch. v. EEOC, 565 U.S. 171 (2012)).

government interests, with a heavy thumb on the scale for religious freedom.[71] We return to that point below.[72] Our point here is that the overall approach should not be substantially weaker than "compelling interest."

2. The flawed analogy to categories with weaker scrutiny

Justice Barrett noted that "this Court's resolution of conflicts between generally applicable laws and other First Amendment rights—like speech and assembly—has been much more nuanced" than strict scrutiny.[73] But if that is meant to propose a weak version of heightened scrutiny for free-exercise conflicts with generally applicable laws, it rests on an analogy that is flawed in many, even most, cases.

Barrett did not specify what she meant by "generally applicable laws" affecting speech or assembly. She might have been referring to cases of symbolic or expressive conduct like *United States v. O'Brien*,[74] which held that a war protester who burned his draft card could not claim exemption, based on the expressive nature of his act, from a general law that prohibited destroying a draft card. *O'Brien* applied a weak version of intermediate scrutiny; the Court accepted reasons of administrative convenience that usually fail anything beyond low-level rational-basis review.[75]

But as we already noted, in multiple other decisions involving conduct with expressive implications, the Court has used strict scrutiny. *Boy Scouts v. Dale*, for example, used it to strike down the application of the general law against discrimination in public accommodations.[76] The Court distinguished *O'Brien*, saying that the nondiscrimination law in *Dale* "directly and immediately affects associational rights . . . that enjoy First Amendment protection," while the draft-card law "only incidentally affects the free speech rights

[71] Douglas Laycock, The Religious Exemption Debate, 11 Rutgers J.L. & Religion 139, 151–52 (2009).

[72] See *infra* Part III.B.4.

[73] Fulton, 141 S. Ct. at 1883 (Barrett, J., concurring).

[74] 391 U.S. 367 (1968).

[75] See, e.g., *id.* at 378–79 (holding that the card gave an "easy and painless" way of showing that the holder had registered and a "potentially useful" reminder to holders to notify the draft board of changed address or status).

[76] Dale, 530 U.S. at 657–58.

of those who happen to use a violation of that law as a symbol of protest."[77]

The Court sometimes calls the effect of generally applicable laws "incidental,"[78] but that was not *Dale's* usage, for the public-accommodations law was generally applicable yet the Court called its effect "direct." The difference between *Dale* and *O'Brien* appears to be that a prohibition on symbolic conduct leaves open many other ways to express the same views. Burning a draft card was dramatic but was far from the only way of protesting the war. Sleeping in the park on the National Mall was far from the only way to call attention to the plight of homeless persons.[79]

Adequate alternative channels are also crucial in the other category of "generally applicable laws" where review is (in Justice Barrett's words) "nuanced": namely, content-neutral time, place, and manner restrictions. The Court permits application of these laws if they "are justified without reference to the content of the regulated speech, . . . are narrowly tailored to serve a significant governmental interest, and . . . leave open ample alternative channels for communication of the information."[80] In other words, the law is often upheld, under moderate review, if—but only if—it leaves ample alternative channels.[81] A total ban on signs on residential property leaves insufficient alternatives.[82] So does a ban on door-to-door canvassing of residences, as applied to religious and political speech.[83] And the law can be invalid in application if alternatives are inadequate for the particular speaker—as alternatives to litigation were inadequate for the NAACP, even if not for all speakers, because the political process was closed to Southern blacks.

---

[77] *Id.* at 659.

[78] See Smith, 494 U.S. at 878.

[79] Clark v. Cmty. for Creative Non-Violence, 468 U.S. 288, 295 (1984).

[80] Ward v. Rock Against Racism, 491 U.S. 781, 791 (1989) (citation omitted).

[81] See generally Geoffrey R. Stone, Content-Neutral Restrictions, 54 U. Chi. L. Rev. 46, 57–58 (1987) (discussing alternative channels of communication as part of overarching question whether a content-neutral law "unduly constrict[s] the opportunities for free expression").

[82] City of Ladue v. Gilleo, 512 U.S. 43, 56 (1994).

[83] Watchtower Bible & Tract Soc'y of N.Y. v. Vill. of Stratton, 536 U.S. 150, 166–68 (2002).

Substantial burdens on religious practice are usually more like the restrictions in *Boy Scouts v. Dale* than like restrictions on symbolic conduct or on the time, place, and manner of expression. By their nature, burdens on religious practice often leave no adequate alternatives. Most obviously, believers who are prohibited from acting on their belief cannot simply change the belief: if Native Americans are barred from using peyote in worship, they can't switch to wine. Nor can the government say they still have the "alternative" of following their other beliefs. In *Holt v. Hobbs*, where a generally applicable prison rule barred a Muslim inmate from wearing a half-inch beard, officials claimed that he'd suffered no substantial burden because he could still use a prayer rug, receive Islamic literature, correspond with a religious advisor, and observe religious diets and holidays.[84] The unanimous Court rejected that argument: "RLUIPA's 'substantial burden' inquiry asks whether the government has substantially burdened religious exercise (here, the growing of a 1/2-inch beard), not whether the RLUIPA claimant is able to engage in other forms of religious exercise."[85]

From the standpoint of the constitutional interest, telling the free-exercise claimant to practice his other beliefs instead of this one would be like telling the free-speech claimant to communicate other messages instead of this one. In that sense, a prohibition on a religious practice is more like a content-based restriction on speech: it is not "practice-neutral," and for a free-exercise claim, the practice is what matters. Put differently, religious practices are rarely fungible. Assessing whether another practice is close enough to the one restricted would involve courts in difficult religious judgments based on a mistaken premise of near fungibility.

Likewise, if a law blocks a person or institution from pursuing a form of religiously motivated service, it does not help that they can switch to another form of service. When CSS lost the ability to provide foster-care services in Philadelphia, it was no answer to say that it could serve vulnerable persons in other ways. When religious progressives prosecuted for assisting undocumented migrants with food and water raised a RFRA defense, it was no answer to say—as one magistrate judge did—that the defendants could have avoided

---

[84] 574 U.S. 352 (2015).
[85] *Id.* at 361–62.

the burden because their beliefs compelled them "only . . . to aid persons in distress," not specifically to "aid undocumented migrants."[86] The district judge in another such case ruled, more sensibly, that punishment for aiding the people you believe are most in need is a substantial burden.[87]

Often, those providing religiously based service believe God commands them to do so. Those who aid migrants follow the scriptural directives to care for the stranger and sojourner; CSS follows the directives to care for the orphan.[88] At a minimum, they have chosen this service as their very mission. The Court properly noted that caring for orphans is "a mission that the Catholic Church has undertaken since ancient times."[89] Excluding a religious entity from a field of service thus imposes a severe burden analogous to that in *Button*. There it was irrelevant that the NAACP could still advocate for civil rights in multiple other ways. Under the circumstances, litigation was its "most effective form of political association."[90]

There are cases in which courts can assess the adequacy of alternative means of exercising religion; we discuss them below.[91] But alternatives are inadequate in several recurring, important contexts: when a law penalizes a practice stemming from religious tenets (like sacramental peyote use), interferes with a religious organization's internal governance, or significantly burdens a religious organization's ability to provide a service. In those cases, judicial scrutiny must be highly demanding.

3. Serious intermediate scrutiny?

Justice Barrett cited one pre-*Smith* case in which the Court asked whether the government's interest was "substantial," not "compelling."[92] *Gillette v. United States* held that applying the draft law to persons with conscientious objections to a particular war was

---

[86] United States v. Warren, No. CR 18-002230TUC-RCC(BPV), 2018 WL 5257807, at *2 (D. Ariz. May 31, 2018).

[87] United States v. Hoffman, 436 F. Supp. 3d 1272, 1285–87 (D. Ariz. 2020).

[88] See, e.g., Matthew 25:31–46; James 1:27.

[89] Fulton, 141 S. Ct. at 1885 (Alito, J., concurring in the judgment).

[90] Button, 371 U.S. at 431.

[91] See *infra* Part III.B.4.

[92] Fulton, 141 S. Ct. at 1883 (Barrett, J., concurring) (citing Gillette v. United States, 401 U.S. 437, 462 (1971)).

"strictly justified by substantial governmental interests that relate directly to the very impacts questioned."[93] That reference to a direct relation incorporated the opinion's earlier conclusion that Congress had acted permissibly when it exempted objectors to all wars but not objectors to particular wars. The Court, after lengthy discussion, had found that granting selective objections, unlike categorical objections, would pose "a real danger of erratic or even discriminatory decisionmaking in administrative practice," including problems in distinguishing moral objections to a particular war from policy arguments committed to the political process.[94]

Perhaps "strictly justified" indicated strict scrutiny; perhaps "substantial" indicated something less. *Gillette* would have reached the same result either way. The Court would certainly hold the interests in conscription compelling in general. And the fairness and consistency problems with selective-objector exemptions, and the heavy overlap with political judgments, could make denying such exemptions the least restrictive means of serving those interests. Assuming that *Gillette* used intermediate scrutiny, it was a serious version, not the weak version used in *O'Brien*.

Serious versions of intermediate scrutiny have appeared in several decisions in recent years. The Court requires that sex classifications rest on an "exceedingly persuasive" justification, with a "'strong presumption'" that they are invalid.[95] It now judges mandatory disclosures of organizational members or donors or of political contributors under at least "exacting scrutiny," which requires not only "a substantial relation" to "a sufficiently important government interest," but also "narrow tailoring" of the mandates."[96]

Serious intermediate scrutiny would be better than *Smith*'s total abdication of review. But intermediate scrutiny often declines into excessive deference, as in *O'Brien*. If lower courts have underenforced the compelling-interest test,[97] they could just as easily underenforce intermediate scrutiny. If the Court wants anything less than strict scrutiny for challenges to generally applicable laws—if

[93] Gillette, 401 U.S. at 462.

[94] *Id.* at 455; see *id.* at 455–60.

[95] United States v. Virginia, 518 U.S. 515, 532–33 (1996) (citation omitted).

[96] Ams. for Prosperity Found., 141 S. Ct. at 2383–84 (Roberts, C.J., for three justices).

[97] See *supra* notes 65–68 and accompanying text.

it wants to confine strict scrutiny to a near absolute presumption of invalidity—then to prevent underenforcement, it must give clear instructions about the demanding nature of the intermediate review.

B. Key Features of Free-Exercise Challenges

Several elements in the logic and purposes of free exercise can help generate a demanding but workable standard for deciding challenges to generally applicable laws.

1. Considering government interests at the margin

One key feature allowing the doctrine to be protective but workable is that religious-exemption claims are as-applied challenges: they seek to invalidate only one application of the law "while leaving other applications in force."[98] Thus they avoid "nullify[ing] more of a legislature's work than is necessary."[99] They allow courts "to tailor their relief to the religious-freedom claimant and avoid undercutting regulation broadly. . . . By examining government interests and ordering relief 'at the margin,' the court can preserve the law's core purposes while also protecting religious freedom."[100]

Because a free-exercise claimant seeks only an exemption at the margin, the court must measure the government's interest at the margin. *Fulton* applied the rule that had controlled previous cases: "[R]ather than rely on 'broadly formulated interests,' courts must 'scrutinize[] the asserted harm of granting specific exemptions to particular religious claimants.'"[101] The Court has held that the interest in preventing illegal drug use may be compelling in general, but not as applied to limited use of a drug as a sacrament in worship services.[102] The interest in preserving the unemployment-benefits fund may be compelling in general, but not as applied to the few claimants who would refuse work for religious reasons.[103] And the state

---

[98] Ayotte v. Planned Parenthood, 546 U.S. 320, 329 (2006).

[99] *Id.*

[100] Thomas C. Berg, Religious Accommodation and the Welfare State, 38 Harv. J.L. & Gender 103, 121–22 (2015).

[101] Fulton, 141 S. Ct. at 1881 (quoting Gonzales v. O Centro Espirita Beneficente Uniao do Vegetal, 546 U.S. 418, 431 (2006)).

[102] O Centro, 546 U.S. at 432–34.

[103] Sherbert, 374 U.S. at 407–09.

interest in requiring education of children is compelling in general, but not as applied to Amish children after eighth grade.[104]

In *Fulton* as in previous cases, the government's interest, "[o]nce properly narrowed" in this way, could coexist with an exemption. "Maximizing the number of foster families and minimizing liability are important goals," the Court said, but "including CSS in the program seems likely to increase, not reduce, the number of available foster parents."[105] Likewise, while the interests underlying nondiscrimination laws may be generally compelling, they are less likely so when there are multiple alternatives to the objecting religious provider or when the alleged discrimination is inside the church itself.

2. Self-interested exemptions: cumulative claims and religious incentives

Even under the marginal-interest analysis, in some cases allowing one exemption will trigger many others and undermine a law's basic coverage, not just a few of its applications. If the free-exercise claim coincides strongly with secular self-interest, or is otherwise highly attractive in this-worldly terms, granting one claim may encourage many other people to assert it. This helps explain why the Court refused religious exemptions from tax laws, even under strict scrutiny; many people want to avoid paying taxes.[106] Draft exemptions likewise could generate multiple claims, which helps explain why the Court lets Congress decide whether to have such exemptions.

The incentive created by a claim that strongly tracks self-interest also implicates a basic purpose of the Religion Clauses. The clauses should prevent government from discouraging religious practices; exemptions from generally applicable laws are warranted precisely because civil or criminal penalties or loss of government benefits profoundly discourages the prohibited religious practice. But neither

---

[104] Yoder, 406 U.S. at 221 (examining "the impediment to [state] objectives that would flow from recognizing the claimed Amish exemption").

[105] 141 S. Ct. at 1881–82.

[106] United States v. Lee, 455 U.S. 252, 260 (1982) (refusing claim of Amish employers who objected to paying Social Security taxes for their Amish employees, reasoning that "[t]he tax system could not function" if multiple exemptions were claimed as a matter of right). One of us has criticized *Lee* on the ground that the specific claim of the Amish, who also refused to receive Social Security benefits, "posed little risk of strategic behavior." Berg, *supra* note 64, at 10, 43 n.193.

should exemptions create affirmative incentives for religious practice. The Religion Clauses "require government to minimize the extent to which it either encourages or discourages religious belief or disbelief, practice or nonpractice."[107] Exemption is appropriate when it "does not have the effect of 'inducing' religious belief, but instead merely 'accommodates' or implements an independent religious choice."[108]

Some exemptions would incentivize assertions of religious belief, sincere or otherwise. Exempting secular income from taxes based on religious objections would encourage people to adopt or claim the religious belief that gained the exemption. Draft exemptions limited to theistic claims could encourage objectors to orient or characterize their beliefs that way. But most exemptions do not have such an effect. Nonbelievers will not suddenly start observing the sabbath, or traveling by horse and buggy, or holding their children out of high school, just because observant Jews or Adventists or Amish are permitted to do so. Most exemptions of religious practices have value only for believers in some particular faith, so most exemptions create neutral incentives, leaving religious choice far less distorted by government than regulation would.

3. Laws with exceptions for other interests

Under *Smith*, exceptions in a law for secular interests—even a small number of such exceptions—can make the law nonneutral or less than generally applicable and trigger strict scrutiny.[109] This protection is important and must not be lost if *Smith*'s unprotective part is overruled. If that part is overruled, neutrality and general applicability will no longer be a threshold hurdle; strict or at least heightened scrutiny will apply to all substantial burdens on religion. But other exceptions in a law will still be relevant to the compelling-interest analysis. To reiterate: the government cannot show a compelling interest "when it leaves

---

[107] Douglas Laycock, Formal, Substantive, and Disaggregated Neutrality toward Religion, 39 DePaul L. Rev. 993, 1001 (1990). See *id.* (connecting this standard to "voluntarism," or protection of choice in religious matters); Thomas C. Berg, Religion Clause Anti-Theories, 72 Notre Dame L. Rev. 693, 703–04 (1997) (same).

[108] Thomas v. Rev. Bd. of Ind. Emp. Sec. Div., 450 U.S. 707, 727 (1981) (Rehnquist, J., dissenting on other grounds).

[109] See *supra* notes 9–11 and accompanying text.

appreciable damage to that . . . interest unprohibited."[110] Even one exception for another activity that undercuts the government's asserted interest can indicate that the government does not regard the interest as compelling. Even if the test is less stringent, any meaningful number of exceptions that undercut the asserted interest indicate that the interest is not so important.

Moreover, if the law includes numerous other exceptions, it clearly discriminates against religion. At the extreme, a minor penalty imposed solely on religious activity is invalid. As Justice Harry Blackmun once said, the targeting of religion is itself the burden.[111]

4. Balancing burdens and government interests, including by categories

Justice Barrett declared herself "skeptical about swapping *Smith's* categorical antidiscrimination approach for an equally categorical strict scrutiny regime."[112] As noted above, we agree that the compelling-interest approach, or heightened scrutiny more generally, should not be all-or-nothing in nature. It is most workable and sensible, as one of us has previously argued, when it balances the burdens on religion against the government interests, with the thumb on the scale for religious exercise; the government interest must "compellingly outweigh the burden on religion."[113]

In weighing the burden on religion, courts cannot be entirely barred from assessing the importance of the religious practice in question. Although such assessments have hazards, to avoid them entirely is very likely to undermine protection. *Smith* argued that it would be "utterly unworkable" to apply the same compelling-interest test to laws preventing people from "throwing rice at church weddings" as to laws preventing church weddings entirely—but also that it was unworkable to decide that one such practice was "central" and the other was not.[114] That supposed dilemma led the Court to say it would no longer order exemptions from generally ap-

---

[110] Lukumi, 508 U.S. at 547 (citation omitted).

[111] *Id.* at 579 (Blackmun, J., concurring in the judgment).

[112] Fulton, 141 S. Ct. at 1883 (Barrett, J., concurring).

[113] See Laycock, *supra* note 71, at 152; Douglas Laycock, The Remnants of Free Exercise, 1990 Sup. Ct. Rev. 1, 31–33.

[114] Smith, 494 U.S. at 887 n.4.

plicable laws. Even if exemptions still exist in theory, an inability to gauge burdens on religion would lead courts to balance by inflating government interests: "watering down" the governing test, as *Smith* warned.[115]

A total refusal to assess the importance of religious practice in religious-exemption cases therefore threatens to invert the proper priority among Religion Clause values. It risks reading the value of nonentanglement in religious questions—a value designed to promote freedom of religious practice—so strictly that it undermines that freedom by undermining any workable doctrine of religious exemptions. It also ignores a kind of waiver argument: claimants who seek an exemption put their sincerity and the significance of their belief or practice at issue. They cannot object to the court inquiring into the belief or practice more than would otherwise be permitted.

All this is consistent with our earlier argument that many restrictions on religious practice by their nature leave no adequate alternatives and thus are unlike permissible time, place, and manner restrictions on speech.[116] Our point there was not that religious practices are never minor; it was that religious practices are often not fungible. If a prohibition on one channel of speech leaves a dozen other channels by which you can communicate the message, there is a good chance that the alternatives are adequate. But if a prohibition on following one significant religious practice or tenet leaves a dozen others you can follow, that fact doesn't matter. A religion can have many significant practices; they are not fungible, so prohibiting any one of them prohibits religious exercise.[117]

Although courts should not refuse entirely to assess the importance of religious practices, such assessments do present dangers. That importance varies from person to person; judges may be prone to substitute what would be important to them for what is important to the person or group being burdened. For these reasons, judgments about importance will usually have to be approximate, with reasonable deference to the claimant's self-understanding. But these difficulties do not mean that courts should wholly ignore the importance

---

[115] *Id.* at 888.

[116] See *supra* notes 73–85 and accompanying text.

[117] Holt, 574 U.S. at 361–62.

of the religious practice when they are asked to decide a claim to exemption. They can distinguish getting married in church from throwing rice at the wedding.

We offer several points and suggestions for striking a workable balance between burdens on religion and government, with the thumb on the scale for protecting religion.

a. The substantiality of the burden, including the importance of the religious interest, should not be an all-or-nothing threshold. Treating it as all or nothing greatly magnifies the cost of misjudging the religious interest: any underestimate leads the court to deny judicial protection entirely, instead of according it somewhat less protection. Rather, the importance of the practice should affect the balance: the greater the burden, the greater the justification required. The test tends to work that way in practice, and sometimes the Court explicitly describes it that way.[118]

b. The prospect of free-form balancing may worry the Court, so balancing can sometimes be resolved into categorical rules. Already such a rule exists for cases involving religious institutions' autonomy over their internal governance. The ministerial exception is absolute within its scope; civil authorities must not interfere with a religious institution's "authority to select, supervise, and if necessary, remove a minister."[119] There is no override, even for compelling interests. Any balancing occurs in drawing the boundaries of the category: for example, defining who is a "minister."

The shield is absolute partly because of the severity of the burden. Interference with a religious organization's key governance decisions, including who should fill "key roles,"[120] tends to affect not just one of its practices but many. "The members of a religious group put their faith in the hands of their ministers"; "a wayward minister's preaching, teaching, and counseling could contradict the church's tenets and lead the congregation away from the faith."[121] In part, the shield is absolute because religious bodies' internal government has

---

[118] See Laycock, *supra* note 71, at 152 n.47 (collecting phrasing from free-exercise and free-speech cases that present the compelling-interest test as weighted balancing of interests).

[119] Our Lady of Guadalupe Sch. v. Morrissey-Berru, 140 S. Ct. 2049, 2060 (2020).

[120] *Id.*

[121] Hosanna-Tabor, 565 U.S. at 188; Our Lady, 140 S. Ct. at 2060.

less effect on societal interests. "All who unite themselves to such a body do so with an implied consent to this government, and are bound to submit to it."[122] Denying someone a position as minister does not generally deny broad employment opportunities. Ministers can find another congregation, denomination, or other religious entity, or any secular occupation.

One of Justice Barrett's questions was whether "entities like [CSS]" should "be treated differently from individuals."[123] Our response is that entities have governance and autonomy interests that rarely or never arise in cases involving individuals. But claims based on conscientious objection—a conflict with religious tenets—should generally be treated the same for both.

c. Sometimes the burden on religion is fully measurable in secular terms. If a law bars a religious entity from providing services at some locations but allows it to do so at others, courts can and should consider whether the alternatives may be adequate. Such laws are essentially time, place, and manner restrictions on religious exercise. If the case involves a land-use regulation, RLUIPA governs, and the adequacy of alternatives is relevant to whether the regulation "substantially burdens" religious exercise. Courts in those cases may be too ready to find alternatives adequate and the burden insubstantial.[124] But there is no bar to them engaging in the evaluation, under RLUIPA or under the Constitution.

d. Some categories of burdens should not by themselves trigger strict or demanding scrutiny. Justice Barrett asked whether the Court should reaffirm *Braunfeld v. Brown*, which rejected strict scrutiny for "indirect burdens" that do not bar a religious practice but bar other behavior and so affect the religious practice.[125] The blue law in *Braunfeld* kept Orthodox Jewish shopkeepers from opening on Sundays, which did not violate their tenets but did hamper the recoupment of business they lost by closing on Saturdays—their Sabbath. *Braunfeld* seems correct that strict review of such indirect burdens would generate an unmanageable range of claims, many

---

[122] Watson v. Jones, 80 U.S. 679, 729 (1872).

[123] Fulton, 141 S. Ct. at 1882 (Barrett, J., concurring).

[124] See Laycock & Goodrich, *supra* note 68, at 1046–48, 1054–57.

[125] 366 U.S. 599 (1961).

of which would involve attenuated or avoidable burdens.[126] The *Braunfeld* shopkeepers should have won, not because they deserved an exemption from a neutral and generally applicable law, but because the Sunday closing law was not religiously neutral; its origins in the Christian-majority sabbath were unmistakable, and it may have been an establishment of religion.[127]

Pre-*Smith* decisions also rejected strict scrutiny in cases challenging the government's internal operations or its management of its own land. The impulse is understandable; again, strict review could cripple government or raise countless claims, often involving attenuated burdens. The Court was correct in *Bowen v. Roy* to find no burden on religious objectors from the government simply assigning them a Social Security number (as opposed to requiring them to provide or use the number).[128] But it was more troubling that the Court found no burden on Native American religion when activities on federal land disturb or even destroy sites that have been vital to tribal religious practices for centuries.[129] Of course the Court was right that the government is generally entitled to manage its own property. But it might have attached significance to the fact that the government acquired the property from its original owners in a coerced transaction, and it might have implied an easement or a duty to protect important religious functions.[130] The harms to tribal sacred sites affect the ability to worship in a concrete, empirical sense: they have "substantial external effects."[131] And the government, by seizing sacred lands, took control over the tribes' ability to practice their traditions fully—in somewhat the same way that prisons control inmates' ability to practice their faith.[132]

---

[126] See *id.* at 606 (noting, as examples, that taxes make it harder for some people to fulfill their tithing obligation, and weekend court closures make scheduling harder for lawyers who observe weekday sabbaths).

[127] McGowan v. Maryland, 366 U.S. 420, 445 (1961), upheld the Sunday laws on the ground that they served the secular purpose in a "uniform day of rest."

[128] 476 U.S. 693 (1986).

[129] Lyng, 485 U.S. at 447.

[130] See Ira C. Lupu, Where Rights Begin: The Problem of Burdens on the Free Exercise of Religion, 102 Harv. L. Rev. 933, 973–76 (1989).

[131] Lyng, 485 U.S. at 470–71 (Brennan, J., dissenting).

[132] Stephanie Hall Barclay & Michalyn Steele, Rethinking Protections for Indigenous Sacred Sites, 134 Harv. L. Rev. 1294, 1320–43 (2021).

The sacred-sites cases dramatize the costs of an all-or-nothing approach; more nuance would resolve them far better. The *Lyng* Court said that because it could not define a practice as "central" to overcome a threshold for strict scrutiny, it had to forego any scrutiny whatsoever.[133] But if, as we have suggested, centrality is a matter of degree—one factor affecting the balance of burdens and government interests—courts can easily consider competent evidence about a given site's historic importance to tribal rites. And if the Court remains concerned that strict scrutiny would cripple federal land management, a serious intermediate level of scrutiny would give the government more flexibility but still push it to avoid harm to sacred sites whenever possible.

e. Still, much of the weighing in religion cases must occur through specification of the government interests that are sufficient to limit religious practice. In general, physical harms, actual or likely, are most likely to implicate overriding interests. As Justice Alito noted in *Fulton*, the original meaning of free exercise harmonizes with Founding-era state constitutional provisions; the majority of those provisions limited the right when it interfered with public "peace or safety."[134] Significant damage to property also fits comfortably within that standard. And the increase in the complexity of modern life expands the scope of government's regulatory interests. But it cannot be that every expansion of regulation produces an equal constriction of freedom to practice religion. Scrutiny of generally applicable laws—especially scrutiny of government interests at the margin rather than in the abstract—prevents that zero-sum result.

Over time, courts can use their experience with cases to develop distinctive rules for categories of cases, much as they have developed categorical rules for different free-speech areas like defamation or incitement of illegal conduct.[135] Consider, for example, liability for different religious actors in cases involving nondiscrimination laws.

---

[133] Lyng, 485 U.S. at 457.

[134] Fulton, 141 S. Ct. at 1901–03 (Alito, J., concurring in the judgment) (collecting provisions). See also McConnell, *supra* note 30, at 1461–66 (same).

[135] See, e.g., N.Y. Times v. Sullivan, 376 U.S. 254, 279–80 (1964) (adopting "actual malice," i.e., recklessness, as the liability standard for defaming a public official); Brandenburg v. Ohio, 395 U.S. 444, 447 (1969) (protecting advocacy of illegal conduct except where it "is directed to inciting or producing imminent lawless action and is likely to incite or produce such action").

Under any serious form of heightened scrutiny, religious nonprofits, like schools and social services, should generally have more protection than ordinary for-profit businesses operated by religious believers, like bakers or florists. The latter are protected; they can face significant burdens. But their exemptions should be narrower, because government's interests are generally stronger, than in nonprofit cases.[136]

The for-profit context increases government's interest in ensuring that all persons have access to basic goods and services and that market actors do not get unfair commercial advantages. Moreover, employees and clients of a religious nonprofit generally have notice that it may adhere to standards stemming from its religious identity; employees or clients of ordinary for-profit businesses often will lack such notice.[137] We do not think that every denial of service necessarily implicates a compelling interest in preventing discrimination. In particular, to the extent that the government's interest is in preventing the customer's offense at the refusal of service, such offensiveness cannot override First Amendment free-exercise rights any more than it overrides speech rights.[138] Nevertheless, it stands to reason that lack of notice will increase the concrete burdens of refusal on customers.

These differences suggest different presumptive rules for a religious nonprofit and an ordinary for-profit. The former should have significant protection from nondiscrimination liability unless it operates as a "choke-point," with market power to reduce services materially, or unless its religious nature is sufficiently attenuated that others no longer have constructive notice that it adheres to religious tenets. But for-profit exemptions should be limited to small vendors in religiously significant contexts like weddings or marriage counseling where alternatives are readily available.

---

[136] For further discussion of the following factors, see Berg, *supra* note 100, at 127–30.

[137] See Micah Schwartzman, Richard Schragger, & Nelson Tebbe, "Hobby Lobby and the Establishment Clause, Part III: Reconciling Amos and Cutter," Balkinization, Dec. 9, 2013, http://perma.cc/VWZ6-JEA6 (noting "the reasonable expectation that employees who work for churches and religious-affiliated non-profits understand that their employers are focused on advancing a religious mission").

[138] Texas v. Johnson, 491 U.S. 397, 414 (1989) (flag burning); Hustler Mag. v. Falwell, 485 U.S. 46, 50–57 (1988) (intentional infliction of emotional distress); Cohen v. California, 403 U.S. 15, 18–26 (1971) (profanity).

Conclusion

Smith's protective rule can do much to shield free exercise of religion, but its unprotective rule still weakens that shield. In answer to Justice Barrett, we think that the logic and purposes of free exercise can generate a protective but workable doctrine for challenges to generally applicable laws.

Americans for Prosperity Foundation v. Bonta: A First Amendment for the Sensitive

*Bradley A. Smith**

Introduction

Americans are living in a new age of "accountability," or what others call "McCarthyism."

Although its roots go much further back, this latest fit of "accountability" burst into mainstream politics in 2008. That year, an organization called Accountable America compiled data from campaign finance disclosure reports to send letters to nearly 10,000 conservative donors, threatening publication of their names and, in the words of the *New York Times*, "digging through their lives" if they continued their financial support of conservative candidates and causes. The group was "hoping to create a chilling effect that will dry up contributions," the *Times* noted.[1] That same year, several websites popped up to facilitate the easy identification and targeting of supporters of Proposition 8, a California initiative that would have barred the state from recognizing same-sex marriages. Using contributor data filed with the state, websites combined information with interactive maps to display

* Josiah H. Blackmore II/Shirley M. Nault Professor of Law, Capital University Law School. Former commissioner (2000–2005) and chairman (2004) of the Federal Election Commission. The author is chairman of the Institute for Free Speech (formerly the Center for Competitive Politics) which had also filed suit challenging the policies challenged by the plaintiffs in *Americans for Prosperity v. Bonta* [hereinafter *AFPF*]. A petition for a writ of certiorari was pending at the time *AFPF* was decided, and after the decision in *AFPF*, the writ was granted, judgment vacated, and the case remanded with instructions to reconsider in light of *AFPF*. Inst. for Free Speech v. Bonta, 2021 U.S. LEXIS 3573 (No. 19-793) (July 2, 2021). Related litigation was reported as Ctr. for Competitive Politics v. Harris, 784 F.3d 1307 (9th Cir. 2015), cert. denied, 577 U.S. 975 (2015). I thank the Cato Institute for the invitation to participate in this edition of the *Cato Supreme Court Review*, Matt Nese and David Keating for comments, and Eric Parker for research assistance.

[1] Michael Luo, "Group Plans Campaign against G.O.P. Donors," N.Y. Times, Aug. 8, 2008, https://nyti.ms/3xhcIOG.

directions to the homes of Prop 8 contributors. A website called "Californians Against Hate" provided addresses and telephone numbers for Prop 8 supporters. Another website allowed users to search for Prop 8 supporters who worked in the user's place of employment.[2]

Marjorie Christoffersen, a manager at El Coyote Restaurant in Los Angeles, is a poster child for this new "accountability." Ms. Christoffersen contributed $100 to "Yes on 8," the lead organization supporting the referendum. Christoffersen had worked without incident at El Coyote, a popular gay hangout, for years. On one occasion, when a regular customer passed away from AIDS, she had personally paid to fly his mother to California for the funeral. But when her contribution to Yes on 8 was publicly disclosed, gay activists boycotted and picketed the restaurant, causing revenues to plunge by 30 percent. A $10,000 contribution by the owner to gay rights causes failed to mollify the boycotters. Eventually, to save the restaurant and the jobs of its 87 employees, Christoffersen tendered her resignation to the owner—her mother.[3]

Proposition 8's opponents claimed many more powerful and higher profile victims than Marjorie Christoffersen, including Richard Raddon, director of the Los Angeles Film Festival, and Scott Eckhern, artistic director of the California Musical Theatre. Numerous accounts of vandalism and harassment aimed at supporters were documented.[4]

Now, less than 15 years after Proposition 8, stories and videos abound of persons both powerful and meek losing jobs, being harassed and threatened by internet mobs or live demonstrators, having their cars and property damaged, being screamed at in restaurants, and sometimes being physically attacked.

In a 2020 Cato Institute/YouGov poll, 62 percent of those under 35 and holding post-graduate degrees (i.e., the leaders of tomorrow) said that an executive who contributed to Donald Trump's presidential campaign should be fired. Not surprisingly, 60 percent of Trump voters under 45 and with post-graduate degrees worried about losing their jobs or "missing out on job opportunities" if their

---

[2] See Thomas Messner, "The Price of Prop 8," Heritage Found., Oct. 22, 2009, https://herit.ag/3fmbwTT.

[3] Steve Lopez, "Prop. 8 Stance Upends Her Life," L.A. Times, Dec. 14, 2008, https://lat.ms/3iien24.

[4] See Messner, *supra* note 2.

political views became known. Overall, only a third of Americans had this concern.[5] In August 2017, a Harvard/Harris poll found that 42 percent of 18- to 34-year-olds believed that it was appropriate to fire a person who expressed views that "tend to reinforce gender stereotypes."[6] Given the trend lines in polling prior to 2017, that percentage is likely higher today.

It is no wonder that in the Cato Institute/YouGov poll, 62 percent of respondents reported that the current climate for free speech had prevented them from stating their true beliefs on public affairs. Although this sentiment was strongest among Republicans (77 percent), a majority of independents (59 percent) and Democrats (52 percent) also reported self-censoring. By ideology, respondents identifying as "strong liberals" were the only group in which a majority disagreed with the statement that "the political climate these days prevents me from saying things I believe because others might find them offensive." A solid majority of "liberals" agreed, as did 64 percent of "moderates." Among both "conservative" and "strong conservative" respondents, 77 percent agreed. And in every category, including strong liberals, there was sharp movement toward self-censorship since Cato had asked the question in 2017.[7]

As this era of blacklists and boycotts matured, sometime in 2011 or 2012—the exact date is unclear—California Attorney General Kamala Harris began demanding that registered charities and other nonprofit organizations operating in the state annually file a list of their major donors as a precondition of continuing to solicit contributions in California. Protective of both their organizations' and their donors' privacy, and perhaps suspicious of the attorney general's motivation, the Americans for Prosperity Foundation (AFPF) and the Thomas More Legal Center (TMLC) sued. The Supreme Court's decision in favor of the plaintiffs, *Americans for Prosperity Foundation v. Bonta (AFPF)*,[8] is arguably the most important decision on the rights of privacy and association in over 60 years.

[5] Emily Ekins, Poll: 62% of Americans Say They Have Political Views They're Afraid to Share, Cato Inst./YouGov, July 22, 2020, https://bit.ly/3fju8UK.

[6] Monthly Harvard-Harris Poll: August 2017, Aug. 23, 2017, https://bit.ly/3lo7X3k.

[7] Ekins, *supra* note 5.

[8] 141 S. Ct. 2373 (2021). Rob Bonta is the current attorney general of California, having replaced Xavier Becerra, who replaced Harris after her election to the U.S. Senate in 2016.

At one level, *AFPF* turns on intricate questions about the proper level of judicial "scrutiny" to be applied, what that scrutiny then requires, and ultimately, what state interests might justify compelled disclosure of donors to and members of various nonprofit organizations. But the case was decided against the background of our social media and "cancel culture," and the questions they raise: What does it mean for Americans to be held "accountable" for peaceful, lawful speech? Should Americans who express views different from our own be "punished" by boycotts, threats, and harassment? And most important for the Court, under what circumstances can government compel Americans to provide their adversaries with the information needed to harass them, and what protections do Americans have when the government itself may be the potential perpetrator of harassment in an effort to squelch views uncongenial to that government?

Part I of this article traces the modern legal development of the right to privacy in speech and group association. Part II reviews the political background against which the *AFPF* litigation took place. In part III I discuss the litigation itself, and in part IV I consider claims that *AFPF* was merely a "stalking horse" for eviscerating campaign finance laws. A brief conclusion follows.

I. A Brief History of a Right

A. NAACP *to* McIntyre

Anonymous speech has a long and often honored history in the United States—think the *Federalist Papers*.[9] But the idea of using compulsory disclosure to silence unwanted speech and shut down unwanted activity is hardly new. Indeed, in the 1950s compulsory disclosure of memberships, financial support, and affiliations was a core strategy in southern segregationists' "massive resistance" to *Brown v. Board of Education*, as well as a tool to root out communists and "subversives" in government and elsewhere in public life.

---

[9] See, e.g., McIntyre v. Ohio Elections Comm'n, 514 U.S. 334, 357 (1995); *id.* at 358–71 (Thomas, J., concurring in the judgment) (citing numerous examples of anonymous speech in the Founding period); Jonathan Turley, Registering Publius: The Supreme Court and the Right to Anonymity, 2001–2002 Cato Sup. Ct. Rev. 57 (2002); Bradley A. Smith, In Defense of Political Anonymity, 20 City J. 74 (2010).

In 1956, as part of an investigation into whether the National Association for the Advancement of Colored People (NAACP) was conducting business in violation of the state's foreign corporation registration statute, Alabama's attorney general demanded that the organization hand over a list of names and addresses of its members. The NAACP refused and was held in contempt by Alabama state courts. The U.S. Supreme Court reversed.[10]

"It is hardly a novel perception," wrote the Supreme Court:

> that compelled disclosure of affiliation with groups engaged in advocacy may constitute [an] effective [] restraint on freedom of association. . . . Inviolability of privacy in group association may in many circumstances be indispensable to preservation of freedom of association, particularly where a group espouses dissident beliefs.[11]

The Court was "unpersuaded" by the state's unspecific claim that the information might prove helpful in its investigation. Citing the NAACP's "uncontroverted showing that on past occasions revelation of the identity of its rank-and-file members has exposed these members to economic reprisal, loss of employment, threat of physical coercion, and other manifestations of public hostility," the Court concluded that, "[u]nder these circumstances, we think it apparent that compelled disclosure of petitioner's . . . membership is likely to affect adversely the ability of petitioner and its members to pursue their collective effort to foster beliefs which they admittedly have the right to advocate."[12]

In a series of decisions over the next decade, the Court built on *NAACP v. Alabama* to recognize a robust right to keep one's memberships and associations private from government.[13]

---

[10] NAACP v. Alabama ex rel. Patterson, 357 U.S. 449 (1958).

[11] *Id.* at 461–462.

[12] *Id.* at 464.

[13] See Bates v. Little Rock, 361 U.S. 516, 525 (1960) (holding unconstitutional a city tax ordinance requiring certain groups, including the NAACP, to publicly disclose donors, and holding that even an otherwise legitimate statute must "bear[] a reasonable relationship to . . . the governmental purpose asserted as its justification"; and further demanding that a court look behind stated reasons where First Amendment rights are at stake: "governmental action does not automatically become reasonably related to the achievement of a legitimate and substantial governmental purpose by mere assertion in the preamble of an ordinance"); Shelton v. Tucker, 364 U.S. 479 (1960) (holding facially unconstitutional a state requirement that public school teachers list all organizations

In 1976, however, in *Buckley v. Valeo*,[14] the Supreme Court backed off this commitment, at least as it pertained to contributions to and expenditures by candidates for political office. The Court upheld the disclosure provisions of the Federal Election Campaign Act (FECA) citing three government interests "sufficiently important to outweigh" the burden on First Amendment rights:[15]

- An "informational interest": Knowing the source of campaign funds and how they were spent by the candidate would aid voters in evaluating candidates, placing them on the political spectrum and "alert[ing] the voter to the interests to which a candidate is most likely to be responsive and thus facilitat[ing] predictions of future performance in office."[16]

- An anti-corruption interest: Disclosure of contributions would "deter actual corruption and avoid the appearance of corruption."[17]

- An enforcement interest: Reporting would help detect violations of the law's limits on the size and sources of campaign contributions.[18]

---

to which they had belonged or contributed in the past five years, even though the list was not public; and requiring a "less drastic means" be used when possible to accomplish the state objective); Talley v. California, 362 U.S. 60, 65 (1960) (holding facially unconstitutional a city ordinance requiring handbills to identify financial supporters, and requiring only a reasonable probability that "identification and fear of reprisal might deter perfectly peaceful discussions of public matters of importance" to satisfy the First Amendment burden on plaintiff).

See also Sweezy v. New Hampshire, 354 U.S. 234 (1957) (overturning contempt conviction where a teacher refused to answer questions regarding memberships and names of other members, during investigation into subversive activities); Gibson v. Fla. Legis. Investigation Comm., 372 U.S. 539 (1963) (contempt citation overturned where head of local NAACP refused to divulge members' names during legislative investigation into communist infiltration of civil rights movement, on grounds that demand lacked an "adequate foundation for inquiry"); Gremillion v. NAACP, 366 U.S. 293 (1961) (finding unconstitutional a Louisiana statute requiring nonprofit organizations to file a membership list with the state); Roberts v. Pollard, 393 U.S. 14 (1968) (summarily affirming district court decision enjoining subpoena demanding names of political party donors where there was no showing of relevance to prosecutor's investigation).

[14] 424 U.S. 1 (1976).

[15] *Id.* at 66–68.

[16] *Id.* at 66–67.

[17] *Id.* at 67.

[18] *Id.* at 67–68, 81.

Against these "sufficiently important" government interests, the Court found it significant that the plaintiffs had not tendered record evidence of actual, specific harassment or threats "of the sort proffered in *NAACP v. Alabama*."[19] Given the "magnitude" of the government interests identified and the "speculative" nature of harms to the plaintiffs, the Court upheld the disclosure requirements targeting political committees.[20]

But *Buckley*'s constitutional blessing of disclosure was not so extensive as is often claimed. The originally sweeping disclosure provisions of FECA were upheld in their original form only for "political committees"—groups formed with "the major purpose" of electing candidates, such as candidate campaign committees, political parties, and political action committees (PACs). When it came to groups and organizations that were not political committees—charities, nonprofits, think tanks, trade associations, and community groups—*Buckley* substantially curtailed FECA's disclosure provisions to protect the rights of anonymous association and speech.

The Court held that for organizations that were not "political committees," the disclosure requirements could constitutionally apply only to "expenditures for communications that expressly advocate the election or defeat of a clearly identified candidate."[21] And the Court elsewhere in *Buckley* defined "to expressly advocate" this way: as "express words of advocacy of election or defeat, such as 'vote for,' 'elect,' 'support,' 'cast your ballot for,' 'Smith for Congress,' 'vote against,' 'defeat,' 'reject.'"[22] This combination severely truncated the reach of FECA's disclosure provisions regarding any organization that was not a "political committee." Further, the Court held that even when making expenditures "expressly advocating" the election or defeat of a candidate, these organizations only needed to report making those specific expenditures. They did not need to report on donors to their organizations unless those donors had specifically earmarked their contribution for the express advocacy of election or defeat of a candidate.[23]

[19] *Id*. at 71.
[20] *Id*. at 66, 70.
[21] *Id*. at 79–80.
[22] *Id*. at 44 n.52.
[23] *Id*. at 79–80.

Since these organizations, not being political committees, were not subject to contribution or spending limits,[24] the government's "enforcement" interest in tracking contributions and expenditures disappeared. And because no money flowed directly to the candidate or the campaign, the anti-corruption interest was, as the Court demurely put it, "significantly different" than when discussing contributions to political committees.[25] Thus, for these organizations, the restrictions that were upheld were justified solely on the basis of the "informational" interest. But that interest was narrowly defined by the Court as helping voters "define a candidate's constituencies,"[26] and, therefore, "the interests to which a candidate is most likely to be responsive."[27] That interest was satisfied simply by knowing the organization doing the spending—little was to be gained from the names of individual donors. The "informational interest," in other words, lay in predicting how a candidate would act in office—it did not encompass public curiosity or the possibility that knowing the source of funding might make some voters more or less skeptical of the merits of the argument. It was certainly not about assuring "accountability" on the part of contributors. To have understood the "informational" interest as some generic "right to know," or as a means to evaluate the merit of arguments, would have undermined *NAACP*, as it would effectively have conceded that Alabama had an important state interest in simply knowing who was funding the NAACP's speech.

In *McIntyre v. Ohio Elections Commission*,[28] the Court again emphasized the narrow reach of the "informational interest." Margaret McIntyre was distributing handbills opposing a local school tax levy. With no candidate in the race, and hence no limits on contributions, both the anti-corruption and enforcement interests were missing. And, with no candidate, there was no compelling informational interest either:

> Insofar as the interest in informing the electorate means nothing more than the provision of additional information that may either buttress or undermine the argument in a

[24] *Id.* at 54–58.
[25] *Id.* at 81.
[26] *Id.*
[27] *Id.* at 67.
[28] 514 U.S. 334.

document, we think the identity of the speaker is no different from other components of the document's content that the author is free to include or exclude.[29]

Further, the Court held that McIntyre really had no need to prove threats or harassment, or even to state a reason for preferring anonymity at all:

> The decision in favor of anonymity may be motivated by fear of economic or official retaliation, by concern about social ostracism, or merely by a desire to preserve as much of one's privacy as possible. Whatever the motivation may be, . . . the interest in having anonymous works enter the marketplace of ideas unquestionably outweighs any public interest in requiring disclosure as a condition of entry.[30]

B. Citizens United *to* Bonta

The Supreme Court's 2010 decision in *Citizens United v. Federal Election Commission* is generally known as the case that, on First Amendment grounds, upheld the right of corporations to make political expenditures.[31] But Citizens United, the nonprofit corporation at the center of the case, also challenged a statutory requirement, included in the Bipartisan Campaign Reform Act of 2002,[32] mandating that it disclose its donors for a small subset of its advertising.

Citizens United went beyond the narrow disclosure regime that had emerged from *Buckley* in two ways. First, it upheld the compulsory disclosure of names and addresses of donors even if those donors did not earmark their contributions for the organization's limited political communications.[33] Second, it upheld disclosure for

---

[29] *Id.* at 348.

[30] *Id.* at 341–42.

[31] Citizens United v. Fed. Election Comm'n, 558 U.S. 310 (2010).

[32] Pub. L. 107-155 (2002).

[33] 558 U.S. at 368. It should be noted, however, that the Court had already crossed this bridge seven years before, in *McConnell v. Federal Election Commission.* 540 U.S. 93 (2003). There, the Court rejected a facial challenge to the same rules. As a practical matter, *McConnell* had not had great effect on this point, mainly because the Federal Election Commission had interpreted the provision narrowly, limiting it, for the most part, to earmarked contributions from donors, consistent with *Buckley.* See 11 C.F.R. § 114.20(c)(9); Van Hollen v. Fed. Election Comm'n, 811 F.3d 486 (D.C. Cir. 2016) (upholding same).

speech, independent from a candidate's campaign, a political party, or a PAC, that did not constitute "express advocacy" or its "functional equivalent"—broadcast ads costing in excess of $10,000 and naming a candidate within 60 days of an election.[34] Still, these holdings were not radical departures from *Buckley*, *McIntyre*, and the *NAACP* line of cases, at least in that they required a tight nexus between the speech and an identified political candidate, during an election season.

But *Citizens United*'s greatest impact came less from these holdings than from its brief discussion of the so-called "informational" interest. The majority quoted *Buckley* for the point that the informational interest in compelled disclosure was to "insure that the voters are fully informed"[35]—but then added something *Buckley* did not say—"about the person or group who is speaking."[36] *Buckley*, in contrast, had stated that the purpose was to inform voters about "the interests to which a candidate is most likely to be responsive."[37] The *Citizens United* opinion then quoted a single sentence of *dicta* from a footnote in *First National Bank of Boston v. Bellotti*, a 1978 case that did not involve a challenge to disclosure laws, for the proposition that "identification of the source of advertising may be required so that the people will be able to evaluate the arguments to which they are being subjected."[38]

Thus, whereas *Buckley* and *McIntyre* had defined the interest in terms of providing information to voters on how candidates were likely to prioritize once in office, *Citizens United* appeared to re-center the interest around an evaluation of the credibility of the speaker. That raised the question: if the purpose of compulsory disclosure is to help the public evaluate the credibility of a speaker, is there any need to restrict it to speech about candidates? Might "information" be helpful to the public—and thus an important government interest—in a variety of settings?

---

[34] 558 U.S. at 368–69. The ads were defined as "electioneering communications." The allowance for compelled disclosure of the "functional equivalency" of express advocacy was also first set forth in *McConnell v. FEC*. 540 U.S. at 206.

[35] 558 U.S. at 368 (quoting Buckley, 424 U.S. at 76).

[36] *Id.*

[37] 424 U.S. at 67.

[38] 558 U.S. at 368 (quoting First Nat'l Bank of Bos. v. Bellotti, 435 U.S. 765, 792, n.32 (1978)).

Five months later, in *Doe v. Reed*, the Court considered a Washington state law compelling publication of the names and addresses of persons who signed a petition to put a marriage referendum, similar to Prop 8, on the statewide ballot.[39] The Court upheld the requirement, but based its decision solely on the state's interest in "preserving the integrity of the electoral process by combating fraud, detecting invalid signatures, and fostering government transparency and accountability." It specifically did not address the state's asserted informational interest.[40] But the various opinions of the justices—six all told—left many believing that the life had gone out of the *NAACP* line.

Justice Samuel Alito noted the breathtaking sweep of the state's asserted informational interest—"Were we to accept [the state's] asserted informational interest, the State would be free to require petition signers to disclose all kinds of demographic information, including the signer's race, religion, political affiliation, sexual orientation, ethnic background, and interest-group memberships"[41]—and discussed at length the record evidence of harassment and the problems of post-disclosure as-applied challenges.[42] But the other justices seemed not to share his concern. Justice Sonia Sotomayor, joined by Justices John Paul Stevens and Ruth Bader Ginsburg, was dismissive of plaintiffs, characterizing their First Amendment burden as "minimal."[43] Next, Justice Stevens, joined by Justice Stephen Breyer, authored a separate opinion arriving at the same conclusion.[44] And Justice Antonin Scalia concluded his concurring opinion with a ringing denunciation of anonymity: "Requiring people to stand up in public for their political acts fosters civic courage, without which democracy is doomed."[45]

---

[39] Doe v. Reed, 561 U.S. 186 (2010). Two organizations, with the bland but, in the circumstances, rather ominous names "Whosigned.org" and "KnowThyNeighbor.org," sought the information from the state for the purpose of placing it online in a searchable format. *Id.* at 193.

[40] *Id.* at 197.

[41] *Id.* at 202, 207 (Alito, J., concurring).

[42] *Id.* at 205–07.

[43] *Id.* at 212, 214 (Sotomayor, J., concurring).

[44] *Id.* at 216 (Stevens, J., concurring in part and concurring in the judgment).

[45] *Id.* at 228 (Scalia, J., concurring in the judgment).

Although both *Citizens United* and *Doe* called for "exacting scrutiny" in reviewing compulsory disclosure regulations, lower courts picked up on the generally lax tenor of the opinions. The "exacting scrutiny" standard of review—a standard intended to be, well, "exacting"—began to look much like the deferential "rational basis" test reserved for economic legislation,[46] with sweeping, vague state interests accepted at face value, privacy interests dismissed as inconsequential or even nonexistent, and no requirement that the state tailor its demands to its asserted interests.[47]

II. The Political Backdrop to the *AFPF* Litigation

As *Citizens United*'s holding on disclosure changed the way judges seemed to think about what was needed to justify compelled disclosure under the "exacting scrutiny" test, its holding that corporations and unions had a constitutional right to spend money to promote their views on candidate elections sent shockwaves through the body politic.

The decision came during a particularly rough patch for the Democratic Party. January 2010 polling showed President Barack Obama with the lowest net approval rating after one year in office of any president in 56 years,[48] with approval for his handling of his signature issue, health care, falling to 37 percent.[49] On January 18, Massachusetts Republican Scott Brown scored a stunning upset in a special election for U.S. Senate. It was the first victory for a Republican in a Massachusetts Senate race in 38 years, and it ended the Democrats' filibuster-proof majority. It also had enormous symbolic impact—the seat was known as "the Kennedy seat," having been held by Edward Kennedy for 47 years until his death five months before, and prior to that by John F. Kennedy.

---

[46] See United States v. Carolene Products, 304 U.S. 144 (1938).

[47] See Ctr. for Competitive Politics, 784 F.3d 1307, a facial challenge to the same practice challenged in *Bonta*. See also Del. Strong Families v. Denn, 793 F.3d 304 (3d Cir. 2015), cert. denied, 136 S. Ct. 2376 (2016); Citizens United v. Schneiderman, 882 F.3d 374 (2d Cir. 2018); Rio Grande Found. v. Santa Fe, 437 F. Supp. 3d 1051 (2021).

[48] Lydia Saad, "Obama Starts 2010 with 50% Approval," Gallup, Jan. 6, 2010, https://bit.ly/3C7Ktp1. See also Stephanie Condon, "Poll: Obama Ends First Year with 50% Approval Rating," CBS News, Jan. 18, 2010, https://cbsn.ws/3C4QUt6.

[49] Jeffrey M. Jones, "Obama Approval on Terrorism Up to 49%," Gallup, Jan. 13, 2010, https://bit.ly/3xiVAaY.

Less than 72 hours after Brown's upset win, the Supreme Court announced *Citizens United*.[50] Coming when it did, to a Democratic Party with much of its base conditioned to view corporate America as its enemy, the psychological impact was enormous. It is not an exaggeration to say that hysteria gripped many on the left. Sen. Russ Feingold (D-WI), for example, warning that the net assets of U.S. corporations were in excess of $23 trillion dollars, claimed, "that is quite a war chest that may soon be unleashed on our political system," as if corporations could or would spend all their assets on political communications.[51]

Within days, however, a strategy to limit unwanted speech began to emerge on the political left: compulsory disclosure. Writing at SCOTUSblog, the *éminence grise* of liberal law professors, Harvard's Laurence Tribe, called for corporate ads to include a statement by the company's chief executive revealing how much was being spent and certifying the CEO's personal conclusion that the expenditure would significantly advance the corporation's business interests. "The impact of a campaign ad," wrote Tribe, "would be cut down to size." He further called for a federally created private cause of action against those corporate CEOs for "corporate waste," with "double or treble damages" and attorney's fees.[52] The intent would be to create an *in terrorem* effect on corporate executives that would prevent corporate ads from being aired at all.

In Congress, Democrats quickly introduced the DISCLOSE Act,[53] the first of many attempts to impose extensive new disclosure requirements on civic organizations engaged in public discourse beyond the

---

[50] 558 U.S. 310.

[51] See Sean Parnell, "Senator Feingold Completely Loses Track of Reality," Inst. for Free Speech, Oct. 26, 2009, https://bit.ly/3zYmBCn. For a few other examples, see, e.g., Sean Parnell, "Waiting for ExxonMobil's One Percent," Inst. for Free Speech, Sept. 7, 2010, https://bit.ly/3jaAmHq; Bradley A. Smith & Allen Dickerson, The Non-Expert Agency: Using the SEC to Regulate Partisan Politics, 3 Harv. Bus. L. Rev. 419, 423–24 (2013).

[52] Laurence H. Tribe, "What Should Congress Do about Citizens United?," SCOTUSblog, Jan. 24, 2010, https://bit.ly/3jbgpQN.

[53] H.R. 5175 and S. 3295, 111th Cong., 2d Sess. (2010). "DISCLOSE" was an acronym created by the gimmicky title, "Democracy Is Strengthened by Casting Light on Spending in Elections."

traditional definitions of political spending.[54] Introducing the legislation, Sen. Chuck Schumer (D-NY) argued that "the deterrent effect [of compulsory disclosure] should not be underestimated."[55]

Elsewhere, liberal activists attempted to pressure a variety of federal agencies, including the Federal Election Commission (FEC), the Federal Communications Commission, and the Securities and Exchange Commission (SEC), into issuing expansive new disclosure requirements.[56] Rep. Chris Van Hollen (D-MD) unsuccessfully sued the FEC twice to try to force it to compel added disclosure.[57] A number of states—mainly, though not exclusively, under Democratic political control—passed new compulsory disclosure laws.

It must be stressed that *Citizens United* made no change to disclosure laws. Corporate PACs would still have to report their contributions and expenditures to the FEC, for public consumption. Any corporation spending money from its treasury on ads expressly advocating the election or defeat of a candidate, or falling within the Bipartisan Campaign Reform Act's definition of "electioneering communications," would be required to disclose those expenditures.

---

[54] For an analysis of DISCLOSE, which has been introduced in each succeeding Congress, see Eric Wang, "Analysis of the DISCLOSE Act of 2017 (S. 1585): New Bill, Same Plan to Crack Down on Speech," Inst. for Free Speech, Sept. 2017, https://bit.ly/3rUHBr6.

[55] T.W. Farnam, "Disclose Act Could Deter Involvement in Elections," Wash. Post, May 13, 2010.

[56] See Fed. Election Comm'n, Independent Expenditures and Electioneering Communications by Corporations and Labor Organizations, 79 Fed. Reg. 62797, Oct. 21, 2014. For the full history of what began as Rulemaking 2010-01, see Fed. Election Comm'n, Reg. 2010-01 at https://sers.fec.gov/fosers/, and see Fed. Election Comm'n, Statement of Vice Chair Ann Ravel on the Citizens United v. FEC and McCutcheon v. FEC Rulemakings, Oct. 9, 2014, https://bit.ly/3jaAzKI. See also Campaign Legal Ctr., Common Cause, and Sunlight Foundation, Letter to Tom Wheeler, Chair, Fed. Commc'ns Comm'n., Oct. 29, 2015, https://bit.ly/3xsz1B7; Comm. on Disclosure of Corporate Political Spending, Petition for Rulemaking, Aug. 3, 2011, https://bit.ly/3C6I8ef. Unions and liberal advocacy groups ginned up literally hundreds of thousands of form letters, many of which were little more than rants against the decision in *Citizens United*, in support of this petition to the SEC. See Smith & Dickerson, *supra* note 51, at 445–47; Bradley A. Smith, "Did Hundreds of Thousands of 'Investors' Really Write 'Personally' to the SEC on Corporate Disclosure? No, Not Really," Inst. for Free Speech, Dec. 22, 2013, https://bit.ly/3fD7t5Z.

[57] See Van Hollen v. Fed. Election Comm'n, 811 F.3d 486 (D.C. Cir. 2016); Ctr. for Individual Freedom v. Van Hollen, 694 F.3d 108 (D.C. Cir. 2012).

Any donations to other people or organizations earmarked for political ads would have to be disclosed.

What, then, was the intended purpose of all this newly proposed, compulsory disclosure? One purpose appears to have been simply to burden speakers and interfere with their message, as in some of Professor Tribe's proposals. Another, however, was to expand the definition of "political" discussion to encompass all spending and memberships that were part of public discourse—including, for example, the type of activities engaged in by past plaintiffs before the Supreme Court, including the NAACP, the anti-discrimination picketer Talley, the teacher Tucker, and the leafleteer McIntyre.[58] This meant greater disclosure of contributions and dues to trade associations, nonprofit advocacy organizations, think tanks, and politically incorrect charities, such as the Boy Scouts. None of this spending had previously counted as "political" or been covered by disclosure laws. The colloquial, loaded term for this spending became "dark money." Well aware of the harassment of donors to conservative ballot initiatives in California and Washington state, the actions of groups such as Accountable America, and the statements and occasional actions of Sen. Schumer and other elected officials in the nation's capital,[59] many conservatives began to see in these demands for compulsory disclosure an effort to "name and shame" and use public pressure to drive conservative voices from the public debate.[60]

It was in this environment that California Attorney General Harris began demanding that charities and other nonprofits supply her office

---

[58] See *supra* note 13.

[59] For example, in 2013, in the wake of the controversial shooting of an unarmed black teenager, Trayvon Martin, Sen. Dick Durbin (D-IL) sent a letter to some 300 businesses and advocacy organizations. In the letter, Sen. Durbin demanded to know if they supported the American Legislative Exchange Council, a bipartisan but predominately Republican organization of state legislators that Democrats viewed as a facilitator of conservative legislation. He also demanded to know if they supported so-called "stand-your-ground" laws, which Democrats at the time denounced as "racist." Durbin let it be known that he would announce their answers publicly in connection with a hearing on "stand-your-ground" laws, one that featured Martin's mother as the star witness. See Sen. Dick Durbin, Letter to Companies on "Stand Your Ground," Aug. 6, 2013, https://bit.ly/3rQq7fw. Patrick Howley, "Dick Durbin Calls in Trayvon Martin's Mother for Anti-ALEC Testimony," Daily Caller, Sep. 19, 2013, https://bit.ly/3zTF8jg.

[60] See generally Kimberly Strassel, The Intimidation Game: How the Left Is Silencing Free Speech (2016).

with copies of "Schedule B," a simple form that lists the names, addresses, and amounts given by donors of over $5,000[61]—as a prerequisite to continuing to do business in the state.[62]

III. The AFPF Litigation

A. The Lower Courts

AFPF and TMLC were two of the many conservative organizations that began receiving deficiency notices from the attorney general's office starting in the spring of 2012. Eventually threatened with deregistration and fines, both organizations sued. The district court granted preliminary injunctions prohibiting the state from requiring the donor list[63] but was overruled by a Ninth Circuit panel, which remanded the cases for trial.[64]

At the ensuing bench trials, the state asserted a compelling interest in enforcing the law and protecting the public from "self-dealing, improper loans, interested persons, or illegal or unfair business practices."[65] The main problem was, it wasn't really true. The court summarized the testimony of the state's own witness, a supervising auditor:

> [O]ut of the approximately 540 investigations conducted over the past ten years . . .only five instances involved the use of a Schedule B. In fact, as to those five investigations identified, the Attorney General's investigators could not recall whether they had unredacted Schedule Bs on file before initiating the investigation. And even in instances where a Schedule B was relied on, the relevant information it contained could have been obtained from other sources.[66]

---

[61] Schedule B is an attachment to the IRS's primary charitable reporting form, Form 990. Although Form 990 is a public document, Schedule B, because of the sensitive nature of donor information, is not; IRS officials are prohibited by law from releasing filed Schedule Bs. 26 U.S.C. §§ 6014(b) & 6014(d)(3)(A).

[62] At about the same time, New York's Democratic Attorney General Eric Schneiderman also began demanding information on donors from charities and other nonprofits seeking to solicit contributions in New York. See Schneiderman, 882 F.3d 374. Thus, nonprofit organizations unwilling to disclose donors found themselves in danger of being shut out of two of the largest, wealthiest states in the union.

[63] Ams. for Prosperity Found. v. Harris, 2015 WL 768778 (No. 14-09448) (C.D. Cal. Feb. 23, 2015).

[64] Ams. for Prosperity Found. v. Harris, 809 F.3d 536 (9th Cir. 2015).

[65] Ams. for Prosperity Found. v. Harris, 182 F. Supp. 3d 1049, 1053 (C.D. Cal. 2016).

[66] Id. at 1054.

"The record," concluded the court, "lacks even a single, concrete instance in which pre-investigation collection of a Schedule B did anything to advance the Attorney General's investigative, regulatory or enforcement efforts."[67]

Eschewing any reliance on the "informational interest," the state instead countered that the bulk collection of Schedule Bs did not constitute a First Amendment harm at all because the information was not disclosed to the public. The primary flaw in this argument, however, was that the trial record showed that nearly 1,800 Schedule Bs had been publicly posted on the state's website.[68] And as the district court pointed out, once such information is disclosed, "it cannot be clawed back."[69]

As to the harm from this disclosure, the district court cited in detail extensive testimony of harassment, non-idle death threats, physical assaults, economic boycotts, and threats to family members, aimed at members and contributors to the two organizations.[70] The court entered judgment for both plaintiffs.

The Ninth Circuit again reversed both decisions on appeal.[71] Although the court claimed to apply the relatively demanding "exacting scrutiny" standard,[72] it actually employed something more akin to the "rational basis" standard typically used in evaluating economic regulation. Except that may be unfair to the "rational basis" test—the Ninth Circuit's actual standard was more akin to a "credulous acceptance" standard of review.

In response to the district court's factual findings that for over a decade the state had not used Schedule B information to police charitable activity, the court of appeals noted that, well, someday it might find it handy to "flag suspicious activity" or improve "efficiency." It also

---

[67] *Id.* at 1055.

[68] *Id.* at 1057.

[69] *Id.* at 1058.

[70] See *id.* at 1055–56; see also Thomas More Law Ctr. v. Harris, 2016 WL 6781090 (No. 15-3048), at *4 (C.D. Cal. Nov. 16, 2016). These included business boycotts; obscene and threatening calls and emails; death threats, including at least one in which the perpetrator was found taking pictures of AFPF employees' autos in the parking garage; numerous physical attacks, including collapsing a heavy event tent on members; pushing; spitting; and threats to grandchildren.

[71] Ams. for Prosperity Found. v. Becerra, 903 F.3d 1000 (9th Cir. 2018).

[72] *Id.* at 1008, 1020.

credited testimony that the state might be able to use Schedule Bs in various hypothetical situations over the testimony that it didn't actually use Schedule B in real situations, and, in fact, had apparently not even noticed for years that many charities were not including Schedule B in their filings.[73] As for the fact that the state had publicly posted almost 1,800 copies of confidential Schedule Bs—and further recognizing that in fact over 350,000 Schedule Bs were readily accessible to any hacker with a modicum of computer knowledge[74]—the court blithely accepted the state's promise that it wouldn't happen again.[75] And in a curious defense of the state's proven inability to maintain confidentiality, the court noted that "[n]othing is perfectly secure on the internet."[76] The plaintiffs were undoubtedly comforted by that bit of wisdom.

The court of appeals then simply dismissed the record of threats, reprisals, and harassment: "Ultimately, we need not decide whether the plaintiffs have demonstrated a reasonable probability that the compelled disclosure of Schedule B information would subject their contributors to a constitutionally significant level of threats, harassment or reprisals . . . [because] we are not persuaded that there exists a reasonable probability that the plaintiffs' Schedule B information will become public."[77]

Over the objections of five judges, a petition for rehearing *en banc* was denied.[78]

B. The Supreme Court

The Supreme Court granted certiorari on January 8, 2021,[79] heard arguments in late April, and reversed the Ninth Circuit in a 6-3 decision on July 1, the last day of the term.[80]

Much of the justices' energy was devoted to debating the proper standard of review and the proper application of that standard.

[73] *Id.* at 1010.

[74] By altering a single URL digit, over 350,000 Schedule Bs were readily available through the state's website. *Id.* at 1018.

[75] *Id.* at 1019.

[76] *Id.* at 1018.

[77] *Id.* at 1017.

[78] Ams. for Prosperity Found. v. Becerra, 919 F.3d 1177 (9th Cir. 2019).

[79] 141 S. Ct. 973 (2021).

[80] Ams. for Prosperity Found. v. Bonta, 141 S. Ct. 2373 (2021).

The lower courts had applied "exacting scrutiny."[81] The TMLC (but not AFPF) urged the Court to apply "strict scrutiny," the Court's most demanding standard.[82] Although "strict scrutiny" generally applies in the First Amendment context, and there are powerful arguments that it should apply to cases of compelled disclosure,[83] the argument for "exacting scrutiny" in the context of compelled disclosure was also strong. Although *NAACP* had used the term "closest scrutiny," *Buckley* declared, "[s]ince *NAACP v. Alabama* we have required that the . . . interests of the State must survive exacting scrutiny."[84] Similarly, *McIntyre* and *Doe* had applied "exacting scrutiny."[85] In the end six justices—Chief Justice John Roberts, joined by Justices Brett Kavanaugh and Amy Coney Barrett, and the three liberal dissenters—opted for "exacting scrutiny." Justice Clarence Thomas would have applied "strict scrutiny"; Justices Alito and Neil Gorsuch left open the possibility that "strict scrutiny" might be applied in the future but believed that it was not necessary to decide the issue in this case because the rule failed under either test.

More important than the standard of review may have been the majority's interpretation of the "exacting scrutiny" standard. Roberts's group, now joined by Justices Alito and Gorsuch, insisted that "exacting scrutiny" has real teeth,[86] while the dissenters, like the Ninth Circuit, interpreted it as little different from "rational basis."

As in *NAACP* and its classic progeny, the majority was skeptical of the state's asserted interest. It recognized, of course, that law enforcement could be an "important" and "substantial" state interest

---

[81] 903 F.3d at 1003; 182 F. Supp. 3d at 1053.

[82] 141 S. Ct. at 2383. The "strict scrutiny" standard generally requires the state to demonstrate a "compelling" government interest in its restriction and to "narrowly tailor" that restriction to arrive at the "least restrictive means" of solving the problem. McCullen v. Coakley, 573 U.S. 464, 478 (2014). For an in-depth review of the standard and its application, see Richard H. Fallon, Jr., Strict Judicial Scrutiny, 54 UCLA L. Rev. 1267 (2007).

[83] See, e.g., Buckley v. Am. Const. L. Found., 525 U.S. 182, 206–09 (1999) (Thomas, J., concurring in the judgment).

[84] 424 U.S. at 64.

[85] McIntyre, 514 U.S. at 334–35; Doe, 561 U.S. at 196.

[86] 141 S. Ct. at 2391 (Alito, J., concurring in part and concurring in the judgment). Justice Thomas's strict scrutiny test would, of course, encompass the majority's version of "exacting scrutiny."

as required under "exacting scrutiny." But the majority looked at the record, and the trial court's findings, and simply doubted that that was really the case. The Court noted the trial court's findings that the state, in fact, rarely if ever used Schedule B to detect or investigate fraud; that only two other states require filing of Schedule B; and that California and those other states had rarely enforced the requirement at all prior to 2010. It concluded, "California's interest is less in investigating fraud and more in ease of administration."[87] And ease of administration simply is not a compelling interest sufficient to override First Amendment burdens.

While not requiring that the state use the "least restrictive means" to accomplish its objectives, the majority held that "exacting scrutiny" did require the statute to be "narrowly tailored" to achieving the state's ends. By that, it appeared to mean something like "strict scrutiny light"—the statute or policy need not be the *least* restrictive, but it ought to be no more extensive in scope than reasonably necessary. Given the thousands of charitable filings in California and the almost nonexistent use of Schedule Bs in enforcement, the policy had no chance of meeting the narrow tailoring requirement.

Finally, the majority addressed the trial court's lengthy record of harassment. But following cases such as *Talley v. California, Shelton v. Tucker,* and *McIntyre,* the majority rejected the suggestion that relief had to be conditioned on such evidence—a reasonable probability of harassment "creates an unnecessary risk of chilling" protected activity.[88] Even as it recited the stark evidence of harassment and threats against the plaintiffs' members, the majority recognized that that would not be true in every case. But "[w]hen it comes to the freedom of association, the protections of the First Amendment are triggered not only by actual restrictions on an individual's ability to join with others to further shared goals. *The risk of a chilling effect on association is enough.*"[89]

In sum, the failure of the state to establish that its demands were at all necessary to its legitimate interests (as in *NAACP, Bates,* and *Gibson*), its unnecessarily broad sweep (as in *Talley* and *Shelton*), and the record of harassment (again, as in *NAACP* and *Bates*) made *AFPF*

[87] *Id.* at 2387.

[88] *Id.* at 2388.

[89] *Id.* at 2389 (emphasis added).

an easy case—as Justice Alito wrote in his concurrence, "[t]he question is not even close."[90]

In contrast, the dissent, authored by Justice Sotomayor and joined by Justices Breyer and Elena Kagan, offered a very different version of "exacting scrutiny." They would not have required "narrow tailoring," but only a "substantial relationship" between the compelled disclosure and an "important" government interest.[91] This might work if "substantial relationship" were given serious consideration. But to the dissent, the term seemed to mean little more than "rational basis." After all, a "rational basis" for a policy will almost always mean some "relationship" to a problem, and thus likely a "substantial one." And once that is established, absent some tailoring requirement, there are no further checks on the state. The dissent's version of "exacting scrutiny" was all but meaningless.

Given the clear inadequacy of that approach to *AFPF*, the dissent decided not to address the absence of any meaningful state reliance on Schedule B for investigative purposes, the broad sweep of the state's bulk collection of Schedule Bs, the proven failure of the state to keep the records out of the public realm, or the record of harassment developed at trial. Instead, the dissent opted to adjudicate a different case in which these problems just weren't present.

"The majority holds that a California regulation requiring charitable organizations to disclose tax forms containing the names and contributions of their top donors unconstitutionally burdens the right to associate *even if the forms are not publicly disclosed,*" wrote the dissenters,[92] ignoring the fact that nearly 1,800 forms were publicly disclosed and tens of thousands of others were easily accessible. This inconvenient fact was brushed aside because "California has implemented security measures to ensure that Schedule B information remains confidential."[93] The dissent didn't consider the possibility of a second fail.

As to the record of harassment, Justice Sotomayor's opinion borders on callous: "The same scrutiny the Court applied when NAACP members in the Jim Crow South did not want to disclose their membership for fear of reprisals and violence now applies equally in the

[90] *Id.* at 2391 (Alito, J., concurring).

[91] *Id.* at 2396 (Sotomayor, J., dissenting).

[92] *Id.* at 2392 (emphasis added).

[93] *Id.* at 2400.

case of donors only too happy to publicize their names across the websites and walls of the organizations they support."[94] But if all these donors were "only too happy to publicize their names," what was the case about? The notion that nothing short of a Jim Crow regime is enough to create meaningful First Amendment burdens ignores a century of jurisprudence and threatens to convert the hard-won victories of the civil rights movement into hollow memories. The *AFPF* record was replete with examples of harassment and physical violence. Would the dissenters have lynchings be a prerequisite to invoking the protections of the Constitution? Complaining that "the vast majority of donors prefer to publicize their charitable contributions"[95] makes no more sense than noting that the vast majority of people don't take to the streets in peaceful protest, so maybe those rights don't matter either. Of course, it may be that some donors were a bit "too happy to publicize their names," but presumably the same could have been said about at least some donors to the NAACP, even back in 1957.

Oddly, in her concluding paragraph, Justice Sotomayor confessed, "[t]here is no question that petitioners have shown that their donors reasonably fear reprisals if their identities are publicly exposed."[96] She just didn't care.

IV. The Campaign Finance Stalking Horse

Early in her dissent, Justice Sotomayor may have revealed what was really bothering her. "Today's analysis marks reporting and disclosure requirements with a bull's-eye."[97] Almost from the start, America's liberal commentariat portrayed the case as one of "dark money" in politics.[98] Recall that Attorney General Harris

---

[94] *Id.* at 2393.

[95] *Id.* at 2403.

[96] *Id.* at 2405.

[97] *Id.* at 2392.

[98] See, e.g., *id.*; Brief of U.S. Senators as Amici Curiae in Support of Respondent, Ams. for Prosperity Found. v. Bonta, 141 S. Ct. 2373 (2021) (Nos. 19-251, 19-255) (the 15 senators—all Democrats—managed to use the phrase "dark money" 42 times in the brief); Jon Skolnik, "Right-wing Funders Are Waging War to Keep Dark Money Secret. Some Liberals Are Joining Them," Salon, May 12, 2021, https://bit.ly/2TNsanP; Matt Ford, "How Far Will the Roberts Court Go to Protect Shadowy Political Donors?," New Republic, Jan. 10, 2020, https://bit.ly/3ljPgxH.

implemented the policy of requiring donor disclosure in the wake of *Citizens United* and in the midst of a concerted effort to expand disclosure beyond its traditional boundary of actual campaigns and elections. At oral argument, Justice Breyer raised the question directly, asking if the case was "really a stalking horse for campaign finance disclosure laws."[99] And the decision was greeted by many—again, primarily on the left—as a major blow to democracy and a victory for "dark money."[100]

The issue arises because charities and nonprofits of all types engage in many activities that affect public policy, and hence have the potential to affect elections. The NAACP's agitation, education, and litigation for civil rights certainly affected American politics and elections, but the organization was at all times in its battles against compelled disclosure a recognized charity. Think tanks such as the Brookings Institution and the Heritage Foundation are intimately involved in public policy. Recognized charities such as the League of Women Voters, the American Society for the Prevention of Cruelty to Animals, and Judicial Watch are well-known entities in public policy debates. Nonpartisan voter registration has long been a staple activity of many charities. Churches preach their teaching on justice and are often intimately involved in political causes. Even what were once the most mainstream of charities, such as the Boy Scouts of America, may become embroiled in hot cultural—and hence, political—disputes. As Justice Oliver Wendell Holmes once put it, "every idea is an incitement. It offers itself for belief and if believed it is acted on."[101] Such action might include voting.

The plaintiffs, AFPF and TMLC, are conservative in their orientation but—like the NAACP in 1958—both are charitable organizations operating under section 501(c)(3) of the Internal Revenue Code. As such, they are prohibited from engaging in partisan political activities

99 Transcript of Oral Argument at 50, Ams. for Prosperity Found. v. Bonta, 141 S. Ct. 2373 (2021) (Nos. 19-251, 19-255) ("I'd like to know what you think of the argument raised in several of the amici briefs anyway that this case is really a stalking horse for campaign finance disclosure laws.").

100 See, e.g., Alison Durkee, "Supreme Court Sides with Conservative Groups, Empowers Dark Money Groups with Ruling Striking Down California Donor Law," Forbes, July 1, 2021, https://bit.ly/3llxg6k; Ian Millhiser, "The Supreme Court Just Made Citizens United Even Worse: It's a Great Day for Dark Money," Vox, July 1, 2021, https://bit.ly/3iiUYhG.

101 Gitlow v. New York, 268 U.S. 652, 673 (1925) (Holmes, J., dissenting).

and campaigns. "Dark money" in politics is, by definition, not money expended by charities. To the extent that *AFPF v. Bonta* was about campaign finance, then, it was not about the plaintiffs attempting to roll back laws, but about efforts of the political left to dramatically expand the reach of campaign finance law to cover most every aspect of public life—precisely what the Supreme Court in *Buckley* had held was unconstitutional and what the *NAACP* line of cases had implicitly rejected.

On its own terms, the "dark money" argument makes no sense. "Dark money"—which makes up about two to four percent of spending in U.S. elections[102]—is legal. It is called "dark" only because the donors to the organization doing the spending are not publicly disclosed.[103] There is no need, therefore, for the state's attorney general to investigate it. Those who argue that the Court's decision will make it hard to fight "dark money" are, in essence, admitting that— at least for them—the game was never about "law enforcement." It is about exposing donors publicly, or perhaps giving government itself the ability to track spenders and create, in essence, a government "enemies list."

Not surprisingly, given that California argued that it did not release the Schedule B information—intentionally, anyway—to the public, the state in *AFPF* did not rely on the "informational" interest. How could it, if it wasn't going to make the information public? Yet even as Harris's successor as California's attorney general was arguing that the state's important interest in bulk disclosure of donor information was to efficiently police self-dealing and fraud,[104] he argued in a letter to the IRS commenting on a proposal to eliminate most Schedule B filings, and joined by the attorneys general of 19 other states (all Democrats), that the state needed the information on Schedule B in order to track "dark money" in

---

[102] Luke Wachob, "Putting 'Dark Money' in Context: Total Campaign Spending by Political Committees and Nonprofits per Election Cycle," Inst. for Free Speech, May 8, 2017, https://bit.ly/2V9GXdo.

[103] See Dark Money Basics, Ctr. for Responsive Politics, https://bit.ly/3A5pKAi (last visited July 29, 2021) ("'Dark money' refers to spending meant to influence political outcomes where the source of the money is not disclosed.").

[104] Brief for Respondent at 7–8, 29–32, Ams. for Prosperity Found. v. Bonta, 141 S. Ct. 2373 (2021) (Nos. 19-251, 19-255), https://bit.ly/2TTfD2m.

the state.[105] That sounds like a broadly defined "informational" interest, and not necessarily a benign one.

Justice Sotomayor, like the Ninth Circuit, seemed to believe that if information was not intended to be publicly disclosed, there is no First Amendment harm.[106] But compelled information can be misused by the state too. The *AFPF* majority only hints, perhaps wisely, at the possibility of harassment by the state itself. Although it implicitly noted that official harassment could be a problem,[107] the Court spoke explicitly only of nonofficial harassment—"bomb threats, protests, stalking, physical violence."[108] And, indeed, other than the probably inadvertent disclosure of hundreds of Schedule B forms, there was no evidence that the state had misused the information. But the Court in the future should not ignore the simple fact that disclosure can be a harm in and of itself. Some people just don't like the idea that the government has information about them, and that is a real harm, even if it seems a nonsensical objection to Justice Sotomayor. More important, once information is in government hands, it can rarely be clawed back. American history is replete with examples of government abusing tax and other information to harass its enemies.[109] And the mere fact that today's government is not using information improperly does not mean that tomorrow's will not. Governments change. And in recent years, we have seen numerous incidents of people being harassed for actions or statements that were not controversial years ago but are today.[110]

[105] Gurbir Grewal et al., Letter to Steven T. Mnuchin & Charles B. Rettig, Dec. 19, 2019, at 2 n.2.

[106] See Ctr. for Competitive Politics v. Harris, 784 F. 3d 1307, 1312–13 (9th Cir. 2015).

[107] 141 S. Ct. at 2388.

[108] *Id.*

[109] Indeed, *NAACP v. Alabama* is itself an example. President Richard Nixon's "enemies list" is another example, and a major reason the IRS now has such tight rules on the handling of donor information, with criminal penalties for its improper release. See Barnaby Zall, "Reviving the 'Enemies List' Using IRS Form 990, Schedule B," Pub. Pol'y Legal Inst., Feb. 3, 2021, https://bit.ly/2Vo3X83.

[110] See, e.g., Noah Manskar, "Boeing Communications Boss Niel Golightly Resigns over Sexist Article," N.Y. Post, July 3, 2020, https://bit.ly/3xkGG40 (executive forced to resign over 33-year-old newspaper column opposing women in combat); David Lee, "Mozilla Boss Brendan Eich Resigns after Gay Marriage Storm," BBC News, Apr. 4, 2014, https://bbc.in/3jc5uX7 (Mozilla founder Brendan Eich ousted from company over political donation made years earlier to a ballot proposition that gained majority support).

Perhaps the state had legitimate law enforcement interests. But consider the timing and political atmosphere of the attorney general's decision to "ramp up" enforcement of donor disclosure, the open statements by prominent politicians and commentators of the intent to use disclosure to deter opposition speech, the actual campaigns of harassment against donors whose political campaign contributions had been disclosed, the prominent leaks of confidential tax information of conservative politicians and groups,[111] and the memories of the IRS's own "tea party" scandal of 2013,[112] could certainly lead a reasonable observer to conclude that the primary reason for the state's policy was to enable harassment, both official and unofficial, of donors to disfavored charities.[113] If *AFPF* was a stalking horse to prevent such harassment, it was a good one to have in the hunt.

If, on the other hand, the purpose of California's compelled donor disclosure was not to harass and intimidate, then laws regulating disclosure of campaign contributions and spending have little to fear. *Buckley* differentiated *NAACP* and its progeny from the campaign finance disclosure provisions of FECA by noting three compelling state interests: enforcement, prevention of corruption, and a narrow informational interest in knowing the organizations a candidate was most likely to prioritize. Those interests simply were not present in *AFPF*, but presumably they still are when the state demands disclosure of contributions to political campaigns.

---

[111] See Stephen Engelberg & Richard Tofel, "Why We Are Publishing the Tax Secrets of the .001%," ProPublica, June 8, 2021, https://bit.ly/3A21y1P ("We obtained the [confidential] information from an anonymous source"); Larry Light, "A Trump Tax Return Revealed," CBS News, Mar. 15, 2017, https://cbsn.ws/3ig3DBo (discussing "leaked copy" of Donald Trump tax returns); Editorial, "IRS Admits to a Smidgeon of a Felony," Investor's Bus. Daily, June 27, 2014, https://bit.ly/3C4UuDw ("The National Organization for Marriage has been awarded a $50,000 settlement from the IRS after the agency admitted wrongdoing in leaking the organization's 2008 tax return and the names and contact information of major donors.").

[112] See, e.g., Peter Overby, "IRS Apologizes for Aggressive Scrutiny of Conservative Groups," NPR, Oct. 27, 2017, https://n.pr/3A7f7gF. For comprehensive, day-by-day coverage of the scandal, see Professor Caron's TaxProf Blog, searching under "IRS Scandal," https://taxprof.typepad.com/ (last viewed July 30, 2021).

[113] It must be noted here that conservatives do not share this fear alone—dozens of "liberal" nonprofits, such as the American Civil Liberties Union, People for the Ethical Treatment of Animals, the Council on Islamic-American Relations, and many more filed amicus briefs in support of the petitioners. A complete list of amicus briefs is available at SCOTUSblog, https://bit.ly/37d4tZc (last viewed July 29, 2021).

Because the state did not raise it, the Court did not consider the scope of the "informational" interest that has caused so many problems since its narrow purpose was blurred in *Citizens United*. But the tougher "exacting scrutiny" test will make it harder for that interest to be used as an all-purpose rationale for expanding compelled disclosure. Further, the general tenor of the majority opinion and Justices Alito's and Thomas's concurrences suggests that the Court will be skeptical of efforts to expand that interest beyond its original narrow scope delineated in *Buckley* and *McIntyre*.

Thus, it is true that by putting some teeth into "exacting scrutiny," campaign disclosure laws might be trimmed at the margin. For example, many states require public disclosure of political contributions at very low levels, and it may be hard to sustain these under the "informational" interest after *AFPF*. That would seem to be a good thing—small-dollar donors to a campaign shouldn't have to run even a minimal risk of harassment and retaliation, a threat that is very real in today's climate. Most other existing rules, however, should remain, for better or worse, undisturbed, just as *Buckley* upheld them in spite of *NAACP v. Alabama*.

If most current laws are not threatened, *AFPF* does cast still further constitutional doubt on the decade-long effort to "deter" speech by expanding the reach of campaign finance disclosure laws to non-candidate, nonelectoral advocacy activities by trade associations, social welfare and advocacy organizations, charities, think tanks, and grassroots networks. Something like the proposed DISCLOSE Act, already of dubious constitutionality, now rests on even soggier ground. Similarly, the IRS's own use of Schedule B—already truncated voluntarily by the service—could come under scrutiny, since there is little evidence that the IRS actually uses the information to enforce the tax code.

And that would be fine. A little trimming here and there is probably overdue.

V. Conclusion

One of the more encouraging aspects of *AFPF* was the majority's recognition of the facts on the ground—not just in the instant case, but in our culture generally. This was apparent at oral argument, when Justice Thomas used a simple question to demonstrate how even noncontroversial causes—such as "puppies"—can today create a raging storm of controversy. Justice Thomas noted as well that "in this era, there seems to be quite a bit of . . . loose accusations about organizations, . . . [that] might be accused of being a white supremacist organization or racist or homophobic."[114] Justice Alito specifically addressed "legitimate fear in our current atmosphere."[115] And this concern found its way into Chief Justice Roberts's majority opinion: "Such risks [of violence and harassment] are heightened in the 21st century and seem to grow with each passing year, as anyone with access to a computer [can] compile a wealth of information about anyone else, including such sensitive details as a person's home address or the school attended by his children."[116]

Supporters of laws and regulations requiring Americans to disclose their associations, memberships, and financial support tend to respond to this problem by speaking in general terms of "the public's right to know." When concerns of boycotts, blacklists, and harassment are raised, they often quote the late, great Justice Scalia's concurring opinion in *Doe v. Reed*. In that case, upholding public disclosure of the names of persons signing petitions to place a referendum on a state ballot, Justice Scalia wrote:

> [H]arsh criticism, short of unlawful action, is a price our people have traditionally been willing to pay for self-governance. Requiring people to stand up in public for their political acts fosters civic courage, without which democracy is doomed. For my part, I do not look forward to a society which, thanks to the Supreme Court, campaigns anonymously *(McIntyre)* and even exercises the direct democracy of initiative and referendum hidden from public scrutiny and protected from the accountability of criticism. This does not resemble the Home of the Brave."[117]

---

[114] Transcript of Oral Argument, *supra* note 99, at 9–10.

[115] *Id.* at 53.

[116] 141 S. Ct. at 2388.

[117] Doe, 561 U.S. at 228 (Scalia, J., concurring) (this passage was quoted in whole or in part in at least three amicus briefs supporting the state of California in *AFPF v. Bonta*); see Brief of U.S. Senators, *supra* note 98, at 34; Brief of Legal Historians in Support of Respondents at 17, Ams. for Prosperity Found. v. Bonta, 141 S. Ct. 2373 (2021) (Nos. 19-251, 19-255); Brief of Campaign Legal Ctr. et al. in Support of Respondents at 13, Ams. for Prosperity Found. v. Bonta, 141 S. Ct. 2373 (2021) (Nos. 19-251, 19-255).

Whether Justice Scalia would have sided with the state in *AFPF* can, of course, never be known for certain. I suspect not.[118] But either way, and with great respect, Justice Scalia was not a typical person. He was possessed of a dominant, outgoing personality; with his keen intellect and dashing rhetorical skills, he relished verbal combat and battles of ideas. Perhaps more important, the justice spent a majority of his adult life in jobs with enormous security—as a tenured law professor and, for the final 34 years of his life, as a federal judge. Moreover, in these positions, Justice Scalia did not have to concern himself with the possibility that something he might say could damage the welfare of share-holders (perhaps retirees counting on their investments to meet expenses), or employees who could lose jobs, if a boycott ensued. And although Scalia was famous for eschewing the company of federal marshals who regularly accompany justices of the Court, it remains true that his workplace and local travel were protected by the Supreme Court Police, and when necessary or desired in his travels outside of Washington he could call on the protection of the U.S. Marshals Service. It almost goes without saying that most Americans, even the rich and powerful, lack such insulation from "cancel culture."

Not everyone is an Antonin Scalia—indeed, and perhaps unfortunately, almost no one is. And so, in a sense, the ultimate questions before the Supreme Court in *Americans for Prosperity Foundation v. Bonta* were these: To what extent does the First Amendment protect not just the "courageous" and "brave," but also the "timid and sensitive,"[119] by protecting them from forced disclosure of their associations, memberships, and financial support, when such disclosure may be used to harass and threaten them and their families? Do the meek have ideas we should hear, and if so, how do we encourage those ideas? And finally, is democracy better served when Americans can offer their opinions without fear of being held "accountable" in

---

[118] Justice Scalia's opinions critical of anonymity came in the context of elections, not, as in *AFPF*, where nonelectoral speech was at issue. See McIntyre, 514 U.S. at 371 (Scalia, J., dissenting); McConnell v. Fed. Election Comm'n, 540 U.S. 93 (in which Justice Scalia joined the Court majority in upholding disclosure rules); Doe, 561 U.S. at 228 (Scalia, J., concurring in the judgment).

[119] See Barsky v. United States, 167 F.2d 241, 249 (D.C. Cir. 1948) (Edgerton, J., dissenting).

the manner favored by today's "woke" and 1950s segregationists? I think it is.

At a minimum, the government should be neither harassing citizens for their beliefs, nor forcing citizens to provide the information for their own undoing, without a darn good reason. In *Americans for Prosperity Foundation v. Bonta*, the Supreme Court indicated that it thinks so, too.

Mahanoy Area School District v. B.L.: The Court Protects Student Social Media but Leaves Unanswered Questions

*David L. Hudson Jr.**

Fifty years ago, the U.S. Supreme Court reasoned that the state of California could not criminally punish Paul Robert Cohen for wearing a jacket bearing the words "Fuck the Draft" in a Los Angeles County courthouse.[1] Justice John Marshall Harlan II began his majority opinion with the memorable line: "This case may seem at first blush too inconsequential to find its way into our books, but the issue it presents is of no small constitutional significance."[2] Fifty years later, the Court addressed another case involving a speaker who used the f-word multiple times in what some might view as trivial expression. But, as in *Cohen*, the Court delivered another significant free-speech victory in *Mahanoy Area School District v. B.L.*, ruling that a public school could not impose discipline upon one of its student for posting a fusillade of f-bombs on social media.[3]

In *Mahanoy*, the Court limited the ability of school officials to police student social media expression that is posted off campus. The Court not only addressed student social media expression but also reaffirmed the vitality of the Court's seminal student speech decision in *Tinker v. Des Moines Independent Community*

* David L. Hudson Jr. is an assistant professor of law at Belmont University College of Law. He also serves as a Justice Robert H. Jackson Fellow for the Foundation for Individual Rights in Education (FIRE) and a First Amendment Fellow for the Freedom Forum.

[1] Cohen v. California, 403 U.S. 15 (1971).

[2] *Id.* at 15.

[3] 141 S. Ct. 2038 (2021).

School District.[4] However, the decision leaves much room for future litigation to flesh out the broad parameters of the Court's ruling.

Part I of this article provides a brief overview of the Court's previous rulings on public school student speech in the K–12 context. Part II discusses the Court's decision in *Mahanoy*. Part III outlines some unanswered questions from the *Mahanoy* decision.

I. Student Speech (K–12) and the U.S. Supreme Court

For the 19th century and a good portion of the 20th, public school students had no First Amendment free-speech rights. Teachers taught and students listened. It was not until the Court's famous flag-salute case in *West Virginia Board of Education v. Barnette* that students possessed some level of free-speech rights in public schools.[5]

The case involved sisters Marie and Gathie Barnett (their last name was misspelled in the case caption), who attended Slip Hill Grade School near Charleston, West Virginia.[6] They and their father, Walter, were devout Jehovah's Witnesses who believed that saluting the flag was akin to idol worship and sanctifying graven images.[7] West Virginia had a law on the books that mandated students salute the flag and recite the Pledge of Allegiance or face expulsion. Not only did students face expulsion, but their parents could face up to 30 days in jail for such nonconformity.

The Barnetts sued, asserting that such action violated their First Amendment rights under the Free Exercise and Free Speech Clauses of the First Amendment. But the timing did not seem propitious for such a lawsuit: the Supreme Court in 1940 had upheld a similar Pennsylvania law from a challenge by students expelled for similar conduct in *Minersville School District v. Gobitis*.[8]

---

[4] 393 U.S. 503 (1969).

[5] 319 U.S. 624 (1943).

[6] David L. Hudson, Jr., "Woman in Barnette Reflects on Flag Salute Case," Freedom F., Apr. 29, 2009, https://bit.ly/3ysatcx.

[7] *Id.*

[8] Minersville Sch. Dist. v. Gobitis, 310 U.S. 586 (1940).

Gobitis had caused many to question the patriotism of Jehovah's Witness students and led to much violence perpetrated against the religious minority.[9] But three justices—William O. Douglas, Hugo Black, and Frank Murphy—had publicly questioned the *Gobitis* decision and candidly admitted that they had made a mistake:

> Since we joined in the opinion in the *Gobitis* case, we think this is an appropriate occasion to state that we now believe that it also was wrongly decided. Certainly our democratic form of government, functioning under the historic Bill of Rights, has a high responsibility to accommodate itself to the religious views of minorities, however unpopular and unorthodox those views may be.[10]

The time was ripe for another flag-salute case. Enter the Barnetts.

In the *Barnette* decision, the Court ruled that public school officials violated the First Amendment when they punished the Barnett sisters in a West Virginia elementary school for refusing to salute the flag and recite the Pledge of Allegiance. The Court famously proclaimed that "[i]f there is any fixed star in our constitutional constellation, it is that no official, high or petty, can prescribe what shall be orthodox in politics, nationalism, religion, or other matters of opinion or force citizens to confess by word or act their faith therein."[11] The Court further emphasized the importance of teaching students the value of constitutional freedoms, writing: "That they are educating the young for citizenship is reason for scrupulous protection of Constitutional freedoms of the individual, if we are not to strangle the free mind at its source and teach youth to discount important principles of our government as mere platitudes."[12]

The decision not only established a constitutional baseline that students possess some level of First Amendment rights in

---

[9] Garret Epps, "America's New Lesson in Tolerance," The Atlantic, Sept. 1, 2016, https://bit.ly/3lzGagq.

[10] Jones v. Opelika, 316 U.S. 584, 623–24 (1942) (Black, Douglas, and Murphy, JJ., dissenting).

[11] W. Va. State Bd. of Educ. v. Barnette, 319 U.S. 624, 642 (1943).

[12] *Id.* at 637.

public school.[13] It also created the no-compelled-speech doctrine: that the First Amendment often prohibits the government from forcing individuals to recite, believe or affirm certain expression.[14]

But the Court in *Barnette* did not establish a legal test to determine when school officials violate students' First Amendment rights.[15] Furthermore, there was some question as to whether the decision was more rooted in the Free Exercise Clause or the Free Speech Clause.[16] It took more than two and a half decades for the Court to create such a legal test in the *Tinker* case.[17] That case involved the wearing of black peace armbands by Mary Beth Tinker, her brother John, Christopher Eckhardt, and a few other students to protest U.S. involvement in the Vietnam War, to support Robert Kennedy's Christmas truce, and to mourn those who had died in the conflict. School officials learned of the impending black armband protest and imposed a rule that selectively targeted and prohibited black armbands.

The Tinkers still wore their armbands and faced suspensions from school. A federal district court ruled against them, a decision affirmed by a deadlocked Eighth Circuit. The Tinkers' last shot was at the Supreme Court. They prevailed by a 7-2 vote in a decision that remains the seminal student speech decision.[18]

The Court ruled that public school students do not "shed their constitutional rights to freedom of speech or expression at the schoolhouse gate."[19] While the Court acknowledged that such rights should be interpreted "in light of the special characteristics of the school environment,"[20] the decision was filled with language

---

[13] Stuart Leviton, Is Anyone Listening to Our Students?: A Plea for Respect and Inclusion, 21 Fla. St. U. L. Rev. 35, 40 (1993).

[14] David L. Hudson, Jr., Let the Students Speak!: A History of the Fight for Freedom of Expression in American Schools 35 (2011).

[15] *Id.* at 45.

[16] David L. Hudson, Jr., Thirty Years of Hazelwood and Its Spread to College and University Campuses, 61 How. L.J. 491, 494 (2018).

[17] Tinker, 393 U.S. at 503.

[18] David L. Hudson, Jr., Losing the Spirit of Tinker v. Des Moines and the Urgent Need to Protect Student Speech, 66 Clev. St. L. Rev. Et Cetera 1, 1 (2018).

[19] Tinker, 393 U.S. at 506.

[20] *Id.*

about the value of freedom of expression for young persons.[21] Consider the following passages from Justice Abe Fortas's majority opinion:

> But, in our system, undifferentiated fear or apprehension of disturbance is not enough to overcome the right to freedom of expression. Any departure from absolute regimentation may cause trouble.[22]
>
> . . .
>
> Any word spoken, in class, in the lunchroom, or on the campus, that deviates from the views of another person may start an argument or cause a disturbance. But our Constitution says we must take this risk; and our history says that it is this sort of hazardous freedom—this kind of openness—that is the basis of our national strength and of the independence and vigor of Americans who grow up and live in this relatively permissive, often disputatious, society.[23]
>
> . . .
>
> In our system, state-operated schools may not be enclaves of totalitarianism. School officials do not possess absolute authority over their students. Students in school as well as out of school are "persons" under our Constitution.[24]
>
> . . .
>
> In our system, students may not be regarded as closed-circuit recipients of only that which the State chooses to communicate. They may not be confined to the expression of those sentiments that are officially approved.[25]

The Court also established a legal test to determine when student speech qualified for First Amendment protection, reasoning that such speech was protected unless school officials could reasonably forecast that the student speech would cause a substantial

[21] Hudson, Losing the Spirit of Tinker, *supra* note 18, at 4.

[22] Tinker, 393 U.S. at 508.

[23] *Id.* at 508–09 (citation omitted).

[24] *Id.* at 511.

[25] *Id.*

disruption or material interference of school activities[26] or that the student speech would infringe or invade the rights of others.[27] The Court explained that "our independent examination of the record fails to yield evidence that the school authorities had reason to anticipate that the wearing of the armbands would substantially interfere with the work of the school or impinge upon the rights of other students."[28]

The Court also explained that school officials needed to be able to point to articulable evidence or at least some facts of disturbance rather than censor or punish student speech based on "undifferentiated fear or apprehension of disturbance."[29] While school officials do not have to wait for an actual riot, they must have some real evidence before censoring student speech.

The *Tinker* decision was the high-water mark of student First Amendment rights.[30] In the 1980s, the Court first carved out an exception for student speech that was vulgar and lewd in *Bethel School District v. Fraser*.[31] The case involved a student who delivered a speech before the school assembly nominating a fellow student for vice president.[32] The speech read in part:

> I know a man who is firm—he's firm in his pants, he's firm in his shirt, his character is firm—but most of all his belief in you, the students of Bethel, is firm. Jeff Kuhlman is a man who takes his point and pounds it in. If necessary . . . he drives hard, pushing and pushing until finally—he succeeds.
>
> Jeff is a man who will go to the very end—even the climax, for each and every one of you.
>
> So vote for Jeff for A. S. B. vice-president—he'll never come between you and the best our high school can be.[33]

---

[26] *Id.* at 509.

[27] *Id.* at 508.

[28] *Id.* at 509.

[29] *Id.* at 508.

[30] Broussard v. Sch. Bd. of Norfolk, 801 F. Supp. 1526, 1534 (E.D. Va. 1992).

[31] 478 U.S. 675 (1986).

[32] *Id.* at 687 (Brennan, J., concurring).

[33] *Id.* (ellipses omitted).

The speech contained sexual references and caused giggles among the student body—but no real disruption. Nevertheless, school officials suspended the offending student, Matthew Fraser. Fraser prevailed before a federal district court and federal appeals court, but school officials appealed and prevailed before the Supreme Court by a 7-2 vote. The Court ruled that public school officials can teach students "the boundaries of socially appropriate behavior"[34] and that includes teaching students not to utter vulgar and lewd language at school.[35] The decision distinguished the political speech of *Tinker* from what it termed the "sexual" speech of Matthew Fraser.

Two years later, in *Hazelwood School District v. Kuhlmeier*, the Court created another exception for so-called school-sponsored student speech, such as the expression in many school newspapers, school plays, or school curricular activities.[36] The case involved a school principal censoring two stories that dealt with teen pregnancy and the impact of divorce upon teens.[37] Principal Robert Eugene Reynolds feared that the article on teen pregnancy would lead to social ostracism for the school's pregnant students and was concerned that the divorce article contained quotes from teens about their parents.[38] He ordered the two articles excised from the school's newspaper, to the consternation of the students, including female student editors Cathy Kuhlmeier, Lee Ann Tippett-West, and Leslie Smart.[39]

The Court held that public school officials can censor school-sponsored student speech when they have a legitimate educational reason to do so.[40] Justice Byron White proclaimed, "we hold that educators do not offend the First Amendment by exercising editorial control over the style and content of school-sponsored expressive activities so long as their actions are reasonably related to legitimate pedagogical concerns."[41] The Court seemingly took this rational

[34] *Id.* at 681.

[35] *Id.*

[36] 484 U.S. 260 (1988).

[37] *Id.* at 263.

[38] *Id.*

[39] William H. Freivogel, "Supreme Court's Rulings Limit Rights of Students," St. Louis Post-Dispatch, Jan. 17, 1988, at 8C.

[40] Hazelwood, 484 U.S. at 273.

[41] *Id.* at 272.

basis–type standard from one of its cases the year before, *Turner v. Safley*.[42] In this prisoner case, the Court proclaimed that "[w]hen a prison regulation impinges on inmates' constitutional rights, the regulation is valid if it is reasonably related to legitimate penological interests."[43] One year later in *Hazelwood*, the Court seemingly substituted "pedagogical" for "penological" and, thus, student First Amendment rights are based on prisoner rights.[44]

This very broad standard in *Hazelwood* included concerns such as avoiding poorly written articles; articles that are inadequately researched; and articles that are prejudiced, vulgar, or "unsuitable for immature audiences."[45] In response, several states passed so-called anti-*Hazelwood* statutes that provide greater statutory protection for students' First Amendment rights.

Nearly 20 years later, the Court established another exception to the *Tinker* standard in *Morse v. Frederick*, an unusual case involving a high school student from Alaska who displayed a "Bong Hits 4 Jesus" banner on a public street right near his high school.[46] Joseph Frederick decided to conduct his ultimate free-speech experiment. He skipped school and went across the street from his public high school where he knew the Olympic Torch Relay was passing. Frederick and several other students displayed the unusual banner with the words "Bong Hits 4 Jesus" written in duct tape. Principal Deborah Morse was less than pleased and rushed across the street, ordering the students to drop the banner. All but Joseph Frederick complied.

Later that day, Frederick went to Principal Morse's office as instructed, where she imposed a five-day suspension. He allegedly quoted Thomas Jefferson to her: "speech limited is speech lost." Morse then doubled the suspension to 10 days.[47]

The Court ruled that public school officials can prohibit student speech that they reasonably regard as advocating the illegal use of drugs.[48]

---

[42] 482 U.S. 78 (1987).

[43] *Id.* at 89.

[44] Hudson, Let the Students Speak, *supra* note 14, at 99.

[45] Hazelwood, 484 U.S. at 271.

[46] 551 U.S. 393 (2007).

[47] Hudson, Let the Students Speak, *supra* note 14, at 109.

[48] Morse, 551 U.S. at 409.

Thus, the Court created a broad protective standard for student speech in *Tinker* and then gradually carved out three exceptions to that ruling. The question was whether the Court would create another exception for student social media expression created off campus. It was a question that the Court had assiduously avoided for years, leading to some division in the circuits.[49] Some courts applied the *Tinker* test as long as they found a clear enough "nexus" or connection between school activities and a student's social media post. Other courts seemingly applied a reasonable foreseeability test. And ultimately, one circuit—the Third Circuit—determined that the *Tinker* test did not apply at all to such speech.[50]

II. *Mahanoy Area School District v. B.L.*

A high school freshman known in court papers as "B.L." (later voluntarily identified as Brandi Levy) was upset at failing to make her varsity cheerleading squad and for not earning the position of choice on a local softball team not affiliated with her high school.[51] One Saturday afternoon, B.L. was with a friend outside a local convenience store when she learned she had not made the varsity squad. She posted a picture on Snapchat of her and a friend with middle fingers raised and the following message: "Fuck school fuck softball fuck cheer fuck everything."[52] She also posted a blank image with the caption, "Love how me and [another student] get told we need a year of jv before we make varsity but tha[t] doesn't matter to anyone else?"[53]

A student who saw the post took pictures of the post and showed it to her mother, who was a cheerleading coach.[54] Ultimately, the coaches and other school officials determined that B.L. should be suspended from the cheerleading squad for a year.[55] Even though

[49] See David L. Hudson, Jr., Time for the Supreme Court to Address Off-Campus, Online Student Speech, 91 Or. L. Rev. 621 (2012).

[50] See Benjamin A. Holden, Tinker Meets the Cyberbully: A Federal Circuit Conflict Round-Up and Proposed New Standard for Off-Campus Speech, 28 Fordham Intell. Prop. Media & Ent. L.J. 233 (2018).

[51] Mahanoy, 141 S. Ct. at 2041.

[52] *Id.* at 2043.

[53] *Id.*

[54] *Id.*

[55] *Id.*

B.L. had apologized, the officials still imposed the harsh penalty. B.L. and her parents sued in federal district court, alleging a violation of her First Amendment free-speech rights. The court ruled in favor of B.L., reasoning that school officials failed to show that the social media post would cause a substantial disruption under *Tinker*.[56] The district court judge reasoned that "[t]he interest that a school or coach has in running a team does not extend to off-the-field speech that, although unliked, is unlikely to create disorder on the field."[57]

On appeal, the Third Circuit affirmed but ruled that the *Tinker* standard did not apply to off-campus student speech.[58] The Third Circuit wrote, "We hold today that *Tinker* does not apply to off-campus speech—that is, speech that is outside school-owned, -operated, or -supervised channels and that is not reasonably interpreted as bearing the school's imprimatur."[59] One judge on the panel concurred in the result, finding that school officials failed to show that the post would cause a substantial disruption under *Tinker*.[60]

The school district appealed, contending that the Third Circuit went too far in categorically ruling that *Tinker* did not apply to off-campus student speech. The Supreme Court agreed that the Third Circuit went too far but still ruled in favor of B.L. Writing for the majority, Justice Stephen Breyer explained that the school retains some regulatory interests in off-campus student speech. He wrote:

> The school's regulatory interests remain significant in some off-campus circumstances. . . . These include serious or severe bullying or harassment targeting specific individuals; threats aimed at teachers or other students; the failure to follow rules concerning lessons, the writing of papers, the use of computers, or participation in other online school activities; and breaches of school security devices, including material maintained within school computers.[61]

---

[56] B.L. v. Mahanoy Area Sch. Dist., 376 F. Supp. 3d 429 (M.D. Pa. 2019).

[57] *Id.* at 443.

[58] B.L. v. Mahanoy Area Sch. Dist., 964 F.3d 170 (3d Cir. 2020).

[59] *Id.* at 189.

[60] *Id.* at 197 (Ambro, J., concurring in the judgment).

[61] Mahanoy, 141 S. Ct. at 2045.

Interestingly, Breyer did not "set forth a broad, highly general First Amendment rule stating just what counts as 'off campus' speech and whether or how ordinary First Amendment standards must give way off campus to a school's special need to prevent, *e.g.*, substantial disruption of learning-related activities or the protection of those who make up a school community."[62]

However, Breyer identified "three features of off-campus speech" that show school officials have a diminished regulatory interest in such speech. These features include:

(1) Schools do not act in loco parentis with regard to off-campus speech. "Geographically speaking, off-campus speech will normally fall within the zone of parental, rather than school-related, responsibility."[63]

(2) School officials would have to serve as monitors of speech that takes place 24 hours a day and that could encompass much political or religious speech that should be protected.[64]

(3) Schools have an interest in protecting unpopular student speech, because "public schools are the nurseries of democracy."[65]

Applying these features, Breyer found that B.L.'s speech amounted to criticism of government officials—the core type of speech the First Amendment is supposed to protect.[66] Furthermore, B.L. spoke outside of school hours from a location outside of school.[67] She also did not identify her school in her posts or target any specific individual.[68]

School officials argued they had a strong interest against vulgarity, but the Court reasoned that this "anti-vulgarity interest is weakened considerably by the fact that B.L. spoke outside the school on her own time."[69] The Court noted that "the school has presented no

---

[62] *Id.*

[63] *Id.* at 2046.

[64] *Id.*

[65] *Id.*

[66] *Id.* at 2046–48.

[67] *Id.* at 2047.

[68] *Id.*

[69] *Id.*

evidence of any general effort to prevent students from using vulgarity outside the classroom."[70]

The Court also focused on the fact that the post simply did not create a substantial disruption at school, identifying the deposition testimony of a cheerleading coach who when asked if the post created such a disruption, responded "no."[71] The school had argued that such a post could substantially disrupt team morale, but there was no evidence of a "serious decline" in team morale.[72]

Justice Samuel Alito, joined by Justice Neil Gorsuch, authored a concurring opinion that emphasized the importance of parental rights, writing, "Parents do not implicitly relinquish all that authority when they send their children to a public school."[73] Alito agreed that there is some student social media speech for which school officials retain regulatory interests. Perhaps most interesting, however, he warned that "[b]ullying and severe harassment are serious (and age-old) problems, but . . . are not easy to define with the precision required for a regulation of speech."[74]

Justice Clarence Thomas was the Court's lone dissenter—no surprise given that he previously authored a concurring opinion in *Morse v. Frederick* calling for the overruling of *Tinker*, writing that it "is without basis in the Constitution."[75] According to Thomas, "in the earliest public schools, teachers taught, and students listened. Teachers commanded, and students obeyed. Teachers did not rely solely on the power of ideas to persuade; they relied on discipline to maintain order."[76]

Justice Thomas once again cited older student speech cases for the principle that, historically, public school officials could punish students even for off-campus speech. He mentioned at some length an 1859 Vermont Supreme Court decision, *Lander v. Seaver*,[77] involving a student who was whipped by a teacher for calling the teacher names

[70] *Id.*

[71] *Id.* at 2048.

[72] *Id.*

[73] *Id.* at 2053 (Alito, J., concurring).

[74] *Id.* at 2057.

[75] Morse, 551 U.S. at 410 (Thomas, J., concurring).

[76] *Id.* at 412 (Thomas, J., concurring).

[77] 32 Vt. 114 (1859).

outside of school.[78] The Vermont high court reasoned that school officials can punish students for off-campus speech that has "merely a remote and indirect tendency to harm."[79]

III. Unanswered Questions

The Court's decision leaves many unanswered questions. For one, the Court never really defined off-campus speech or explained precisely the boundaries between on-campus and off-campus speech. Obviously, B.L.'s speech took place off campus—outside the Cocoa Hut on a Saturday afternoon. But there exists the possibility that speech created off campus might come on campus or be treated as on-campus speech. For example, a student could post on social media while off campus, then others actively distribute or share the post while on campus.

More litigation over these boundaries is likely. Free-speech expert Catherine J. Ross explains:

> The Supreme Court's failure to define off-campus speech and to provide guidance to school administrators and lower courts about whether, when, and on what grounds schools may regulate and punish students for what they say on their own time from their own equipment, is likely to lead to much additional litigation—and to even more incidents in which schools punish off-campus expression that never reach a court.[80]

Another unsettled question is how to handle Breyer's "three features" of student speech. Lawyers are familiar with multifactor or multiprong tests, but that is not what Breyer delivered in his opinion. He specifically referred to three features. One would think that the three features mean that many school districts will take a more hands-off approach when it comes to much online, off-campus student speech. That certainly would appear to be a primary lesson of Breyer's opinion, but only time will tell if that's the case.

However, Breyer—as mentioned earlier—did explain that school districts retain regulatory authority over several types of speech.

[78] 141 S. Ct. at 2060 (Thomas, J., dissenting).

[79] Lander, 32 Vt. at 20–21.

[80] Catherine J. Ross, "One 'Vulgar' Cheerleader Vindicated—But Other Students May Still Face Discipline for Off-Campus Speech," First Amend. Watch, July 6, 2021, https://bit.ly/3ypTxU9.

The first category mentioned was "serious or severe bullying or harassment targeting particular individuals."[81] Most states have laws that require schools to address both bullying and cyberbullying in their codes of conduct.[82] One question is when such bullying or harassment is considered "serious or severe." Another is what does it take to target a particular individual. One could conceive of student social media posts that mainly address grievances or the venting of frustration but that also may name a particular individual. In other words, student social media speech could mainly be protected unpopular expression but also might involve the specific targeting required to constitute bullying or harassment. Justice Alito offered another trenchant observation regarding laws or policies targeting bullying and harassment, noting that it is quite difficult to draft such laws with the required precision.

A related unsettled question is when does student speech invade or infringe on the rights of others. Presumably, speech that constitutes severe harassment would fall into this category, but the Court has never explained or fleshed out this language from *Tinker*.[83] A few lower courts have delved into this issue, but it remains the "forgotten" part of *Tinker*.[84] Then-Judge Alito of the Third Circuit expressed it well when he wrote, "[t]he precise scope of *Tinker*'s 'interference with the rights of others' language is unclear."[85]

Another unanswered question concerns student social media speech that does have more of an impact on a team or extracurricular activity. Justice Breyer made much of the fact that one of B.L.'s cheerleading coaches candidly acknowledged that her post did not cause a substantial disruption. But what if coaches or team members claim that a student's post did cause much more of a disruption of team morale?

---

[81] Mahanoy, 141 S. Ct. at 2045.

[82] David L. Hudson, Jr., Freedom of Speech and Cyberbullying, 50 N.M. L. Rev. 287, 292 (2020).

[83] David L. Hudson, Jr., Unsettled Questions in Student Speech Law, 22 U. Pa. J. Const. L. 1113, 1121 (2020).

[84] *Id.* at 1121. See also David L. Hudson, Jr., "Tinkering with Tinker Standards?," Freedom F., Aug. 9, 2006, https://bit.ly/2TSembG (referring to the invasion of the rights of others as the "forgotten part" of the *Tinker* case).

[85] Saxe v. State Coll. Area Sch. Dist., 240 F.3d 200, 217 (3d. Cir. 2001).

Still another unanswered question concerns a school that has made combatting vulgarity and profanity part of its mission, even vulgarity and profanity uttered off campus. Justice Breyer emphasized that there was no evidence that the school district in *Mahanoy* had emphasized problems of off-campus vulgarity. But what if a school district has started some anti-profanity campaign? Would that lead to a different result?

Conclusion

While critics may contend that Justice Breyer's opinion in *Mahanoy* left much to be desired, it remains a victory for student rights. It remains the first pure student speech case in which the U.S. Supreme Court has ruled in favor of the student litigant since *Tinker* itself. Furthermore, Justice Breyer's opinion recognizes the animating spirit of the *Tinker* decision, that free-speech protection "must include the protection of unpopular ideas, for popular ideas have less need for protection."[86]

Justice Breyer's opinion quoted Justice Fortas's language in *Tinker* about students not losing their free-speech rights at the schoolhouse gate, recognized that school officials must be able to point to student speech causing a substantial disruption before censoring it, and emphasized that school officials must rely on actual facts rather than "undifferentiated fear or apprehension of disturbance."[87]

The decision also can be viewed as a victory for parental rights. The Court ultimately determined that it was B.L.'s parents who should have the primary disciplinary authority over her offensive postings on social media rather than school officials. Both Justice Breyer's majority opinion and Justice Alito's concurring opinion mention that most social media speech posted off campus falls within the zone of parental, rather than school, authority.

The Supreme Court identified several areas of student speech—even off campus—that will still arguably fall within the zone of school officials' regulatory authority. Some may question the wisdom of the Court's decision to protect a speaker who, like Paul Robert Cohen 50 years earlier, used profanity to convey a message.

---

[86] Mahanoy, 141 S. Ct. at 2046.

[87] David L. Hudson, Jr. "Students, Parents, and Free Speech Win in Cheerleading Case," Freedom F., June 30, 2021, https://bit.ly/37lFTWc.

But the Court's decision in *Mahanoy* holds true to what Justice Fortas famously proclaimed back in *Tinker*:

> Any departure from absolute regimentation may cause trouble. Any variation from the majority's opinion may inspire fear. Any word spoken . . . that deviates from the views of another person may start an argument or cause a disturbance. But our Constitution says we must take this risk; and our history says that it is this sort of hazardous freedom—this kind of openness—that is the basis of our national strength and of the independence and vigor of Americans who grow up and live in this relatively permissive, often disputatious, society.[88]

Mahanoy, whatever its shortcomings, remains a victory not only for student and parental rights but also for individual liberty and the hazardous freedom spoken of in *Tinker*. A decision in favor of the school district could have led to an Orwellian, 24-hour-a-day monitoring of student social media posts, and turned school officials into the social media police.

---

[88] Tinker, 393 U.S. at 508–09 (citation omitted).

Unreviewable: The Final Installment of the "Epic" Obamacare Trilogy

*Josh Blackman**

Introduction

By fate or design, my young career has tracked the trajectory of Obamacare. In September 2009, shortly after I graduated from law school, I launched a blog to focus on constitutional and other legal issues. On my fourth day of blogging, I covered this new bill called the Patient Protection and Affordable Care Act (ACA, also known as "Obamcare"). The cornerstone of the law was an individual mandate that commanded people to purchase health insurance. In November 2009, I was by chance present at a meeting where the legal strategy to challenge the individual mandate was hatched.

Over the next decade, I followed and wrote about the ACA. During that period, Obamacare faced three existential legal challenges. And in each "installment [of the] epic Affordable Care Act trilogy,"[1] the Supreme Court rebuffed those attacks. First, *National Federation of Independent Business v. Sebelius* (*NFIB*) saved the ACA's individual mandate as an exercise of Congress's taxing power.[2] Second, *King v. Burwell* held that the ACA, which subsidizes only health care exchanges "established by the State," also subsidizes the federal exchange.[3] And this past term, *California v. Texas* held that the latest challenge to Obamacare was unreviewable.[4] After three rounds, Obamacare remains undefeated before the Supreme Court.[5]

* Professor, South Texas College of Law Houston. Adjunct Scholar, Cato Institute.

[1] California v. Texas, 141 S. Ct. 2104, 2123 (2021) (Alito, J., dissenting).

[2] Nat'l Fed'n of Indep. Bus. v. Sebelius, 567 U.S. 519 (2012); see Josh Blackman, Unprecedented: The Constitutional Challenge to Obamacare (2013).

[3] King v. Burwell, 576 U.S. 473 (2015); see Josh Blackman, Unraveled: Obamacare, Religious Liberty, and Executive Power (2016).

[4] Texas, 141 S. Ct. at 2120.

[5] Josh Blackman, Undefeated: Trump, Obamacare, and the Roberts Court (forthcoming 2022).

California v. Texas began when President Donald Trump signed the Tax Cuts and Jobs Act of 2017 (TCJA).[6] This law did not repeal the individual mandate. Rather, it reduced the ACA's penalty to $0.[7] Arguably, this revision toppled *NFIB*'s saving construction. Soon, a cohort of conservative attorneys general, as well as two private plaintiffs, filed suit.[8] The plaintiffs contended that the penalty-less law could no longer be saved as a tax. And, they argued, the unconstitutional mandate could not be severed from the remainder of the law. Therefore, the entire law was unconstitutional.

The arguments were familiar. But *Texas* felt different. *NFIB v. Sebelius* had united the conservative legal movement and the Republican political apparatus.[9] This confluence moved novel arguments about the unconstitutionality of the mandate from *off-the-wall* to *on-the-wall*.[10] In *NFIB*, 26 states joined the challenge against the federal government. These combined forces came within one vote of killing the most important social-welfare legislation in decades. Four years later, the support for *King v. Burwell* was still strong. The conservative legal movement largely backed the challenge, which was grounded in a conventional reading of the ACA.[11]

Yet, by 2017 the politics were different. The ACA had finally surpassed the 50 percent mark for popularity.[12] Indeed, this surge in popularity was triggered by failed efforts in Congress to repeal the law. Millions of Americans now rely on the ACA. The threat of unraveling Obamacare rallied people to support the law. As a result, many red states that joined *NFIB* did not support Texas's case. Only 18 states joined the challenge. Moreover, the *Wall Street Journal* and

[6] Tax Cuts and Jobs Act of 2017, Pub. L. No. 115–97, 131 Stat. 2054 (2017).

[7] *Id.* at § 11081.

[8] Jenny Deam, "The Journey from Wisconsin to Texas and the Ruling that Struck Down the ACA," Hous. Chron., Jan. 11, 2019, https://perma.cc/D8AD-B5JN.

[9] Josh Blackman, Popular Constitutionalism and the Affordable Care Act, 27 Pub. Aff. Q. 3 (2013).

[10] Jack M. Balkin, "From Off the Wall to On the Wall: How the Mandate Challenge Went Mainstream," Atlantic, June 4, 2012, https://perma.cc/2FWB-TQ9M.

[11] Robert Pear, "Flood of Briefs on the Health Care Law's Subsidies Hits the Supreme Court," N.Y. Times, Feb. 21, 2015, https://perma.cc/RQ85-MFMX.

[12] Dan Mangan, "Obamacare Tops 50 percent Popularity among Americans for First Time in New Poll, after Senate Unveils Bill to Gut Health-care Law," CNBC, June 23, 2017, https://perma.cc/EGD6-KVMX.

other bellwethers of right-of-center thought opposed the challenge.[13] And the conservative legal movement ridiculed the challenge. Indeed, the architects of *King v. Burwell* lampooned *Texas*.[14] For some time, I was the "only prominent dissenting voice,"[15] though Professor Randy Barnett joined the fray.[16]

Still, the new Obamacare challenge was consistent with my long-standing views about *NFIB*.[17] First, I long ago concluded that the private plaintiffs had standing to challenge the ACA, even with a $0 penalty. For nearly a decade, I argued that the injury-in-fact from *NFIB* was premised solely on the individual mandate and did not rely on the penalty. Second, for that same period, I vigorously contended that the individual mandate imposed an unconstitutional command to purchase insurance, without regard to the penalty. And only through Chief Justice John Roberts's saving construction could the ACA be read to compel a *choice* between buying insurance and paying a tax. Once the penalty was reduced to $0, the saving construction failed, and that choice vanished. I advanced these views in the Cato Institute's *California v. Texas* amicus brief.[18]

Alas, the Supreme Court disagreed. The vote wasn't even close. Seven members of the Court found that plaintiffs lacked standing. Justice Stephen Breyer wrote the majority opinion, which was joined by Chief Justice Roberts and Justices Clarence Thomas, Sonia Sotomayor, Elena Kagan, Brett Kavanaugh, and Amy Coney Barrett. Justice Samuel Alito dissented with Justice Neil Gorsuch. They found that the state plaintiffs had standing, the mandate was

[13] "Texas ObamaCare Blunder," Wall St. J., Dec. 16, 2018, https://perma.cc/SU3X-QDTD.

[14] Jonathan H. Adler & Abbe R. Gluck, "What the Lawless Obamacare Ruling Means," N.Y. Times, Dec. 15, 2018, https://perma.cc/EQZ9-ENTP; Michael F. Cannon, "ObamaCare's Enemy No. 1 Says This Is the Wrong Way to Kill It," N.Y. Post, March 28, 2019, https://perma.cc/RNB4-T4KL.

[15] Michael C. Dorf, "Can an 'Off the Wall' Procedural Argument (Invalidating Obamacare) Climb the Wall?," Dorf on Law, Dec. 18, 2018, https://perma.cc/8SL7-PJB2.

[16] Randy E. Barnett, "Texas v. U.S.: Why the Individual Mandate Is Still Unconstitutional," Volokh Conspiracy, July 8, 2019, https://perma.cc/3N3X-BUPX.

[17] Josh Blackman, "How I Approach Unpopular and Unconventional Legal Views," Volokh Conspiracy, July 28, 2021, https://perma.cc/NT7K-5W2W.

[18] Brief for Cato Institute as Amicus Curiae Supporting Respondents, California v. Texas, 141 S. Ct. 2104 (2021) (No. 19-840) [hereinafter Cato Amicus], https://perma.cc/6RYA-SQDU.

unconstitutional, and certain portions of the ACA that injure the states should be enjoined. However, the majority and dissent did not address my preferred theory of standing-through-inseverability, which was also advanced by the solicitor general.

This article for the *Cato Supreme Court Review*—my fourth—considers the legal arguments that *California v. Texas* declined to reach.

Part I revisits *NFIB*. In that case, the private plaintiffs established standing based entirely on the mandate, without regard to the penalty. Moreover, *NFIB* held that the ACA imposes a command to purchase insurance. Outside the saving construction, the ACA does not provide people with a choice between buying insurance and paying a tax. In *Texas*, the Fifth Circuit accepted both of these premises.

Part II turns to severability. The Cato brief, as well as the solicitor general, advanced a theory of standing premised on inseverability: *standing-through-inseverability*. In short, the private plaintiffs could establish Article III jurisdiction based on the ACA's insurance reforms that were inseverable from the unconstitutional mandate. Taken together, these provisions established an injury-in-fact, traceability, and redressability.

Part III turns to *California v. Texas*. The majority found that the plaintiffs could not trace their injuries to the individual mandate because the mandate is not enforced. And the Court found that the plaintiffs waived the standing-through-inseverability argument. In dissent, Justices Alito and Gorsuch accepted standing-through-inseverability for the state plaintiffs but declined to consider it for the private plaintiffs. Justice Thomas concurred and cast some doubt on standing-through-inseverability. In the end, the ACA survived once again.

I. The Individual Mandate Injures the Private Plaintiffs and Does Not Offer a "Choice," without Regard to the Penalty

California v. Texas was *NFIB v. Sebelius* redux. Indeed, my position on *Texas* was informed by two of my long-held views about *NFIB*. First, standing in *NFIB* was premised entirely on the pocketbook injury inflicted by the mandate and did not turn on the enforcement of the penalty. Second, the ACA could only be read to grant people a "choice"—buy insurance or pay a tax—under the auspices of the saving construction. My writings on these two points affected the proceedings before the Fifth Circuit.

A. *Standing in* NFIB *Was Premised on the Mandate, Not the Penalty*

Many critics ridiculed the jurisdictional argument in *Texas*. They said that a mandate without a penalty could not impose an Article III injury. A "toothless" mandate, they claimed, was not a mandate at all.[19] California argued that "the TCJA rendered Section 5000A(a) *toothless*" because there are no longer any "'negative legal consequence[s]' of not buying health insurance."[20] To these critics, the jurisdictional arguments in *Texas* were unprecedented. But, from my vantage point, the arguments were familiar. Indeed, I wrote about them in *Unprecedented*.[21] Questions Chief Justice Roberts and Justice Kagan asked in 2012 augured, with a remarkable degree of clarity, two issues presented in *Texas*. First, is the mandate separate from the penalty? Second, would someone who is subject to the mandate, but not the penalty, have standing? We will revisit these questions, which were presented in *NFIB* and then resurfaced before the Fifth Circuit.

1. Oral arguments in *NFIB*, revisited

On Monday, March 26, 2012, the Supreme Court heard the first of four oral argument sessions in *NFIB v. Sebelius*. At the time, most people focused on the second day, which considered the constitutional basis of the mandate. However, the first day proved to be the most pivotal for the saving construction.[22] And, in hindsight, the first day was also a critical day for standing.

Gregory Katsas (now a judge on the D.C. Circuit) argued on behalf of the private plaintiffs. Justice Kagan asked Katsas whether "a person who is subject to the mandate but not subject to the penalty would have standing?" This question addresses the dispute in *Texas*: The private plaintiffs were subject to the mandate but did not have to pay a penalty for going uninsured. Justice Kagan's question demonstrates that the question presented in *Texas* was not new.

---

[19] Henry J. Aaron, "The Supreme Court Procrastinates: No Decision Now on a Baseless Challenge to the Affordable Care Act," Brookings Inst., Feb. 10, 2020, https://perma.cc/3FWQ-KQ74.

[20] Opening Brief for Petitioners at 15, 38, California v. Texas, 141 S. Ct. 2104 (2021) (No. 19-840), https://perma.cc/GHD8-E6N8 (emphasis added).

[21] Unprecedented, *supra* note 2, at 176–84.

[22] *Id.* at 181.

Indeed, even in 2012, there were some people who were subject to the mandate but were statutorily exempt from having to pay the penalty. The law exempted five categories of people from having to pay the shared responsibility payment: "no penalty shall be imposed" for (1) individuals who cannot afford coverage, (2) taxpayers with income below the filing threshold, (3) members of Indian tribes, (4) people with short gaps in coverage, and (5) those who have "suffered a hardship" as defined by the secretary.[23] Individuals covered by § 5000A(e) are *still* subject to the mandate but are exempt from the penalty.

Katsas answered that for people exempted by § 5000A(e), the mandate still causes an injury-in-fact. "[T]hat person is injured by compliance with the mandate," he explained. Justice Kagan was incredulous. She asked what that injury would "look like." Katsas replied that the person subject to the mandate, but not the penalty, still suffers a "classic pocketbook injury" through the "forced acquisition of an unwanted good."

Consider the declarations of the private plaintiffs from *NFIB*. Mary Brown, for example, wrote that she would be harmed because she was "required to obtain and maintain such insurance, which [she] neither need[s] nor want[s], or to pay the prescribed penalties for non-compliance."[24] Starting in 2014, the payment of the penalty could have caused a separate Article III injury. But when the case was being litigated, the penalty had *not yet been assessed*. Rather, standing was premised entirely on the mandate. Brown wrote, "to comply with the individual insurance mandate, and well in advance of 2014, [she] must now investigate whether and how to rearrange [her] personal finance affairs." Indeed, the penalty could not provide the injury-in-fact because Brown *never* planned to pay the penalty. Why? The plaintiffs were "*law-abiding* citizens who intend[ed] to comply with the mandate unless it is invalidated." The plaintiffs challenged the mandate and not the penalty, because the penalty

---

[23] 28 U.S.C. § 5000A(e).

[24] Declaration of Plaintiff Mary Brown in support of Plaintiffs' Motion for Summary Judgment at 2, Florida v. United States HHS, 780 F. Supp. 2d 1256 (N.D. Fla. 2011) (No. 3:10-cv-91-RV/EMT) [hereinafter Declaration of Plaintiff], https://perma.cc/EJ6W-BUPG.

would never injure them. Indeed, enjoining the penalty would not redress their injuries.

Earlier in the argument, Gregory Katsas elaborated on this theme in a colloquy with the chief justice. Roberts asked, "why would you have a requirement that is completely toothless? You know, buy insurance or else. Or else what? Or else nothing." Katsas replied in much the same way that the *Texas* plaintiffs would respond: "Because Congress reasonably could think that at least some people will follow the law precisely because it is the law."

Katsas's brief cited a 2008 Congressional Budget Office (CBO) report, which found that "many individuals . . . would comply with a mandate, even in the absence of penalties, because they believe in abiding by the nation's laws."[25] The brief added that CBO's "finding readily confirms the common-sense proposition that the interest of law-abiding citizens in challenging burdensome legal requirements *exists independently of the sanction* that would be imposed for non-compliance."[26] This argument is precisely the same argument that the *Texas* private plaintiffs advanced.

Some critics, both then and now, may think that Katsas's argument was wrong—maybe even silly. During oral argument, Chief Justice Roberts seemed genuinely skeptical. But in his written opinion, Roberts put his skepticism aside. Though he did not directly address the standing question, he *had* to accept NFIB's position to reach the merits. Otherwise, the plaintiffs would have lacked standing to challenge the mandate in 2012. But he did not dismiss the case due to a lack of standing.

The *Texas* private plaintiffs suffered an injury-in-fact for the same reason that the *NFIB* private plaintiffs suffered an injury-in-fact: the mandate imposes a legal obligation to purchase insurance, without regard to any collateral legal consequences.[27] Indeed, the *Texas* plaintiffs had a far more imminent injury in fact: they needed to maintain insurance at present, whereas the *NFIB* plaintiffs had to make financial arrangements to purchase insurance in the future.

[25] U.S. Cong. Budget Off., Pub. No. 3102, Key Issues in Analyzing Major Health Insurance Proposals 53 (2008), https://perma.cc/BA6E-VEK7.

[26] Brief for Private Respondents (Anti-Injunction Act) at 15, HHS v. Florida, 565 U.S. 1088 (2011) (No. 11-398), https://perma.cc/E6UV-V6MX.

[27] Declaration of Plaintiff, *supra* note 24.

2. Obamacare stands down in the Fifth Circuit

On the eve of oral arguments before the Fifth Circuit, I blogged about Katsas's colloquies with the chief justice and Justice Kagan.[28] This writing, based on my 2013 book *Uprecedented*, had a discernible impact on oral arguments.

Robert Henneke of the Texas Public Policy Foundation represented the private plaintiffs. He explained that the "individual mandate carries the force of a command, because [certain] categories of persons are subject to it, without the penalty."[29] Judge Jennifer Walker Elrod asked if people who were "in one of those exempted categories" from 28 U.S.C. § 5000A(e) would still "have standing." She referenced the "original argument" from *NFIB* in 2012. Judge Elrod recalled that "Justice Kagan asked . . . [w]hether or not people who don't have to pay the penalty . . . have standing?" Henneke returned to the "case history of *NFIB*." He explained that the "sole basis for the *NFIB* individual plaintiffs' [standing,] as set forth in their declarations, was the individual mandate. Not the penalty." Henneke recounted that this argument "was addressed during the first day of oral argument, in questions from both the Chief Justice and Justice Kagan." Henneke then recited the colloquy between Justice Kagan and Katsas.

Ultimately, the Fifth Circuit found that the private plaintiffs had standing. Judge Elrod wrote the majority opinion, which was joined by Judge Kurt Engelhardt. The majority explained that "[t]he standing issues presented by the individual plaintiffs are not novel."[30] Rather, "the Supreme Court faced a similar situation when it decided *NFIB* in 2012."[31] The majority then quoted from Justice Kagan's colloquy with Katsas. Justice Kagan asked "whether [Katsas] thought 'a person who is subject to the [individual] mandate but not subject to the [shared responsibility payment] would

---

[28] Randy E. Barnett & Josh Blackman, "NFIB v. Sebelius Already Addressed the 'Injury in Fact' Question in Texas v. U.S.," Volokh Conspiracy, July 8, 2019, https://perma.cc/R75B-YJBE.

[29] Oral Argument at 1:25:14, Texas v. United States, 945 F.3d 355 (5th Cir. 2019) (No. 19-10011), https://bit.ly/2VnSg1o.

[30] Texas v. United States, 945 F.3d 355, 378 (5th Cir. 2019).

[31] *Id.*

have standing.'"[32] Under Congress's design, some people were subject to the mandate but not the penalty. Katsas replied that such people would have standing because they would be "injured by compliance with the mandate."[33] He explained, "when that person is subject to the mandate, that person is required to purchase health insurance. That's a forced acquisition of an unwanted good. It's a classic pocketbook injury."[34] The majority further cited Mary Brown's declaration.[35] The court also relied on the 2008 CBO report.[36] Based on this report, the majority quoted once again from Katsas's argument: "Congress reasonably could think that at least some people will follow the law precisely because it is the law."[37]

Judge Carolyn Dineen King dissented. She found that the private plaintiffs lacked standing. And she dismissed the relevance of Justice Kagan's colloquy with Katsas: "counsel's answer to a Justice's hypothetical question does not bind this court."[38] Of course, the panel was not bound by hypothetical questions. But those questions highlighted a necessary aspect of *NFIB*. And the majority drew that essential inference: "To bring a claim against the individual mandate, therefore, the [*NFIB*] plaintiffs needed to show injury from the individual mandate—not from the shared responsibility payment."[39] The *NFIB* plaintiffs advanced only this single argument for standing. And *California v. Texas* teaches that waived theories of standing are forfeited—at least in ACA cases. Judge Elrod concluded, "[t]he evidentiary basis for this injury is even stronger than it was in *NFIB*."[40]

B. *The ACA Imposes a Mandate, Not a Choice*

Over the past decade, I have confronted a persistent argument about *NFIB*: the ACA does not impose a mandate, but instead affords

[32] *Id.* (citations omitted).

[33] *Id.*

[34] *Id.*

[35] *Id.* at 379.

[36] *Id.* at 385 n.27.

[37] *Id.* at 379.

[38] *Id.* at 410 n.5 (King, J., dissenting).

[39] *Id.* at 378.

[40] *Id.* at 380.

people a choice between buying insurance or paying a tax.[41] This premise is half-right. Chief Justice Roberts accepted the *choice* reading of the ACA. But only in the context of the saving construction does "the shared responsibility payment merely impose[] a tax citizens may lawfully *choose* to pay in lieu of buying health insurance."[42] Outside the saving construction, Chief Justice Roberts rejected the *choice* reading. And this rejection is evident from the structure of *NFIB*. In *Texas*, the Fifth Circuit recognized this structure.

1. The structure of *NFIB*

For years, I debated the *choice* argument in many fora. And consistently advocates and scholars quoted the chief's *choice* reading, without noting that his reading was only permissible for the saving construction. To address this frequent mischaracterization of *NFIB*, I turned to a simple structure: roman numerals. I broke down the structure of *NFIB* based on the subsections of Part III of the opinion.[43]

Part III of *NFIB* considered the constitutionality of the individual mandate. Part III-A held that the mandate could not be sustained under the Commerce or Necessary and Proper Clauses. Part III-B held that the mandate could be sustained under Congress's taxing power. Five justices agreed with Parts III-A and III-B. But the opinion did not stop there.

Part III-C developed and applied the "saving construction." Chief Justice Roberts explained that "[t]he exaction the Affordable Care Act imposes on those without health insurance"—that is, the shared responsibility payment—"looks like a tax in many respects."[44] And because the penalty raised revenue, the Court could save § 5000A as a single entity. The saving construction fused together the mandate and the penalty. When combined, this chimera presented an individual with "a lawful *choice* to do or not do a certain act, so long as he is

---

[41] See, e.g., Marty Lederman, "There Is No 'Mandate,'" Balkinization, Dec. 15, 2018, https://perma.cc/F2VB-4UU7 ("But the ACA doesn't contain any mandate, or legal requirement, for anyone to maintain health insurance. What § 5000A contains, instead, is a choice.").

[42] NFIB, 567 U.S. at 568.

[43] See Josh Blackman, Undone: The New Constitutional Challenge to Obamacare, 23 Tex. Rev. of Law & Politics 3, 9–11, 20–22 (2019).

[44] NFIB, 567 U.S. at 563.

willing to pay a tax levied on that choice."[45] The saving construction may be treated as a gloss on the ACA. Outside the saving construction, however, "[t]he most straightforward reading of the mandate is that [§ 5000A] commands individuals to purchase insurance."[46] The shared responsibility payment, as drafted by Congress, was not a tax. And § 5000A, as drafted by Congress, did not offer a "lawful choice." Instead, it imposed an unconstitutional mandate to purchase insurance.

The TCJA reduced the shared responsibility payment to $0. As a result, § 5000A can no longer be read as offering a "lawful choice" to purchase insurance or pay a tax. Congress thus peeled off the ACA's protective gloss, leaving only the unvarnished and unconstitutional individual mandate. Part III-C, and much of Part III-B, are no longer controlling. Rather, Part III-A controls: "the 'most straightforward' reading of that provision [is] a command to purchase insurance."[47]

My sequential framing of the structure of *NFIB* had a discernible impact on the proceedings before the Fifth Circuit.

2. The Fifth Circuit recognized a mandate, not a choice

Before the Fifth Circuit, Texas Solicitor General Kyle Hawkins concisely explained why Part III-A is now the only relevant portion of *NFIB*, and how Parts III-B and III-C became irrelevant.[48] He began, "it is crucial to understand the structure of Chief Justice Roberts's opinion." Hawkins continued, "in Part III-A," Chief Justice Roberts "says that the best way to read [§ 5000A(a)] is as a command to buy insurance." Critically, the chief "looks at the mandate" and "not the penalty." But in Parts "III-B and III-C" Roberts, "says that we can glue the individual mandate provision to the penalty provision, and once they are glued together, then they function as a tax." The chief could apply that saving construction only because "the penalty is raising revenue for the government." However, in 2017, "Congress took away everything that supported III-B and III-C." Because of the TCJA, the penalty "is no longer raising any revenue for the federal government"

---

[45] *Id.* at 574 (emphasis added).

[46] *Id.* at 562 (opinion of Roberts, C.J.).

[47] Texas v. United States, 945 F.3d at 391 (quoting NFIB, 567 U.S. at 562).

[48] Oral Argument, *supra* note 29, at 56:36.

and "no longer can be fairly characterized as a tax." Hawkins stated that "in light of the [TCJA], Part III-B and III-C . . . are irrelevant." "[T]he only thing we are left with then is Part III-A . . . where [Roberts] holds that [§ 5000A(a)] is a command to buy insurance." At that point, Judge Elrod asked if the court should "sever" Parts III-B and III-C from *NFIB*. Hawkins replied, "the entire basis for III-B and III-C is now off the table."

Ultimately, the Fifth Circuit's majority opinion followed the structure of *NFIB*. Judge Elrod explained that "Chief Justice Roberts's opinion functioned in the following way."[49] First, "[i]n Part III-A, Chief Justice Roberts said that the individual mandate was most naturally read as a command to buy insurance."[50] And that mandate "could not be sustained under either the Interstate Commerce Clause or the Necessary and Proper Clause."[51]

Second, "in Part III-B, the Chief Justice wrote that . . . the most natural reading of the individual mandate was unconstitutional."[52] Still, "the Court . . . needed to determine whether it was 'fairly possible' to read the provision in a way that saved it from being unconstitutional."[53] And as part of "an exercise in constitutional avoidance," the Court found "the mandate could be read not as a command but as an option to purchase insurance or pay a tax."[54] The "'option' interpretation of the statute could save the statute from being unconstitutional" as an exercise of "Congress' taxing power."[55] Critically, however, this "option," or *choice* reading was only feasible because the penalty raised revenue.

Third, in "Part III-C," the Court "concluded that [§ 5000A] could be construed as constitutional" under the saving construction.[56] The majority would "read[] the individual mandate, in conjunction with the shared responsibility payment, as a legitimate exercise of

[49] Texas v. United States, 945 F.3d at 387 n.12.

[50] *Id.*

[51] *Id.*

[52] *Id.*

[53] *Id.*

[54] *Id.* at 388.

[55] *Id.*

[56] *Id.* at 387 n.12.

Congress' taxing power."[57] The provisions were, in Solicitor General Hawkins's words, "glued together." The choice argument works *only* within the context of the saving construction. Judge Elrod concluded "that the individual mandate was [*only*] constitutional as saved."[58]

The Supreme Court would echo this reading of the ACA—sort of.[59]

II. Sensing Severability

As a general matter, I felt confident about the standing and merits arguments in *Texas*. But I was conflicted about severability in this case, and in general. I have long struggled with the notion that courts can halt an entire law, even though only part of it is unconstitutional. In *Unprecedented*, I carefully avoided taking any firm position about what should happen if the mandate was unconstitutional. I tentatively agreed with the Obama administration's position: the ACA's central insurance reforms were inseverable from the "essential" mandate. But I didn't commit. Ultimately, the *NFIB* majority did not need to reach the severability question because it saved the mandate. The joint dissent, by contrast, would have halted the *entire* ACA. All of it. Still, in hindsight, at least one *NFIB* dissenter may have become uncertain about that sweeping holding. In *Murphy v. NCAA*, Justice Thomas advanced a different approach to severability. *Murphy* changed how I think about severability. And Justice Thomas's writings on severability affected how I approached standing.

This part will explain the relationship between standing and severability in *Texas*. First, I will reconsider the severability analysis in *NFIB*'s joint dissent in light of Justice Thomas's *Murphy* concurrence. Second, I will introduce the concept of standing-through-inseverability. In a rare sliver of cases, courts have Article III jurisdiction to redress injuries caused by inseverable provisions. Indeed, third, a careful analysis of *NFIB* shows that standing in that case could have been established only through inseverability. Fourth, under modern, purposivist doctrine, the severability analysis in *Texas* would be straightforward: the Congress that enacted the TCJA did not want to kill the entire law. But the unstated legislative intent from

[57] *Id.*

[58] *Id.*

[59] See *infra* Part III.C.

2017 was a nullity. Instead, fifth, the plaintiffs established standing to challenge the mandate by showing that their injuries were traceable to the enforcement of the ACA's insurance reforms. And those injuries could be redressed by enjoining the reforms. I thought that approach was consistent with Justice Thomas's *Murphy* concurrence. So did the solicitor general. We were wrong.

A. NFIB's *Joint Dissent, Reconsidered after* Murphy

In *Murphy v. NCAA*, Justice Thomas wrote a significant concurring opinion, which Justice Gorsuch joined.[60] Justice Thomas recognized that the Court's severability precedents are "in tension with traditional limits on judicial authority."[61] Modern "severability doctrine," he wrote, "often requires courts to weigh in on statutory provisions that no party has standing to challenge, bringing courts dangerously close to issuing advisory opinions."[62] When one provision of a statute is declared unconstitutional, "every other provision" of that statute is "at risk of being declared nonseverable and thus inoperative," regardless of "whether the plaintiff has standing to challenge those other provisions."[63] Justice Thomas cited a recent example of this dynamic: the *NFIB* joint dissent, which found that the *entire* ACA was inseverable from the unconstitutional mandate.[64] Yes, Justice Thomas cast some doubt on his own opinion from six years earlier. (If only we were all able to so easily admit our own fault.) Justice Thomas observed that "severability doctrine is thus an unexplained exception to the normal rules of standing, as well as the separation-of-powers principles that those rules protect."[65] Justice Thomas, as he often does, urged the Court to "reconsider these precedents, at some point."[66]

The *Murphy* concurrence had a large impact on how I view severability, as well as standing.

---

[60] Murphy v. NCAA, 138 S. Ct. 1461, 1485 (2018) (Thomas, J., concurring).

[61] *Id.*

[62] *Id.* at 1487.

[63] *Id.*

[64] *Id.* (citing NFIB, 567 U.S. at 696–97).

[65] *Id.* at 1487.

[66] *Id.*

B. *Standing-through-Inseverability*

To establish Article III standing, "a plaintiff must show (i) that he suffered an injury in fact that is concrete, particularized, and actual or imminent; (ii) that the injury was likely caused by the defendant; and (iii) that the injury would likely be redressed by judicial relief."[67] "[S]tanding and remedies are joined at the hip: Article III permits a court only to provide 'a remedy that redresses the plaintiffs' injury-in-fact.'"[68] For example, a plaintiff argues that he is injured by an unconstitutional provision and the court redresses that injury by enjoining the injurious unconstitutional provision.

Conversely, if a court can afford a remedy that redresses the plaintiffs' injury-in-fact, then a court has Article III jurisdiction. Or does it? Placing the remedial inquiry *before* the standing inquiry seems backwards. Crafting a remedy often involves statutory interpretation—an inherently *merits*-style question. How can a court resolve a remedial question before establishing Article III standing? Engaging in this task prior to establishing Article III jurisdiction could amount to something like an advisory opinion. I'll admit this argument is powerful and—in most cases—persuasive. But I think the adjudicatory order of operations can be flipped for a narrow sliver of cases that involve inseverability.

Often, legislatures include severability clauses in statutes: Courts should sever an unconstitutional provision of a statute from the remainder of a law to save as much of the statute as possible. By contrast, inseverability clauses are rare. With these provisions, legislatures group together central provisions of a statute. If *any* aspect of that grouping is declared unconstitutional, the entire grouping must fall.

Consider a hypothetical statute with three sections: Section A, Section B, and Section C. Congress adds an inseverability clause to this statute, finding that Section A is "essential" to the operation of Section B. If Section A is declared unconstitutional, then the court should also enjoin Section B. Congress would not want Section B to operate in the absence of Section A. However, Section A is not

---

[67] Transunion, L.L.C. v. Ramirez, 141 S. Ct. 2190, 2203 (2021).

[68] Collins v. Yellen, 141 S. Ct. 1761, 1796 n.34 (2021) (Gorsuch, J., concurring) (quoting Collins v. Mnuchin, 938 F.3d 553, 609 (5th Cir. 2019) (Oldham, J., concurring in part and dissenting in part)).

"essential" to the operation of Section C. Thus, Section C can be severed from Sections A and B. But Section A cannot be severed from Section B.

In a hypothetical case, the enforcement of Section A injures the plaintiff. The plaintiff alleges that Section A is unconstitutional. Moreover, that injury can be traced to the enforcement of Section A. And that injury can be redressed by enjoining Section A. But Section B does not satisfy any of the three elements of Article III standing. Yet, in light of the inseverability clause, Section B would be enjoined, *regardless* of whether Section B is unconstitutional. Under modern doctrine, the court would not even ask if Section B injures the plaintiff, or whether enjoining Section B redresses any injury.

This analysis is not controversial. But it should be. Here, the court enjoined Section B, which was constitutional and never injured the plaintiff. For the reasons Justice Thomas identified in *Murphy*, this approach seems to conflict with the rigors of Article III standing. The courts should only have the power to enjoin laws that in fact injure the plaintiffs. Yet, under settled doctrine, this analysis is valid.

Now consider another statute with two sections: Section A and Section B. Congress adds an inseverability clause to this statute, finding that Section A is "essential" to the operation of Section B. Section A imposes an unconstitutional-but-unenforced mandate: a command to buy a commercial product. Section A inflicts on the plaintiff a classic pocketbook injury. And the plaintiff alleges that Section A is unconstitutional. However, that injury cannot be traced to the government's enforcement of Section A because the government does not enforce Section A. Accordingly, there is no government defendant to enjoin. Thus, the plaintiff's injury cannot be redressed by enjoining Section A. Section B likewise injures the plaintiff. The government does enforce Section B. And the injury from Section B could be redressed by enjoining the enforcement of Section B. But there is no allegation that Section B is unconstitutional.

In this second hypothetical, the plaintiff mixes and matches the Article III analysis based on inseverability. The injury in fact is premised on the injurious-and-unconstitutional-but-unenforced Section A, while traceability and redressability are premised on the injurious-and-constitutional-and-enforced Section B. Sections A and B both injure the plaintiff. And Section B, which is inseverable from Section A, can be enjoined to redress the injuries caused by

Sections A and B jointly. The inseverability clause expressly holds this triptych together. The theory underlying this second hypothetical can be described as *standing-through-inseverability*.

This second analysis should not be controversial, but it is under modern doctrine. The Supreme Court has approved of enjoining constitutional provisions of law that do not satisfy any of the three elements of Article III standing, solely by virtue of inseverability. See the first hypothetical. But the Supreme Court has not approved of enjoining an unconstitutional provision of law that satisfies the first element of Article III standing and also satisfies the other two elements by virtue of inseverability. Justice Thomas observed that the Court "has not addressed standing-through-inseverability in any detail, largely relying on it through implication."[69] Still, standing-through-inseverability is far less objectionable than inseverability-without-standing.

Standing-through-inseverability has several virtues. First, unlike with hypothetical 1, in hypothetical 2 all of the enjoined provisions actually injure the plaintiff. The latter example avoids the problems identified in *Murphy* where the courts enjoin noninjurious provisions. Second, standing-through-inseverability prevents Congress from creating unenforceable-but-unconstitutional mandates that cannot be challenged in court. Some law-abiding citizens will still follow a mandate even if there is no penalty for ignoring the mandate. Nudges can sometimes be just as effective as shoves. These sorts of requirements are novelties in federal jurisprudence and should not be encouraged.

The third virtue was illustrated during oral arguments in *California v. Texas*. Justice Alito asked about a statute with two sections, in which Section A is unconstitutional but imposes no injury.[70] For example, Section A has a "clearly racially discriminatory provision."[71] Section B is constitutional but does not injure the plaintiff. And Sections A and B are inseverable. If you reject standing-through-inseverability, no plaintiff could challenge this statute. Donald Verrilli, who defended the ACA on behalf of the House of Representatives, recognized that

---

[69] Texas, 141 S. Ct. at 2122 (Thomas, J., concurring).

[70] Transcript of Oral Argument at 42, California v. Texas, 141 S. Ct. 2104 (2021) (No. 19-840).

[71] *Id.* at 94.

Alito's hypothetical statute likely could be challenged in court.[72] He said that Alito's question "definitely tests the limits of our objection to standing-through-inseverability."[73] He stated that "it would be hard to maintain [the House's] position in the face of a statute like that.'"[74]

As a theory, standing-through-inseverability cannot be rejected out of hand. Indeed, standing-through-inseverability was the *only* basis for standing in *NFIB*.

C. Standing in NFIB, *Revisited*

What was the basis for standing in *NFIB*? Let's consider each of the three elements of Article III jurisdiction. First, the individual mandate imposed an injury-in-fact. And that injury was imposed without regard to the penalty—see part III.A above. But what about the other two elements: traceability and redressability? These elements could not be supported by the penalty. The plaintiffs forfeited any standing arguments premised on the penalty. Nor could traceability and redressability be supported by the individual mandate standing by itself. To understand why, we have to consider what a mandate actually means.

NFIB found that the "most straightforward reading of the mandate is that it commands individuals to purchase insurance."[75] I agree. In a legal sense, there is indeed a command that people must buy insurance. But the ACA does not actually require people to maintain insurance. *Actual* mandates, backed by government compulsion, are exceedingly rare in the law. And many legal regimes described as mandates are not really mandates. To use a topical example, *Jacobson v. Massachusetts* is usually cited to support compulsory vaccine mandates.[76] Not quite. Under the Cambridge law, people could receive a free vaccine or pay a modest $5 fine.[77] The city of Cambridge did

[72] *Id.* at 42.

[73] *Id.*

[74] *Id.*

[75] NFIB, 567 U.S. at 562 (opinion of Roberts, C.J.).

[76] See Buck v. Bell, 274 U.S. 200, 207 (1927) (citing Jacobson v. Massachusetts, 197 U.S. 11 (1905)) ("The principle that sustains compulsory vaccination is broad enough to cover cutting the Fallopian tubes.").

[77] Roman Cath. Diocese of Brooklyn v. Cuomo, 141 S. Ct. 63, 70–71 (2020) (Gorsuch, J., concurring). See also, Josh Blackman, "Told You So about Jacobson v. Massachusetts," Volokh Conspiracy, Nov. 26, 2020, https://perma.cc/2MCW-RZN9.

not forcibly strap Henning Jacobson to a gurney and jab a needle in his arm. By contrast, *Buck v. Bell* involved an actual mandate. Carrie Buck was forced to undergo an involuntary tubal ligation. She was sterilized for being an "imbecile." Buck did not have the choice to pay a fine.

With the ACA, bureaucrats are not empowered to garnish wages or withdraw funds to pay a person's insurance premiums. No federal agent can accost scofflaws on the street, take their wallets, and deposit money on the health-insurance exchanges. Even those people who paid the penalty—a sum less than the cost of policies—could still remain uninsured. In short, no government officer can actually enforce the individual mandate in § 5000A(a)—not today, and not in 2012.

During oral arguments in *NFIB*, Solicitor General Verrilli made an important representation. He "confirm[ed] that if someone chooses to pay [the penalty] rather than obtain health insurance, they have fully complied with the law."[78] This representation proved essential to the chief justice's saving construction.[79] But it should not have been particularly difficult for the government to make this representation. Congress gave the federal government no mechanism to actually force people to purchase insurance. At most, uninsured people could be required to pay a penalty. But as far as the government was concerned, no further action can be taken because the government was not authorized to take any further action. Here, the executive branch could not actually make people buy insurance.

Imagine a different statute in which people who failed to buy insurance were subject to wage garnishment, and those funds would then be used to automatically enroll a person in an insurance policy. That law would amount to a true mandate. But the ACA did not create this mechanism. By contrast, the ACA "bars the IRS from using several of its normal enforcement tools, such as criminal prosecutions and levies."[80]

The individual mandate is *unprecedented* in many regards. Section 5000A(a) has *always* imposed an unenforced command to purchase insurance. Indeed, the ACA provided that several people would be

---

[78] NFIB, 567 U.S. at 568 (citing Brief for United States 60–61; Transcript of Oral Argument 49–50 (Mar. 26, 2012)).

[79] Unprecedented, *supra* note 2, at 180, 274.

[80] NFIB, 567 U.S. at 539.

subject to the mandate but not to the penalty.[81] For these people, the government expressly established an unenforceable mandate without adverse consequences.

Some critics argue that an unenforced command is not a command at all. This position may be grounded in the nuances of federal standing law, but often it amounts to a philosophical debate: When the government says "thou shalt," are the people are under no obligation unless the government also says "or else . . ."? I disagree with this approach from both a legal and a moral perspective. Some people follow the law simply for the sake of following the law. That respect for the law is a value our polity should praise, not deride. These actions are not self-inflicted injuries; citizens are responding to a very rare sort of command from their government. During oral arguments in *California v. Texas*, Justice Kavanaugh questioned whether Congress had ever enacted a "true mandate with no penalties" "to do something" or "to purchase a good or service."[82] In reply, Texas Solicitor General Hawkins said that the mandate was "unprecedented."[83]

Still, an injury-in-fact is not enough to establish Article III standing. The problem with an unenforced mandate concerns the other two elements of the Article III inquiry: traceability and redressability. Imagine that Congress enacted a variant of the ACA in which § 5000A(a) was completely severable from the remainder of the statute. In this case, I do not think private plaintiffs would have standing to challenge the individual mandate. Plaintiffs could claim an injury-in-fact, but the court could not redress that injury through an injunction of the unconstitutional-but-unenforced mandate. They would have no luck in federal court.

In *NFIB*, § 5000A(a) by itself was not enough to support standing. The plaintiffs' injuries could not be *traced* to the enforcement of § 5000A(a) because the provision was not enforced. And the plaintiffs' injuries could not be *redressed* by enjoining § 5000A(a) because there is no defendant to enjoin. Injunctions run against the enforcement of a law, not the mere existence of a statute. Moreover, enjoining the penalty would not have redressed the plaintiffs' injury in 2012 because the penalty had not been assessed. Additionally, some

---

[81] See 28 U.S.C. § 5000A(e).

[82] Transcript of Oral Argument, *supra* note 70, at 84.

[83] *Id.*

people were—and still are—subject to the mandate but not to the penalty. Enjoining the penalty would never redress their injuries. Plus, the *NFIB* plaintiffs forfeited any standing argument premised on the penalty. Thus, to satisfy traceability and redressability, some *other* provision of the ACA had to be enjoined. In *NFIB*, the only path to satisfy traceability and redressability involved standing-through-inseverability.

Specifically, in *NFIB* the plaintiffs and the federal government agreed that the mandate was inseverable from insurance reforms known as guaranteed issue and community rating (GICR).[84] Under these regulations, insurers (1) are required to issue policies to customers regardless of their pre-existing conditions, and (2) cannot charge customers higher rates because of their pre-existing conditions.

Congress included two statutory findings about the relationship between the individual mandate and GICR.[85] First, Congress concluded that the "individual responsibility requirement"—the individual mandate—was *"essential* to creating effective health insurance markets in which improved health insurance products that are guaranteed issue and do not exclude coverage of pre-existing conditions can be sold."[86] Second, Congress found that the individual mandate was *"essential* to creating effective health insurance markets that do not require underwriting and eliminate its associated administrative costs."[87] In short, the individual mandate was "essential" to GICR. Chief Justice Roberts cited these findings in his controlling opinion.[88] In *NFIB*, the Obama administration read these two statutory findings as the functional equivalent of an inseverability clause. The government argued that if the individual mandate was unconstitutional, then the Court should also enjoin GICR.[89]

I agree with the Obama administration's argument: The statutory findings functioned as an inseverability clause. The mandate and GICR operated together. This cohesive grouping required people to

---

[84] 42 U.S.C. §§ 300gg, 300gg-1, 300gg-3, 300gg-4, 18032(c), and some related provisions.

[85] 42 U.S.C. § 18091(2)(J).

[86] *Id.* at § 18091(2)(I) (emphasis added).

[87] *Id.*

[88] NFIB, 567 U.S. at 556 (opinion of Roberts, C.J.).

[89] *Id.* at 542.

purchase insurance that provided "minimum essential coverage." For some people—the elderly and sick—this grouping potentially lowered the cost of insurance. For other people—the young and healthy—this grouping potentially raised the cost of insurance. Catastrophic policies, for example, would not comply with the mandate. Rather, to comply with the mandate people would have to purchase comprehensive and expensive policies.

Now, the full scope of the standing inquiry comes into view. The mandate, standing by itself, imposes an injury in fact. Alternatively, the mandate, in conjunction with GICR, imposes an injury in fact. (In *California v. Texas*, the U.S. solicitor general favored the latter view and Cato favored the former view.). Both injuries are classic pocket-book injuries: The purchase of an unwanted product. And those products are unwanted because of GICR, which can raise prices and reduce selection. In either case, those injuries can be traced to officials who enforce GICR, and those injuries can be redressed by enjoining the enforcement of GICR. In *NFIB*, traceability and redressability could only have been satisfied if the mandate was inseverable from GICR. Many observers simply assumed the penalty provided the basis for standing in *NFIB*. The penalty did not, and could not, have played a role in the Article III inquiry for the *NFIB* private plaintiffs.

Standing-through-inseverability established Article III jurisdiction in 2012. But was this theory still available after the Tax Cuts and Jobs Act of 2017?

D. Congressional Intent Before and After 2017

In popular discourse, the severability analysis in *California v. Texas* was largely informed by realpolitik. After President Trump's surprise victory in 2016, congressional Republicans spent nearly a year trying to repeal large portions of the ACA. Those efforts failed. Instead, Congress relied on the budget reconciliation process to reduce the penalty to $0. Republican politicos from Trump on down boasted that the Tax Cuts and Jobs Act "repealed" the individual mandate. The TCJA did no such thing. The mandate remained in place; the penalty was simply zeroed out. How did this change affect the severability analysis?

Under modern severability doctrine, purpose matters—a lot. If one portion of a law is declared unconstitutional, courts imagine what Congress would have wanted to do with the remainder of the statute. "'Would Congress still have passed' the valid sections 'had it known' about the constitutional invalidity of the other portions of the statute?"[90] For the ACA, the answer to this question is straightforward. Had congressional Republicans and Democrats been polled in late 2017, I speculate that a super-majority would have agreed: If the mandate was declared unconstitutional, the remainder of the ACA should remain unchanged. The sense of Congress—on both sides of the aisle—was that the TCJA made a surgical excision from the ACA.

Before the Supreme Court, this understanding of legislative history was articulated by the Democratic-controlled House of Representatives[91] and 47 Democratic senators.[92] No Republican members of Congress signed an amicus brief to the contrary, suggesting they did not disagree with the Democrats. The Cato brief acknowledged this dynamic: "if the Court were to defer to the will of the [2017] Congress, the severability analysis would be straightforward: the unconstitutional individual mandate should be severed from the rest of the ACA."

Still, I do not hold the handiwork of the 2017 Congress in very high regard. The *NFIB* saving construction was straightforward: The ACA could be saved because the penalty raised revenue. Any competent attorney should have recognized that zeroing out the penalty risked toppling the saving construction and throwing the ACA into constitutional jeopardy. Before 2017, the ACA was dangling by a constitutional thread. The TCJA severed that thread. In my view, the actions of the 2017 Congress were a constitutional "nullity."[93]

But on a deeper level, I profoundly disagree with the purposivist nature of modern severability doctrine. "Instead of requiring courts to determine what a statute means, the severability doctrine requires courts to make 'a nebulous inquiry into hypothetical

---

[90] United States v. Booker, 543 U.S. 220, 258 (2005) (quoting Denver Area Educ. Telecomm. Consortium, Inc. v. FCC, 518 U.S. 727, 767 (1996) (plurality op.)).

[91] Opening Brief for the United States House of Representatives as Respondent Supporting Petitioners, California v. Texas, 141 S. Ct. 2104 (2021) (No. 19-840), https://perma.cc/RCZ8-FQ46.

[92] Brief of 47 Members of the United States Senate as Amici Curiae in Support of Petitioners, California v. Texas, 141 S. Ct. 2104 (2021) (No. 19-840), https://perma.cc/3SCG-VXHK.

[93] Blackman, Undone, *supra* note 43, at 47–48.

congressional intent.'"[94] Often, "the enacting Congress [lacked] any intent" on the severability question.[95] That problem does not concern the TCJA. Here individual members of Congress were quite forthright: If the mandate was declared unconstitutional, then the rest of the ACA should remain in effect. But so what? Intentions only count if "they are enshrined in a text that makes it through the constitutional processes of bicameralism and presentment."[96] In 2017, Congress did not repeal the statutory findings that linked the "essential" mandate to GICR—the very findings that the Obama administration treated as an inseverability clause in *NFIB*.

Finally, I recognize that members of Congress who supported and opposed the TCJA did not expect any other portions of the ACA to fall. Again, so what? Congress can enact a statute with one intent, which can later be interpreted to achieve radically different policy outcomes. "[L]egislators' . . . intended expected applications" or "a statute's purpose is [not] limited to achieving applications foreseen at the time of enactment."[97] And frankly, the consequences of zeroing out the penalty should have been entirely foreseeable—at least it was obvious to the attorneys general who challenged the ACA.

As a matter of first principles, the inseverability analysis should have been the same in 2012 and in 2017. The penalty played no role in resolving severability in *NFIB*. And nothing in the TCJA altered that analysis. Furthermore, the standing analysis should have been the same in 2012 and in 2017. The penalty played no role in resolving standing in *NFIB*. And zeroing out the penalty did not change the linkage between the mandate and GICR. "[S]tanding and remedies are joined at the hip."[98] They rise together, and they fall together. In *California v. Texas*, the Supreme Court should have "fashion[ed] a remedy that actually redresses Plaintiffs' harms."[99] Or at least that is what I hoped would happen.

---

[94] Murphy, 138 S. Ct. at 1486 (Thomas, J., concurring) (quoting Booker, 534 U.S. at 320 n.7 (Thomas, J., dissenting)).

[95] *Id.* at 1487.

[96] *Id.*

[97] Bostock v. Clayton Cty., 140 S. Ct. 1731, 1750 (2020).

[98] Collins, 141 S. Ct. at 1796 n.34 (Gorsuch, J., concurring) .

[99] Collins v. Mnuchin, 938 F.3d 553, 611 (5th Cir. 2019) (Oldham, J., concurring in part and dissenting in part).

E. *Cato's and the U.S. Solicitor General's "Novel" Theory of Standing-through-Inseverability*

The Cato brief argued that the two private plaintiffs had standing based on provisions that were inseverable from the unconstitutional mandate. The U.S. solicitor general also contended that the individual plaintiffs had standing-through-inseverability.[100] Cato and the solicitor general advanced very similar theories about traceability and redressability, though we parted company on the nature of the injury in fact. In *California v. Texas*, both Justice Breyer's majority opinion and Justice Alito's dissent referred to our theories as "novel."[101] Ultimately, both opinions declined to consider standing-through-inseverability for the private plaintiffs. This part will address what could have been on standing.

1. Injury in fact

The Cato brief contended that *NFIB* stands for a simple proposition: The individual mandate inflicted a pocketbook injury without regard to the penalty. Congress imposed a command to purchase health insurance. Nothing in the TCJA altered that injury. The solicitor general did not advance this argument directly. Rather, the United States established the injury in fact through inseverability. The Department of Justice argued that "[t]he individual plaintiffs have shown that the ACA's insurance-reform provisions," like GICR, "injure them by limiting their options with regard to insurance coverage and by raising their costs."[102] Specifically, "the plaintiffs challenge[d] the insurance-reform provisions that do injure them, and the basis for their challenge is that the insurance-reform provisions are inseverable from the mandate, which is invalid."[103]

Stated differently, the individual mandate—working in conjunction with the ACA's insurance-reform provisions—force the plaintiffs to buy unwanted, overpriced products. The plaintiffs claimed they were injured by regulations, which were inseverable from the

---

[100] Brief for the Federal Respondents, California v. Texas, 141 S. Ct. 2104 (2021) (Nos. 19-840, 19-1019) [hereinafter Brief for the Federal Respondents], https://perma.cc/HZZ5-4MT9.

[101] Texas, 141 S. Ct. at 2116; *id.* at 2126 (Alito, J., dissenting).

[102] Brief for the Federal Respondents, *supra* note 100, at 11–12.

[103] *Id.* at 20.

individual mandate. This approach to standing-through-inseverability can be referred to as a *bootstrap* theory: The individual mandate and other inseverable insurance reforms are bootstrapped together for the standing inquiry.

I have no problem with the solicitor general's approach to the injury-in-fact prong. It has the virtue of avoiding an unconventional reading of *NFIB* that was not directly addressed by the Court. But the more direct approach is to argue that the plaintiffs are injured by the unconstitutional individual mandate.

2. Traceability

The individual mandate, standing by itself, creates an injury-in-fact. But the unenforced requirement, standing by itself, creates problems for the second prong of Article III standing: traceability. During oral arguments, Justice Barrett asked Texas Solicitor General Hawkins how the alleged injuries with respect to the mandate were "traceable to the defendants that the individual[] [plaintiffs] have actually sued here."[104] She asked, "Why is it [the defendants'] action that's actually inflicting the injury?"[105] Later in the argument Acting Solicitor General Jeffrey Wall acknowledged that "Justice Barrett [asked] some very difficult questions about traceability with respect to the individual" plaintiffs.[106]

The private plaintiffs' injuries cannot be traced to § 5000A(a), standing by itself, as that provision is not actually enforced. But the insurance reforms, like GICR, are enforced. The bootstrap theory addresses Justice Barrett's questions. The U.S. solicitor general argued that the plaintiffs established "a cognizable injury traceable to the insurance-reform provisions," such as GICR.[107] Here, the plaintiffs' injury can be traced to the defendants' "'allegedly unlawful conduct,'" and not to the allegedly unlawful "provision of law that is challenged."[108] And "[t]he individual plaintiffs can make this merits argument regardless of whether they would have Article III standing

---

[104] Transcript of Oral Argument, *supra* note 70, at 88.

[105] *Id.*

[106] *Id.* at 107.

[107] Brief for the Federal Respondents, *supra* note 100, at 19.

[108] Collins, 141 S. Ct. at 1765 (quoting Allen v. Wright, 468 U. S. 737, 751 (1984)).

to challenge the individual mandate by itself."[109] Traceability could only be established through inseverability. This premise was true in *NFIB*, and it was true in *California v. Texas*.

3. Redressability

The third element of Article III standing—redressability—can also be satisfied through inseverability. It is unclear how a court could enjoin a requirement that is not enforced. But a court could enjoin the ACA's inseverable insurance reforms, such as GICR. The solicitor general contended that "the individual plaintiffs have standing to obtain an injunction barring enforcement against them of the insurance reforms that injure them."[110] And this redressability analysis was "joined at the hip" with the remedial analysis.[111] The federal government argued that "the relief the Court orders should be limited to redressing the injury actually incurred—that is, the relief should reach only the enforcement of the ACA provisions that injure the individual plaintiffs."[112]

Cato likewise urged the Court to "fashion a remedy that actually redresses [the plaintiffs'] harms."[113] I thought that this approach to standing and severability threaded the needle between the Court's modern severability doctrine and the *Murphy* concurrence. Alas, I only garnered one of the *Murphy* concurrers: I got Justice Gorsuch, but lost Justice Thomas.

III. *California v. Texas* Is Unreviewable

California v. Texas split 7-2. Justice Breyer wrote the majority opinion, which was joined by Chief Justice Roberts and Justices Thomas, Kagan, Sotomayor, Kavanaugh, and Barrett. Justice Thomas concurred. And Justice Alito dissented with Justice Gorsuch.

The majority held that the challenge to the mandate was unreviewable. The Court only considered the second standing prong and ruled that the plaintiffs' alleged injuries were not traceable to

---

[109] Brief for the Federal Respondents, *supra* note 100, at 14.

[110] *Id.* at 23 n.4.

[111] See Collins, 141 S. Ct. at 1796 (Gorsuch, J., concurring).

[112] Brief for the Federal Respondents, *supra* note 100, at 12.

[113] Cato Amicus, *supra* note 18, at 29 (quoting Collins v. Mnuchin, 938 F.3d 553, 611 (5th Cir. 2019) (Oldham, J., concurring in part and dissenting in part)).

any governmental action. Both the majority and dissent declined to consider standing-through-inseverability with respect to the private plaintiffs. But Justice Alito, in dissent, concluded that the state plaintiffs established standing-through-inseverability. Justice Thomas maintained that none of the plaintiffs had standing.

A. Standing-through-Inseverability

Justice Breyer's majority opinion declined to consider the solicitor general's "alternative theory" of standing-through-inseverability.[114] Breyer wrote that this position was "raised for the first time" before the Supreme Court, "was not directly argued by the plaintiffs in the courts below," and "was nowhere presented at the certiorari stage."[115]

Justice Alito also declined to consider standing-through-inseverability with respect to the private plaintiffs.[116] Rather, he relied on standing-through-inseverability for the state plaintiffs. He wrote that "costly obligations imposed on [the states] by other provisions of the ACA cannot be severed from the mandate."[117] In other words, the ACA's insurance reforms were *inseverable* from the unconstitutional mandate. The dissent found this line of reasoning was "conceptually sound."[118] Finally, the dissent rejected the argument that the state plaintiffs' forfeited the standing-through-inseverability argument.[119]

Only Justice Thomas addressed the bootstrap theory for the private plaintiffs. Justice Thomas acknowledged that "[t]his theory" of standing-through-inseverability "offers a connection between harm and unlawful conduct."[120] And, he explained, this theory "might well support standing in some circumstances."[121] But Justice Thomas would not address standing-through-inseverability in this case. First, he agreed with the majority that the issue was forfeited. Second, he

---

[114] Texas, 141 S. Ct. at 2116.

[115] *Id.*

[116] *Id.* at 2127 (Alito, J., dissenting).

[117] *Id.*

[118] *Id.*

[119] *Id.* at 2134.

[120] *Id.* at 2122 (Thomas, J., concurring).

[121] *Id.*

wrote that "this Court has not addressed standing-through-inseverability in any detail, largely relying on it through implication."[122] Third, and most damning, he cast doubt on the validity of the theory. He wrote that "standing-through-inseverability—*assuming* it is a legitimate theory of standing—is fundamentally a merits-like exercise."[123] He concluded, "standing-through-inseverability could only be a valid theory of standing to the extent it treats inseverability as a merits exercise of statutory interpretation."[124]

Justice Gorsuch apparently viewed the issue differently. He had joined the *Murphy* concurrence and also joined the *California* dissent. He was content to consider inseverability at the standing stage. Justice Thomas, alas, was not. Here, we see a fracture between the Court's two most conservative members. In the end, Justice Thomas cast the seventh vote against the plaintiffs.

B. No Standing-without-Inseverability

Justice Breyer declined to consider whether the individual mandate imposes an injury in fact. Rather, the entire majority opinion turned on traceability. Even if the Court "assume[d] that [the plaintiffs'] pocketbook injury satisfies the injury element of Article III standing," the plaintiffs still failed to show "that the injury they will suffer or have suffered is 'fairly traceable' to the 'allegedly unlawful conduct' of which they complain."[125]

The Court recognized that the minimum essential coverage requirement "has no means of enforcement."[126] Justice Breyer concluded, "there is no action [by the government]—actual or threatened—whatsoever."[127] Here, the majority echoed Justice Barrett's questions from oral argument. Thus, the private plaintiffs could not trace their injuries to any governmental action.

Justice Breyer also rejected the state plaintiffs' arguments for standing. The Court concluded that "the plaintiffs in this suit failed to show a concrete, particularized injury fairly traceable to the

[122] *Id.*
[123] *Id.* at 2122 n.2 (emphasis added).
[124] *Id.* at 2122.
[125] *Id.* at 2113–14.
[126] *Id.* at 2114.
[127] *Id.* at 2115.

defendants' conduct in enforcing the specific statutory provision they attack as unconstitutional."[128]

C. The ACA Imposes a Mandate—Not a Choice—That Is Unconstitutional

The majority did not "reach" any "questions of the Act's validity."[129] Still, language in Justice Breyer's majority opinion seems inconsistent with the argument that the ACA imposed a *choice*. First, the Court accurately described § 5000A(a): "As originally enacted in 2010, the Patient Protection and Affordable Care Act *required* most Americans to obtain minimum essential health insurance coverage."[130] There was a "requirement," not a choice. Indeed, § 5000(A) is described as a requirement throughout the majority opinion. Second, the words "choice" or "choose" appear nowhere in the decision. Third, the Court described the penalty as an altogether separate provision from the requirement.[131] The ACA imposes a requirement to buy insurance; it does not offer a choice to pay a tax-penalty. That fact was true in 2010. It was true in *NFIB*. And it remains true today.

Justice Alito found that the individual mandate does not "fall[] within a power granted to Congress."[132] However, *NFIB* saved "the mandate [as] a lawful exercise of Congress's taxing power"—in part because the penalty raised revenue.[133] And "raising revenue is an 'essential feature' of any exercise of the taxing power."[134] But in 2017, the TCJA reduced the penalty to zero. It no longer raised revenue. "Now, in the trilogy's third episode," Justice Alito wrote, "the Court is presented with the daunting problem of a 'tax' that does not tax."[135] He asked rhetorically, "[c]an the taxing power, which saved the day in the first episode, sustain such a curious creature?"[136] No, he answered. "[T]he slender reed that supported the decision in *NFIB*

---

[128] *Id.* at 2120.

[129] *Id.* at 2112.

[130] *Id.* (emphasis added).

[131] *Id.*

[132] *Id.* at 2135 (Alito, J., dissenting).

[133] *Id.*

[134] *Id.* at 2136.

[135] *Id.* at 2123.

[136] *Id.*

was seemingly cut down" by Congress.[137] The saving construction no longer holds. And the taxing power argument that garnered five votes in 2012 "is no longer defensible."[138]

The final "installment [of the] epic Affordable Care Act trilogy" ended not with a bang, but a whimper.[139]

Conclusion

In dissent, Justice Alito wrote that "in all three episodes, with the Affordable Care Act facing a serious threat, the Court has pulled off an improbable rescue."[140] Justice Alito lamented, "once again the Court has found a way to protect the ACA."[141] Justice Alito predicted, "[o]ur Affordable Care Act epic may go on."[142]

The unconstitutional individual mandate will remain until a party with standing challenges it. For example, a person who is subject to an ACA enforcement action can raise the mandate's unconstitutionality as a defense. Soon enough, the trilogy will become a quadrilogy. You can check out of the Hotel *California v. Texas* any time you like. But I can never leave.

[137] *Id.*

[138] *Id.*

[139] *Id.* at 2123.

[140] *Id.*

[141] *Id.*

[142] *Id.*

Three Views of the Administrative State: Lessons from *Collins v. Yellen*

*Aaron L. Nielson**

Introduction

As I was preparing for oral argument in *Collins v. Yellen*,[1] the thought came to me that David Thompson—counsel for the plaintiffs—had a tough job. I had spent hundreds of hours on just the constitutional aspect of this enormous case. Thompson, however, had two additional issues to cover: a complex statutory argument and an important remedial argument. Thompson is a world-class lawyer and was able to handle each issue skillfully, but even so, it is challenging to argue essentially three cases at once. Yet to understand *Collins*—and, indeed, key aspects of the administrative state—one needs to view all three parts at the same time: the statutory debate, the constitutional question, and the remedy.

First, *Collins* concerns the "nationaliz[ation]"—Justice Stephen Breyer's word[2]—of the Federal National Mortgage Association and the Federal Home Loan Mortgage Corporation, better known as Fannie Mae and Freddie Mac or just Fannie and Freddie. Following the housing-market collapse in 2007 and 2008, Congress created the

* Professor of Law, J. Reuben Clark Law School, Brigham Young University. In *Collins v. Yellen*, the Supreme Court appointed Professor Nielson to brief and argue in support of the position that the Federal Housing Finance Agency's structure does not violate the separation of powers. Professor Nielson would like to thank Brock Mason for excellent research assistance.

[1] 141 S. Ct. 1761 (2021).

[2] Transcript of Oral Argument at 12, Collins v. Yellen, 141 S. Ct. 1761 (2021) (Nos. 19-422, 19-563) ("[Y]ou could . . . view the shareholders' claim as saying we bought into this corporation, it was supposed to be private as well as having a public side, and then the government nationalized it. That's what they did. If you look at their giving the net worth to Treasury, it's nationalizing the company.").

Federal Housing Finance Agency (FHFA), which promptly placed Fannie and Freddie in conservatorships. As of 2021, those conservatorships remain in place. Since 2012, moreover, following what is called the "Third Amendment" (by the United States and the Supreme Court) or the "Net Worth Sweep" (by the *Collins* plaintiffs), most of Fannie's and Freddie's profits have gone to the U.S. Treasury rather than staying with the companies for the benefit of their private shareholders.[3] In *Collins*, the Court dealt a sharp blow to those private shareholders, unanimously concluding that the FHFA did not exceed its statutory authority as conservator when it adopted the Third Amendment.

Second, *Collins* may be the most pro-"unitary executive" decision in history.[4] In addition to their argument that the FHFA abused its conservatorship authority, the *Collins* plaintiffs also argued that the FHFA is unconstitutionally structured because the president can only remove the FHFA's director "for cause." On this point, the Court agreed with the plaintiffs. Building on—but significantly expanding—the holding in *Seila Law LLC v. CFPB*,[5] the Court held that the president has the constitutional power to remove the head of an agency regardless of how much authority the agency exercises. This reflects the vision of the unitary executive from *Myers v. United States*,[6] but with a twist: Whereas almost all of *Myers's* broad language was *dicta*, in *Collins*, it's a *holding*.

And third, *Collins* is also a case about constitutional remedies. Despite prevailing—decisively—on the constitutional merits question, it is possible that the plaintiffs will never see a penny of relief; indeed, both Justices Clarence Thomas and Elena Kagan wrote

[3] See Collins, 141 S. Ct. at 1774.

[4] See, e.g., Steven G. Calabresi & Saikrishna B. Prakash, The President's Power to Execute the Laws, 104 Yale L.J. 541, 544 (1994) ("The claim made by unitary executivists [is] that the Constitution creates only three branches of government and that the President must be able to control the execution of all federal laws. . . .").

[5] 140 S. Ct. 2183 (2020); see also Ilan Wurman, The Removal Power: A Critical Guide, 2019–2020 Cato Sup. Ct. Rev. 157 (2019) (explaining *Seila Law*).

[6] See Myers v. United States, 272 U.S. 52, 163–64 (1926) ("[A]rticle II grants to the President the executive power of the Government, i.e., the general administrative control of those executing the laws, including the power of appointment and removal of executive officers—a conclusion confirmed by his obligation to take care that the laws be faithfully executed. . . .").

separately to predict that very outcome.[7] Although agreeing with the *Collins* plaintiffs that Congress cannot restrict the president's ability to remove the head of the FHFA, the Court also held that the mere presence of an unconstitutional restriction on removal does not mean that the agency's actions are per se invalid. Instead, at least when seeking retrospective relief, a plaintiff must show that without the unconstitutional restriction, the agency would have behaved differently—which is no easy task, especially because the evidence necessary to make such a showing may not be publicly available. As a consequence, going forward, many plaintiffs may conclude that the trouble (and expense) of litigating removal issues just isn't worth the candle.

When these three aspects of *Collins* are considered at the same time, the true picture emerges: Federal power is ubiquitous in the housing sector, the White House has extensive control over that power, and the Supreme Court is reluctant to provide much relief to private plaintiffs.

I. Background

Collins is an important case. But it is also complicated. Accordingly, to understand what the Court decided, it is necessary to first appreciate the case's context, which is set forth below.

A. Fannie, Freddie, and the Collapse of the Housing Market

Collins is ultimately a case about Fannie and Freddie, two peculiar— yet consequential—companies. Congress chartered Fannie in 1938 to help "create[] liquidity in the mortgage market."[8] Originally, Fannie was a federal agency, but Congress later turned it "into a public-private, mixed ownership corporation" and then later into "a for-profit, shareholder-owned company."[9] In 1970, Congress chartered Freddie "to help thrifts manage the challenges associated with interest rate risk" and allowed both Fannie and Freddie to "to buy and sell mortgages not

---

[7] See Collins, 141 S. Ct. at 1795 (Thomas, J., concurring); *id.* at 1802 (Kagan, J., concurring in part and concurring in the judgment in part).

[8] Off. of Inspector General, FHFA, A Brief History of the Housing Government-Sponsored Enterprises 2, https://bit.ly/2TMbXiK.

[9] *Id.* at 2–3.

insured or guaranteed by the federal government."[10] In 1989, Freddie also became a for-profit company with private shareholders.[11]

Although they are open to private investment, however, Fannie and Freddie are not ordinary businesses. To the contrary, Fannie and Freddie serve "important public missions,"[12] including encouraging "housing for low- and moderate-income families" and increasing "credit" for "central cities, rural areas, and underserved areas."[13] Fannie and Freddie also enjoy special privileges, including exemptions from some regulation and taxation; without such privileges, Fannie and Freddie may not be able to survive in the marketplace, at least in their current form.[14] Thus, although Congress chartered Fannie and Freddie as for-profit entities, the Court has aptly characterized them as "not purely private actors."[15]

Beginning in 1992, Fannie and Freddie were regulated by the Office of Federal Housing Enterprise Oversight within the Department of Housing and Urban Development, which required them to meet certain mortgage goals.[16] "[F]rom about 2004 through 2007, Fannie Mae and Freddie Mac embarked on aggressive strategies to purchase mortgages and mortgage assets originated under questionable underwriting standards," including buying mortgage-backed securities "collateralized by subprime mortgages."[17]

---

[10] *Id.* at 3.

[11] See *id.* at 4.

[12] 12 U.S.C. § 4501(1).

[13] *Id.* §§ 1716(3)-(4).

[14] See, e.g., Harold Seidman, The Quasi World of the Federal Government, 6 Brookings Rev. 23, 26 (1988) ("In objecting to Reagan administration proposals to cut off its special privileges—its line of credit with the Treasury, tax exemptions, eligibility of obligations for purchase by federal trust funds, exemption from Securities and Exchange Commission regulations—[Fannie Mae] protested that 'Congress established Fannie Mae to run efficiently as an agency, not as a fully private company.' Without these special ties to the government, Fannie Mae says it would be forced out of business.").

[15] Seila Law, 140 S. Ct. at 2202.

[16] See A Brief History of the Housing Government-Sponsored Enterprises, *supra* note 8, at 5.

[17] *Id.*; see also Mark Calabria, Fannie, Freddie, and the Subprime Mortgage Market, Cato Inst. Briefing Paper no. 120, Mar. 7, 2011, https://bit.ly/3yhLqZz ("Foremost among the government-sponsored enterprises' deleterious activities was their vast direct purchases of loans that can only be characterized as subprime.").

In 2007 and 2008, the U.S. housing bubble burst, pushing Fannie and Freddie "to the brink of collapse."[18] Combined, their portfolios were worth "approximately $5 trillion," so when housing prices fell, so did their value.[19] Further, "many feared that their troubling financial condition would imperil the national economy."[20] In response, Congress enacted the Housing and Economic Recovery Act of 2008.

B. The FHFA and the Conservatorship

As part of the Recovery Act, Congress created the FHFA and tasked it with regulating Fannie and Freddie for safety and soundness.[21] In so doing, Congress declared that the FHFA is an "independent agency" to be headed by a single director whom the president appoints following Senate confirmation.[22] The director enjoys a five-year term but can be removed by the president "for cause," which the Recovery Act does not define.[23] Should the director be "absen[t]," the president may choose from one of three deputy directors to serve as acting director.[24] The statute does not expressly provide any tenure protection for an acting director.

The FHFA has two types of authority—the power to regulate and the power to act as conservator or receiver. As regulator, the FHFA examines Fannie and Freddie to ensure their financial soundness.[25] As conservator, the FHFA succeeds to "all rights, titles, powers, and privileges of the regulated entity, and of any stockholder, officer, or

[18] Perry Capital LLC v. Mnuchin, 864 F.3d 591, 598 (D.C. Cir. 2017).

[19] Collins, 141 S. Ct. at 1771; see also id. ("In fact, they lost more [in 2008] than they had earned in the previous 37 years combined. Though they remained solvent, many feared the companies would eventually default and throw the housing market into a tailspin.").

[20] Id. at 1770.

[21] The FHFA also regulates the 11 Federal Home Loan Banks, though they were not at issue in Collins.

[22] 12 U.S.C. §§ 4511(a), 4512(b)(1).

[23] Id. § 4512(b)(2).

[24] Id. § 4512(f). The president also potentially can use the Federal Vacancies Reform Act to select among other officials to serve as the acting director. See generally 5 U.S.C. §3345(a); Off. of Legal Couns., U.S. Dep't of Justice, Designating an Acting Director of the Federal Housing Finance Agency, 2019 WL 6655656, at *7 (Mar. 18, 2019); Anne Joseph O'Connell, Actings, 120 Colum. L. Rev. 613, 668–71 (2020).

[25] See, e.g., 12 U.S.C. § 4631(a)(1).

director of such regulated entity with respect to the regulated entity" (the succession clause) and may take "such action as may be—(i) necessary to put the regulated entity in a sound and solvent condition; and (ii) appropriate to carry on the business of the regulated entity and preserve and conserve the assets and property of the regulated entity."[26] As receiver, the FHFA "place[s] the regulated entity in liquidation," thus "immediately terminat[ing] any conservatorship. . . ."[27] Furthermore, when the FHFA acts as conservator or receiver, it may act "in the best interests of the regulated entity *or the Agency.*"[28] Finally, Congress limited judicial review of the FHFA's actions, declaring in the Recovery Act's so-called anti-injunction clause that "no court may take any action to restrain or affect the exercise of powers or functions of the Agency as a conservator or a receiver."[29]

Shortly after Congress enacted the Recovery Act, James Lockhart, the first FHFA director, put Fannie and Freddie into conservatorships.[30] The FHFA—acting as conservator—and the Treasury Department then made a deal: In exchange for commitments from the U.S. Treasury of $100 billion to both companies, Fannie and Freddie would provide the Treasury Department with senior liquidation preferences, "a dollar-for-dollar increase [in that preference] every time [one of them] drew on the capital commitment," a fixed right to dividends based on the size of the liquidation preference, warrants to acquire 79.9 percent of their common stock, and periodic commitment fees "to compensate Treasury for the support provided by the ongoing access to capital."[31]

The United States' commitments of funds, however, did not prove sufficient. Accordingly, in 2009, the FHFA—still acting as conservator—and the Treasury Department entered into the First Amendment to their contractual relationship, in which the United States

---

[26] *Id.* at §§ 4617(b)(2)(A)(i), 4617(b)(2)(D).

[27] *Id.* at §§ 4617(b)(2)(E), 4617(a)(4)(D).

[28] *Id.* at § 4617(b)(2)(J)(ii) (emphasis added). This power is found in a subsection listing "[i]ncidental powers," rather than in the subsection of "[p]owers as conservator." Compare *id.* at § 4617(b)(2)(D).

[29] *Id.* at § 4617(f).

[30] See Collins, 141 S. Ct. at 1770.

[31] *Id.* at 1773.

doubled its funding commitment to Fannie and Freddie.[32] Lockhart afterwards resigned and was replaced by an acting director, Edward DeMarco.[33] Later that year, the FHFA and the Treasury Department entered into the Second Amendment, in which "Treasury agreed to provide as much funding as the companies needed through 2012, after which the cap would be reinstated."[34] After several years, Fannie and Freddie had drawn over $180 billion from that funding commitment and often did not have cash on hand to pay the required dividend to the U.S. Treasury. Fannie and Freddie thus "began the circular practice of drawing funds from Treasury's capital commitment just to hand those funds back as a quarterly dividend."[35]

In August 2012, the Treasury Department and Acting Director DeMarco agreed to amend the 2008 agreement again. This Third Amendment suspended Fannie and Freddie's requirement to pay the periodic commitment fee and replaced their obligation to pay fixed dividends with a requirement to pay variable dividends equal to the amount by which their net worth exceeds a capital buffer.[36] In effect, this means that when times are bad, Fannie and Freddie do not need to pay anything, but when times are good, there is essentially nothing left over.[37]

In 2013, the Senate confirmed a new FHFA director (Melvin Watt), who served until early 2019, at which point President Donald Trump tapped Joseph Otting to serve as acting director until Mark Calabria was confirmed in April 2019.[38]

Since the Third Amendment, Fannie and Freddie's financial situation has improved, so much that they have transferred at least $124 billion more to the U.S. Treasury than they would have had to pay under the pre-Third Amendment formula.[39] In January 2021, the FHFA and the Treasury Department amended the agreement again.

[32] See *id.*

[33] See Rop v. Fed. Hous. Fin. Agency, 485 F. Supp. 3d 900, 912–15 (W.D. Mich. 2020) (describing chronology).

[34] Collins, 141 S. Ct. at 1773.

[35] *Id.* at 1774.

[36] See *id.*

[37] See *id.*

[38] See, e.g., Rop, 485 F. Supp. 3d at 915.

[39] See Collins, 141 S. Ct. at 1774.

147

Fannie and Freddie now can begin to build up capital, but the Treasury Department also receives larger liquidation preferences; eventually, Fannie and Freddie may again begin paying dividends and periodic commitment fees.[40]

C. The Fifth Circuit's Proceedings

In October 2016, Patrick Collins, Marcus Liotta, and William Hitchcock sued both the Treasury Department and the FHFA in the Southern District of Texas, alleging that the FHFA exceeded its statutory authority as conservator by entering into the Third Amendment, that the Treasury Department exceeded its statutory authority, and that the Treasury Department acted arbitrarily and capriciously. They also alleged that even apart from its statutory failings, the Third Amendment should be vacated because it "was adopted by FHFA when it was headed by a single person who was not removable by the President at will."[41]

The district court rejected the statutory claims, concluding that the Recovery Act's anti-injunction clause barred the plaintiffs' statutory claims and that the FHFA's structure was constitutional in light of cases like *Humphrey's Executor v. United States*[42] and *Morrison v. Olson*.[43] On appeal, a divided Fifth Circuit panel affirmed as to the statutory claims but concluded that the Recovery Act's "for cause" tenure provision for the FHFA director unconstitutionally limited the president's removal authority.[44] Yet rather than invalidating the Third Amendment, the panel instead "str[uck] the language

---

[40] See *id.* at 1774–75.

[41] Complaint ¶ 189, Collins v. Fed. Hous. Fin. Agency, 254 F. Supp. 3d 841 (S.D. Tex. 2017) (No. H-16-3113).

[42] 295 U.S. 602 (1935) (rejecting separation-of-powers challenge to removal of FTC commissioner).

[43] 487 U.S. 654 (1988) (rejecting separation-of-powers challenge to independent counsel).

[44] See Collins v. Mnuchin, 896 F.3d 640, 646 (5th Cir. 2018); see also *id.* at 674 ("We conclude that the FHFA's structure violates Article II. Congress encased the FHFA in so many layers of insulation—by limiting the President's power to remove and replace the FHFA's leadership, exempting the Agency's funding from the normal appropriations process, and establishing no formal mechanism for the Executive Branch to control the Agency's activities—that the end 'result is a[n] [Agency] that is not accountable to the President.'") (quoting Free Enter. Fund v. Pub. Co. Acct. Oversight Bd., 561 U.S. 477, 495 (2010)).

providing for good-cause removal."[45] Judge Don Willett dissented from the panel's statutory holding—lamenting that the court had left "Fannie Mae and Freddie Mac . . . forever trapped in a zombie-like trance as wards of the state, bled of their profits quarter after quarter in perpetuity"[46]—while Chief Judge Carl Stewart dissented from the panel's constitutional holding.[47]

The Fifth Circuit then reheard the case *en banc*. Writing for a majority, Judge Willett concluded that the *Collins* plaintiffs plausibly stated a statutory claim against the FHFA. In so doing, Willett explained that the Recovery Act's bars on judicial review—the anti-injunction clause and the succession clause—did not bar the court's decision because the plaintiffs plausibly alleged that the FHFA exceeded its authority as conservator and because the Administrative Procedure Act made the plaintiffs' claim direct rather than derivative.[48] Particularly important, the Willett majority also concluded that the FHFA director's "for cause" tenure provision—which the court held applied with equal force to an acting director—is unconstitutional.[49]

Thus, one might have thought that the *Collins* plaintiffs had won. Another majority, however, headed by Judge Catharina Haynes and including some members of the Willett majority and other judges who dissented from the Willett majority, concluded that the remedy for the constitutional violation was to sever the "for cause" provision and otherwise keep the Third Amendment in place.[50] Haynes reasoned that the White House had "full oversight" over the Third Amendment because it had plenary control over the secretary of the Treasury, and that but for the Treasury Department's participation

---

[45] *Id.* at 676.

[46] *Id.* at 679 (Willett, J., dissenting in part).

[47] *Id.* at 678 ("Neither the for-cause removal restriction nor the single-leader feature of the FHFA's structure place the agency outside the Presidents purview in violation of the Constitution or the Supreme Court's removal jurisprudence.") (Stewart, C.J., dissenting in part).

[48] Collins v. Mnuchin, 938 F.3d 553, 569–85 (5th Cir. 2019) (en banc).

[49] See *id.* at 587–91. The Fifth Circuit reached the constitutional claim even though the statutory claim was still pending because, in theory, if the constitutional claim was valid, the court could provide the plaintiffs relief without requiring further factual development.

[50] *Id.* at 595.

in the deal, there would be no Third Amendment at all.[51] Willett (and others) dissented from that remedy; for her part, Haynes (and others) dissented from the court's statutory holding; and still others dissented from the court's constitutional holding, including Judge Gregg Costa, who concluded there was no standing to challenge the Third Amendment because the president could freely remove an acting FHFA director.[52]

D. Seila Law

Both the plaintiffs and the United States petitioned for certiorari—the United States as to the Fifth Circuit's statutory holding, and the plaintiffs as to the constitutional remedy. Those petitions, however, were put on hold pending *Seila Law*—an important separation-of-powers case.

Seila Law concerned the Consumer Financial Protection Bureau (CFPB). In response to the same financial crisis that prompted the Recovery Act, Congress in 2009 created the CFPB as part of the Dodd-Frank Wall Street Reform and Consumer Protection Act. Congress's goal was to create a powerful financial regulator with political independence. Thus, the CFPB—headed by a single person—was tasked with enforcing 19 consumer-protection statutes, including authority to punish "unfair, deceptive, or abusive act[s] or practice[s]," and to regulate "any person that engages in offering or providing a consumer financial product or service."[53] At the same time, the president could only remove the CFPB director for "'inefficiency, neglect of duty, or malfeasance in office,'"[54] a standard that does not allow removal based on policy disagreement alone. That combination of expansive power and insulation from presidential control meant that—with the lone exception of the president—the CFPB director arguably "enjoy[ed] more unilateral authority than any other official in any of the three branches of the U.S. Government."[55]

---

[51] *Id.* at 594.

[52] See *id.* at 621 (Costa, J., dissenting).

[53] 12 U.S.C. §§ 5536(a)(1)(B), 5481(6)(A).

[54] *Id.* § 5491(c)(3).

[55] PHH Corp. v. Consumer Fin. Prot. Bureau, 881 F.3d 75, 166 (D.C. Cir. 2018) (en banc) (Kavanaugh, J., dissenting).

The CFPB's structure prompted years of litigation, including a lengthy *en banc* decision in the D.C. Circuit that upheld the CFPB's constitutionality over then-Judge Brett Kavanaugh's dissent.[56] After Justice Kavanaugh joined the Supreme Court, a 5-4 majority held in *Seila Law* that the CFPB's structure is unconstitutional because its director "wield[ed] significant executive power," yet was free to disagree with the president about how to use that power.[57] Writing separately, Justices Clarence Thomas and Neil Gorsuch urged the Court to overrule *Humphrey's Executor*, one of the most discussed separation-of-powers cases in the Court's history.[58] By contrast, Justice Kagan—joined by Justices Ruth Bader Ginsburg, Breyer, and Sonia Sotomayor—vigorously dissented from the constitutional holding.[59]

E. My Involvement

After deciding *Seila Law*, the Court granted both the United States's petition and the plaintiffs' petition. That's where I came into the picture. Because the Department of Justice chose not to defend the constitutionality of the FHFA's "for cause" provision, the Court appointed me to try to distinguish the FHFA from the CFPB. With the help of friends and a team of talented students, I identified several potential ways to do that, discussed below. Several months later, in one of the most surreal moments of my life, I found myself arguing constitutional issues with the justices on the telephone during the COVID-19 pandemic.

II. The Supreme Court's Three Answers

In *Collins*, the Court—per Justice Samuel Alito—addressed all three issues identified by the Fifth Circuit: The plaintiff's statutory claim, the plaintiff's constitutional claim, and the appropriate

[56] See *id.* at 77 ("We . . . hold that the . . . provision of the Dodd-Frank Wall Street Reform and Consumer Protection Act shielding the Director of the CFPB from removal without cause is consistent with Article II.").

[57] Seila Law, 140 S. Ct. at 2192.

[58] See *id.* at 2211–12 (Thomas, J., concurring in part).

[59] See *id.* at 2225 ("The text of the Constitution allows these common for-cause removal limits. Nothing in it speaks of removal. And it grants Congress authority to organize all the institutions of American governance, provided only that those arrangements allow the President to perform his own constitutionally assigned duties.") (Kagan, J., dissenting in part).

constitutional remedy. The Court unanimously concluded that the plaintiffs' statutory claim was barred by the Recovery Act's anti-injunction clause; seven justices (all but Justices Breyer and Sotomayor) concluded that the FHFA's structure is unconstitutional, although Justice Kagan concurred only in the judgment; and eight justices (all but Justice Gorsuch) rejected the plaintiffs' argument that the constitutional remedy should be automatic *vacatur* of the Third Amendment.

A. The Scope of the FHFA's "Conservatorship" Authority

The scope of the FHFA's conservatorship authority divided the lower courts.[60] Yet the Supreme Court quickly and unanimously rejected the plaintiffs' statutory arguments. Justice Alito focused on the Recovery Act's unusual provision that allows the FHFA, as conservator or receiver, to act "in the best interests of the regulated entity or the Agency."[61] Suffice it to say, this is not how conservatorship normally works. According to the Court, the FHFA "may aim to rehabilitate the regulated entity in a way that, while not in the best interests of the regulated entity, is beneficial to the Agency and, by extension, the public it serves."[62] Thus, the Court determined that it does not matter "whether the FHFA made the best, or even a particularly good, business decision when it adopted the third amendment"; either way, the Recovery Act's broad anti-injunction clause bars judicial review.[63]

The plaintiffs protested that by precluding Fannie and Freddie from rebuilding capital reserves—and thus potentially dooming them to perpetual conservatorships—the Third Amendment was really a step towards liquidation, which should have triggered the FHFA's receivership rather than conservatorship authority. The Court

[60] In addition to Judge Willett's panel dissent in the Fifth Circuit, Judge Janice Rogers Brown dissented at length in the D.C. Circuit. See Perry, 864 F.3d at 635 ("[E]ven in a time of exigency, a nation governed by the rule of law cannot transfer broad and unreviewable power to a government entity to do whatsoever it wishes with the assets of these Companies.") (Brown, J., dissenting).

[61] 12 U.S.C. § 4617(b)(2)(J)(ii).

[62] Collins, 141 S. Ct. at 1776.

[63] *Id.* at 1778; see also *id.* (declining to opine whether the FHFA made a good decision).

disagreed, concluding that Fannie and Freddie continue to function "at full steam in the marketplace," despite the conservatorships.[64] At the same time, however, the Court did not deny that it may be "years" before Fannie and Freddie can "build up enough capital" to act as (more) ordinary companies.[65]

The Court's reliance on the anti-injunction clause was somewhat surprising—the Justice Department's lead argument concerned the Recovery Act's succession provision, which directs that when the FHFA acts as conservator, it succeeds to "all rights, titles, powers, and privileges of the regulated entity, and of any stockholder, officer, or director of such regulated entity with respect to the regulated entity and the assets of the regulated entity."[66] According to the solicitor general's brief to the Court, this provision barred shareholders from bringing a derivative claim regarding injuries allegedly suffered by Fannie and Freddie that only indirectly harmed shareholders. The plaintiffs countered, however, that their challenge to the Third Amendment was a direct claim. Because the Supreme Court rested its statutory decision on the anti-injunction clause, it did not resolve this issue.[67]

Notably, the plaintiffs raised a nondelegation objection to the Court's reading of the anti-injunction clause, observing that if the FHFA truly has discretion whether to conserve assets, the Recovery Act would not contain an "intelligible principle."[68] The Fifth Circuit agreed and relied on this point as a reason to read the Recovery Act narrowly.[69] The Supreme Court, however, did not address this argument—suggesting that it did not see any nondelegation concerns with the FHFA's broad authority.

---

[64] *Id.*

[65] *Id.* at 1774; see also *id.* (explaining that the solicitor general told the Court that this process "is expected to take years").

[66] 12 U.S.C. § 4617(b)(2)(A)(i).

[67] The Court did hold that the succession clause was not an obstacle to the plaintiffs' constitutional claim. See Collins, 141 S. Ct. at 1781 ("Here, the right asserted is not one that is distinctive to shareholders of Fannie Mae and Freddie Mac; it is a right shared by everyone in this country.").

[68] Brief for Petitioners at 43, Collins v. Yellen, 141 S. Ct. 1761 (2021) (Nos. 19-422, 19-563).

[69] Collins v. Mnuchin, 938 F.3d 553, 580 (5th Cir. 2019) (en banc).

B. The Continued Rise of the Unitary Executive

Justice Alito, for the Court, also addressed the constitutional question—and here, he authored arguably the strongest endorsement to date of the idea that the president has the constitutional authority to remove anyone in the executive branch. Even limits on removal recognized last year in *Seila Law*—most notably, that the president's removal power applies to those offices that exercise "significant executive power"— no longer apply.[70] The Court also concluded that an acting FHFA director is removable at will and, in so doing, reiterated that Congress must clearly state its intention if it wants removal restrictions.

This is my part of the story. As court-appointed amicus, my job was to defend the FHFA's structure despite *Seila Law's* holding that the president must be able to remove agency heads. My lead argument focused on the fact that *Collins* concerned an acting director. In their complaint, the plaintiffs challenged the Third Amendment on the ground that it "was adopted by FHFA when it was headed by a single person who was not removable by the President at will."[71] Yet *Acting* Director DeMarco agreed to the Third Amendment, and nothing in the Recovery Act bars the president from firing an acting director for any reason. Even so, the *en banc* Fifth Circuit concluded that the director's removal provision also applies to an acting director because Congress declared that the FHFA is an "independent" agency. According to Judge Willett, allowing the president to remove an acting director at will would "override . . . FHFA's central character."[72] In dissent, Judge Costa objected that the court's conclusion that Congress implicitly gave an acting director protection from removal "is a stark departure from textualist principles."[73]

I put Judge Costa's analysis front and center in my brief. Indeed, I suspected that the Court would unanimously hold that an acting FHFA director is removable at will and that the Court would remand because the Fifth Circuit's constitutional holding rested on an

[70] Seila Law, 140 S. Ct. at 2192.

[71] Complaint ¶ 189, *supra* note 41.

[72] Collins, 938 F.3d at 589. In support, Judge Willett cited *Wiener v. United States*, a 1958 decision in which the Supreme Court inferred removal restrictions for a member of the War Claims Commission. 357 U.S. 349, 353 (1958).

[73] See Collins, 938 F.3d at 621 (Costa, J., dissenting in part).

erroneous premise. I was almost right about the first half of my prediction but very wrong about the second. Eight justices—everyone but Justice Sotomayor[74]—concluded that an acting FHFA director is removable at will.[75] The Court also rejected the suggestion that the term "independent" has a talismanic quality, given that some agencies labeled by Congress as "independent" have no removal restrictions at all, such as the Peace Corps, while other agencies do have removal restrictions but are not labeled "independent," such as the Federal Trade Commission.[76] Rather than remanding, however, the Court concluded that the plaintiffs' "harm is alleged to have continued after the Acting Director was replaced by a succession of confirmed Directors, and it appears that any one of those officers could have renegotiated the companies' dividend formula with Treasury."[77] The Fifth Circuit did not reach this issue, which is debatable. As far as I am aware, nothing suggests that the Treasury Department wanted to renegotiate the Third Amendment in a way beneficial to private shareholders but that the FHFA director stood in the way.

Nonetheless, the Court proceeded to address the constitutional merits of the FHFA director's "for cause" removal restriction. In *Seila Law*, the majority distinguished the FHFA from the CFPB on the ground that the FHFA "regulates primarily Government-sponsored enterprises, not purely private actors," and does "not involve regulatory or enforcement authority remotely comparable to that exercised by the CFPB."[78] Based on those distinctions in *Seila Law*, I offered a number of reasons why *Seila Law* should not control for the FHFA, but none of them succeeded.

First, the Court rejected my argument that an agency must exercise "significant executive power"[79] before the president's removal authority applies, explaining that "the nature and breadth

---

[74] It is unclear why Justice Sotomayor did not join this portion of the majority opinion; she did not explain herself, and Justice Breyer—who joined her dissent—*did* join this portion of the majority opinion.

[75] See Collins, 141 S. Ct. at 1782.

[76] See *id.* at 1782–83.

[77] *Id.* at 1781.

[78] Seila Law, 140 S. Ct. at 2202.

[79] *Id.* at 2192.

of an agency's authority is not dispositive in determining whether Congress may limit the President's power to remove its head."[80] This expansion of *Seila Law* prompted Justice Kagan to concur only in the judgment; although she believed that *Seila Law* required her to rule against the FHFA's structure, she did so because, in her view, the FHFA *does* exercise "significant executive power."[81] Yet she observed that "[w]ithout even mentioning *Seila Law*'s 'significant executive power' framing, the majority announces that, actually, 'the constitutionality of removal restrictions' does not 'hinge[]' on 'the nature and breadth of an agency's authority.'"[82] Justice Sotomayor (joined by Justice Breyer) dissented on this point, concluding that *Seila Law*'s observation that the FHFA's authority is nothing like the CFPB's means that the FHFA's structure should be upheld.[83]

Second, the Court disagreed that the FHFA's conservatorship function materially distinguishes it from the CFPB. After all, the Court explained, the FHFA does not always act as a conservator—it's a regulator, too.[84] And even as a conservator, "its authority stems from a special statute, not the laws that generally govern conservators and receivers," and "'[i]nterpreting a law enacted by Congress to implement the legislative mandate is the very essence of 'execution' of the law.'"[85] Furthermore, the Court reiterated that FHFA is not a typical conservator, explaining that "[i]t can subordinate the best

---

[80] Collins, 141 S. Ct. at 1784.

[81] See *id.* at 1800 ("[The FHFA] wields 'significant executive power,' much as the agency in *Seila Law* did.") (Kagan, J., concurring in part and concurring in the judgment in part).

[82] *Id.* at 1801. Justice Kagan also disputed the majority's "political theory." *Id.* Yet on this point, the majority simply repeated the reasoning from *Seila Law*.

[83] *Id.* at 1803 ("[T]he Court today holds that the FHFA and CFPB are comparable after all, and that any differences between the two are irrelevant to the constitutional separation of powers. That reasoning cannot be squared with this Court's precedents, least of all last Term's *Seila Law*.") (Sotomayor, J., concurring in part and dissenting in part).

[84] *Id.* at 1785.

[85] *Id.* (quoting Bowsher v. Synar, 478 U.S. 714, 733 (1986)). This line from *Bowsher* is puzzling. The Supreme Court also "interpret[s] a law enacted by Congress to implement the legislative mandate." See, e.g., 28 U.S.C. § 2072 ("The Supreme Court shall have the power to prescribe general rules of practice and procedure and rules of evidence . . . [but shall not prescribe rules that] abridge, enlarge or modify any substantive right."). Yet no one says that involves *executive* power.

interests of the company to its own best interests" and its "decisions are protected from judicial review."[86]

Third, the Court disagreed that it is significant that the FHFA's authority is limited to a handful of government-sponsored enterprises (GSEs). In *Seila Law*, the Court observed that the FHFA does not regulate "purely private actors."[87] In *Collins*, however, the Court stressed that "the President's removal power serves important purposes regardless of whether the agency in question affects ordinary Americans by directly regulating them or by taking actions that have a profound but indirect effect on their lives."[88] The Court therefore implicitly rejected a distinction between public and private rights. The CFPB regulates private citizens and can prevent them from engaging in types of commerce that people have been doing for centuries. By contrast, no one must invest in Fannie and Freddie. In either situation, however, *Collins* holds that the president can remove the agency's head.

Fourth, the Court agreed with my argument that a "for cause" provision is much less restrictive on the president than other removal provisions and that the president can fire the FHFA director for not obeying his commands.[89] Even so read, however, the Court still concluded that the Recovery Act's "for cause" provision is unconstitutional because it prevents the White House from having "confidence" in the official.[90]

Last, the Court declined to say how far its decision goes. Instead, the majority opinion includes this footnote, which should not give much comfort to those who support removal restrictions:

> Amicus warns that if the Court holds that the Recovery Act's removal restriction violates the Constitution, the decision will "call into question many other aspects of the Federal Government."

---

[86] Collins, 141 S. Ct. at 1785. Why the fact that the FHFA's decisions as conservator "are protected from judicial review" makes its authority "clearly . . . executive," *id.* at 1786, is a mystery. Members of Congress are also protected from judicial review, see U.S. Const. art. I, § 6, cl. 1, yet do not exercise executive power.

[87] Seila Law, 140 S. Ct. at 2202.

[88] Collins, 141 S. Ct. at 1786.

[89] See *id.* ("We acknowledge that the Recovery Act's 'for cause' restriction appears to give the President more removal authority than other removal provisions reviewed by this Court.").

[90] *Id.* at 1786–87.

> Amicus points to the Social Security Administration, the Office of Special Counsel, the Comptroller, "multi-member agencies for which the chair is nominated by the President and confirmed by the Senate to a fixed term," and the Civil Service. None of these agencies is before us, and we do not comment on the constitutionality of any removal restriction that applies to their officers.[91]

The fact that the Court was unwilling to offer a limiting principle suggests that there may not be one. Granted, because of *stare decisis*, the Court may not be willing to overrule *Humphrey's Executor*—a case that the *Collins* majority essentially ignored, but that Justice Sotomayor's dissent repeatedly cited. Still, it seems safe to say that the Court will not extend the principle from *Humphrey's Executor* any further.

C. Constitutional Remedies

Finally, the Court addressed remedies. The *Collins* plaintiffs had opened their reply brief by warning that "[n]o one would bring a separation of powers lawsuit if the only remedy were a judicial declaration years after the fact that the Constitution was violated."[92] Yet it is possible that such a declaration will be the only remedy in *Collins*.

The *Collins* majority—here, everyone but Justice Gorsuch—rejected the argument that the Third Amendment should be set aside, reasoning that the Third Amendment was approved by Acting Director DeMarco, whom the president could remove at will.[93] The Court instead focused on whether subsequent actions taken by confirmed directors "to *implement* the third amendment during their tenures" merit a retrospective remedy.[94] Whereas cases like *Lucia v. SEC*[95] concern "a Government actor's exercise of power that the actor did not lawfully possess" (in *Lucia*, the administrative law judge's

---

[91] *Id.* at 1787 n.21.

[92] Reply Brief of Petitioners at 1, Collins v. Mnuchin, 141 S. Ct. 1761 (2021) (Nos. 19-422, 19-563).

[93] Collins, 141 S. Ct. at 1787.

[94] *Id.*

[95] 138 S. Ct. 2044 (2018) (holding that an administrative law judge was an officer of the United States for purposes of the Appointments Clause).

appointment violated the Appointments Clause), *Collins* holds that an unconstitutional restriction on removal does not automatically mean that an official "lack[s] the authority to carry out the functions of the office."[96] Thus, unless plaintiffs can demonstrate that the unconstitutional removal restriction caused them harm in the real world, a court should not provide a retrospective remedy. For example, if a court—after concluding there was no cause for dismissal—barred the president from removing the official, or if the president were to say that he would have removed the official but for the removal restriction, and then that official harmed a plaintiff, *vacatur* may be warranted.[97]

After announcing this standard, the Court remanded for the Fifth Circuit to determine whether in a world without the removal restriction, a president may "have replaced one of the confirmed Directors who supervised the implementation of the third amendment, or a confirmed Director might have altered his behavior in a way that would have benefited the shareholders."[98] It may be difficult for the *Collins* plaintiffs to make such a showing, though this issue is worth watching going forward. As Justice Kagan explained—and as the Haynes's majority opinion in the Fifth Circuit concluded—the president always could supervise the Third Amendment's implementation because the agreement was between the FHFA and the Treasury Department.[99] Justice Thomas—who wrote separately to address his view of the proper way to conceptualize the remedial question[100]— similarly observed that he "seriously doubt[s] that the shareholders

---

[96] Collins, 141 S. Ct. at 1788.

[97] *Id.* at 1788–89.

[98] *Id.* at 1789.

[99] *Id.* at 1802 ("[Judge Haynes's] reasoning seems sufficient to answer the question the Court kicks back, and nothing prevents the Fifth Circuit from reiterating its analysis. So I join the Court's opinion on the understanding that this litigation could speedily come to a close.") (Kagan, J., concurring in part).

[100] In particular, Justice Thomas emphasized that it is necessary to identify an unlawful action, not just a statute that conflicts with the Constitution. He observed that a misunderstanding of the law—including that a removal restriction is valid when, in reality, it conflicts with the Constitution—might render agency action arbitrary and capricious under the Administrative Procedure Act, but he did not pursue the issue because it was not raised. See *id.* at 1791–95 (Thomas, J., concurring).

can demonstrate that any relevant action by an FHFA Director violated the Constitution."[101]

Justice Gorsuch alone did not join the Court's remedial holding. He faulted his colleagues for distinguishing appointment from removal—a distinction that, in his view, defies "230 years of history"[102] and ignores the fact that removal may be more important than appointment in terms of the president's ability "to shape his administration and respond to the electoral will that propelled him to office."[103] Further, he warned that this distinction cannot be administered: "[H]ow are judges and lawyers supposed to construct the counterfactual history" required to determine what the President would have done without the removal restriction?[104] He thus would have invalidated the Third Amendment and left it to Congress to decide what should happen next.

III. What *Collins* Tells Us about the Administrative State

Collins is essentially three cases in one, each of which teaches a different lesson. Accordingly, to better understand the administrative state, it is helpful to view those three lessons together.

A. Agency Power Is Ubiquitous

The Court's curt and unanimous rejection of the *Collins* plaintiffs' statutory arguments demonstrates just how ubiquitous agency power is when it comes to the housing sector. The Court did not bat an eye at the idea that Congress allowed the FHFA as conservator to take over massive companies and to make decisions based on the FHFA's own interests. To be sure, the situation here is complicated by the fact that Fannie and Freddie have never been purely private. Those who invested in Fannie and Freddie before the housing

---

[101] *Id.* at 1795.

[102] *Id.* (Gorsuch, J., dissenting in part).

[103] *Id.* at 1796.

[104] *Id.* at 1798; see also *id.* at 1799 ("The Court declines to tangle with any of these questions. It's hard not to wonder whether that's because it intends for this speculative enterprise to go nowhere. Rather than intrude on often-privileged executive deliberations, the Court may calculate that the lower courts on remand in this suit will simply refuse retroactive relief.").

collapse presumably received returns beyond what they would have earned if the federal government had not been in the background. In fact, because "[m]ost purchasers of the GSEs' debt securities believe that this debt is implicitly backed by the U.S. government," the companies may have received an "implicit government subsidy" of "between $122 and $182 billion."[105]

Collins, however, confirms that the federal government now acts as more than just an implicit backstop. Under the FHFA's conservatorship authority, Fannie and Freddie can themselves be seen in a sense as de facto federal instruments. Because the FHFA is not required to act "in the best interest of" Fannie and Freddie but instead can act in ways "beneficial to the Agency and, by extension, the public it serves," the FHFA (largely) can do what it thinks best.[106] The Court's holding finds support in the Recovery Act's text, although the question is closer than the lopsided 9-0 vote may suggest. *Collins*, however, demonstrates that the Court is not going to stretch statutory law to constrain the FHFA's authority.

B. *The Continued Rise of Presidentialism*

The constitutional holding in *Collins* further confirms that this is the age of presidentialism. For decades, the White House has increasingly directed how agencies use their authority. As Professor Elena Kagan explained, for example, once it became clear that Congress would not enact the legislation that President Bill Clinton wanted, "Clinton and his White House staff turned to the bureaucracy to achieve, to the extent it could, the full panoply of his domestic policy goals."[107] This approach has been repeated by presidents of both parties, who seek to use "'an executive style of governing

---

[105] Wayne Passmore, The GSE Implicit Subsidy and the Value of Government Ambiguity, 33 Real Est. Econ. 465, 465–66 (2005); see also Jacobs v. Fed. Hous. Fin. Agency, 908 F.3d 884, 887 (3d Cir. 2018) ("Although Fannie and Freddie are privately owned and publicly traded companies, the public has long viewed their securities as implicitly backed by the federal government's credit. That perceived government guarantee has helped them to borrow money and to buy mortgages more cheaply than they otherwise could have.").

[106] Collins, 141 S. Ct. at 1776.

[107] Elena Kagan, Presidential Administration, 114 Harv. L. Rev. 2245, 2248 (2001).

that aims to sidestep Congress more often.'"[108] Cases like *Collins* and *Seila Law* make it easier for the White House rather than agency heads to direct policy.

The Court's strong embrace of the unitary-executive theory may strike some readers as strange because it enables more aggressive uses of agency power, which seems in tension with the view that the Court is concerned about regulatory overreach.[109] Here, for example, hours after the Court decided *Collins*, President Joe Biden fired Director Calabria and replaced him with an acting director who presumably will use the FHFA's authority more aggressively.[110] Relying on *Collins*, Biden also fired the head of the Social Security Administration several weeks later.[111] Yet the principle cuts both ways. After all, *Collins* also increases political accountability for how the FHFA exercises its authority and going forward may lead to less aggressive regulation in future administrations. The key point is that presidential elections are now even more important—an observation that may become more significant still if the Court takes *Collins* and *Seila Law* further and revisits *Humphrey's Executor*.

C. Narrow Remedies

Finally, *Collins* says something important about remedies. After years of litigation, the plaintiffs may end up recovering nothing. True, the president has more control over the executive branch, but that does not directly help the plaintiffs and may discourage

[108] Aaron L. Nielson, Deconstruction (Not Destruction), 150(3) Dædalus 143, 147 (2021) (quoting Scott Wilson, "Obama's Rough 2013 Prompts a New Blueprint," Wash. Post., Jan. 25, 2014).

[109] See, e.g., Christopher J. Walker, Attacking Auer & Chevron Deference: A Literature Review, 16 Geo. J.L. & Pub. Pol'y 103 (2018) (explaining the Court's wariness with deference). This point should not be overstated. The unitary-executive theory does not define the *breadth* of executive power but instead only identifies who wields *whatever* power exists. Accordingly, the Court may restrict agency-empowering tools like deference, for example, while still concluding that whatever power agencies have should be subject to the president's control.

[110] See, e.g., Katy O'Donnell, "Biden Removes FHFA Director after Supreme Court Ruling," Politico, Jun. 23, 2021, https://politi.co/3ly3N9p.

[111] See, e.g., Andrew Saul, "Biden Politicizes the Social Security Administration," Wall St. J., July 18, 2021 (op-ed from dismissed SSA Commissioner); Aaron L. Nielson, The Logic of Collins v. Yellen, Yale J. on Reg.: Notice & Comment (Jul. 9, 2021), https://bit.ly/3ly3Ull.

future litigation.[112] Justice Kagan made this point, arguing that although the SSA may be "next on the chopping block" because it too "has a single head with for-cause removal protection," most individual SSA decisions "would not need to be undone."[113] Thus, in her view, *Collins's* remedial analysis should "prevent[] theories of formal presidential control from stymying the President's real-world ability to carry out his agenda."[114]

That prediction may prove accurate for suits by private parties seeking retrospective relief. That said, it is unclear whether *Collins* will prevent a party subject to ongoing agency action from seeking forward-looking injunctive relief. The majority did not resolve this issue, so we'll have to wait and see.[115] Regardless, however, *Collins* certainly limits the circumstances in which meaningful relief is available.

Conclusion

Collins is difficult to describe because, at bottom, it is three cases in one. We learn from the Court's statutory holding just how deeply embedded federal authority is in today's economy. We learn from the Court's constitutional holding that the White House can direct how that power is used. And we learn from the Court's remedial holding that the justices are not looking to tear everything down. When those three holdings are put together, what does it all mean? Well, it's probably best to avoid simple narratives about the Court's views on administrative law.

---

[112] The Court's standing analysis is noteworthy—a court can declare that a removal restriction is invalid, even though doing so may not benefit the plaintiff. In *Collins*, the Court was aware of this potential oddity, but concluded that "for purposes of traceability, the relevant inquiry is whether the plaintiffs' injury can be traced to 'allegedly unlawful conduct' of the defendant, not to the provision of law that is challenged." 141 S. Ct. at 1779 (quoting Allen v. Wright, 468 U.S. 737, 751 (1984)).

[113] Collins, 141 S. Ct. at 1802 (Kagan, J., concurring in part and concurring in the judgment in part).

[114] *Id.*

[115] See *id.* at 1780 (focusing only on "retrospective relief").

Cedar Point: Lockean Property and the Search for a Lost Liberalism

Sam Spiegelman* and Gregory C. Sisk**

Introduction

This October term, in *Cedar Point Nursery v. Hassid*, the Supreme Court heard a case with the potential to (finally) move regulatory-takings doctrine in a coherent direction. Two strawberry growers argued that a decades-old California law permitting union activists to trespass on facilities like theirs and disrupt production for up to three hours per day for almost *one-third* of the year was a taking of their "right to exclude" others.[1] The Court agreed, ruling in a 6-3 split that despite its durational and conceptual limits, the law constituted a per se taking of that right.[2]

The Takings Clause protects against the "tak[ing]" of "property" for "public use" unless the government provides "just compensation."[3] Unfortunately, the clause at times poses more questions than it answers. What qualifies as property? Where is the line between public use and private transfer? How do we calculate just compensation when the purpose of an eminent-domain action—the construction of an interstate highway, for example—may increase a property's value tenfold? While outright confiscations create questions too, these are far less complicated than those that takings-like

* Legal associate, Cato Institute, Robert A. Levy Center for Constitutional Studies. J.D., University of Virginia School of Law; B.A., University of Michigan.

** Pio Cardinal Laghi Distinguished Chair in Law, professor and co-director of the Terrence J. Murphy Institute for Catholic Thought, Law and Public Policy, University of St. Thomas School of Law. J.D., University of Washington School of Law; B.A., Montana State University.

[1] Cedar Point Nursery v. Hassid, 141 S. Ct. 2063, 2072 (2021).

[2] *Id.*

[3] U.S. Const. amend. V.

regulations produce. In an era of ubiquitous governmental involvement in the private sector, any meaningful right to possess property would be eviscerated if all regulations of property were regarded as exceptions to the Takings Clause.

Property regulations—directives that restrict specified uses (or non-uses) but do not confiscate anything tangible—have grown more varied over time. Between ratification of the Constitution and the dawn of the 20th century, the United States, alongside other Western countries, underwent substantial industrial and urban growth. Railroads replaced rivers and canals as the primary channels of commerce, while new (and more dangerous) manufacturing and agricultural technologies, alongside novel financing and employment arrangements, transformed the social and cultural landscapes, pressing political forces into greater oversight of an increasingly complex private sector.[4] Despite these changes, many American courts during this period continued to distinguish ordinary regulations from proto-regulatory takings based on whether a challenged state action was public-harm-preventing (regulatory) or public-benefit-conferring (takings).[5] This development tracked the classical liberal understanding of the state's police power as permissible only to the extent of protecting the public from private externalities, and not as a means of redistributing private wealth.[6]

That approach emerged in English common law and crossed the Atlantic through the writings of eminent philosopher John Locke. Long before John Stuart Mill formulated his famous "harm principle,"[7] the

[4] See generally G. Edward White, 2 Law in American History: From Reconstruction Through the 1920s (2016).

[5] Scott M. Reznick, Empiricism and the Principle of Conditions in the Evolution of the Police Power: A Model for Definitional Scrutiny, 1978 Wash. U. L.Q. 1, 2–3 (1978) [hereinafter Evolution of the Police Power] ("During its early manifestations and throughout the nineteenth century, definitional scrutiny incorporated a substantive component derived from the common law of nuisance—the maxim *sic utere tuo ut alienum non laedas*. Under this maxim, courts limited the states' use of the police power to the prospective prevention of harms (negative externalities) to the community and its inhabitants.").

[6] See Richard A. Epstein, The Classical Liberal Constitution: The Uncertain Quest for Limited Government 353 (2014) ("The proper ends under the police power are those of the private law of nuisance, no more and no less. The means are regulations that fit well with the chosen ends, by being neither overbroad nor underinclusive. . . . It is instead necessary to make sure that differential systems of enforcement do not result in the hidden wealth transfers that are prohibited under the Takings Clause.").

[7] See generally John Stuart Mill, On Liberty (1859).

Lockean conception of property—as inviolable save for a superseding public *need*—permeated American legal culture from before the Founding. It was thus that the bulk of judicially recognized police powers during the first half of American history operated under the banner of *sic utere tuo alienum non laedas*—roughly, using one's property in such a manner as not to injure that of another.[8] *In re Jacobs* is a perfect example of this principle in action. There the New York Court of Appeals (the state's highest court) struck down a law that prohibited commercial home cigar-rolling, an activity that produces no harmful effects. The court reasoned that laws

> must have some relation to [the ends of protecting public health and securing the public comfort and safety]. Under the mere guise of police regulations, personal rights and private property cannot be arbitrarily invaded, and the determination of the legislature is not final or conclusive. If it passes an act ostensibly for the public health, and thereby destroys or takes away the property of a citizen, or interferes with his personal liberty, then it is for the courts to scrutinize the act and see whether it really relates to and is convenient and appropriate to promote the public health. It matters not that the legislature . . . declare that it is intended for the improvement of the public health.[9]

The Supreme Court affirmed this approach in the latter half of the 19th century.[10] But then, on the heels of an emergent legal realism that began to question tried-and-true elements of Anglo-American law, Justice Oliver Wendell Holmes in 1922 unhelpfully declared in *Pennsylvania Coal v. Mahon* that a regulation could "go[] too far" and become a taking, even if the owner retained control; though he hinted that the state had substantial latitude before that bridge

---

[8] See Reznick, Evolution of the Police Power, *supra* note 5, at 10 ("*Sic utere* is the fountainhead maxim from which both the common law of nuisance and the police power arose. As originally applied, *sic utere* 'operated to protect real property from what the courts thought were injuries resulting from the use of another of his real property.' That is, the courts used *sic utere* principles to resolve cost spillover conflicts between the existing uses of neighboring landowners. This relationship in tort between property owners originally caused the maxim and the emerging police power to be defined in terms of the prevention of harms.").

[9] In re Jacobs, 98 N.Y. 98, 110 (1885).

[10] See Pumpelly v. Green Bay Co., 80 U.S. 166 (1871); Mugler v. Kansas, 123 U.S. 623 (1887).

was crossed.[11] However significant Holmes's proviso, it offered no practical instruction on *when* it should be applied, besides implying that it would be on rare occasion. Since *Pennsylvania Coal*, the precedents have grown only more complicated. Regulatory-takings doctrine seems doomed to incoherence.[12] *Cedar Point*, despite its flaws, might yet mark the beginning of the end of this muddle.[13]

To help secure that end, this article will proceed as follows: Part I will briefly discuss the evolution of regulations and takings, from Norman England to 20th-century America. It will place special emphasis on how American courts tended toward the classical liberal distinction between harmful and innocent property uses that had long guided the public-private relationship, and that fit neatly within Locke's seminal "social contract" theory. It will then discuss the early-20th-century turn from the classical liberal approach to the legal realist one, and the regressive impact this had on property rights. Part II will discuss *Cedar Point* in greater detail and in the context of the broader takings muddle, focusing on the ruling's pros and cons. Pros include its strong Lockean language, which borrows heavily from precedent, and its self-saving preservation of mere governmental trespasses and invasions falling under the "background limitations" of state law. Cons include its failure (perhaps due to institutional timidity more than doctrinal disagreement) to escape the shadow of the confounding *Penn Central Transportation Co. v. New York City* decision.[14] *Cedar Point* did not recognize that the "background limitations" of state law denote, primarily (though not universally), those public actions that through longstanding practice and judicial distillation prove to be public-harm-preventing rather than public-benefit-conferring. While *Cedar Point* did exempt the "right to exclude" from *Penn Central's* notoriously pro-government multifactor "balancing" test, it stopped short of replacing *Penn Central* altogether. Combine this with its failure to use "background limitations" to return takings doctrine to the classical liberal approach that predominated before

[11] Pa. Coal, 260 U.S. 393, 415 (1922).

[12] See generally Mark Fenster, The Stubborn Incoherence of Regulatory Takings, 28 Stan. Envtl. L.J. 525 (2009).

[13] See generally Carol M. Rose, Mahon Reconstructed: Why the Takings Issue Is Still a Muddle, 57 S. Cal. L. Rev. 561 (1984).

[14] Penn Cent. Transp. Co. v. New York City, 438 U.S. 104 (1978).

the doctrinal changes of the 20th century, and *Cedar Point* has left much to finish. Part III will discuss how *Cedar Point* barely impacts *Robins v. Pruneyard Shopping Center*, in which the Court endorsed a far-too-generous police power—one that is incompatible with the classical liberal approach. Ideally, this article will be but an early contribution to a prodigious scholarship that nudges the post–*Cedar Point* Court to return takings jurisprudence to its classical liberal roots.

II. A Brief History of Regulations and Takings

A. The Evolution of "Property" from 1066 to 1791

The bundle of property rights familiar to an Anglo-American audience did not begin with the Constitution but with the solidification of an English common law after the Norman Conquest in 1066. Under William the Conqueror, lands were divided among reliable feudal lords who in turn controlled the division of those lands among vassals. Possession would escheat to the lord upon a felony conviction and was relinquished upon death.[15] This version of feudalism "implied land *holding* rather than land *owning*, save in the case of those few great lords and princes who had no superior, and therefore owned their lands, both those they retained and those which they granted out, by absolute right."[16] And so while there was ownership, such was a *privilege* reserved to the king's deputies, and not a *prerogative*, or a right; landlords' claims, in turn, depended on their "perform[ing] the required duties," including military service.[17] "Private transactions in land . . . were insecure until [the sovereign] had confirmed them, and he had a right to be consulted before a man of any position commended himself to a new lord."[18]

For his successors, William the Conqueror's discretion crystallized into habit. "[B]y the year 1100, it became settled that the king and his tenants-in-chief would automatically accept the eldest son of a deceased feudal lord as his replacement," though still "upon the

---

[15] Theodore F. T. Plucknett, A Concise History of the Common Law 508 (5th ed. 1956).

[16] *Id.* (emphasis added).

[17] Bruce L. Benson, The Evolution of Eminent Domain: A Remedy for Market Failure or an Effort to Limit Government Power and Government Failure?, 12 Indep. Rev. 423, 424 (2008).

[18] F. M. Stenton, Anglo-Saxon England 616 (1943).

payment of a sum of money."[19] Though "feudal lands became increasingly alienable,"[20] it was not until 1215—when King John's aggrieved barons compelled him to sign Magna Carta—that ownership became a *right* in the modern sense: free from sovereign intervention without due procedural safeguards.[21] But Magna Carta did not make ownership inviolable. By the 16th century, the conception of property as a bundle of rights still did not prevent the English sovereign from seizing land or chattel; though it now required the taken property serve a public purpose rather than enriching the sovereign.[22]

The shift from state-crafted to natural-right property found its most eloquent articulation in the writings of John Locke. The 17th-century philosopher's views on property made their way to the American continent, where they had a profound influence.[23] Locke argued that, whether it emerged from scripture or "natural reason," things are made property through labor: "[L]abour, in the beginning, gave a right of property, wherever any one was pleased to employ it, upon what was common. . . ."[24] As such, ownership implies a *vested interest*. "Hence it is a mistake," Locke declared,

> to think that the supreme or legislative power of any commonwealth can do what it will, and dispose of the estates of the subject arbitrarily, or take any part of them at pleasure. . . . For a man's property is not at all secure, though there be good and equitable laws to set the bounds of it between him and his fellow-subjects, if he who commands those subjects have power to take from any private man what part he pleases of his property, and use and dispose of it as he thinks good.[25]

---

[19] Steven J. Eagle, Regulatory Takings 48 (3d ed. 2005) (citing Plucknett, *supra* note 15, at 13).

[20] *Id.*

[21] Magna Carta art. 39 ("No free man shall be seized or imprisoned, or stripped of his rights *or possessions* . . . except by the lawful judgments of his equals or by the law of the land.") (cleaned up) (emphasis added).

[22] William B. Stoebuck, A General Theory of Eminent Domain, 47 Wash. L. Rev. 553, 561 (1972).

[23] James W. Ely, Jr., The Sacredness of Private Property: State Constitutional Law and the Protection of Economic Rights Before the Civil War, 9 N.Y.U. J.L. & Liberty 620, 621–22 (2015) [hereinafter The Sacredness of Private Property].

[24] John Locke, The Rational Basis of Private Property, in Francis William Coker, Readings in Political Philosophy 537, 546 (1938).

[25] *Id.* at 563–64.

While Locke's contributions to the 13 colonies' intellectual development is undisputed,[26] there are at least two contrasting views of its extent on pre-Revolution law and jurisprudence, particularly on eminent domain and land-use regulation. Professor William Michael Treanor for majoritarian republicanism and Professor James Ely for classical liberalism draw two far different conclusions from what is quite a mixed historical record.

In Treanor's view, there is little consistency in the property law of colonial America. The colonists did *everything*, from making owners of taken property whole to providing them no compensation at all.[27] Treanor notes that "there was no consensus among the framers that majoritarian decisionmakers"—legislatures as opposed to common-law courts—"could not be trusted to determine the appropriate level of protection for property interests."[28] From this he concludes that "[m]any of the framers believed that government could . . . limit individuals' free use of their property," with the "balancing [of] societal needs against individual property rights . . . left in large part to the political process."[29]

Ely, on the other hand, sees a country enamored with the idea of ownership—and believing strongly in its protection: "To the colonial mind, property and liberty were inseparable, as evidenced by the colonists' willingness to break with England when the mother country seemingly threatened property ownership."[30] Ely continues, contra Treanor, that "[a] review of the historical evidence amply demonstrates the wide acceptance of the compensation principle by colonial Americans from the time of initial settlement."[31] This "wide

[26] Jeffrey M. Gaba, John Locke and the Meaning of the Takings Clause, 72 Mo. L. Rev. 525, 526 (2007).

[27] William Michael Treanor, The Origins and Original Significance of the Just Compensation Clause of the Fifth Amendment, 94 Yale L.J. 694, 695–98 (1985) [hereinafter Original Significance]; James W. Ely, Jr., "That Due Satisfaction May Be Made": The Fifth Amendment and the Origins of the Compensation Principle, 36 Am. J. Legal Hist. 1, 4–13 (1992) [hereinafter Origins of the Compensation Principle].

[28] William Michael Treanor, The Original Understanding of the Takings Clause and the Political Process, 95 Colum. L. Rev. 782, 818 (1995) [hereinafter Original Understanding].

[29] *Id.* at 783.

[30] James W. Ely, Jr., The Guardian of Every Other Right: A Constitutional History of Property Rights 13, 16–17 (3d ed. 2008).

[31] *Id.*

acceptance" indicates a general recognition that private property rights trumped public benefits, and so the public ought to compensate owners for disruptions. Who is correct—Treanor or Ely—depends upon the question asked. If the question is how the colonists *practiced* eminent domain, then Treanor's position might win by a whisker. But if the question is what the colonists *wanted* the public-private relationship to look like, then Ely's portrait, of a nascent people striving to reach the Lockean ideal, is the clear favorite:

> Revolutionary Americans shared a pervasive concern with the security of property rights against governmental interference. Far from representing an innovation, the [T]akings [C]lause simply codified a long-standing constitutional principle upholding the right of compensation for property taken for public use.[32]

The Framers recognized the dangers that freewheeling republicanism posed to property rights.[33] But they understood that majoritarian needs could supersede individual lives, liberties, and estates.[34] Requiring compensation offered a mostly[35] novel compromise—allowing public needs to be fulfilled, with payment ensuring that the intrusions made into the private realm were truly necessary.[36] The Takings Clause was thus one of the means to protect American constitutionalism and its Lockean foundations from the vagaries of civic republicanism.[37] In this sense, the clause suggests a *fusion*

[32] Ely, Origins of the Compensation Principle, *supra* note 27, at 4.

[33] The Federalist No. 10 (James Madison), in The Essential Debate on the Constitution: Federalist and Antifederalist Speeches and Writings 125 (Robert J. Allison & Bernard Bailyn eds., 2018) (1787) ("Hence it is, that such Democracies have ever been spectacles of turbulence and contention; have ever been found incompatible with personal security, or the rights of property.").

[34] Treanor, Original Significance, *supra* note 27, at 699–701 (discussing the balancing of public and private rights, including the insight that "a major strand of republican thought held that the state could abridge the property right in order to promote common interests").

[35] See Vt. Const. (1777), ch. I, art. II ("[W]henever any particular man's property is taken for the use of the public, the owner ought to receive an equivalent in money."); Mass. Const. (1780), part I, art. X ("[W]henever the public exigency requires that the property of any individual should be appropriated to public uses, he shall receive a reasonable compensation therefor.").

[36] Treanor, Original Understanding, *supra* note 28, at 825–34.

[37] Ely, Origins of the Compensation Principle, *supra* note 27, at 2.

of Treanor's and Ely's renditions of the American conception of the public-private relationship. It shows a striving toward Locke's vision, which within it included doing what was necessary to *protect* the public (not to benefit it). While the Takings Clause and the Framers' discussion around property rights offers clues, it would take the course of the 19th century for the jurisprudential results of this fusion to fully emerge.

B. *After Ratification: Strengthening, then Weakening, the Classical Liberal Approach to Regulations*

In the century after ratification, immense social and technological changes led to more complex regulations.[38] Yet despite these changes, many courts still used the harm/benefit distinction to differentiate noncompensable police-power actions from regulations that Justice Holmes would in the next century deride as "go[ing] too far."[39] While some courts acquiesced to legislative uber-expansions of the police power, the tendency was to defer only on the assumption that the challenged regulations were preventing private parties from harming the public, instead of redistributing wealth.[40] Some of the most prominent legal scholars, both before and after the Civil War, shared this view.[41]

Notable among the state-court decisions, and paradigmatic of the harm/benefit doctrine of the time, was *Commonwealth v. Alger*,[42]

---

[38] For a general discussion of the doctrinal complications these changes created, see Errol E. Meidinger, Public Uses of Eminent Domain: History and Policy, 11 Envtl. L. 1 (1980).

[39] Pa. Coal, 260 U.S. at 415.

[40] The best example of this is the mid-19th-century treatment of prohibition-driven bans on alcohol production, a treatment that mirrors the Supreme Court's in *Mugler*. While some courts "endorsed the view that alcoholic beverages could be defined as a nuisance by the legislature, and were thus subject to forfeiture without compensation," other "jurists and commentators expressed concern that the prohibition laws amount to an uncompensated destruction of property." James W. Ely, Jr., Are Eminent Domain and Confiscation Vehicles for Wealth Redistribution? A Skeptical View, 6 Brigham-Kanner Prop. Rts. Conf. J. 211, 228 (2017).

[41] See, e.g., Joseph Postell, The Misunderstood Thomas Cooley: Regulation and Natural Rights from the Founding to the ICC, 18 Geo. J.L. & Pub. Pol'y 75, 85 (2020) (discussing post–Civil War legal giant Thomas Cooley's view that "the purpose of the police power . . . is to ensure that citizens are able to enjoy their rights more fully by preventing injuries by one citizen upon the rights of another").

[42] 61 Mass. 53 (1851).

which Justice Lemuel Shaw of the Massachusetts Supreme Judicial Court authored in 1851. While some believe *Alger* to have articulated an almost limitless police power,[43] this is a common misconception. At the time, Shaw's opinion was correctly regarded "as a textbook restatement of the *scope* of the police power"[44]—one reflective of the general trend. As Shaw put it:

> Rights of property, like all other social and conventional rights, are subject to such reasonable limitations in their enjoyment *as shall prevent them from being injurious*, and to such reasonable restraints and regulations established by law as the legislature, under the governing and controlling power vested in them by the constitution, may think necessary and expedient.[45]

Professor Ely concludes from the *Alger*-esque class of rulings that "[u]nder the police power, state officials enjoyed broad authority to prevent an individual from using property in a manner detrimental to public order or safety."[46] Still, acknowledging that "new methods are needed to deal with new problems"[47] does not mean that modern exercises of the police power are no longer limited to the "overruling necessity" of protecting the public from *harm*.[48]

Professor William Novak argued that the concept of *salus populi suprema lex* ("the welfare of the people is the supreme law"—to some

---

[43] See generally, e.g., Kevin P. Arlyck, What Commonwealth v. Alger Cannot Tell Us about Regulatory Takings, 82 N.Y.U. L. Rev. 1746 (2007).

[44] Eric R. Claeys, Takings, Regulations, and Natural Property Rights, 88 Cornell L. Rev. 1549, 1599 (2003) [hereinafter Natural Property Rights] (emphasis added).

[45] Alger, 61 Mass. at 85 (emphasis added).

[46] Ely, Guardian of Every Other Right, *supra* note 30, at 61 ("To modern eyes, most of these economic regulations appear modest. Far from comprehensive, they were typically piecemeal and directed against specific problems. Although many of these controls did impose costs on businesses or property owners, their objective was to safeguard the general public interest. Antebellum regulations were not generally designed to transfer wealth from one portion of the population to another, and thus they produced little redistributive effect.").

[47] Robert Kratovil & Frank J. Harrison, Jr., Eminent Domain—Policy and Concept, 42 Cal. L. Rev. 596, 609 (1954).

[48] Scott M. Reznick, Land Use Regulation and the Concept of Takings in Nineteenth Century America, 40 U. Chi. L. Rev. 854, 860 (1973) [hereinafter Takings in Nineteenth Century America] (citing Sir Edward Coke's Mouse's Case, 12 Coke 63 (c. 1600), as an early use of what we now call the "police power").

meaning the public's benefit) was as influential to 19th-century regulatory rulings as *sic utere* (harm-preventing) was.[49] He concluded that the public welfare theme convinced many courts to expand traditional police powers to cover civic-republican (read: benefit-conferring) aims rather than just anti-harm purposes. Novak's argument is incorrect, both in view of courts' longstanding depiction of such cases in harm-preventing versus benefit-conferring terms, and in their general tendency to view regulations as protective enterprises, not as means for the majority to secure windfalls at the expense of the private realm.[50] Projecting a 20th-century understanding of "regulation," Novak overlooks that most of the categories of 19th-century regulation he cites were designed to prevent physical, moral, or economic injury.[51] They were not, as some modern utilitarians view them, understood as means for resource redistribution.[52] Nineteenth-century regulations of property were much easier to stomach because, at bottom, they sought (even if they did not always succeed) to advance a public-private relationship that gave individuals free

---

[49] See generally William J. Novak, The People's Welfare: Law & Regulation in Nineteenth-Century America (1996) [hereinafter The People's Welfare]. See Claeys, Natural Property Rights, *supra* note 44, at 1562 ("The examples Novak gives," to justify *salus populi* regulations, "closely track a conception of the police powers similar to" those relating to "health and safety laws, public morals controls, and laws regulating the use of public commons.").

[50] Danaya C. Wright, A Requiem for Regulatory Takings: Reclaiming Eminent Domain for Constitutional Property Claims, 49 Envtl. L. 307, 336 (2019) [hereinafter A Requiem for Regulatory Takings] ("[C]ourts had relied for nearly two centuries on the distinction between harm-prevention and benefit-conferr[al]" to distinguish between permissible and impermissible interferences with property.); Glenn H. Reynolds & David B. Kopel, The Evolving Police Power: Some Observations for a New Century, 27 Hastings Const. L.Q. 511, 519 (2000) ("The limitations on the police power . . . cast considerable doubt on the correctness of the conventional-wisdom interpretation of *salus populi*. . . . [T]he notion that the government can rob A for B's benefit, and conclusively pronounce the robbery to be 'for the public good' and therefore beyond judicial review is not the dominant view of nineteenth-century legal thought.").

[51] See generally Novak, The People's Welfare, *supra* note 49.

[52] Claeys, Natural Property Rights, *supra* note 44, at 1621–22. Claeys argued that *Pennsylvania Coal's* focus on "values" of property over property as a value in itself exemplified the utilitarian view: "Property consists of 'value,' and this value is subject to 'implied limitation[s]' to make room for government action. The government is presumed to have the power to pursue any object that has public value for society at large. To secure public value, the government may increase, diminish, transfer, or even abolish private uses of property." *Id.* at 1622 (quoting Pa. Coal, 260 U.S. at 413).

use of what they owned up to the point at which such uses began to interfere with others' freedoms. As Professor Eric Claeys puts it:

> If one could ask nineteenth-century jurists to reduce the natural-right approach to a slogan, they might say that the object of all property regulation is to secure to every owner an "equal share of freedom of action" over her own property. On this understanding, every owner is entitled to some zone of non-interference in which to use her possessions industriously, productively, and consistent with the health, safety, property, and moral needs of her neighbors.[53]

Regarding public health and safety measures, Claeys explains that 19th-century courts "were obliged to uphold state laws as 'regulations' whenever legislatures could demonstrate a 'real' or 'actual' nuisance"—that is, a harm—but "in the few cases where legislatures passed laws that could not credibly be called 'health and safety' regulations," those laws were swiftly struck down.[54] The same goes for public morals, such as prohibitions on the production or consumption of spirts. Here "courts . . . were inclined to presume that prohibition prevented alcoholism and its concomitant social problems."[55] Professor Scott Reznick summarized these courts' general understanding of the scope of states' "chartered" police powers—that is, "delegations of legislative power to deal with problems of local concern":[56]

> Exercise of this power was implicitly limited to conditions within the traditional, narrow common law nuisance categories. Generally, police regulations dealt with such matters as fire limits, the storage of gunpowder, and placement of cemeteries, and perpetuated a narrow application of the principle that no man should use his property so as to injure that of his neighbor—*sic utere tuo alienum non laedas*.[57]

In 1871, in *Pumpelly v. Green Bay Co.*, the Supreme Court reasoned "[i]t would be a very curious and unsatisfactory result" that "if the government refrains from the absolute conversion of real

---

[53] *Id.* at 1556.
[54] *Id.* at 1579.
[55] *Id.* at 1582.
[56] Reznick, Takings in Nineteenth Century America, *supra* note 48, at 862.
[57] *Id.*

property . . . it is not taken for the public use, . . . in the narrow-
est sense of that word."⁵⁸ Regulatory takings now had the Court's
theoretical endorsement. In 1887, in *Mugler v. Kansas,* the Court
elaborated that a state statute restricting production of liquor on
premises was a valid exercise of the state's police power, rather
than a taking, because it did "not disturb the owner in the control
or use of his property for *lawful* purposes, nor restrict his right to
dispose of it."⁵⁹ And what does lawful mean? The statute was not
targeting an innocent use without compensation, but "merely prohibited a use of property that the legislature had determined 'to
be *injurious* to the health, morals, or safety of the community.'"⁶⁰
In a word, it means *harmful.* "In contrast to the government action
in *Pumpelly,* which took 'unoffending property . . . away from an
innocent owner,' the Kansas statute only abated a nuisance. As a
result, the [law in *Mugler*] was a noncompensable police power regulation, while the physical invasion in *Pumpelly* was a compensable
taking."⁶¹

Pumpelly and *Mugler* should have put to rest the notion that the
regulation/confiscation distinction was somehow dispositive in takings analysis. And for a time it did. The natural-rights/harm-prevention
mode of analyzing the public-private relationship culminated in
Lochner v. New York, decided at the turn of the 20th century. *Lochner* held
that freedom to contract was a substantive right immune from unjusti-
fied social-management-style regulatory efforts (as opposed to harm-
preventing regulations, which under *sic utere* were still permitted).⁶²
But soon, a new generation of legal-realist thinkers and jurists derided
Lochner's supposed anti-regulationism. Courts increasingly blurred
the lines between *sic utere* (i.e., harm-preventing) and *solus populi* (i.e.,
benefit-conferring) regulations.⁶³ Justice Holmes exemplified this drift

---

⁵⁸ 80 U.S. at 177–78.

⁵⁹ 123 U.S. at 669 (emphasis added).

⁶⁰ Glynn S. Lunney, Jr., Responsibility, Causation, and the Harm-Benefit Line in Takings Jurisprudence, 6 Fordham Envtl. L.J. 433, 442 (1995) (quoting Mugler, 123 U.S. at
668).

⁶¹ *Id.*

⁶² Lochner v. New York, 198 U.S. 45 (1905).

⁶³ Claeys, Natural Property Rights, *supra* note 44, at 1605 ("The nineteenth-century
constitutional order did not recede during the New Deal in the face of an external
political assault; it collapsed from 50 years' worth of internal dry rot.").

in *Pennsylvania Coal* when he offered that "[g]overnment hardly could go on if to some extent *values* incident to property could not be diminished without paying for every such change in the general law."[64] *Penn Central*, decided five decades after *Pennsylvania Coal*, represents the apex (or nadir) of the takings muddle.

II. *Cedar Point* and the Classical Liberal Approach to Regulations and Takings

A. Existing Regulatory Takings Doctrine Is a Mess

The Supreme Court's modern reluctance to impose bright-line rules has created confusion about the definition and scope of regulatory takings. Claims brought in the last four decades have for the most part been analyzed under the *Penn Central* test.[65] That test holds that whether a regulation effects a taking depends upon an ad hoc, factual inquiry into the economic impact on, and the distinct investment-backed expectations of, the owner, as well as the character of the government action (i.e., its purpose and the plan to achieve it).[66] In *Loretto v. Teleprompter Manhattan CATV Corp.* and *Lucas v. South Carolina Coastal Council*, the Court carved out per se exceptions for permanent physical occupations and regulations resulting in total value loss, respectively.[67] Once the plaintiff proves one or the other (or both), the regulation is a taking, regardless of the government's purpose, and there is no need for *Penn Central* balancing.

But even these seemingly bright lines become dimmer at second or third glance. When is an occupation permanent? What if the occupation is a boon to the owner rather than a burden? What if the government proves that a parcel retains .0001 percent of its preregulation value? In seeking to rescue takings jurisprudence from its post–*Penn Central* tangle, *Loretto* and *Lucas* moved a few steps forward, but also a couple back. The Court acknowledged that certain property rights are fundamental, their disruption requiring overwhelming justification. But it declined to limit these justifications, primarily, to those

---

[64] Pa. Coal, 260 U.S. at 413.

[65] Cedar Point, 141 S. Ct. at 2082 (Breyer, J., dissenting).

[66] Penn Cent., 438 U.S. at 124.

[67] Loretto v. Teleprompter Manhattan CATV Corp., 458 U.S. 419 (1982); Lucas v. S.C. Coastal Council, 505 U.S. 1003 (1992).

that prevented public harms.[68] Harm-prevention, though not the *only* basis for restricting the essential elements of ownership,[69] was the most pervasive one for centuries. Its "perpetual appeal" is the result of its "beguiling simplicity."[70]

But since *Pennsylvania Coal*, and especially after *Penn Central*, the Supreme Court has rejected this "beguiling simplicity." For instance, in *Miller v. Schoene*, decided six years after *Pennsylvania Coal*, the Court held:

> [T]he state does not exceed its constitutional powers by deciding upon the destruction of one class of property in order to save another which, *in the judgment of the legislature*, is of greater value to the public. . . . [W]here the public interest is involved preferment of that interest over the property interest of the individual, to the extent even of its destruction, is one of the distinguishing characteristics of every exercise of the police power which affects property.[71]

Then, in *Berman v. Parker*, the Court declared that "when the legislature has spoken, the public interest has been declared in terms well-nigh conclusive."[72] By the time the Court decided *Penn Central* in 1978, it had all but abandoned the classical liberal approach to judging regulations.

In *Lucas*, Justice Antonin Scalia did not seek a return to the harm/benefit distinction. Indeed, he outright rejected it. Yet the decades of *Berman*-esque deference to legislators' view of what was harmful, or even merely in the "public interest" to stop or prevent, troubled the

---

[68] See Lucas, 505 U.S. at 1026 ("When it is understood that . . . the distinction between regulation that 'prevents harmful use' and that which 'confers benefits' is difficult, if not impossible, to discern on an objective, value free basis[,] it becomes self-evident that noxious-use logic cannot serve as a touchstone to distinguish regulatory 'takings'. . .").

[69] Penn Cent., 438 U.S. at 145 (Rehnquist, J., dissenting) ("The nuisance exception to the taking guarantee is not coterminous with the police power itself."). See, e.g., John D. Echeverria, The Public Trust Doctrine as a Background Principles Defense in Takings Litigation, 45 U.C. Davis L. Rev. 931, 933 (2012) (describing the "public trust" doctrine—under which some lands are held under implied public ownership even if a private party holds title—e.g., a stretch of beachfront—to "certainly qualif[y] as a background principle that defeats a takings claim").

[70] Joseph L. Sax, Takings and the Police Power, 74 Yale L.J. 36, 48 (1964).

[71] Miller v. Schoene, 276 U.S. 272, 279–80 (1928) (emphasis added).

[72] Berman v. Parker, 348 U.S. 26, 32 (1954).

late justice. To limit it, Scalia invented a new phrase—"restrictions that background principles of the [s]tate's law of property and nuisance already place upon land ownership"[73]—in other words, restrictions on one's use of property that have stood the test of time. "[A] law or decree" does "no more than duplicate the result that could have been achieved in the courts—by adjacent landowners . . . under the [s]tate's law of private nuisance, or by the [s]tate under its complementary power to abate nuisances that affect the public generally. . . ."[74] Scalia's slight detour did not help clear the takings muddle. Instead, it added an extra layer of confusion, with some courts bending "background principles" to include those state actions that in their normative view should *become* longstanding practice. This is not a logical stretch if the court presumes, not without some doctrinal merit, that background principles have to start somewhere.

In 1980, in *Agins v. Tiburon*, the Court ruled that a regulation of property is only permissible if it "substantially advance[s] legitimate state interests."[75] In 2005, in *Lingle v. Chevron*, it reversed itself.[76] In 1987, in *First English Evangelical Lutheran Church v. County of Los Angeles*, it held that temporary takings "deny a landowner all use of his property" and thus "are not different in kind from permanent takings, for which the Constitution clearly requires compensation."[77] But then in 2002, in *Tahoe-Sierra Preservation Council v. Tahoe Regional Planning Agency*, the Court ruled, on a slightly different set of facts, that "a permanent deprivation of the owner's use of the entire area is a taking . . . whereas a temporary restriction that merely causes a diminution in value is not."[78] These and other doctrinal zigzags have sowed confusion in the lower courts, alongside *Penn Central*'s muddle and *Lucas*'s "background principles" miasma.[79] Returning

---

[73] Lucas, 505 U.S. at 1029.

[74] *Id.*

[75] Agins v. Tiburon, 447 U.S. 255, 260 (1980).

[76] Lingle v. Chevron U.S.A. Inc., 544 U.S. 528, 531 (2005).

[77] First English Evangelical Lutheran Church v. Cty. of Los Angeles, 482 U.S. 304, 318 (1987).

[78] Tahoe-Sierra Pres. Council v. Tahoe Reg'l Planning Agency, 535 U.S. 302, 332 (2002).

[79] See generally Michael C. Blumm & Lucus Ritchie, Lucas's Unlikely Legacy: The Rise of Background Principles as Categorical Takings Defenses, 29 Harv. Envtl. L. Rev. 321 (2005) (surveying lower-court interpretations of "background principles" to uphold a number of regulations that Scalia likely would not have expected).

to the classical liberal approach—distinguishing regulations as takings based on a harm-versus-benefit analysis—could solve a great many of the takings puzzles that the 20th-century departure has produced.

B. Cedar Point's *Strong Lockean Approach*

Especially in light of the Takings Clause's recent poor treatment, there is much in Chief Justice John Roberts's opinion in *Cedar Point* for property-rights advocates to celebrate. Not only does it designate a crucial element of ownership for per se takings analysis, it is steeped in Lockean views of property and the public-private relationship, and even references William Blackstone's "exuberant" definition of ownership.[80] Roberts cited with approval a number of previous rulings that emphasized the special position property occupies in the Anglo-American legal tradition. He began with "the Founders['] recogni[tion] that the protection of private property is indispensable to the promotion of individual freedom," quoting with approval John Adams's adage that "[p]roperty must be secured, or liberty cannot exist."[81] Roberts agreed with the Court's proposition, in *Murr v. Wisconsin*, that "protection of property rights is 'necessary to preserve freedom' and 'empowers persons to shape and to plan their own destiny in a world where governments are always eager to do so for them.'"[82]

But the majority was not prepared to extend Adams's view of property—as the essence of liberty—to its logical conclusion, whereby any non-harm-preventing regulation that causes even a *partial* (rather than a *Lucas*-esque *total*) value loss works a total taking *of that interfered-with portion*, regardless of whether the regulation effects a physical interference. If this were not so, then *Murr*'s recitation that property "'empowers persons to shape and to plan their own destiny'" would be meaningless in practice. Under *Lucas*, so long as even .0001 percent of a property's value remains, regulations could impose

---

[80] Cedar Point, 141 S. Ct. at 2072 (citing 2 William Blackstone, Commentaries on the Laws of England 2 (1766) [hereinafter Commentaries] (describing ownership as "that sole and despotic dominion which one man claims and exercises over the external things of the world, in total exclusion of the right of any other individual in the universe").

[81] *Id.* at 2071. (citing Discourses on Davila, in 6 Works of John Adams 280 (C. Adams ed. 1851)).

[82] *Id.* (quoting Murr v. Wisconsin, 137 S. Ct. 1933, 1943 (2017)).

burdens functionally equivalent to confiscation. If the majority had applied *Lucas*, as some might have expected, the union-trespass law would almost certainly have been upheld because it does not result in a total-value loss. Thankfully, the Court instead used a remarkably expansive view of *Loretto*'s physical-invasion test, finding that "the duration of an appropriation—just like the size of an appropriation . . . bears only on the amount of compensation."[83] The majority read that case, alongside its progenitors and progeny, to have carved out a special status for the "right to exclude" stick in the proverbial "bundle of rights." It found that *any* abrogation of the right to exclude is subject to a per se analysis, which involves a far more exacting standard than *Penn Central*'s "factual inquiries." As Roberts put it:

> The upshot of [*Loretto*, its predecessors, and successors] is that government-authorized invasions of property—whether by plane, boat, cable, or beachcomber—are physical takings requiring just compensation.[84]

The "invasions" Roberts referred to are quite varied in form and scope. Some, like *Loretto*, involved permanent and continuous invasions. Those that did not, like *United States v. Causby*, together teach that the rules in *Loretto* and *Lucas* do not comprise the sole exemptions to the *Penn Central* test—even though until *Cedar Point*, the Court had refrained from expressly extending the per se category beyond them. *Causby*, decided three decades before *Penn Central*, involved the federal government's recurrent flight of "military aircraft low over the Causby farm, grazing the treetops and terrorizing the poultry."[85] This constituted "a servitude . . . imposed upon the land," even though it was not continuous and did not "take" any portion of the land itself.[86] In *Kaiser Aetna v. United States*, decided the term after *Penn Central*, the Court held that the right to exclude "'falls within [the] category of interests that the [g]overnment cannot take without compensation.'"[87] As in *Causby*, the taking in *Kaiser Aetna* was of a "servitude," this time "navigational," stemming from the

---

[83] *Id.* at 2074.

[84] *Id.*

[85] *Id.* at 2073 (summarizing United States v. Causby, 328 U.S. 256 (1946)).

[86] *Id.*

[87] *Id.* (quoting Kaiser Aetna v. United States, 444 U.S. 164, 180 (1979)).

government's assertion that a marina "could not exclude the public" because the dredging of the pond that had opened the marina's waters to "a nearby bay and the ocean" rendered them "navigable" and therefore open as a matter of public right.[88]

Before *Loretto* or *Lucas*, *Causby* and *Kaiser Aetna* went the furthest in establishing a baseline perimeter for owners' exercise of their "sole and despotic dominion," as Blackstone had put it.[89] And in both cases, that line was not drawn at "continuous" invasion; the invasion in each was or would have been intermittent. The flights in *Causby* were frequent, but not unending. And while in *Kaiser Aetna* the public would have been allowed to cross the marina's waters, it would not have been permitted to dock. Thus as long as there is no superseding public need to interfere with private property—the essence of the classical liberal approach—the form an invasion takes is irrelevant. Whether a confiscation of an owner's fee simple estate or a mere "taking" of access (i.e., a gross easement), what is taken in *Causby*, *Kaiser Aetna*, and *Cedar Point* is a "right to exclude"—which Professor Thomas Merrill called the *"sine qua non"* of ownership.[90]

The majority's use of these and similar cases is telling. It reveals something of a return to Locke's "life, liberty, and estates." According to James Madison, the latter—synonymic of property—"embraces every thing to which a man may attach a value and have a right; and *which leave to every one else the like advantage."*[91] After *Penn Central*, the protections afforded to the sticks in the bundle of rights seemed to have become negotiable. As long as one or more remained, then the others could be scrambled with relative ease. *Cedar Point*, in finally affording the "right to exclude" per se protection, moves the needle in favor of the Lockean over the positivistic view. And though it did not do so through the classical liberal approach of distinguishing public-harm-preventing from public-benefit-conferring regulations (the latter properly viewed as takings), it has at least not closed this door.

---

[88] *Id.* (summarizing Kaiser Aetna, 444 U.S. 164).

[89] Blackstone, Commentaries, *supra* note 80, at 2.

[90] Thomas Merrill, Property and the Right to Exclude, 77 Neb. L. Rev. 730, 730 (1998) (emphasis original).

[91] James Madison, Property, Nat'l Gazette (Mar. 29, 1792), in James Madison: Writings 515 (Jack N. Rakove ed. 1999) (emphasis original).

C. Cedar Point's *Weak Classical Liberalism*

Despite the majority's strong commitment to the Lockean view of property, its attachment to the classical liberal view of takings versus regulations is anything but. Chief Justice Roberts backed the majority into something of a corner in responding to Justice Stephen Breyer's suggestion, in dissent, that the holding threatens "large numbers of ordinary regulations in a host of different fields that, for a variety of purposes, permit temporary entry onto (or an 'invasion of') a property owner's land."[92] Roberts used "background limitations" or "restrictions"—akin to *Lucas*'s "background principles"—to preserve some essential state interferences of private property rights. Roberts failed to recognize that these traditions, like "standard health and safety inspections,"[93] are not carveouts that empower state interference where it would otherwise constitute a taking. Instead, these are better described as examples of the broad (but not boundless) universe of police-power actions that Anglo-American courts since at least Edward Coke's time have recognized as necessary for the public's protection from harm to its safety, health, welfare, or morals.[94] This is the approach the Supreme Court endorsed in *Pumpelly* and *Mugler*, before the era of high deference began in the first quarter of the 20th century. Scalia's focus in *Lucas* on background principles maintained the post–*Pennsylvania Coal* break from the classical liberal approach—necessary if *Penn Central*'s balancing test was to be preserved. Scalia apparently was not prepared to abandon it:

> The transition from our early focus on control of "noxious" uses to our contemporary understanding of the broad realm within which government may regulate without compensation was an easy one, since the distinction between "harm-preventing" and "benefit-conferring" regulation is often in the eye of the beholder.[95]

Never mind that courts were able to make this distinction for centuries, producing common-law rules and standards that Englishmen

---

[92] Cedar Point, 141 S. Ct. at 2087 (Breyer, J., dissenting).

[93] *Id.* at 2080 (majority op.).

[94] Mouse's Case, 12 Coke 63 (c. 1600).

[95] Lucas, 505 U.S. at 1024.

everywhere—from the Americas to Australia—sought to emulate.[96] Roberts continues the modern error of distinguishing "background principles" or "limitations" from the common-law core of anti-harm justifications to which most of them belong:

> Unlike a mere trespass, the regulation grants a formal entitlement to physically invade the growers' land. Unlike a law enforcement search, *no traditional background principle of property law* requires the growers to admit union organizers onto their premises. And unlike standard health and safety inspections, *the access regulation is not germane to* any benefit provided to agricultural employers[97] or *any risk posed to the public.*[98]

It is difficult to see how the italicized phrases are distinguishable: "[B]ackground principles" refer, in almost all cases, to public-harm-preventing measures. As discussed in Part I, the historical treatment of regulations, as in line with the Lockean (though perhaps not Blackstonean) view of property—acceptable *only* insofar as they are harm-preventing—strongly suggests that the two are indistinguishable. Roberts alludes to this logic, noting, "[w]ith regard to the complexities of modern society, we think they only reinforce the importance of safeguarding the basic property rights that help preserve individual liberty, as the Founders explained."[99] But "safeguarding" must mean more than protecting a select few property rights (e.g., the right to exclude) from *Penn Central's* ad hoc-ery, mustn't it?

Professor Lynda Oswald made a persuasive case for placing the harm/benefit distinction at the center of regulatory-takings analysis, as had been the Court-endorsed practice before the rise of legal realism.[100] Oswald argued that the harm principle "provides a rough-and-ready analytical tool for resolving most takings questions."[101] Oswald's approach leans on Professor Robert

[96] Wright, A Requiem for Regulatory Takings, *supra* note 50, at 336.

[97] That is, it is not comparable to a safety inspection directly related to a commercial enterprise's maintenance of its license from the relevant state board.

[98] Cedar Point, 141 S. Ct. at 2080 (emphasis added).

[99] *Id.* at 2078.

[100] Lynda J. Oswald, The Role of the "Harm/Benefit" and "Average Reciprocity of Advantage" Rules in a Comprehensive Takings Analysis, 50 Vand. L. Rev. 1447 (1997).

[101] *Id.* at 1481.

Ellickson's insight that "[e]valuative terms like good, bad, beneficial, and harmful are easily used because people have remarkably consistent perceptions of normal conditions and thus can agree in characterizing deviations."[102] These "perceptions of normal conditions" sound an awful lot like the process by which communities develop behavioral norms and ordering, perhaps originating outside the law,[103] that through gradual, widespread acceptance evolve into the "background principles" of state law. As the Court sought to clarify in *Palazzolo v. Rhode Island*, "[o]ur description [in *Lucas*] of the concept [of background principles] is explained in terms of those common, shared understandings of permissible limitations derived from a State's legal tradition."[104]

And what are more permissible limitations than those that prevent harm to others? After all, protecting members' lives, liberties, and estates from the violence and vagaries of others is the very purpose for which individuals enter into the social contract to leave the Hobbesian state of nature and adopt a Lockean rule of law.[105] Roberts could have easily grounded *Cedar Point*'s reasoning in the harm/benefit distinction at the core of the classical liberal formulation of the public-private relationship. His failure to do so means that *Cedar Point* is far from the end of the story. The return to a full "safeguarding [of] the basic property rights that help preserve individual liberty" will require a more comprehensive ruling than one that depends upon an unknown set of exempted "background limitations" to commend it.

---

[102] Robert C. Ellickson, Alternatives to Zoning: Covenants, Nuisance Rules, and Fines as Land Use Controls, 40 U. Chi. L. Rev. 681, 729 (1973).

[103] See Robert C. Ellickson, Order without Law: How Neighbors Settle Disputes 1 (1991) (formulating a theory "to predict the content of informal norms, to expose the processes through which norms are generated, and to demarcate the domain of human activity that falls within—and beyond—the shadow of the law").

[104] Palazzolo v. Rhode Island, 533 U.S. 606, 630 (2001).

[105] Vanhorne's Lessee v. Dorrance, 2 U.S. 304, 310 (1795) ("The preservation of property . . . is a primary object of the social compact.").

III. *Pruneyard*, *Cedar Point*, and the Dangers of a Generous Police Power

There remains one more problem with *Cedar Point* that will require correction: its "read[y] distinguish[ment]" of *Robins v. Pruneyard Shopping Center*.[106] In that case, the California Supreme Court granted political activists a state constitutional right to solicit petition signatures in the common area of a privately owned shopping center.[107] The U.S. Supreme Court affirmed the California Supreme Court and rejected the argument that this state-sanctioned trespass constituted a taking.[108] For four decades, *Pruneyard* has stuck out like a sore thumb in takings jurisprudence and highlights the dangers of overbroad police-power justifications, which *Cedar Point* failed, expressly, to condemn.

Today, "the constitutional legitimacy of state-sanctioned trespass in the name of speech into a private shopping center has become increasingly difficult to sustain."[109] Explicit adoption of the classical liberal approach would deal a fatal blow to the *Pruneyard* detour, and the whataboutist cover it could provide critics of *Cedar Point* and its future progeny. In each of the Court's post–*Pruneyard* rulings upholding private property rights against state overreach, the Court has distinguished *Pruneyard* rather than revisit it. In *Nollan v. California Coastal Commission*, for example, the Court observed in a footnote that the shopping center owner in *Pruneyard* "had already opened his property to the general public."[110] *Cedar Point* made the same distinction: "*Pruneyard* was open to the public, welcoming 25,000 patrons a day."[111] *Cedar Point* apparently has carved out a different takings rule for "how a business generally open to the public

---

[106] 592 P.2d 341 (Cal. 1979), aff'd, Robins v. Pruneyard Shopping Ctr., 447 U.S. 74 (1980).

[107] *Id.* at 341–42, 347–48.

[108] Pruneyard, 447 U.S. 74.

[109] Gregory C. Sisk, Returning to the Pruneyard: The Unconstitutionality of State-Sanctioned Trespass in the Name of Speech, 32 Harv. J.L. & Pub. Pol'y 389, 393 (2009) [hereinafter Returning to the Pruneyard].

[110] Nollan v. Cal. Coastal Comm'n, 483 U.S. 825, 832 n.1 (1987).

[111] Cedar Point, 141 S. Ct. at 2076.

may treat individuals on the premises."[112] But factual differences like this would—and should—become meaningless when using the harm-preventing-versus-benefit-conferring distinction.

The right to trespass at a private shopping center to engage in political or other social expression falls on the public benefit side of the harm/benefit distinction. Nothing about a claimed state right for the public to enter a business for a political or social cause could be framed as abating a public harm *created* by that business. Indeed, the argument for access to prevent a public harm was stronger in *Cedar Point*, where the labor organizers sought to empower the property owners' own agricultural workers to organize for better pay and working conditions. But in *Cedar Point*, the unions had ample means of accessing and communicating with employees without trammeling the employers' rights,[113] as did the trespassers in *Pruneyard* in exercising their political views.

When a state invents a new right,[114] it is attempting to extend a benefit to the public. The state is free to expand the venues for political or social speech, whether that be requiring shopping malls to accommodate political gatherings or requiring homeowners to permit political protests on their front lawns. But the state may do so only if it compensates the burdened private parties. The just compensation principle "prevents the public from loading upon one individual more than his just share of the burdens of government."[115] Germane to *Pruneyard* and *Cedar Point*, "[a] state court declaration of a permanent easement on private property for third-party political speech is the exercise of eminent domain for which the state must pay."[116]

Put simply, when the state seeks to expand the places open to would-be trespassers to exercise their constitutional rights, as in *Pruneyard*

[112] *Id.* at 2077.

[113] *Id.* at 2080–81 (Kavanaugh, J., concurring).

[114] For an extended critique of the California Supreme Court's decision in *Pruneyard* as a policy decision untethered to the constitutional text, history, context, and developed legal reasoning, together with a careful analysis of the typical state liberty-of-speech clause and an examination of original historical sources on state constitutional drafting, see generally Gregory C. Sisk, Uprooting the Pruneyard, 38 Rutgers L.J. 1145 (2008).

[115] Monongahela Navigation Co. v. United States, 148 U.S. 321, 325 (1893).

[116] Sisk, Returning to the Pruneyard, *supra* note 109, at 414.

and *Cedar Point*, or to confer some other public benefit, it risks creating new police powers that are far from justified under the common law, background limitations of state law, or a version of the harm principle that tracks the classical liberal approach to regulations. As long as it remains good law, *Pruneyard* could at any point be used to limit *Cedar Point* to fact-patterns identical to its own. Therefore, any post–*Cedar Point* opinion worth its weight must overturn *Pruneyard* and any other precedents keeping open the door to ostensible exercises of the state's police power that, on closer inspection, are takings.

Conclusion

Cedar Point moves regulatory takings in a direction that accords far better with the history of Anglo-American property law than does *Pennsylvania Coal*—at least as that ruling has been understood in the post–*Penn Central* cases. Instead of balancing competing values, it focuses on the claimed right or interest interfered with, asking whether the ancient common law or evolving "background principles" of state law removes that claimed right or interest from the ambit of ownership, almost invariably because its use does or will produce a public harm.

Still, *Cedar Point* omitted some crucial pieces from the latter-day takings puzzle. What is the content, scope, and elasticity of the "exceptions" to the otherwise absolute character of ownership? *Cedar Point* recites a few examples of when the state may appear to take the right to exclude but is in fact exercising its legitimate police powers. But the majority does not discover in those the thread of the classical liberal approach to regulations, by which the question is whether or not the regulation stops or prevents a harm, not whether it physically deprives an owner of their property. Its distinguishing of *Pruneyard* demonstrates this oversight. Despite arguments that it is too subjective to be workable,[117] the harm/benefit distinction controlled much of the public-private relationship for centuries[118] and aligns far better with Locke's social contract—with

[117] See, e.g., John S. Harbison, Constitutional Jurisprudence in the Eyes of the Beholder: Preventing Harms and Providing Benefits in American Takings Law, 45 Drake L. Rev. 51, 55–57 (1997).

[118] See generally Daniel R. Coquillette, Mosses from an Old Manse: Another Look at Some Historic Property Cases about the Environment, 64 Cornell L. Rev. 761 (1979) (surveying the early English treatment of indirect *injuria* to property).

its ultimate end of preserving individual life, liberty, and estates—
than does the modern positivistic style. The survival of the Lockean view of property could well depend upon whether the Court
has in it the want and wherewithal to move its takings jurisprudence back in a classical liberal direction.

Police as Community Caretakers: *Caniglia v. Strom*

*Christopher Slobogin**

What *is* the proper role of the police? That question has been at the forefront of debates about policing for quite some time, but especially in the past year. One answer, spurred by countless news stories about black people killed by law enforcement officers, is that the power of the police should be reduced to the bare minimum, with some in the Defund the Police movement calling for outright abolition of local police departments.[1] Toward the other end of the spectrum is the notion that the role of the police in modern society is and must be capacious. Police should function as "community caretakers," because "a police officer—over and above his weighty responsibilities for enforcing the criminal law—must act as a master of all emergencies, who is 'expected to aid those in distress, combat actual hazards, prevent potential hazards from materializing, and provide an infinite variety of services to preserve and protect community safety.'"[2]

That commodious language comes from the First Circuit Court of Appeals in the case of *Caniglia v. Strom*.[3] The court relied on the "special role of the police in our society" to hold that police may enter the home of a suicidal individual to seize his guns, when he is not present, in the absence of consent, and without a warrant.[4] As a matter

---

*Milton Underwood Professor of Law, Vanderbilt University.

[1]See Asha Ransby Sporn, "Campaigns to Defund Police Have Seen Major Wins—and They're Not Stopping," Truthout, May 25, 2021, https://bit.ly/3j7DAx2 (describing Defund movement and quoting one leader stating that "[i]t would be a failure to . . . try to gently bend policing to make it friendlier. We are proposing something that has not been done yet, which is to dismantle the policing and prison systems.").

[2]Caniglia v. Strom, 953 F.3d 112, 124 (1st Cir. 2020).

[3]*Id.*

[4]*Id.*

of formal legal doctrine, the First Circuit purported to be applying what courts have long called the "community caretaker exception" to the Fourth Amendment rule that warrants are usually required to carry out a search of a home and the seizure of items in it.

The First Circuit's holding did not stand for long, however. In an opinion written by Justice Clarence Thomas, a unanimous Supreme Court (not a common phenomenon these days) reversed the First Circuit, taking only four pages to do so (also unusual in recent years).[5] While recognizing that one of its earlier cases, *Cady v. Dombrowski*,[6] had alluded to a community caretaker exception to the warrant requirement when police are engaged in something other than crime-fighting, Justice Thomas noted that *Cady* had involved a warrantless search of a disabled car and had "repeatedly stressed" that there is "a constitutional difference" between houses and cars.[7] Rebuking the First Circuit for extrapolating from *Cady* "a freestanding community-caretaking exception that applies to both cars and homes," the Court admonished, "What is reasonable for vehicles is different from what is reasonable for homes."[8] It concluded that Edward Caniglia's lawsuit for damages against the city of Cranston, Rhode Island, and its police department was viable.

There were three concurring opinions, each agreeing with the result but carefully laying out what the majority opinion did *not* prohibit. Chief Justice John Roberts, joined by Justice Stephen Breyer, provided a reminder that earlier decisions had allowed warrantless home entries to prevent violence, restore order, and render first aid.[9] Similarly, Justice Samuel Alito suggested that the Fourth Amendment would not be violated by warrantless entries of residences when an occupant presents an imminent risk of suicide or is otherwise in "urgent need of medical attention and cannot summon help."[10] Finally, Justice Brett Kavanaugh reviewed the cases in which the Court had allowed warrantless entries to fight a fire and investigate its cause, to prevent imminent destruction of evidence, to

[5]Caniglia v. Strom, 141 S. Ct. 1596 (2021).

[6]413 U.S. 433 (1973).

[7]Caniglia, 141 S. Ct. at 1599 (quoting Cady, 413 U.S. at 439).

[8]*Id.* at 1600.

[9]*Id.* at 1600 (Roberts, C.J., concurring).

[10]*Id.* at 1601 (Alito, J., concurring).

engage in hot pursuit of a fleeing felon, and to handle a number of other "exigent circumstances."[11]

The seizure of guns in *Caniglia* fit none of these scenarios because it was not necessary to prevent imminent harm to anyone or to respond to some other emergency. The day before the seizure Edward Caniglia had placed a handgun on his dining room table and asked his wife to "shoot me and get it over with." Rather than obliging, his wife left the home and spent the night at a hotel. The next morning, when she was unable to reach her husband by phone, she called the police and accompanied them to the house, where Edward was sitting on the porch. After some dialogue, the police convinced Edward to go to the hospital for a psychiatric evaluation and arranged for an ambulance to take him there. Only then, after Edward was gone, did the police go in to get the guns.

So the *Caniglia* opinion, on its face, is a narrow one: police cannot go into a home without a warrant in the absence of some type of extenuating circumstance. But the case still provides a springboard for raising a number of issues about the proper role of the police. The first is why the police were involved in this case at all. Edward Caniglia was not committing a crime, nor was he about to do so. His wife said she did not fear for her life, only for Edward's. If something needed to be done about the situation, wouldn't a team of mental health professionals have been a better fit? This is the type of question that many in the Defund the Police movement are asking.

A second set of issues, pertinent even when the police are the only option, is raised by the Court's firm conclusion in *Caniglia* that police cannot excuse the failure to obtain a warrant with the mere fact that they are engaging in "tasks that go beyond criminal law enforcement," to use Justice Alito's phrase.[12] Justice Thomas's opinion seemed to reject the idea of a "freestanding" caretaker exception in connection with home entries,[13] and Justice Alito interpreted the Court's opinion to reject it in *any* setting.[14] At the same time, the various opinions in

[11] *Id.* at 1604–05 (Kavanaugh, J., concurring).

[12] *Id.* at 1600 (Alito, J., concurring).

[13] *Id.* at 1598 (noting that "the First Circuit extrapolated a freestanding community-caretaking exception that applies to both cars and homes" and holding that the exception did not apply to homes).

[14] *Id.* ("The Court's decision in [*Cady*] did not recognize any such 'freestanding' Fourth Amendment category.").

Caniglia, including Alito's, appear to contemplate that at least some tasks that go beyond criminal law enforcement do permit warrantless entry even when there is time to get a warrant. So the question is raised, what *are* police allowed to do in the name of "caretaking"? The suggestion made here is that, given the potential for police misuse of force and for pretextual actions by the police, warrantless home entries in the absence of real exigency should never be part of policing's mission, even when a "caretaking" goal can be articulated.

Then there is the possibility, admittedly speculative, that *Caniglia* could also affect searches and seizures outside the home. First, if there is no such thing as a freestanding caretaker exception, then *Cady* itself—involving a nonexigent warrantless search of a vehicle—might be questioned, or at least framed more accurately. *Caniglia* could also lead to a rethinking of what the courts call "special needs" doctrine. This doctrine—like the community caretaking exception—relaxes the usual Fourth Amendment strictures when a search or seizure purports to be facilitative rather than aimed at "ordinary crime control."[15] Under the special-needs rubric, the Supreme Court has permitted searches of school children and public employees for disciplinary infractions not only in the absence of a warrant but also on something less than probable cause. It has also sanctioned warrantless and *suspicionless* searches and seizures in connection with government inspections for dangerous conditions, checkpoints set up for various regulatory purposes, and drug testing programs aimed at safety rather than prosecution. While the Court has offered various rationales for these decisions, *Caniglia's* concern about an overly expansive community caretaking exception resonates with similar criticisms aimed at the elastic nature of its special needs cases. Perhaps some finetuning is necessary here as well.

I. Who Are the Best "Caretakers"?

Police are heavily involved in dealing with people who have a mental illness. From 10 to 20 percent of 911 calls involve mental health crises.[16] In many communities, the response to those calls is

---

[15]See *infra* Part III; City of Indianapolis v. Edmond, 531 U.S. 32, 44 (2000).

[16]The 20 percent figure comes from Eugene, Oregon; see *infra* text following note 28. A nationwide estimate is that 10 percent of 911 calls require some sort of mental health intervention. Mike Maciag, "The Daily Crisis Cops Aren't Trained to Handle," Governing.com, Apr. 27, 2016, https://bit.ly/2Sno8Sm.

to send the police; in fact, even when the 911 caller is a concerned family member, he or she often *asks* for the police, as Caniglia's wife in fact did.

But that is probably the wrong move most of the time. Nearly a quarter of all people killed by the police in the past five years have been people with mental illness.[17] That statistic raises an obvious question. Why are people who are trained to use deadly force, and have the means to use it, the primary response to a suicide threat or to a person who is beyond the control of family members? Presumably the goal in these cases is to talk the person down, not shoot them or otherwise harm them. Yet the latter is often what happens. Two recent cases are illustrative. The first ended with police shooting a 13-year-old boy with an autism-related disorder whose mother had called because he was having a "mental breakdown."[18] The second involved Daniel Prude, a 43-year-old black man who was wandering in the streets naked and babbling. Police put a hood over his head (to prevent him from spitting on them), pressed him to the ground a la Chauvin, and killed him.[19]

Even when a person with mental illness has a weapon (neither the 13-year-old nor Prude did), bringing in the police is probably a bad idea. For instance, in *Kisela v. Hughes*,[20] someone called the police to report a woman hacking at a tree with a kitchen knife. Three officers responded and were met by the caller, who told them the woman had been behaving erratically and then had disappeared. Soon afterward, the police saw Hughes, who fit the caller's description, emerge from a house carrying a large knife and walk within six feet of another woman, who turned out to be a housemate named Chadwick. The three officers, separated by a chain link fence, drew their weapons and twice told Hughes to drop the knife. Although Chadwick told the police to "take it easy" and later

---

[17] Hasan T. Arslan, Examining Police Interactions with the Mentally Ill in the United States, in Enhancing Police Service Delivery (James F. Albrecht & Garthden Heyer eds., 2021).

[18] Rachel Treisman, "13-Year-Old Boy with Autism Shot by Salt Lake City Police," NPR, Sept. 9, 2020, https://n.pr/3jazWm1.

[19] Michael Gold & Troy Closson, "About Daniel Prude's Case and Death: What We Know," N.Y. Times, Apr. 16, 2021.

[20] 138 S. Ct. 1138 (2018).

testified she did not feel endangered, and although Hughes appeared "calm" throughout, within less than a minute Officer Kisela had shot Hughes.

Mario Woods also had a weapon. The police received a call from a man who said Woods had slashed his arm with a knife, after walking back and forth on the sidewalk, talking nonsense, and appearing to be "under the influence of something."[21] A video shows Woods, a few hours later, standing against a wall with a knife in his hands, surrounded by six to eight officers, most of them pointing guns. When he doesn't put the knife down and starts limping away from the officers, he's shot 20 times, many of the bullets hitting him in the back.[22]

The police might not be to blame in these situations. In Hughes's case, the Supreme Court held that the police acted "in good faith" (although Justice Sonia Sotomayor, joined by Justice Ruth Bader Ginsburg, stated in dissent that "it is 'beyond debate' that Kisela's use of deadly force was objectively unreasonable").[23] Woods had hurt someone with his knife. But the question remains whether cops were the best first responders.

A typical reaction to these types of situations is to push for better training of the police—training on how to handle people with mental illness, how to talk to people with delusions and hallucinations, how to de-escalate. A number of jurisdictions have established crisis intervention teams (CITs) that rely either entirely on specially trained police officers or on teams of officers and mental health professionals.[24] But the research is, at best, equivocal on whether CITs work or are used properly. In Rochester, New York, where Prude was killed, a CIT program had existed for 15 years.[25] A national study of

---

[21] Phil Matier & Andy Ross, "Mario Woods' Last Moments: 'You Better Squeeze That . . . and Kill Me,'" SFGate, Jan. 23, 2016, https://bit.ly/3gS98p6.

[22] Julia Carrie Wong, "Mario Woods, Black Man Killed by Police, 'Had 20 Gunshot Wounds,'" The Guardian, Feb. 12, 2016, https://bit.ly/3xVoxuB.

[23] 138 S. Ct. at 1161 (Sotomayor, J., dissenting).

[24] Univ. of Memphis, CIT Ctr.: Overview, https://bit.ly/3gPyN1I (last accessed May 20, 2021) (reporting over 2,700 CIT programs nationwide as of 2017).

[25] Noelle E.C. Evans, "One Year After Daniel Prude's Death, Has Mental Health Care for People of Color Changed?," NPR, Mar. 21, 2021, https://bit.ly/3hfbsFF.

CITs found that, while the programs resulted in more people with mental illness being diverted out of the criminal justice system to psychiatric treatment, they did not significantly decrease the number of people killed or injured.[26]

An award-winning documentary called "Ernie and Joe: Crisis Cops" depicts two officers with the San Antonio Police Department "diverting people away from jail and into mental health treatment, one 911 call at a time."[27] There are several powerful moments in the film that show how well-trained, compassionate police officers can effectively de-escalate a situation without having, much less using, a weapon, and without any show of force. Perhaps the most potent message of the film, however, is that the officers are, in effect, mental health professionals. Not only do Ernie and Joe not have weapons, they often do not wear uniforms, and the techniques they use are similar to those that a good clinical social worker routinely uses in hospital wards. As Ernie says, they do not rely on the typical police academy use-of-force spectrum of "ask, tell, make"; instead, they listen, empathize, and hug.

Following that line of reasoning to its logical conclusion is a program called CAHOOTS (for Crisis Assistance Helping Out on the Streets) in Eugene, Oregon.[28] CAHOOTS teams are composed entirely of civilians, usually a medic and a behavioral specialist who, when on call, endeavor to avoid "pseudo-professional" demeanors, and are often people who at one time needed services themselves. In 2019, these teams responded to 24,000 calls, about 20 percent of all dispatches in Eugene. They called for police backup in about 150 of those cases. But most of the time they responded on their own to a wide range of situations, including "substance addiction crises, psychotic episodes, homeless residents and threats of suicide, [and] depressed children."[29] The efficacy of the program is hard to measure, but Eugene's chief

[26] Michael Rogers, Dale E. McNiel, & Renee L. Binder, Effectiveness of Crisis Intervention Programs, 47 J. Am. Acad. Psychiatry & L. 1 (2019).

[27] Ernie & Joe: Crisis Cops (HBO 2019).

[28] See CAHOOTS, Crisis Assistance Helping Out on the Streets, https://whitebirdclinic.org/cahoots.

[29] Scottie Andrew, "This Town of 170,000 Replaced Some Cops with Medics and Mental Health Professionals. It's Worked for Over 30 Years," CNN, July 6, 2020, https://cnn.it/3jmQmrr.

of police, who works closely with the CAHOOTS organization, says "When they show up, they have better success than police officers do. We're wearing a uniform, a gun, a badge—it feels very demonstrative for someone in crisis."[30] No deaths or injuries have been attributed to the teams. Note also the important role of the 911 dispatcher in this system. If *Caniglia* had happened in Eugene, the dispatcher might have resisted the request for police assistance from Edward's wife, and instead sent a CAHOOTS team.

The kink in the CAHOOTS program is a lack of dispositional options. The teams can usually avoid putting people in jail (which is where they often end up when the police are involved). But if a detox program or a homeless shelter is full, clients may have to be left on the streets, making many of them repeat players.

CAHOOTS deals primarily with issues of mental health and homelessness. "Civilian" responses are also possible for many other types of situations that police have traditionally been called on to handle, including potentially violent ones. In post–George Floyd Minneapolis, for instance, four teams of 20 to 30 members, including former felons and gang members, roam high-crime zones and try to intervene "before verbal taunts give way to fists or firearms."[31] They themselves are not armed. Their effectiveness, according to one journalistic account, "relies on quick thinking, calm persuasion, and a credibility that derives, in part, from who they aren't."[32] Also in Minneapolis, armed police in schools are being replaced by "civilian safety specialists" who are not armed and are trained to handle conflict. In the wake of the nation's many mass school shootings, the move is not uncontroversial, but is seen as a way of, among other things, easing racial tensions that uniformed officers can create.[33] Most dramatically, beginning in 2022, the police department in Ithaca, New York will be replaced by a "Community Solutions and Public Safety Department," composed of a significant number

---

[30] *Id.*

[31] Martin Kuz, "No Badges. No Guns: Can Violence Interrupters Help Minneapolis?," Christian Sci. Monitor, Apr. 13, 2021.

[32] *Id.*

[33] Chelsea Sheasley, "In a Roiled Minneapolis, Schools Are Testing a New Model for Safety," Christian Sci. Monitor, Apr. 20, 2021.

of unarmed public servants, and a smaller number of armed officers who will respond to serious life-threatening situations.[34]

In terms of sheer numbers, perhaps the move that could have the largest impact on changing the role of the police and their relationship with the community is in the domain of traffic enforcement. Across the country, police make 32 million car stops a year.[35] The number could easily be much higher, given the dozens of laws that all of us violate daily, including not just speeding and failure-to-stop rules, but laws on seat belts, outdated license plates, defective equipment, use of cellphones, crossing the median or shoulder, and failing to signal. Given the huge discretion traffic laws give the police, the potential for disparate application is also huge.

An unmeasurable but undoubtedly large number of traffic stops are pretextual—meaning that the real agenda behind the stop is not enforcement of the traffic laws but something much less benign, and perhaps racist.[36] The Supreme Court has held that pretextual stops do not violate the Constitution, in part for the understandable reason that discerning a cop's motives is very difficult.[37] Even so, many black and brown people are convinced that traffic laws are applied in a discriminatory manner, and they are backed up by research, which shows that people of color are proportionately more likely to be stopped than whites, yet proportionately less likely to have evidence of crime in their cars.[38] Unfortunately, a not insignificant number of traffic stops also result in serious injuries, usually to the car's occupants, sometimes to the police, and the occupants are often black.[39] All of this provides still another reason for communities of

[34]City of Ithaca & Tompkins Cty., N.Y., Reimagining Public Safety Collaborative, https://bit.ly/3hZPGXU (click on City of Ithaca Resolution, Apr. 21, 2021).

[35]Andrew Hurst, "Police Stop More than 32 Million Americans per Year for Traffic Violations," ValuePenguin.com, June 24, 2021.

[36]Charles R. Epp et al., Pulled Over: How Police Stops Define Race and Citizenship 72–73, 155 (2014).

[37]Whren v. United States, 517 U.S. 806 (1996).

[38]The latest study, of many, to so find is reported in Emma Pierson et al., A Large-Scale Analysis of Racial Disparities in Police Stops Across the United States, 4 Nat. Human Behav. 736 (2020).

[39]For instance, in 2015 more than 100 people were shot by police during traffic stops, one in three of them black. Wesley Lowery, "A Disproportionate Number of Black Victims in Fatal Traffic Stops," Wash. Post, Dec. 25, 2015.

color to distrust the police, and still another plank in the Defund the Police campaign.

One response to this state of affairs is to separate traffic enforcement from other policing tasks and make it a job for civilians, as Ithaca may soon do.[40] Another is to rely on technology to catch traffic violators, who are then sent a summons, a process that avoids potentially lethal police-citizen confrontations (but also riles powerful constituencies, as the short life of many red-light camera programs attests).[41] A third solution is simply to discontinue stops for non-moving violations such as defective equipment and failing to signal. When the police chief in Fayetteville, North Carolina, ordered a move in that direction in the years 2013 through 2016, "investigative stops" went to zero and stops of blacks plummeted 50 percent.[42]

Many of these moves toward reducing the police role are still experimental, and some could backfire. But they all have in common the idea that, in situations that do not call for the immediate use of force, alternatives to armed police might function just as well, if not better. Conversely, as Egon Bittner, the renowned sociologist, suggested a half century ago, police might be most useful when there is an emergency calling for the use of physical or armed force. As he put it, "[t]he policeman, and the policeman alone, is equipped, entitled, and required to deal with every exigency in which force may have to be used, to meet it."[43] That concept of the police role, in turn, gets us back to *Caniglia* and what it has to say about exigency and force.

II. Caretaking of Home Emergencies

Caniglia involved entry into the home, an entry the lower courts and the Supreme Court assumed was nonconsensual, and thus involved force.[44] Under the Fourth Amendment, such force must

---

[40]For a discussion of this approach, see Jordan Blair Woods, Decriminalization, Police Authority and Traffic Stops, 62 UCLA L. Rev. 672, 754–59 (2015).

[41]Elizabeth E. Joh, Discretionless Policing: Technology and the Fourth Amendment, 95 Cal. L. Rev. 199 (2007).

[42]Ahmed Jallow, "What Would Happen If Cops Didn't Make Certain Traffic Stops? This North Carolina City Offers a Case Study," Burlington (N.C.) Times-News, Apr. 15, 2021, https://bit.ly/3qB8mzZ.

[43]Egon Bittner, Florence Nightingale in Pursuit of Willie Sutton: A Theory of the Police, in The Potential for Reform of Criminal Justice 17, 35 (Herbert Jacob ed., 1974).

[44]Caniglia, 141 S. Ct. at 1599; 953 F.3d at 122–23.

usually be authorized by a warrant. "A basic principle of Fourth Amendment law," the Supreme Court has declared, "is that searches and seizures inside a home without a warrant are presumptively unreasonable."[45] This rule protects the home—the ultimate sanctuary of individuals from state interference—from the unchecked discretion of officers in the field. However, the Court has also long made clear that police may enter a home without a warrant when there are "exigent circumstances."[46] The Court has generally described exigent circumstances to include "hot pursuit of a fleeing felon, . . . imminent destruction of evidence, . . . the need to prevent a suspect's escape, or the risk of danger to the police or to other persons inside or outside the dwelling."[47]

Only the last exigency—sometimes called the "emergency aid exception"[48]—involves Justice Alito's "tasks that go beyond criminal law enforcement" and thus might justify warrantless police entry on caretaker grounds. Consistent with this language, the sole exigency of this type that Justice Thomas mentioned in *Caniglia* was "emergency assistance to an injured occupant or to protect an occupant from imminent injury."[49] Recall that most, if not all, of the other examples of permissible warrantless entries cited by the concurring justices also fit comfortably with this language. So the question naturally arises whether any noncriminal goal *besides* emergency aid authorizes warrantless entry under the Fourth Amendment.

The majority opinion in *Caniglia*—which references the exigent circumstances exception and then states that "[t]he First Circuit's 'community caretaking' rule . . . goes beyond anything this Court has recognized"[50]—suggests the answer is no. Nonetheless, the four

---

[45] Payton v. New York, 445 U.S. 573, 586 (1980).

[46] *Id.* at n.25 (citing Coolidge v. New Hampshire, 403 U.S. 443, 474–75 (1973)).

[47] Minnesota v. Olson, 495 U.S. 91, 100 (1990).

[48] See, e.g., Root v. Gauper, 438 F.2d 361 (8th Cir. 1971) ("police officers may enter a dwelling without a warrant to render emergency aid and assistance to a person whom they reasonably believe to be in distress and in need of that assistance"). *Gauper* was one of dozens of cases cited by the Supreme Court in *Mincey v. Arizona*, in stating that "[n]umerous state and federal cases have recognized that the Fourth Amendment does not bar police officers from making warrantless entries and searches when they reasonably believe that a person within is in need of immediate aid." 437 U.S. 385, 392 (1978).

[49] Caniglia, 141 S. Ct. at 1599.

[50] *Id.*

justices who signed on to the three concurring opinions seem to be hesitant about a warrant-unless-exigency rule, either because they believe there needs to be an additional exception, beyond the emergency-aid exception, or because they are worried that "emergency" will not be defined broadly enough. The tension on these issues came out during oral argument, through a series of hypotheticals thrown out by Chief Justice Roberts and the other justices. For instance, Roberts asked Caniglia's attorney whether the Fourth Amendment would be violated by a warrantless entry after police received a call from neighbors of an elderly woman, who express concern that the woman had agreed to come over for dinner two hours earlier but had not shown up, could not be reached, and had not been seen leaving her home.[51] The answer given by the attorney was that police could not enter the woman's home without a warrant even after 24 hours had gone by, and that, even after several days, they could enter only after obtaining "a warrant for a missing person." That reply clearly was not satisfactory to most of the justices.[52]

Justice Breyer (who ultimately joined Chief Justice Roberts's concurring opinion) also asked a series of questions, beginning with this commentary:

> There are so many situations where it's obvious the police should enter. You know—a baby's been crying for five hours, nobody seems to be around. A rat's come out of a house at a time when rats carry serious disease and have to be stopped. A person goes into the house . . . but the people inside the house don't know that that person has a serious communicable disease. . . . If we call those "exigent circumstances" we weaken the exigent circumstances [rule]. And if we move to a whole new thing like caretaker, I don't know *what* we do.[53]

Caniglia's attorney did not directly address all of Justice Breyer's hypotheticals, but he did insist that there must be a "true emergency" to justify a warrantless entry.[54]

There are certainly definitions of the emergency-aid component of exigency that address "true emergencies" without going down the

---

[51] Transcript of Oral Argument at 8, Caniglia v. Strom, 141 S. Ct. 1596 (2021) (No. 20-157).

[52] *Id.* at 8–9.

[53] *Id.* at 16 (emphasis added).

[54] *Id.* at 18.

rabbit hole that Caniglia's attorney did in answering Chief Justice Roberts's elderly woman hypothetical. Any such formulation must address: (1) the seriousness of the harm or threat that can trigger the exception, (2) the certainty the harm has occurred or will occur, and, if it hasn't occurred yet, (3) the imminence of the harm. In light of the observations in Part I, the test should also consider (4) the need for *police* to address the situation. An exigency standard that aims at limiting warrantless caretaker entries to "true emergencies" might prohibit warrantless caretaker entries unless police have *probable cause* to believe that *serious physical injury* to a person either *has occurred* or is *likely to occur,* and that *immediate* assistance *from the police* is therefore needed.

This definition of exigency is relatively narrow. But it is consistent with the Court's exigency exceptions in noncaretaker situations (*"hot* pursuit of a fleeing *felon," "imminent* destruction of evidence," "the *need to prevent* a suspect's escape"). It thus strongly reinforces "the basic Fourth Amendment principle" that warrantless entries into the home are presumptively unreasonable. At the same time, it signals, in tune with the first part of this article, that other government actors besides the police might be more appropriate responders. Yet, despite these various restrictions, this narrower definition would probably produce the result Chief Justice Roberts seemed to want in his hypothetical, at least if the police were the only available option: if an officer was dispatched after the neighbors' 911 call, checked on their story, knocked on the woman's door, and got no answer, warrantless entry would be permitted under this formulation. Whether it would resolve Justice Breyer's quandaries would depend on the relevant facts. But to the extent his hypotheticals do not involve real exigency, a visit from the welfare or public health agency, not the police department, would be a much more appropriate response.

In short, one could, and arguably should, read *Caniglia* to mean there is no caretaker exception independent of the emergency aid exception. Yet numerous courts have resisted that position.[55] And, again, at least some of the justices may be hesitant about adopting it.

---

[55] See, e.g., Hunsberger v. Wood, 570 F.3d 546, 554 (4th Cir. 2009) (noting that, while the two exceptions "overlap conceptually," they are "not the same," because "[t]he community caretaking doctrine requires a court to look at the *function* performed by a police officer, while the emergency exception requires an analysis of the *circumstances* to determine whether an emergency requiring immediate action existed") (emphasis original).

One source of this reluctance could stem from a concern that the traditional warrant regime is not a good fit in situations that do not involve crimefighting. For instance, in his concurring opinion in *Caniglia*, Justice Alito stated that "circumstances are exigent only when there is not enough time to get a warrant, and warrants are not typically granted for the purpose of checking on a person's medical condition."[56] Similarly, the "missing person warrant" conjectured by Caniglia's attorney would be a new phenomenon.

But the argument that warrants should not be required in such situations because they have not been in the past is, at best, unimaginative. As the Court has recognized in the investigative context, the advent of telephonic warrants means that judicial authorization can be obtained relatively expeditiously,[57] meaning that the process of obtaining a court order today is nowhere near as cumbersome as in the days when *Cady* was decided. And the judicial process can easily be adapted to the nonemergency caretaker scenario. Justice Alito himself speculates, after noting the atypicality of caretaker warrants, "[p]erhaps States should institute procedures for the issuance of such warrants."[58] In fact, that is precisely what many states have done in addressing situations like the one in *Caniglia*. Today at least 19 states—including Rhode Island, where Edward Caniglia lived—have enacted "red flag laws" that provide for "Extreme Risk Protection Orders" or "Gun Violence Restraining Orders" authorizing confiscation of weapons from people with mental illness who are considered dangerous.[59] Some of these laws can be triggered only by a mental health professional; in others, family members, school administrators, and the police can do so. In some states, such orders can also be issued in response to other people considered possible threats, such as domestic abusers and those who abuse substances.[60] While these orders are normally not called "warrants," they fulfill

---

[56] Caniglia, 141 S. Ct. at 1602 (Alito, J., concurring).

[57] Missouri v. McNeely, 569 U.S. 141, 154–55 (2013) (making this observation in a case in which a warrantless draw of the defendant's blood occurred 25 minutes after his arrest).

[58] Caniglia, 141 S. Ct. at 1602 (Alito, J., concurring).

[59] Sean Cambpell, Alex Yablon, & Jennifer Mascia, "Red Flag Laws: Where the Bills Stand in Each State," The Trace, Dec. 22, 2020, https://bit.ly/3h25fxP.

[60] *Id.*

the same role by identifying the place to be searched and the item to be seized (or, in the case of missing or injured persons, the person to be searched for).

A closely related argument on behalf of a relaxed exigency exception in caretaker situations is that a more restrictive approach is not flexible enough to allow police to respond to all of the important circumstances in which they are needed. Requiring probable cause to believe a person is hurt or in danger, it might be said, is too onerous a standard given the potential harm involved. This may be Justice Kavanaugh's main concern. In his concurring opinion in *Caniglia*, Kavanaugh approvingly cited a lower court judge's law review article noting that "municipal police spend a good deal of time responding to calls about missing persons, sick neighbors, and premises left open at night" and asserting that "the responsibility of police officers" to carry out these tasks "has never been the subject of serious debate."[61] Justice Kavanaugh then posits two hypotheticals, one involving a woman who calls 911 saying she is contemplating suicide and who does not respond when police knock, and the second an elderly man who uncharacteristically misses church services, repeatedly fails to answer his phone through the day and night, and does not answer to police performing a wellness check. In both cases, Kavanaugh declared that "of course" police may enter the home without a warrant.[62]

The point of these hypotheticals may have been to demonstrate that there are many instances when the injury or potential for injury is not certain, but police should be able to act anyway. Of course, the "probable cause" standard, which can be satisfied on something less than a "preponderance of the evidence,"[63] takes that fact into account. But there are signs the Court believes that this standard is insufficiently malleable. In fact, in another caretaker-type case, *Brigham City v. Stuart*,[64] the Court said as much. *Brigham City* involved

---

[61]Caniglia, 141 S. Ct. at 1604 (Kavanaugh, J., concurring) (citing Debra Livingston, Police, Community Caretaking, and the Fourth Amendment, 1998 U. Chi. Legal F. 261, 263 (1998)).

[62]*Id.* at 1604–05.

[63]See Am. L. Inst., Model Code of Pre-Arraignment, §§ 120.1(2), 210.1 (the comments to both sections make this point).

[64]547 U.S. 398 (2006).

police entry of a home after they had been called to the scene by a noise complaint and witnessed a struggle through a screen door. In upholding the warrantless entry, the Court eschewed probable cause language in favor of a test requiring "an objectively reasonable basis for believing" that aid is needed.[65] Some lower courts have been explicit about lowering the certainty required for police to act on caretaking rationale.[66]

Although this stance has occasioned some academic criticism, it is consistent with the idea that when the government's objective is prevention, rather than investigating an already completed act, the requisite justification may be relaxed. This, for instance, is one explanation for the Court's well-known decision in *Terry v. Ohio*,[67] authorizing a "protective frisk" on reasonable suspicion, a lower standard than probable cause. It is also one basis for the Court's decision in *Addington v. Texas*,[68] which refused to require that, in civil commitment proceedings, dangerousness to self or others be proven beyond a reasonable doubt, and instead permitted involuntary hospitalization on the less demanding clear and convincing standard of proof. My proposed exigency rule, which refers to probable cause to believe that harm is *likely* to occur, rather than probable cause to believe it *will* occur, in fact recognizes this point. Perhaps, with that understanding, Justice Kavanaugh would be satisfied with the rule.[69]

---

[65] *Id.* at 399.

[66] One often-cited case is *People v. Mitchell*, which held that, for the exception to apply, "(1) The police must have reasonable grounds to believe that there is an emergency at hand and an immediate need for their assistance for the protection of life or property. (2) The search must not be primarily motivated by intent to arrest and seize evidence. (3) There must be some reasonable basis, approximating probable cause, to associate the emergency with the area or place to be searched." 39 N.Y.2d 173, 177–78 (1976).

[67] 392 U.S. 1 (1968).

[68] 441 U.S. 418 (1979).

[69] Justice Kavanaugh elaborated on his view of *Sanders v. United States*. 956 F.3d 534 (8th Cir. 2020). There, the dispatcher received a call from the grandmother of an 11-year-old child, who had called her saying that her mother and her boyfriend were "fighting real bad"; the grandmother added that there were three children inside the house and that she couldn't tell from the child's report whether a weapon was involved. Upon arrival, police saw the child through a window "acting excited" and gesturing. When they knocked on the door, the mother came outside, had red marks on her face, was emotionally unstable, and told police not to tell her boyfriend that the 11-year-old had called. When the police asked to talk

A final reason for favoring a relaxed exigency requirement may simply be the assumption that the motives of the police in these types of cases are benign, and thus that the usual restrictions are not needed. Of course, if the police are really there to help, consent will often be forthcoming. And when it is not, benign motives do not necessarily eliminate the violation experienced by those whose homes are mistakenly or precipitously invaded by the police (as evidenced by the many lawsuits that are brought in such situations[70]). Most important, as many courts have recognized, police motives can be mixed.[71] For instance, some cases have held that the caretaker exception applies when police serving a court order knock on a door and receive no response, under circumstances suggesting there should be one.[72] That rule creates an incentive for the police to use service of process as a pretext to carry out a house search they cannot get a magistrate to authorize, simply by waiting until a person is not home and then using the lack of response to enter, out of "concern" the person may

---

to the boyfriend, the mother said she would get him to come outside, but when she opened the door, the police heard a baby crying. The police entered at that point, despite the mother saying everything was okay and making clear she did not want the police to enter, and despite the boyfriend, who was just inside the door, also telling them not to enter. The Eighth Circuit upheld the entry under the caretaker exception, but the Supreme Court remanded in light of *Caniglia*'s rejection of that exception. Justice Kavanaugh wrote an opinion agreeing with the remand but stating that the Eighth Circuit's conclusion was not necessarily wrong, given the Court's decision in *Brigham City*. Sanders v. United States, 141 S. Ct. 1646, 1647 (2021) (Kavanaugh, J., concurring). Since the police had probable cause to believe an assault had occurred and that children inside the house were fearful, the emergency aid component of exigency, as defined here, was present. Consider, however, whether a CAHOOTS-type intervention would have been preferable.

[70]See, e.g., Smith v. Kan. City, Mo. Police Dep't, 586 F.3d 576, 580–81 (8th Cir. 2009) (officer not entitled to qualified immunity when he entered a third party's home looking for a domestic violence suspect without a warrant); Briones v. City of San Bernardino, 2012 WL 13124164 (C.D. Cal. 2012) (officer denied summary judgment on claim that entering a locked gate, opening closed door and shooting dog was justified under caretaker exception because of belief that a "hung up" 911 call was from plaintiff's home).

[71]See, e.g., Mitchell, *supra* note 66.

[72]United States v. Quezada, 448 F.3d 1005, 1007 (8th Cir. 2006); Phillips v. Peddle, 7 Fed. Appx. 175, 179 (4th Cir. 2001).

be injured.[73] Many other caretaking pretexts, real or imagined, are available—from hearing loud noises to Justice Breyer's rats.[74] Most disturbingly, the government has frequently argued that warrantless entry should be permitted on a caretaker rationale even when it is clear the real goal of the police was obtaining evidence of crime; unfortunately, occasionally courts have agreed.[75]

There are at least four responses to the pretext problem. The first is to allow individuals to argue that the police used the community caretaker exception as a pretext. But motive is very difficult to prove, and, in any event, the Court held in the aforementioned *Brigham City* case (where there was some dispute as to the real agenda of the cops who entered), that "as long as the circumstances, viewed objectively, justify the action," police motives are irrelevant.[76] A second solution is to require exclusion of any evidence found during a community caretaker entry, regardless of motive.[77] While this rule may deter some pretextual actions, in many such cases the police have nothing to lose by going ahead since, by definition, they know they cannot make their case through a legally authorized investigation. Further, if they do find evidence of a crime, it can always be confiscated even if it isn't admissible, and it could also facilitate subsequent legitimate investigation. In any event, the Supreme Court, already antagonistic

[73]Cf. Vale v. Louisiana, 399 U.S. 30 (1970) (excluding evidence found inside Vale's home after police, with warrants to detain him for a court appearance, delayed execution of the warrants until Vale came outside the house and engaged in suspicious behavior that gave them grounds for conducting a search of his home incident to arrest).

[74]Cf. United States v. Rohrig, 98 F.3d 1506, 1523 (6th Cir. 1996) (officers responding to loud noise report entered back door and went into basement after getting no response at front door).

[75]United States v. Pichany, 687 F.2d 204, 207 (7th Cir. 1983) (finding exception did not apply when officers were searching for stolen property); United States v. Erickson, 991 F.2d 529, 530–31 (9th Cir. 1993) (finding exception did not apply when officers were investigating a burglary); United States v. Bute, 43 F.3d 531, 540 (10th Cir. 1994) (same); State v. Pinkard, 785 N.W.2d, 594–95 (Wis. 2010) (finding exception did apply when police entered to investigate an anonymous tip that cocaine was inside and found door open).

[76]547 U.S. at 404.

[77]Mark Goreczny, Taking Care While Doing Right by the Fourth Amendment: A Pragmatic Approach to the Community Caretaker Exception, 14 Cardozo Pub. L. Pol'y & Ethics J. 229, 251 (2015).

to the exclusionary rule,[78] is not likely to extend it unless its application is likely to bring significant deterrence.

The solution to the pretext problem that is closest to the majority's holding in *Caniglia* is to require police to obtain a court order in the absence of real exigency, just as they must do when they want to enter a home for investigative purposes. While police control the storyline whether they appear before a magistrate *ex post* (in a suppression hearing) or *ex ante* (when seeking a warrant), at least in the latter situation they do not have the advantage of hindsight bias when they try to explain their community caretaking reason for entering the home.[79] Pretextual searches of homes are harder to pull off if the pretext has to be justified before entry occurs.

The fourth solution, of course, is to avoid police involvement entirely, for all the reasons explored in Part I. If the bulk of caretaker situations are handled by civilians, there will be fewer entries (because pretexts will not be manufactured as a ruse to obtain criminal evidence) and fewer pretextual entries (because civilians are not interested in criminal evidence). This solution also suggests how the courts might approach the many searches and seizures that the courts have said involve "special needs."

III. Caretaking Outside the Home

In *Cady v. Dombrowski*,[80] the police, looking in a car for the revolver of another officer after he had crashed the car, came upon evidence eventually connected with a murder. Dombrowski, the officer, argued that, since at the time of the search the car had been impounded and he had been in jail on drunk driving charges, there was no exigency and the officers should have obtained a warrant. The police claimed that their only goal in searching the car was to find Dombrowki's gun, which was supposed to be in an officer's

---

[78]Herring v. United States, 555 U.S. 135, 144 (2009) (in expanding the good faith exception to the rule, stating that "[t]o trigger the exclusionary rule, police conduct must be sufficiently deliberate that exclusion can meaningfully deter it, and sufficiently culpable that such deterrence is worth the price paid by the justice system").

[79]This was one of William Stuntz's arguments in favor of a warrant requirement. See William Stuntz, The Role of Warrants in an Exclusionary Rule System, 77 Va. L. Rev. 881, 910–18 (1991).

[80]413 U.S. 433 (1973).

possession at all times and had not been found on his person. They did not see the revolver in the car. But they did find, in the trunk of the car, clothes and various other items covered with blood. The Supreme Court upheld the search, despite the lack of a warrant.

In so doing, *Cady* used the language that became the focus of attention in *Caniglia*. The *Cady* Court noted that police "frequently investigate vehicle accidents in which there is no claim of criminal liability and engage in what, for want of a better term, may be described as community caretaking functions, totally divorced from the detection, investigation, or acquisition of evidence relating to a violation of a criminal statute."[81] In *Caniglia* Justice Thomas emphasized that this language in *Cady* was closely linked to searches of cars, with *Cady* stressing throughout that "for purposes of the Fourth Amendment there is a constitutional difference between houses and cars."[82] On its face, then, *Caniglia*, which involved the search of a house, had nothing to say about the caretaker exception and car searches.

It does not necessarily follow, however, that *Caniglia's* concern about a "freestanding" caretaker exception disappears when the caretaker search is of a car rather than a home. As demonstrated in Part I, pretextual searches of cars are exceedingly common, probably much more so than pretextual searches of houses. Of course, in the typical car search case, the Court has already made clear that, because of their mobility and the lesser expectation of privacy associated with them, automobiles can usually be searched without a warrant.[83] But a warrant might still be required when a car is within the police's control and there is clearly time to get a warrant; the question then arises whether a caretaker exception should apply.

One could be excused for concluding that *Cady* held precisely that. At one point, the Court stated that the search of the car was needed "to protect the public from the possibility that a revolver would fall into untrained or perhaps malicious hands" because the car was in a lot over which no guard had been posted.[84] In support of a caretaker

[81]*Id.* at 441.
[82]*Id.* at 439.
[83]See Robbins v. California, 453 U.S. 420, 424–25 (1981).
[84]Cady, 413 U.S. at 443.

exception, one could point to this language and argue that, so long as police have some reason to believe the contents of a car pose a danger to the public, warrantless entry is permissible, even if no immediate exigency exists.

However, read more closely and with the aid of hindsight, *Cady* is not about a freestanding caretaker exception at all. Rather, it was based on a nascent version of what would come to be called the inventory exception to the warrant requirement, which is meant to allow police departments to conduct warrantless searches of impounded cars for dangerous items and valuables that might otherwise be stolen, and to protect the police against false claims of theft. As developed in cases like *Opperman v. South Dakota*,[85] decided three years after *Cady*, warrantless searches of cars are authorized if (1) the car has been lawfully impounded, (2) the search is conducted pursuant to a written policy, and (3) the search is not pretextual.[86] *Cady* was not as specific as one might desire on all three of these points, but it did point out both that Dombrowski's car had been properly impounded after the accident and that the police followed "standard procedure" in looking for weapons in the car.[87] Further, relevant to the pretext point, the Court emphasized that "at the time the search was conducted Officer Weiss was ignorant of the fact that a murder, or any other crime, had been committed."[88]

All of this is important not only because it constrains use of caretaker language in cases involving cars, but also because it could have significant implications for police involvement in a large set of search-and-seizure scenarios that have come to be called "special needs" cases. The first Supreme Court opinion using this phrase, *New Jersey v. T.L.O.*,[89] involved the search of a school child's purse for cigarettes, in the absence of a warrant and on only minimal suspicion. The Court upheld the search because, in the words of Justice Harry Blackmun's concurring opinion, school searches involve "exceptional circumstances in which special needs, beyond the normal need for law enforcement, make the warrant and probable-cause

[85] 428 U.S. 364 (1976).
[86] *Id.* at 374–76 (citing *Cady* in support).
[87] Cady, 413 U.S. at 443.
[88] *Id.* at 447.
[89] 469 U.S. 325 (1984).

requirements impracticable."[90] This language later found its way into an entirely different type of case—involving health and safety inspection regimes; license, sobriety, and immigration checkpoints; school and work drug-testing programs; and other "programmatic" searches and seizures—where the Court has permitted searches and seizures of *groups* conducted in the *absence* of suspicion with respect to any particular person or entity, so long as there is an "adequate substitute" for a warrant.[91]

A key reason the Court has been willing to relax traditional Fourth Amendment strictures in these cases is that, at least in the Court's eyes, the searches and seizures they involve are not focused on "a general interest in crime control" but rather on enforcement of disciplinary infractions and regulatory violations.[92] Concomitantly, these searches and seizures typically are carried out not by police but by "civilians"—public school teachers, public employers, and bureaucrats working for agencies like the Occupational Safety and Health Administration. Indeed, one reason the Court has been willing to relax the warrant and probable-cause requirements in these cases is that it does not want to burden civilian officials with a warrant process and worries about the "niceties" of probable cause.[93]

The Court's special-needs jurisprudence has been roundly criticized for blinking at the fact that criminal prosecution often lurks in the background of these cases, and for too readily giving up on the probable-cause requirement. But the point here is more circumscribed. Whatever may be the right interpretation of the Fourth Amendment when civilian officials are carrying out these searches and seizures, when the *police* are conducting them, the Fourth Amendment should apply with full force. When civilians are the government's emissaries, concerns about misuse of force and pretextual actions may be minimal. But when the

---

[90] *Id.* at 351 (Blackmun, J., concurring).

[91] Eve Brensike Primus, Disentangling Administrative Searches, 111 Colum. L. Rev. 254, 275–76 (2011) (pointing out these two variants).

[92] See, e.g., Los Angeles v. Patel, 576 U.S. 409, 420 (2015) ("Search regimes where no warrant is ever required may be reasonable where 'special needs . . . make the warrant and probable-cause requirement impracticable,' and where the 'primary purpose' of the searches is '[d]istinguishable from the general interest in crime control.'") (citing inspection, parolee, and checkpoint cases).

[93] T.L.O., 469 U.S. at 340–43 (involving searches by school teachers); O'Connor v. Ortega, 480 U.S. 709, 724 (1987) (involving searches by employers).

police are the government's agents, those concerns are at their height, and traditional Fourth Amendment constraints should apply.

With respect to the first special-needs variant—focused on a particular individual—those constraints are clear. The usual warrant, probable-cause, and exigency rules should govern. That would mean, for instance, that if a "school resource officer" is an off-duty police officer or a cop in disguise, armed with a gun and trained in investigative techniques, even a search aimed at enforcing a school disciplinary rule would require a warrant in the absence of exigency.

If, instead, a special-needs search or seizure is programmatic—as with checkpoints, inspections, and drug testing—the group nature of the police action means an individualized suspicion requirement cannot work. But a stricter version of the inventory model broached in *Cady* (also alluded to in a smattering of other Supreme Court cases[94]) could. As I have argued elsewhere,[95] the most effective way of preventing arbitrary police action in programmatic search-and-seizure situations is to require statutory authorization of the program, even-handed implementation across the entire target group, and a ban on pretextual action. The latter prohibition could be enforced by exclusion of any evidence found that is not within the statutory remit (a sanction that is likely to have greater deterrent impact here than in individual home entry cases because it applies program-wide). Or, as the Court itself recently required in some inspection settings, the pretext concern could be addressed by allowing targets to argue to a neutral decisionmaker, pre-search, that the inspection is not consistent with the statutory mandate or an even-handed application of it.[96]

---

[94] The best case in this regard is Donovan v. Dewey, 452 U.S. 594 (1981), which involved inspections of coal mines. The Court upheld the inspection scheme because that statute (and accompanying regulations) "requires inspection of *all* mines and specifically defines the frequency of inspection," and establishes "the standards with which a mine operator is required to comply . . . rather than leaving the frequency and purpose of inspections to the unchecked discretion of Government officers. . . ." *Id.* at 603–04 (emphasis original). However, the Court has been less than punctilious in following the rules developed in cases like *Cady*, *Opperman*, and *Dewey*. See Christopher Slobogin, Advanced Introduction to U.S. Criminal Procedure § 4.8 (2020).

[95] Christopher Slobogin, Policing as Administration, 165 U. Pa. L. Rev. 91 (2016).

[96] Patel, 576 U.S. at 420. See also Camara v. Mun. Ct. of S.F., 387 U.S. 523, 539–40 (1967) (requiring an "area warrant" before nonconsensual entry by inspectors).

Thus, for instance, field officers would not be permitted to set up "license checkpoints" on a whim, in whatever neighborhood they want, with drug-sniffing dogs waiting in the wings.[97] Instead, the legislature would have to authorize such checkpoints and set out general guidelines for their use. Further, the police agencies implementing the statute would have to create a neutral plan (for instance, one calling for checkpoints at every major thoroughfare—including those in predominantly white neighborhoods—a certain number of times a year), make sure it is neutrally applied (by requiring, for instance, that every driver is stopped), and avoid engaging in any action that goes beyond the scope of a license check (including have dogs standing by). While there are good reasons for requiring this type of regulatory regime in every programmatic special-needs situation, it is crucial when the police, or facsimiles thereof, are the instigators, as is the case not only with license checkpoints, but sobriety and immigration checkpoints as well. The same holds true for inspections when police are involved. For instance, in *City of Los Angeles v. Patel*,[98] the police, acting under authority of a city ordinance, arbitrarily checked hotel registries for evidence of drug dealing or prostitution. In such cases, objectors should be entitled to pre-compliance review, regardless of the rules that might apply when the inspectors are civilians. Otherwise, as the Supreme Court noted in *Patel*, the statutory authorization "creates an intolerable risk that searches . . . will exceed statutory limits, or be used as a pretext to harass. . . ."[99]

Finally, to repeat the central point of this article, if the special needs situation does not require armed officers trained to detect and deter crime, police should not be involved at all. In *Ferguson v. City of Charleston*,[100] decided in 2001, the Supreme Court came close to saying as much. There the Court invalidated a police-initiated drug testing program for pregnant women, despite claims that the program was designed primarily to obtain treatment for the women. Unfortunately, however, earlier Court decisions involving programmatic searches and seizures had no difficulty allowing police to conduct

---

[97] A common practice, apparently. See, e.g., Lujan v. State, 331 S.W.3d 1668 (Tex. Ct. Crim. App. 2011) (upholding such a checkpoint); McCray v. State, 601 S.E.2d 452 (Ga. 2004) (same).

[98] 576 U.S. 409.

[99] *Id.* at 421.

[100] 532 U.S. 67 (2001).

them even in the absence of serious restrictions, at least if no other agency was available to take up the task.[101]

Perhaps *Caniglia*, along with *Patel* and *Ferguson*, signal a change in attitude. While *Caniglia* does not purport to pronounce anything about special-needs doctrine, it does bolster *Ferguson*'s rejection of the notion that Fourth Amendment protections can be diluted simply on the ground that the police are engaged in something other than investigation of crime. In describing the First Circuit's holding in *Caniglia*, Justice Thomas was clearly displeased with that court's justification for its broad caretaker exception and its application to Edward Caniglia's case:

> [T]he First Circuit saw no need to consider whether anyone had consented to respondents' actions; whether these actions were justified by "exigent circumstances"; or whether any state law permitted this kind of mental-health intervention. All that mattered was that respondents' efforts to protect petitioner and those around him were "distinct from 'the normal work of criminal investigation,'" fell "within the rule of reason," and generally tracked what the court viewed to be "sound police procedure."[102]

Relying on *Caniglia*'s disdain for the First Circuit's formulation, the argument is strong that, when a nonexigent search or seizure is carried out by police, the assertion that it is not aimed at "ordinary crime control" should be irrelevant to Fourth Amendment analysis, regardless of whether it occurs inside or outside the home.

---

[101]See in particular, *New York v. Burger*, involving searches of junkyards for stolen car parts under a state statute that allowed police to conduct warrantless searches during business hours, any time and as many times as they wanted to do so. There the Court stated:

> [W]e fail to see any constitutional significance in the fact that police officers, rather than "administrative" agents, are permitted to conduct the . . . inspection. . . . [S]tate police officers . . . have numerous duties in addition to those associated with traditional police work. . . . As a practical matter, many States do not have the resources to assign the enforcement of a particular administrative scheme to a specialized agency. So long as a regulatory scheme is properly administrative, it is not rendered illegal by the fact that the inspecting officer has the power to arrest individuals for violations other than those created by the scheme itself. 482 U.S. 691, 717 (1987).

[102]Caniglia, 141 S. Ct. at 1599.

Conclusion

Among government officials, police have a near monopoly on the use of physical force and the greatest incentive to hide their motives. An expansive interpretation of *Caniglia v. Strom*'s rejection of a free-standing caretaker exception would help curb both police misuse of force and police use of pretexts to pursue illegitimate agendas, because it would limit police-initiated searches and seizures purporting to be for benign purposes. It might also provide doctrinal support for the fledgling movement to de-police those government services that, whatever might be the tradition, do not require the intervention of armed individuals trained to fight crime, at the same time it would put guardrails around the special-needs doctrine. It may be that, outside of real emergencies, the last thing we want police to do is function as "caretakers" of the community.

Brnovich v. DNC: Election Litigation Migrates from Federal Courts to the Political Process

Derek T. Muller[*]

We are in a time of public skepticism over elections. The losing side doubts the fairness of the outcome, attributing the loss to suppression, fraud, foreign influence, or late-breaking changes to laws—some "true reason" outside the legitimate political process why a preferred candidate failed. The winning side is a sour contest or a sore loser away from doubting the legitimacy of the election.

It's hard to tell whether the sharp rise in litigation over elections is the cause or the effect. Major political parties are spending more money than ever on lawyers and litigation in federal elections, from $7.5 million in 2012 to more than $66 million in 2020.[1] Seemingly minor changes to schedules, deadlines, or how forms are mailed immediately prompts the filing of a legal complaint. Every corner of election administration is up for a lawsuit as major political parties vie for the smallest competitive advantage—actual or perceived.

While *Brnovich v. Democratic National Committee* was a case about the Voting Rights Act, the hallmark voting legislation of the civil-rights era, it began as one of these efforts by a political party to litigate relatively minor issues of state election administration. A district court rejected the lawsuit. But on appeal, the case took on outsized

[*] Bouma Fellow in Law and Professor of Law, University of Iowa College of Law. Special thanks to Trevor Burrus and the Cato Institute for their invitation to write and for their assistance in publishing this piece. Portions are derived from two of my shorter articles in the aftermath of *Brnovich*: "Brnovich, Election-Law Tradeoffs, and the Limited Role of the Courts," SCOTUSblog, July 6, 2021, https://bit.ly/2TQ8HCY; and "Supreme Court Raised the Bar for Challenge to GA Election Law," RealClearPolitics, July 23, 2021, https://bit.ly/3irVkmd.

[1] Derek T. Muller, Reducing Election Litigation, Fordham L. Rev. (forthcoming), https://bit.ly/3xxnG2J.

importance as an appellate court found that Arizona enacted a statute with racially discriminatory intent, opening the door to judicial oversight of newly enacted election rules. That caught the attention of the Supreme Court, which in turn weighed in for the first time on an entire class of claims under the Voting Rights Act.

The decision in *Brnovich* likely limits opportunities for plaintiffs litigating certain classes of election-law cases, at least compared to the baseline of what some federal courts had permitted in the last few years. But it's also the latest in a 20-year string of Supreme Court cases emphasizing that the political process, not the federal courts, remains the principal place to address most election-law issues. Litigation continues to rise even as plaintiffs are increasingly likely to find themselves on the losing side of the case. And it remains unclear whether public confidence, through litigation or otherwise, will rise anytime soon.

I. Lower-Court Skirmishes

A. The DNC Initiates a Lawsuit

In March 2016, Arizona's presidential primary went off poorly. Significant numbers of unaffiliated or independent voters attempted to vote when they were not permitted to do so, and Maricopa County's move from specific precincts to vote centers caused long lines and significant confusion.[2]

Weeks later, the Democratic National Committee (DNC) sued the state. As Amy Dacey, the chief executive of the DNC, explained when justifying the lawsuit, "What Arizona voters experienced during the presidential primary goes beyond the bounds of what anyone would consider reasonable."[3] The DNC's lawsuit targeted two particular practices that would become the core of the dispute before the Supreme Court.

First, the DNC challenged a prohibition on out-of-precinct voting. Under a law stretching back to at least 1970, if a voter appeared in the wrong precinct, that voter ought to be directed to the proper precinct to cast a vote. If not, she might cast a provisional ballot.

---

[2] AJ Vicens, "The Election in Arizona Was a Mess," Mother Jones, Mar. 24, 2016, https://bit.ly/3rTDjjr.

[3] Amy Dacey, "This Is Why the Democratic Party Is Suing the State of Arizona," Medium, Apr. 14, 2016, https://bit.ly/3rTehAY.

But that ballot would not be counted if the voter was not from that precinct. If the voter was an eligible voter, no votes would be counted, even in statewide races like presidential or gubernatorial elections. Only if the voter actually resided in that precinct but was erroneously excluded from the voting roster would the ballot be counted.

Second, the DNC challenged a statute that Arizona had enacted only weeks earlier and that had not yet gone into effect, H.B. 2023. The bill limited third-party ballot collection, or "ballot harvesting." Only specified third parties (postal workers, election officials, caregivers, family members, or household members) could collect a completed and sealed vote-by-mail ballot. While Arizona had long limited which parties could deliver *blank* ballots to voters, H.B. 2023 was a new rule, one that extended a parallel prohibition to the collection of *completed* ballots. Opponents of ballot harvesting worried that collectors could exert pressure on voters or fraudulently alter or destroy ballots. Such instances are rare, but they have occurred around the country. After failed efforts to enact a similar law in 2011 and 2013, the Arizona legislature succeeded enacting the statute in 2016.

Notably, neither of these practices caused problems in the 2016 presidential primary. Neither would fix long lines, undersized vote centers, or confusion among nonparty members. Arizona's new ballot harvesting law hadn't been enacted, much less taken effect. And Arizona's out-of-precinct voting rule might alter canvassed totals but would certainly not change anything about voter-facing election administration.

At the time, the *Washington Post* reported that it was "unclear" whether the Justice Department "has the evidence to file a lawsuit under Section 2 of the Voting Rights Act."[4] Attorneys in President Barack Obama's Justice Department did not file a lawsuit. Nor did attorneys at a civil rights organization like the NAACP or the Mexican American Legal Defense and Educational Fund.

The lawsuit was instead initiated by the DNC. Indeed, the DNC's complaint squarely framed the litigation on its own behalf

---

[4] Sari Horwitz, "Democratic Party, Clinton and Sanders Campaigns to Sue Arizona over Voting Rights," Wash. Post, Apr. 14, 2016, https://wapo.st/3ymKeEh.

as a matter of partisan advantage, only incidentally about racial effect.[5]

Among other plaintiffs, including individual voters and the Navajo Nation, the lawsuit was joined by Ann Kirkpatrick (a Democratic challenger to Sen. John McCain) and presidential candidate Hillary Clinton. These two individuals had an interest in challenging the out-of-precinct voting rule. The remedy asked for ballots cast in the wrong precinct to be counted for offices for which the voter was otherwise eligible. The Senate and presidential races were statewide elections—and the Democrats understandably hoped to secure an advantage for their candidacies.

The complaint was filed, and the stage was now set to challenge the statutes in federal court. But the choice to file under Section 2 of the Voting Rights Act merits further examination.

B. Recent Section 2 Litigation

The DNC alleged that Arizona's laws disproportionately affected racial minorities, and that H.B. 2023 was enacted with discriminatory intent. But why did the DNC bring an action under Section 2 of the Voting Rights Act? Although the DNC did bring other claims, the Section 2 claims ended up driving the case. It reflects litigation decisions after a pair of Supreme Court decisions in the decade before the 2016 presidential primary—*Crawford v. Marion County Election Board* and *Shelby County v. Holder*.

---

[5] Complaint at 12–13, Feldman v. Ariz. Secretary of State's Off. (D. Ariz. Apr. 15, 2016) (No. 16-01065) ("The DNC has members and constituents across the United States, including eligible voters in Arizona. To accomplish its mission, among other things, the DNC works closely with Democratic public officials and assists state parties and candidates by contributing money; making expenditures on their behalves; and providing active support through the development of programs benefiting Democratic candidates. The lack of oversight for Maricopa County's allocation of polling locations; Arizona's policy of not counting provisional ballots cast in a precinct or voting area other than the one to which the voter is assigned; and the State's recent criminalization of the collection of signed and sealed absentee ballots with the passage of H.B. 2023 directly harm the DNC, its members, and constituents by disproportionately reducing the turnout of Democratic voters and increasing the likelihood that those voters who do turnout will not have their vote counted. These practices and provisions further decrease the likelihood that the DNC will be successful in its efforts to help elect candidates of the Democratic Party to public office. . . . In particular, among the voters most harmed by Arizona's policies are some of the DNC's core constituencies, including Hispanic, Native-American, and African-American voters. . . .").

In 2008, the Supreme Court considered a challenge to Indiana's voter identification law. Its decision in *Crawford* concluded that the law passed constitutional scrutiny.[6] The Court drew upon its precedents that developed a balancing test to determine whether election laws excessively burdened voting rights under the Constitution. A slight burden on the right to vote generally survived judicial review when it advanced the state's "important regulatory interests."[7] A "severe" burden, however, must be "narrowly drawn" to achieve a "compelling interest."[8] In *Crawford*, the Court concluded that the voter-identification law did not place an excessive burden on any class of voters.[9] It did not create a "substantial" burden, "or even represent a significant increase over the usual burdens of voting."[10]

Plaintiffs trying to challenge election laws after *Crawford* would face barriers. The Court approved a voter-identification law, which, on the surface, seems like a more onerous regulation that an out-of-precinct voting rule or a limitation on the third-party collection of ballots. Litigants have had some success challenging some election laws post-*Crawford*.[11] But litigants would consider alternative claims.

Then, in 2013, the Supreme Court decided *Shelby County v. Holder*.[12] It concluded that part of Congress's 2006 extension of the Voting Rights Act was unconstitutional. Specifically, it concluded that Section 4(b), which identified a group of states and localities that would be subject to preclearance under Section 5 of the act, exceeded Congress's power because it no longer paralleled the incidence of racial discrimination in voting. Section 4(b) had not been materially updated since 1975, so the Court concluded that Congress no longer had constitutional justification for continuing to require the covered jurisdictions to preclear their election laws.

Section 4(b) identified a number of jurisdictions, mostly states in the South, that had lagged in voter registration or turnout. But after 50 years, the Court explained that "things have changed dramatically"

---

[6] 553 U.S. 181 (2008) (plurality op.).

[7] Burdick v. Takushi, 504 U.S. 428, 434 (1992).

[8] *Id.*

[9] Crawford, 553 U.S. at 202.

[10] *Id.* at 198.

[11] See Derek T. Muller, The Democracy Ratchet, 94 Ind. L.J. 451 (2019).

[12] 570 U.S. 529 (2013).

in the South when it came to racial discrimination and voting rights.[13] Section 5 required preclearance, or federal approval of all election laws for a jurisdiction covered under Section 4(b). It was a "stringent" and "potent" remedy when first introduced in 1965.[14] And it was a remedy that the Court concluded could not continue to target selected states in 2013.[15]

After *Shelby County*, preclearance no longer applied to the places that had been covered by Section 4(b). One of those places was Arizona. Litigants who disapproved of statutes that once-covered states enacted sought alternative litigation outlets. One of those outlets was Section 2.

In 2016, such Section 2 lawsuits were a novelty.[16] Academics had begun to build out interpretive mechanisms and evaluate how lower courts were beginning to use such tests in nascent litigation, but the Supreme Court had never applied the provision outside the redistricting context.[17]

The decision to use Section 2 as the basis of this litigation reflected a couple of strategic determinations. A decades-old statute like the out-of-precinct voting rule would never have faced Section 5 preclearance, even before *Shelby County*, as it was a longstanding rule rather

---

[13] *Id.* at 547.

[14] South Carolina v. Katzenbach, 383 U.S. 301, 308, 315 (1966).

[15] See generally Derek T. Muller, Judicial Review of Congressional Power Before and After Shelby County v. Holder, 8 Charleston L. Rev. 287 (2013) (scrutinizing effect of *Shelby County*).

[16] Daniel P. Tokaji, Applying Section 2 to the New Vote Denial, 50 Harv. C.R.-C.L. L. Rev. 439, 448 (2015) ("Historically, § 2 vote denial claims have been few and far between. . . . Section 2 vote denial claims have become more prominent since the Shelby County decision, which effectively ended § 5 preclearance."); Derek T. Muller, The Democracy Ratchet, *supra* note 11, at 465–69.

[17] Daniel P. Tokaji, *supra* note 16, at 464–65 (describing courts' tests and proposing a new test for Section 2 claims after *Shelby County*); Christopher S. Elmendorf & Douglas M. Spencer, Administering Section 2 of the Voting Rights Act after Shelby County, 115 Colum. L. Rev. 2143, 2147 (2015) ("This Article takes up the question of whether section 2 can be made to function like erstwhile section 5 in the post-*Shelby County* world."); Michael J. Pitts, Rescuing Retrogression, 43 Fla. St. U. L. Rev. 741, 749 (2016) ("The basic framework for rescuing retrogression is a simple one—make the retrogression test from section 5 a part of the substantive standard of section 2. I would propose to do that by adding a gloss on the current framework for finding a violation of section 2. . . ."); Gilda R. Daniels, Voting Realism, 104 Ky. L.J. 583, 595–97 (2015) (describing how lower courts have used Section 2 after *Shelby County*).

than a recent change. Section 2 thus allowed a new litigation opportunity, beyond what Section 5 would have permitted. And Section 2 applied nationwide, not just in jurisdictions that had once been covered, like Arizona. Additionally, parties had been having some success on matters like voter-identification laws or changes to early voting since *Crawford*—some, but not overwhelming, success. Section 2 might provide a useful outlet, particularly if there was evidence that racial minorities were disproportionately affected. Section 2 spoke of discriminatory effect, not simply discriminatory intent.

A finding of intentional discrimination would also provide a powerful remedial mechanism under Section 3 of the Voting Rights Act.[18] That provision allows for a jurisdiction to be "bailed in" for preclearance of all election laws for a period of time if the jurisdiction is found to have engaged in intentional discrimination.[19] Like preclearance under Section 5, no voting law would then take effect without federal approval. But unlike Section 4(b), which relied on a stale formula to identify covered jurisdictions, Section 3 turns on a recent finding of intentional discrimination and a judicially tailored remedy. For those who lamented that Arizona, among other states, was no longer subject to preclearance, a finding of intentional discrimination could subject Arizona to preclearance once again and restore a remedy lost after *Shelby County*.

Plaintiffs had begun to develop Section 2 as a promising opportunity to curtail disfavored laws that disproportionately affected racial minority voters. It might prove more powerful than the balancing tests used in other cases—and it might pick up some slack after *Shelby County*.

C. The Path to the Supreme Court

The DNC's complaint against Arizona made three claims that the Supreme Court would ultimately address. First, that the out-of-precinct rule excessively burdened racial minorities' opportunities to vote. Second, that H.B. 2023 excessively burdened minority voters. Third, that the Arizona legislature enacted H.B. 2023 with racially

---

[18] See Roseann R. Romano, Devising a Standard for Section 3: Post-Shelby County Voting Rights Litigation, 100 Iowa L. Rev. 387, 392, 405–07 (2014) (describing context and limitations of Section 2 litigation after *Shelby County*).

[19] 52 U.S.C. § 10302(c).

discriminatory intent. The district court and the Ninth Circuit grappled over how to construe and apply Section 2, but this part will focus on the evidence the lower courts considered and the inferences to be drawn from that evidence.

The district court took evidence over a 10-day trial to weigh the merits of the allegations. It considered statistical and anecdotal evidence. It ultimately issued a lengthy and detailed opinion carefully rejecting the claims. For example, the district court noted that the percentage of ballots invalidated under the "out of precinct" rule was 0.15 percent of all ballots cast in 2016 (3,970 ballots of 2,661,497 cast statewide), and that this number was decreasing.[20] Even though the district court found that racial minorities cast such ballots at a disproportionately higher rate, that disparity was not "meaningfully disparate" given how small the numbers were.[21] "As a practical matter," the court concluded, it did not "result in minorities having unequal access to the political process."[22] The district court made similar findings with regard to H.B. 2023, as there was "no quantitative or statistical evidence" of how the rule might affect minority voters.[23]

The district court also rejected the claim that Arizona enacted H.B. 2023 with racially discriminatory intent. The majority of the bill's supporters were "sincere" in their beliefs that it would reduce the risk of fraud.[24] Some proponents had partisan motivations, but partisan motives differ from racial motives, and the district court was careful to distinguish between the two.[25]

The DNC appealed the case to the Ninth Circuit. A divided three-judge panel affirmed, in an opinion written by Judge Sandra Ikuta.[26] But an *en banc* panel reversed, in an opinion by Judge William Fletcher.[27] The court concluded that both bills constituted impermissible vote

---

[20] Democratic Nat'l Comm. v. Reagan, 329 F. Supp. 3d 824, 872 (D. Ariz. 2018).

[21] *Id.*

[22] *Id.*

[23] *Id.* at 886.

[24] *Id.* at 879.

[25] *Id.* at 882.

[26] Democratic Nat'l Comm. v. Reagan, 904 F.3d 686 (9th Cir. 2018).

[27] Democratic Nat'l Comm. v. Hobbs, 948 F.3d 989 (9th Cir. 2020) (en banc).

denial under the Voting Rights Act, and that Arizona had acted with discriminatory intent when it enacted H.B. 2023.

Judge Fletcher's opinion traced Arizona's history of discrimination back to the Treaty of Guadalupe Hidalgo in 1848, well before statehood in 1912.[28] And it also provided a different framing of how to consider the disparate burden on voters. The *en banc* court considered disparate impact with a much narrower focus. For example, "The proper baseline to measure [out of precinct] ballots to is thus not all ballots, but all *in-person* ballots."[29] In extreme cases, "Section 2 is violated based on [a] single denial."[30] A "facially neutral" policy might require a larger number of voters affected—a "substantial number"—and a couple of thousand voters affected could invalidate the policy.[31] The court found that plaintiffs had advanced sufficient evidence to demonstrate an unlawful disparate impact, and the district court clearly erred in concluding otherwise.

A majority of the Ninth Circuit *en banc* panel also concluded that Arizona had acted with discriminatory intent, although one judge dropped off the majority opinion on this point.[32] The majority embraced a theory known as the "cat's paw" to get there.

One of Aesop's fables tells of a monkey that persuades a cat to use its paws to take chestnuts from hot coals for the monkey to eat. The monkey's malice causes the cat to burn its paws. In the employment context, the "cat's paw" is an analogy for when a supervisor's bias can be attributed to the ultimate decision to terminate employment, even if the supervisor was not a part of the final decision. Likewise, the Ninth Circuit concluded that the racially charged allegations from one of the bill's proponents could be attributed to the rest of the legislature, even if those legislators argued for the bill on its merits in good faith. Indeed, the court acknowledged that many of the legislators argued sincerely in support of the law but traced

---

[28] *Id.* at 1017–18.

[29] *Id.* at 1015.

[30] *Id.*

[31] *Id.* at 1016 (comparing potential voting margin to 537-vote margin for George W. Bush in Florida in 2000).

[32] *Id.* at 1046 (Watford, J., concurring) ("I join the court's opinion to the extent it invalidates Arizona's out-of-precinct policy and H.B. 2023 under the results test. I do not join the opinion's discussion of the intent test.").

the legislature's discriminatory intent back to one member.[33] That, in turn, doomed HB 2023.

II. The Supreme Court

Immediately after the Ninth Circuit's *en banc* decision, election observers predicted that the Supreme Court would take up the case, largely driven by the intentional-discrimination finding.[34] *Brnovich* might simply be called an "overreach of a case,"[35] and the Supreme Court took the case at the very least to correct that finding. Even the Justice Department under President Joe Biden agreed ahead of oral argument that Arizona's laws did not have an unlawful discriminatory effect, let alone discriminatory intent.[36] But the Court also took the opportunity for a broader construction of Section 2, construction designed to guide lower courts in the future.

Arizona "generally makes it quite easy for residents to vote."[37] That line early in Justice Samuel Alito's opinion for the Supreme Court set the path for the six-justice majority to reject the challenges to Arizona's laws. Justice Alito's opinion was joined by Chief Justice John Roberts and Justices Clarence Thomas, Neil Gorsuch, Brett Kavanaugh, and Amy Coney Barrett. Justice Elena Kagan wrote a dissenting opinion, joined by Justices Stephen Breyer and Sonia Sotomayor. Apart from a brief concurring opinion from Justice Gorsuch, joined by Justice Thomas, these two opinions provided the Court with clean alliances and direct battle between the Court's wings.

The majority opinion framed the case as a "neutral time, place, and manner" rule, and not, as plaintiffs had often characterized it, as a "vote denial" case. This framing squarely puts the Court's analysis in terms of state power: When has the state violated the Voting Rights Act? What are the appropriate bounds of state power to regulate elections?

---

[33] *Id.* at 1039–40.

[34] Kimberly Strawbridge Robinson, "Arizona Ballot Laws Tossed, U.S. Supreme Court Review Likely," Bloomberg Law, Jan. 27, 2020, https://bit.ly/3fDQn7K.

[35] Richard L. Hasen, "A Partisan Battle in an Overreach of a Case," SCOTUSblog, Feb. 22, 2021, https://bit.ly/3rYx269.

[36] Letter from Edwin S. Kneedler, Deputy Solicitor General, U.S. Dep't of Justice, to Scott S. Harris, Clerk, U.S. Sup. Ct. (Feb. 16, 2021) (on file with U.S. Supreme Court), https://bit.ly/3AlkwAW.

[37] Brnovich v. Democratic Nat'l Comm., 141 S. Ct. 2321, 2333 (2021).

A. Textualism and Open-Ended Language in Statutes

The statutory language the Court construed is open-ended. Consider the text at issue in Section 2(b) of the Voting Rights Act: "A violation of subsection (a) is established if, based on the *totality of circumstances*, it is shown that the political processes leading to nomination or election in the State or political subdivision are not *equally open* to participation by members of a class of citizens protected by subsection (a) *in that* its members have *less opportunity* than other members of the electorate to participate in the political process and to elect representatives of their choice."[38]

The Court's opinion is textualist in nature. Admittedly, not everyone agrees with that characterization, including Justice Kagan, who in her dissent called the majority opinion a "law-free zone."[39] A fair reading of the majority opinion reveals otherwise; the critique that it is not textualist is misplaced.

The Court spends a couple of pages of its opinion parsing the meaning of "equally open," the phrase "in that," and the subsequent reference "less opportunity" as it relates to "equally open." It employs traditional tools of statutory interpretation, including dictionary definitions and contextual interpretation.[40]

First, "equally open" means "without restrictions," or "requiring no special status," according to contemporary dictionary definitions.[41] The phrase "in that," the Court continued, gives the respect in which the political processes may not be "equally open," in an ensuing clause: "in that its members have less opportunity."[42] The Court reasoned that "equal opportunity helps to explain the meaning of equal openness."[43] And "opportunity" means a favorable time, place, occasion, or circumstance.[44]

This parsing of the statute—looking at dictionary definitions, context, and phrasing—continued with perhaps the most challenging phrase: "totality of circumstances." Another lengthy portion of

---

[38] 52 U.S.C. § 10301(b) (emphasis added).

[39] 141 S. Ct. 2321, 2361 (Kagan, J., dissenting).

[40] *Id.* at 2337–38 (majority op.).

[41] *Id.* at 2337.

[42] *Id.*

[43] *Id.* at 2338.

[44] *Id.*

the opinion opens by noting that Section 2 "requires consideration of 'the totality of circumstances.'"[45] The Court defines "totality of circumstances" as "any circumstance that has a logical bearing on whether voting is 'equally open' and affords equal 'opportunity' may be considered."[46]

This definition of "totality of circumstances" and its place within the statute is consistent with the text of Section 2—and, significantly, it is extremely generous. The Court says that "any" circumstances "may be considered," as long as a circumstance has "a logical bearing" on the ensuing words in the statute. "Equally open" could have been placed into the statute without the qualification of "totality of circumstances," but the phrase "totality of circumstances" phrase must perform independent work.[47]

"Any," of course, is exceedingly broad, so the Court's next move is to say that it will "not attempt to compile an exhaustive list, but several important circumstances should be mentioned." The five ensuing guideposts all meet the definition of circumstances that have a logical bearing. The five guideposts are:

1. "the size of the burden imposed by a challenged voting rule";
2. "the degree to which a voting rule departs from what was standard practice when § 2 was amended in 1982";
3. "[t]he size of any disparities in a rule's impact on members of different racial or ethnic groups";
4. "the opportunities provided by a State's entire system of voting"; and
5. "the strength of the state interests."[48]

Lower courts, litigants, and law professors drafting future law review articles may well develop more factors to consider, factors that have "a logical bearing" on "equally open" and "less opportunity." Undoubtedly, however, when the Supreme Court enumerates five "guideposts," these guideposts will influence how lower courts frame their discussion of ensuing cases. They will be the starting

[45] *Id.*
[46] *Id.*
[47] *Id.*
[48] *Id.* at 2338–39.

point, the focus of judicial analysis. And they will dominate how litigants frame their cases.

Three moves that the Court made merit special attention. First, the Court looked back to its 2008 decision in *Crawford*. Even though *Crawford*, as discussed earlier, did not examine the Voting Rights Act but a constitutional balancing test, the plurality opinion in *Crawford* acknowledged that the right to vote must allow for the "usual burdens of voting," including, in some cases, presenting identification. That language—the "usual burdens of voting"—appeared repeatedly in the Court's *Brnovich* opinion as a factor among the "totality of circumstances."

Every voting rule, the court explained, places some burden on voters. Voting inevitably takes time and travel, even when going to the mailbox; there is no constitutional right to have election administrators read a voter's brain waves, or allow voters to text or tweet their votes. And the Court embraced the argument that "mere inconvenience" alone will not be sufficient to win under the Voting Rights Act.[49] An open process that has the "usual burdens of voting" will typically not violate Section 2. The "usual burdens of voting" will be an important framing for litigants moving forward.

Second, the present version of Section 2 was amended by Congress in 1982, and the Supreme Court instructed lower courts to look at voting burdens as they existed that year as the baseline. States had narrow absentee-voting rules in 1982, and voting opportunities are dramatically more generous today. That means few rules will depart significantly from the 1982 baseline, and it means more laws will pass muster under Section 2. Intriguingly, few states had voter identification laws back then, so it's an open question whether Section 2 offers more opportunity for plaintiffs who seek to challenge such provisions.

Third, the relationship of the third and fourth prongs deserves particular attention. The Court rejected the Ninth Circuit's framing, which focused on how a particular law in isolation affects even a small group of voters. Instead, it looked at the place of the law in the overall voting system, as the district court did. Laws that affect a very small percentage of voters, or laws that affect voters who have myriad opportunities to vote in a different fashion,

[49] *Id.* at 2338.

likely survive Section 2 scrutiny. Again, "mere inconvenience" alone is not enough.

The Court went on to reject the challenge to Arizona's laws. The two rules affected a tiny fraction of voters and there was little disparity between how minority and nonminority voters behaved. The rules were well within the "usual burdens of voting," especially given ample opportunities to vote. The "totality of circumstances" included 27 days of vote-by-mail and early in-person voting, coupled with voting in person on election day. The Court approved of the district court's holding—but in doing so, offered an important gloss on Section 2.

Justice Kagan called the majority's analysis "extra-textual"[50] or "remak[ing]"[51] the statute, but the analysis above shows a fairly robust textualist approach. She, instead, simply has a different method of statutory interpretation—purposivism, not textualism. She approaches the interpretation of the Voting Rights Act by citing why Congress "mainly added"[52] the language of "totality of circumstances." In her view, "The totality inquiry requires courts to explore how ordinary-seeming laws can interact with local conditions—economic, social, historical—to produce race-based voting inequalities."[53]

Justice Alito's opinion does not disagree: he notes that factors like racial polarization, racially tinged campaign appeals, and election of minority-group candidates can inform whether the minority group has suffered discrimination in the past and whether it persists.[54] These do have "any" logical bearing, after all.

The "totality of circumstances," Justice Kagan continues, looks at "law and background conditions," including "facts on the ground." It also allows courts to "take into account strong state interests supporting an election rule."

Justice Kagan's dissent argues that the gloss of "equally open" and "less opportunity" should be "whenever the law makes it harder for

---

50 *Id.* at 2362, 2372 (Kagan, J., dissenting).

51 *Id.* at 2373.

52 *Id.* at 2362.

53 *Id.*

54 *Id.* at 2340 (majority op.).

citizens of one race than of others to cast a vote."[55] But then she introduces some caveats in footnote four of her opinion: "very small differences" do not matter (she agrees with Justice Alito here), including those that are "not statistically significant," or those that are statistically significant but not of "practical significance."[56] "Equal," then, is a legal term of art.

In a way, Justices Alito and Kagan are talking past each other. Both opinions agree that "totality of circumstances" involves looking at items not expressly enumerated in the text. And both agree that even statistically significant variance in the voting practices of racial groups is insufficient to win on a Section 2 claim. But, I think, there is a sharp difference in approach to statutory interpretation. Justice Kagan's approach is avowedly purposivist, as her antepenultimate paragraph makes clear in her critique of the majority opinion:

> One does not hear much in the majority opinion about that promise. One does not hear much about what brought Congress to enact the Voting Rights Act, what Congress hoped for it to achieve, and what obstacles to that vision remain today. One would never guess that the Act is, as the President who signed it wrote, "monumental." . . . For all the opinion reveals, the majority might be considering any old piece of legislation—say, the Lanham Act or ERISA.[57]

Justice Kagan looks at the historical context, the congressional "vision," and the reflections of the president who signed the original version of the act—hallmarks of a purposivist approach.

B. "Intentional" Discrimination?

While the Court split 6-3 on whether Arizona's statutes had a discriminatory *effect*, the lineup looked slightly different on the question of whether H.B. 2023 was enacted with discriminatory *intent*. On that question, the Court, by a 6-0 vote—with the three dissenters not addressing the question—concluded that Arizona did not act with discriminatory intent.

---

[55] *Id.* at 2358 (Kagan, J., dissenting).
[56] *Id.* at 2358 n.4.
[57] *Id.* at 2372.

The Court emphasized that the district court, which concluded that the state legislature did not act with discriminatory intent, should have received deference on its factual findings. The majority cited the ample support in the record to sustain the district court's findings in rebuking the Ninth Circuit.

The Court also looked at the historical context of H.B. 2023. Arizona had considered similar measures in 2011 and 2013, so its efforts in 2016 were nothing new or the product of some recent racial animus. The Court further emphasized that racial divides often overlap with partisan divides, and lower courts should not conflate the two. Lower courts must "carefully distinguish[]" between these distinct motives.[58]

Finally, the Court rejected the "cat's paw" theory as applied to legislatures. Legislators are not "agents" of a bill's sponsor or proponents. Legislators "have a duty to exercise their judgment." It was "insulting" for the Ninth Circuit to conclude that legislators could be "mere dupes or tools."[59] The six justices in the majority on the matter of discriminatory effect thus also agreed that there was no intentional discrimination.

In her dissenting opinion, Justice Kagan had concluded that H.B. 2023 had an unlawful discriminatory effect. But in a footnote, she explained that she "need not pass" on the holding that the laws were enacted with discriminatory intent.[60]

It is a curious footnote. A finding of intentional discrimination is not merely an alternative basis for relief. Indeed, the finding might entitle litigants to "bail in" Arizona under Section 3 of the Voting Rights Act. It is a significant and different remedy. The three dissenting justices really ought to have weighed in on the finding of intentional discrimination.

There are at least a few plausible, if speculative, reasons for Justice Kagan's move. It might be that the three dissenters disagreed about how to handle the intentional-discrimination claim, so they deferred the matter to provide a united front. Or it might be that they agreed that there was no intentional discrimination, but worried that such

[58] *Id.* at 2349 (majority op.).

[59] *Id.* at 2350.

[60] *Id.* at 2366 n.10 (Kagan, J., dissenting).

agreement with the majority would soften the impact of the biting dissent. Or maybe it's simply a tacit acknowledgement that the Ninth Circuit should not have reversed on these grounds and should have just stuck with the discriminatory effect holding.

III. A Return to Politics

It is perhaps only a small overstatement to say that the Court is less interested in plaintiffs' election law challenges than at any point since the 1940s and 50s. That was an era of the Court's decisions in *Colegrove v. Green*, concluding that federal courts would not enter the "political thicket" of remedying malapportioned districts; and *Lassiter v. Northampton County Board of Elections*, in which the Court unanimously concluded that a literacy test for prospective voters— at least one "fair on its face"—passed constitutional muster.[61]

By 1962, the Court's decision in *Baker v. Carr* opened the door to "one person, one vote" challenges;[62] and its decisions in cases spanning poll taxes to ballot access rules were plentiful.[63] The Court broadly approved and broadly construed the Voting Rights Act.[64] Plaintiffs successfully challenged state voting laws for decades.

Since *Bush v. Gore*, however, when the Court intervened in Florida's recount in the 2000 presidential election, one is hard-pressed to find a significant victory for plaintiffs challenging election rules (and even in *Bush v. Gore* the Court sided with the defendant).[65] There is a risk of oversimplifying the history, of course, but a few cases will illustrate the concept.

In 2006, the Court issued a brief opinion in *Purcell v. Gonzalez*, warning that federal courts should disfavor late changes to election laws: "Court orders affecting elections, especially conflicting orders, can themselves result in voter confusion and consequent incentive to remain away from the polls. As an election draws closer, that risk

[61] Lassiter v. Northampton Cty. Bd. of Elections, 360 U.S. 45 (1959); Colegrove v. Green, 328 U.S. 549 (1946) (plurality op.).

[62] Baker v. Carr, 369 U.S. 186 (1962).

[63] See, e.g., Harper v. Va. State Bd. of Elections, 383 U.S. 663 (1966); Williams v. Rhodes, 393 U.S. 23 (1968).

[64] See, e.g., South Carolina v. Katzenbach, 383 U.S. 301 (1966); Allen v. State Bd. of Elections, 393 U.S. 544 (1969).

[65] 531 U.S. 91 (2000) (per curiam).

will increase."[66] The *"Purcell* principle" has been the basis, explicitly or implicitly, for myriad decisions of the federal courts in general, and the Supreme Court in particular, in recent years refusing to enjoin election laws close in time to an election.[67] That includes a decision in 2020, when the Court turned back a challenge to the timing of Wisconsin's primary election in the middle of the novel coronavirus pandemic in *Republican National Committee v. Democratic National Committee.*[68]

In the 2008 decision in *Crawford*, discussed above, the Court approved Indiana's photo identification law in elections. In 2015, it rejected a challenge to Arizona's independent redistricting commission in *Arizona State Legislature v. Arizona Independent Redistricting Commission.*[69] In 2016, it considered a challenge to Texas's state legislative map that had been drawn on the basis of total population, and its decision in *Evenwel v. Abbott* rejected the argument that Texas needed to draw districts on some basis more closely approximating voting population.[70]

In 2019, in *Rucho v. Common Cause*, the Court concluded that partisan gerrymandering claims arising under the Constitution were not to be heard in federal courts.[71] And it fended off a tranche of plaintiffs' challenges to the 2020 presidential election, including *Republican Party of Pennsylvania v. Degraffenreid*, concerning Pennsylvania courts' alteration of mail-in voting deadlines;[72] and *Texas v. Pennsylvania*, as states sued other states about how they chose presidential electors.[73]

These cases were brought by Democrats and Republicans. They were brought by states and civic organizations. They put their arguments in terms of state power or in terms of individual rights. All failed. And this is by no means an exhaustive list.

[66] 549 U.S. 1, at 4–5 (2006) (per curiam).

[67] See, e.g., Richard L. Hasen, Reining in the Purcell Principle, 43 Fla. St. U. L. Rev. 427 (2016) (chronicling cases).

[68] 140 S. Ct. 1205 (2020) (per curiam).

[69] 576 U.S. 787 (2015).

[70] 577 U.S. 937 (2016). See generally Derek T. Muller, Perpetuating "One Person, One Vote" Errors, 39 Harv. J.L. & Pub. Pol'y 371 (2016).

[71] 139 S. Ct. 2484 (2019).

[72] 141 S. Ct. 732 (2021) (mem.).

[73] 141 S. Ct. 1230 (2021) (mem.).

That's not to say litigants haven't had some success—*Alabama Legislative Black Caucus v. Alabama*[74] and *Cooper v. Harris*[75] come to mind. But the former was a dying interpretation of Section 5 of the Voting Rights Act, and the latter a fact-specific racial gerrymandering case in a decades-long dispute. Litigants have had tremendous success challenging campaign finance rules, too.[76] And of course plaintiffs may succeed in lower courts in cases the Supreme Court never hears.

Even these cases could be parsed more carefully. *RNC v. DNC*, for instance, may well have come out the way it did precisely because the RNC only appealed certain aspects of the DNC's lower court victory.[77] Supreme Court cases are only a fraction of overall election litigation. And its "shadow docket,"[78] or its refusal to take up cases or summary reversal of a lower court's interim relief or relief close in time to an election, further complicates the portrait.

That's not to say that litigants will stop trying to bring such cases in the federal courts. Days before the Court's decision in *Brnovich*, the Justice Department sued Georgia on several provisions of its recently enacted S.B. 202. Among its many provisions, this omnibus election law prohibits mailing unsolicited absentee ballot applications, requires an identification number or proof of identification to request an absentee ballot, shortens the absentee ballot period, limits "drop boxes" to collect ballots, prohibits third-party distribution of food and water to voters who wait in line, and forbids counting ballots cast outside a voter's precinct unless cast after 5 p.m. on election day. Whether a federal court agrees that some portions of S.B. 202

---

[74] 575 U.S. 254 (2015).

[75] 137 S. Ct. 1455 (2017).

[76] See, e.g., McCutcheon v. Fed. Election Comm'n, 572 U.S. 185 (2014) (holding that aggregate contribution limit in federal elections violated the First Amendment); Citizens United v. Fed. Election Comm'n, 558 U.S. 310 (2010) (concluding that ban on independent campaign expenditures by corporation violated the First Amendment).

[77] See Republican Nat'l Comm., 140 S. Ct. at 1206 (describing lower court's extension of the deadline to receive absentee ballots and emphasizing, "[t]hat extension, which is not challenged in this Court, has afforded Wisconsin voters several extra days in which to mail their absentee ballots").

[78] See William Baude, Foreword: The Supreme Court's Shadow Docket, 9 N.Y.U. J.L. & Liberty 1 (2015).

were enacted with racially discriminatory intent, as the Justice Department alleges, remains to be seen.[79]

But I think it is fair to say that *Brnovich* is the latest in a line of cases suggesting that the federal courts should play a smaller role in the patrolling of how states administer elections. *Brnovich* means that future plaintiffs will have greater difficulty raising similar challenges under Section 2 of the Voting Rights Act. This key provision will, however, continue to play a role in redistricting, its important place in recent decades—at least, unless and until the Supreme Court chooses to weigh in further on this part of the statute.

Voting rights proponents and election law challengers do have other outlets to press against state statutes besides the federal courts. State courts might review election laws under state constitutions. The people can act by ballot initiative in many states. Congress can enact specific rules on these matters if it desires, at least in federal elections. Some such specific rules are a part of H.R. 1, the "For the People Act."[80]

The long-term impact of *Brnovich* remains to be seen, but it is perhaps fairly small. First, it continues the Court's path away from federal judicial involvement in election rules and toward a greater deference to state power. That now includes certain questions of racial discrimination. Second, and relatedly, it reflects the perils of short-sighted litigation strategy or federal court overreach in the face of a Supreme Court that has had a fairly consistent approach for two decades. And finally, it trims little litigation, as such cases were nonexistent even a decade ago. Instead, it tightens up how federal courts should scrutinize these claims that had been churning about the lower courts for the last few years. How lower courts handle *Brnovich*'s totality-of-circumstances test remains to be seen. But it seems unlikely that even these trends will stem the tide of litigation in the politically polarized years ahead.

---

[79] For a nonacademic argument that the answer is "no," see Ilya Shapiro, "The Voter Suppression Lie," Wash. Exam'r, Apr. 22, 2021, https://washex.am/3CjZ4y1.

[80] H.R. 1, 117th Cong., 1st Sess. (2021), https://bit.ly/3yuc0i9.

Declaring Computer Code Uncopyrightable with a Creative Fair Use Analysis

*Adam Mossoff**

The past 50 years have been a period of massive innovation in computer technology—the personal computer revolution, the internet, and the mobile revolution. This half-century has been bookended by Stephen Breyer's writings on copyright protection for computer programs. In 1970, then-Professor Breyer at Harvard Law School first expressed his now well-known intellectual property skepticism in *The Uneasy Case for Copyright*.[1] He argued, among other things, that "[c]omputer programs should not receive copyright protection at the present time."[2] Five decades later, now-Justice Breyer wrote the majority opinion in *Google v. Oracle*,[3] holding that Google is not liable for copyright infringement for its unauthorized copying of approximately 11,500 lines of the "declaring code" in Oracle's Java computer program.

Google was a blockbuster copyright case. It was a legal dispute between two titans in the tech industry arising from Google's unauthorized copying of a computer program that has been integral to the interconnected digital world we all live in today—Java. The lawsuit filed by Oracle against Google took a decade to work its way through the courts with multiple trials and appeals. Oracle claimed billions in damages.

* Professor of Law, Antonin Scalia Law School at George Mason University. Thank you to Devlin Hartline for his insights and his comments on a draft of this article. For research assistance, thank you to Kevin Beck, Matthew Dollett-Hemphill, and Juliet Lomeo.

[1] See Stephen Breyer, The Uneasy Case for Copyright: A Study of Copyright in Books, Photocopies, and Computer Programs, 84 Harv. L. Rev. 281 (1970).

[2] *Id.* at 351.

[3] 141 S. Ct. 1183 (2021).

Legally, it was just as significant. The Supreme Court promised to decide for the first time the scope of protection for computer programs under the Copyright Act.[4] It was also the first case in over two decades in which the Court addressed a fair use defense, and this was the first time the Court considered how fair use applied to the copying of a computer program. To add icing to the cake, the Court separately added a third issue concerning the standard of review for the fair use doctrine. Fifty-nine amicus briefs were filed with the Court after certiorari was granted, in addition to the filing by the solicitor general. Everyone seemed to have something to say about this case.[5]

Surprisingly, Google won in a 6-2 decision with the majority opinion written by Justice Breyer and a dissent by Justice Clarence Thomas (joined by Justice Samuel Alito). The oral argument appeared to go badly for Google, so many observers thought Google was going to lose. But the majority opinion was surprising beyond just the outcome itself. Justice Breyer's majority opinion is unusual in both the form and substance of copyright law.

As a matter of fair use doctrine, the Court held for the first time that a commercial firm that copied a copyrighted work without authorization for a commercial purpose, namely to create a competing product in the marketplace, was immune from liability. The Court appeared to punt on the question of copyrightability, assuming for the purposes of the opinion that the computer program at issue was copyrightable. But that punt will prove to be a false hope for owners of computer programs like Java. Justice Breyer's fair use analysis breaks new ground from prior Court decisions in both form and substance, providing a very expansive fair use defense for anyone who engages in

---

[4] The Supreme Court almost ruled on this issue in 1995 in *Lotus Dev. Corp. v. Borland Int'l,* but the Court split 4-4 due to the happenstance of a snowstorm that prevented Justice John Paul Stevens from participating in oral argument. 516 U.S. 233 (1996). Similar tribulations struck again in *Google.* The COVID-19 pandemic delayed oral argument, originally scheduled for late March 2020, until October 2020. Shortly before oral argument, Justice Ruth Bader Ginsburg passed away. Justice Ginsburg was known for her copyright jurisprudence, and she was often on opposite sides of cases from that of Justice Breyer. Thus, only eight justices (again) heard and decided *Google.*

[5] This included me, as I joined one of several amicus briefs filed by academics in support of Oracle.

the unauthorized copying of a computer software program.[6] The end result is that, despite the Court's denial, *Google* was a decision about the copyrightability of the computer code at issue in the case—the "declaring code" in the Java computer program.[7]

Of course, this article cannot possibly address all the legal and policy issues for copyright law in Justice Breyer's pathbreaking opinion. It would be surprising to see any single law journal article do this, even one of the monstrously long law journal articles that certainly will be published on *Google* in the years to come. Thus, I will focus here on the surprising and novel elements in the opinion in this academic version of a "hot take" to *Google*. First, I will briefly detail the background to the case—the nature of the technology and the licensing-negotiation breakdown between Google and Oracle. Second, I will discuss the copyrightability issue, which is necessary to properly frame the fair use analysis that follows. Third and finally, I will focus in depth on the Court's fair use analysis, as it drives the legal result in the case and opens up whole new vistas of doctrine and policy in copyright law. Along the way, Justice Thomas will make appearances in the discussion for various insights from his dissent. I hope the reader will enjoy the ride, as it has lots of twists and turns.

How *Google v. Oracle* Came to Be

First, a description of the background to the case, detailing the technology and the interactions between Google and Oracle, is necessary. Of course, this history is necessarily abridged, so professional programmers and legal experts will likely be unhappy with the details omitted in this survey. For those unhappy with this section, please consider it version 1.0. Later, longer, and more bloated versions will certainly patch the holes and debug the glitches.

Marc Andreessen, the programmer of Mosaic (the first web browser) and now venture capitalist, put it perfectly: software has

---

[6] See Google, 141 S. Ct. at 1213–14 (Thomas, J., dissenting) (observing that "the majority's application of fair use is far from ordinary").

[7] The third issue on the standard of review ended up being the proverbial dog that did not bark: commentators thought the Court would reverse and remand on the grounds that the Federal Circuit applied the wrong standard of review, but the Court decided this issue without having to reverse.

eaten the world.[8] It's omnipresent in our lives today. It goes far beyond computers, tablets, and smartphones. It runs planes, trains, and automobiles. It runs elevators, thermostats, and coffee machines. There are more transistors at work today than there are leaves on all the trees on the planet—approximately *15 quintillion* transistors as of 2018—and all of them are running computer programs.[9]

Everyone knows the computer programs we use daily (such as Outlook, Chrome, Word, or iTunes), but innumerable computer programs are running under the hood of our devices beyond the computer programs we directly use—which is why tech geeks call us "end-users." The programs that are buried deep in our operating systems and apps are the means by which all these programs interface with each other so that our computers, smartphones, and other devices work. For instance, your email client interfaces with your operating system, which interfaces with a company server, which interfaces with the structural code of the internet, which interfaces with the server receiving the email, and so on, and so on.

One such under-the-hood program is Java, which contains numerous software interfaces known as Application Programming Interfaces (APIs). APIs allow different computer programs to communicate with each other. Java, created by Sun Microsystems in 1995, has been integral to the interconnected world of the internet and mobile revolution of the past several decades. Programmers could use Java to write a program to run on any electronic device that had the Java Virtual Machine, another computer program, installed on it without having to write separate programs to run on each type of device; thus, Sun's famous slogan, "write once, run anywhere."

Java has been massively successful. Over the decades, Sun Microsystems and Oracle, which purchased Sun Microsystems in 2009, have earned billions through licensing of Java to companies creating computer programs to run on a myriad of digital devices and

[8] See Marc Andreessen, "Why Software Is Eating the World," Wall St. J., Aug. 20, 2011, https://bit.ly/2VgD7hW.

[9] See Simon Winchester, The Perfectionists: How Precision Engineers Created the Modern World 280 (2018).

products. (Since Oracle now owns Java and Oracle was the plaintiff that sued Google in 2010, I'll refer to Oracle as the owner of Java, even if a date occurs before 2009.)

Enter Google and its Android smartphone platform. In competition with Apple's iPhone, Google designed the Android smartphone to be open source, but not on the same basis as the well-known General Public License (GPL) that governs most open-source programs. Google gives away Android for free and permits customization of this smartphone operating system, but it does so with another open-source license (the Apache License). Google's business model isn't licensing; rather, it earns tens of billions annually by collecting and monetizing end-user data via targeted advertising and other uses. So, Google wanted Android to be free and available as open source for modification in different smartphone devices—thus the differences between a Samsung Galaxy and an old Motorola Droid—but it didn't want the universal interoperability required by Oracle for devices using Java.

Still, Google wanted programmers familiar with the widely known and used Java API to easily start making lots of new apps for Android. This would immediately create positive network effects, resulting in tons of sales of Android smartphones. More end users creating data with Android and its accompanying apps would create even more revenue for Google through its ad-based business model. Google thus copied the computer code in Java used by programmers in writing APIs, known as the "declaring code." This fact is undisputed, and Justice Breyer acknowledged it in his opinion: "Because Google wanted millions of programmers, familiar with Java, to be able easily to work with its new Android platform, it also copied roughly 11,500 lines of code from the Java SE program."[10]

Google didn't have to copy the code from Java to make an out-of-the-gate-successful device. Apple and Microsoft developed their own declaring code in their own APIs. Justice Thomas made this point in his dissenting opinion, since it is unacknowledged in Justice Breyer's majority opinion.[11] No one would think Apple

---

[10] Google, 141 S. Ct. at 1191.

[11] See *id.* at 1212, 1214 (Thomas, J., dissenting).

or Microsoft is hurting for innovation or commercial success. But Google didn't have to go the Apple or Microsoft route, either, and write its own API program. Google could have licensed Java. Oracle offered three separate licensing options for Java, two of which were paid-for licenses for proprietary versions of Java and a third which was a free, open-source GPL.[12] In fact, Google at first engaged in extensive licensing negotiations with Oracle to obtain permission to use Java in its new Android smartphone platform.

These negotiations were unsuccessful. Google embraced an open-source, proprietary model for Android, and thus none of Oracle's licensing options worked for Google. The open-source GPL did not work because Google wanted programs designed for Android to be proprietary to Android and not interoperable on any other device—Android is free and open source for only Android. Oracle's second licensing option permitted Google to have a proprietary API, as it could license the valuable declaring code and develop its own proprietary API program, but this license still required interoperability with any device or machine with a Java Virtual Machine. Again, Google did not want this result; Google did not want Android apps to be interoperable beyond Android. Google did not want to pay for a license for a proprietary version of the Java API that required interoperability, and the free, open-source GPL for Java was incompatible with Google's open-source and proprietary licensing model for Android. Given its plans for Android, Google was unwilling to take any of the three license options from Oracle.

Acknowledging the value in the Java declaring code known to programmers worldwide, Google copied the 11,500 lines of declaring code. It released Android in 2008, first available on an HTC device but really taking off commercially with the Motorola Droid released in 2009 (my own first smartphone). The rest is history. Android is the top-selling smartphone platform in terms of numbers of devices sold worldwide. More people worldwide have smartphones now than have access to potable water, and most of these smartphones are Android devices.

---

[12] Oracle v. Google, 750 F.3d 1339, 1350 (Fed. Cir. 2014) (describing the three licensing programs for Java).

But before Google made smartphone history, Oracle sued Google for patent and copyright infringement in 2010. The patent claims were later dropped, but this is how the case ended up before the United States Court of Appeals for the Federal Circuit, which is the appellate court that hears all patent appeals. The jury found for Oracle that Google infringed its copyright, but the district court ruled as a matter of law that the Java declaring code was uncopyrightable. Oracle appealed, and the Federal Circuit reversed and remanded for a trial on Google's fair use defense. Google then filed for certiorari with the Supreme Court on the copyrightability issue, but the Court denied the petition. After the second trial, the jury found that Google was immune from liability under the fair use doctrine. Oracle appealed again and won a second reversal by the Federal Circuit. Embracing the adage, "if at first you don't succeed, try, try again," Google filed for certiorari again. This time, the Court granted Google's petition on all the issues raised in the case—the copyrightability of the Java API and Google's fair use defense—as well as a third issue of the standard of review for an appeal from a district court's fair use decision.

The Copyrightability of Computer Software Programs

The first issue in *Google* was whether a software program like an API is copyrightable. This has been a longstanding dispute in copyright law and policy reaching back to when the digital revolution took off like a rocket in the 1960s and 1970s. (The Apollo program would not have been possible without computers, as the newly invented integrated circuits got us to the moon.)

Initially, courts and commentators were strongly divided on whether computer code was copyrightable. Congress resolved this debate when it enacted the Computer Software Copyright Act of 1980.[13] Coincidentally, that same year, the Supreme Court ruled in *Diamond v. Chakrabarty* that biotech innovations were patentable inventions.[14] Nineteen eighty was thus an important year in intellectual property law. That year Congress and the Court established a

---

[13] Pub. L. No. 96-517, § 117, 94 Stat. 3015, 3028 (1980).
[14] Diamond v. Chakrabarty, 447 U.S. 303 (1980).

stable legal foundation for the biotech and personal computer revolutions that developed in the ensuing years.[15]

The Computer Software Copyright Act is clear and straightforward: computer programs are copyrightable. The legislation very broadly defines a copyrightable computer program as "a set of statements or instructions to be used directly or indirectly in a computer in order to bring about a certain result."[16] The broad statutory definition in the Computer Software Copyright Act makes sense. The purpose of this legislation was to resolve definitively the split in the courts in favor of the copyrightability of computer software programs.[17]

Since Java is a computer program that represents "a set of . . . instructions to be used directly or indirectly in a computer in order to bring about a certain result," it seems to easily fall within the scope of the text of the Computer Software Copyright Act. Ergo, it is copyrightable. The statutory text does not distinguish between different types of computer programs, such as operating systems, applications, or the many programs that work below the surface that end users never directly experience. This is the meaning of "indirectly" as an adjective in the statutory definition of a computer program "used . . . to bring about a certain result." Nor does the statutory language distinguish between types of code, such as source code or object code.[18] This is the meaning of the "set of statements or instructions" in the statutory definition, the subject of the proposition that encompasses all computer programs and code.

Not so fast, argued Google. In defending its unauthorized copying of the 11,500 lines of code in the Java program, Google first argued

---

[15] See Adam Mossoff, A Brief History of Software Patents (and Why They're Valid), 56 Ariz. L. Rev. Syllabus 62, 74 (2014) ("It is significant that the Computer Software Copyright Act was enacted in the early 1980s because it was during this time—the late 1970s and early 1980s—that the personal computer ('PC') Revolution began."); Adam Mossoff & Kevin Madigan, Turning Gold to Lead: How Patent Eligibility Doctrine Is Undermining U.S. Leadership in Innovation, 24 Geo. Mason L. Rev. 939, 943–44 (2017) (discussing how *Chakrabarty* launched the biotech revolution).

[16] 17 U.S.C. § 101.

[17] Mossoff, A Brief History of Software Patents, *supra* note 15, at 73–74.

[18] See Comput. Assocs. Int'l v. Altai, Inc., 982 F.2d 693, 702 (2d Cir. 1992).

that the code that it copied was not copyrightable. Google copied the declaring code, which is the code representing commands entered by the programmer to make the implementing code in Java function as an API—it is the implementing code that interfaces between apps and other programs. Thus, Google argued that the declaring code is inherently or entirely functional because it represents a "method of operation" for programmers in writing a Java API, and a "method of operation" is excluded from copyright protection under § 102(b) in the Copyright Act.[19] By the time of oral argument, Google's copyrightability argument had morphed from one of statutory exclusion into a broader merger doctrine argument that expression is uncopyrightable if it is inextricably intertwined (merged) with an idea and functionality.[20]

Google likely shifted in its argument because, as Justice Thomas pointed out in his dissent, the statutory text in the Computer Software Copyright Act is clear: "Congress rejected any categorical distinction" between types of computer code when it amended the Copyright Act to protect code that functioned "directly or indirectly" in a computer software program.[21]

Much time at oral argument was spent on the copyrightability issue, and, as a result, many commentators on both sides concluded that Google was likely going to lose.[22] During oral argument, Justice Elena Kagan said that she was "surprised or confused" by Google's

[19] 17 U.S.C. § 102(b) ("In no case does copyright protection for an original work of authorship extend to any . . . method of operation.").

[20] The merger doctrine is a longstanding doctrine in copyright law that creates an exception for the copyrightability of a written work. When an idea can only be expressed in one or a few ways in writing, the expression becomes inextricably bound up with the idea being expressed and thus cannot be protected. Protecting the expression would mean protecting the idea, which is impermissible in copyright law. See Baker v. Selden, 101 U.S. 99 (1879). In this case, the Federal Circuit held that there were numerous options available to both Google and Oracle in expressing their ideas and thus the merger doctrine did not apply. See Oracle 750 F.3d at 1358–62 (Fed. Cir. 2014).

[21] Google, 141 S. Ct. at 1213 (Thomas, J., dissenting).

[22] See, e.g., Timothy B. Lee, "Google's Supreme Court Faceoff with Oracle Was a Disaster for Google," Ars Technica, Oct. 8, 2020, https://bit.ly/3ibRHiU; Kevin Madigan, "Media Coverage of Google v. Oracle Oral Arguments Recounts Tough Day in Court for Google," Copyright Alliance, Oct. 20, 2020, https://bit.ly/3hGtvWA.

copyrightability argument.[23] Justice Neil Gorsuch agreed with her, confessing that he was "stuck in a similar place as Justice Kagan."[24] Expressions of surprise or confusion are not what a lawyer wants to hear during oral argument before the Court, and not just by one justice, but by two justices from across the jurisprudential spectrum. The general mood after oral argument was that Google was going to lose, and not just on the issue of copyrightability, but the entire case.[25]

Surprise and confusion continued to be the refrain when the Court issued its decision on April 5, 2021. Despite the concerns and skepticism expressed at oral argument, the Court soundly ruled in favor of Google and punted on the copyrightability issue, at least nominally. The *Google* Court addressed the copyrightability issue in a single sentence: "We shall assume, but purely for argument's sake, that the entire Sun Java API falls within the definition of that which can be copyrighted."[26]

This was surprising for several reasons. First, Justice Breyer's opinion for the Court was clear that its affirmation of the copyrightability of the API computer program was "purely for argument's sake." If there was any doubt about this, Justice Breyer reiterated this caveat—"if copyrightable at all"—later in the opinion, in the conclusion of his fair use analysis, holding that declaring code was far "from the core of copyright" and thus received minimal protection.[27] Yet, the Court could easily have held that the declaring code copied by Google is copyrightable, but that, after a balancing of the fair use factors, Google was still safe from liability. It is a head scratcher, to say the least, why the Court believed that it could conclude only for the sake of argument and in a single sentence an issue that consumed

[23] See Transcript of Oral Argument at 24–25, Google v. Oracle, 141 S. Ct. 1183 (2021) (No. 18-956).

[24] *Id.* at 29–30.

[25] See, e.g., Connor Hansen & Stefan Szpajda, "Google v. Oracle: What We Learned from Oral Argument," JDSupra.com, Oct. 22, 2020, https://bit.ly/2Ujjhm9 (noting that "the Justices . . . on balance[] signaled skepticism of Google's positions on each of the issues before the Court"); Eileen McDermott, "Justices Look for Reassurance That the Sky Won't Fall When They Rule in Google v. Oracle," IPWatchdog.com, Oct. 7, 2020, https://bit.ly/3hHXm0R (quoting Gene Quinn that "it seems to me that unless the Supreme Court fundamentally changes the law, Google will lose").

[26] Google, 141 S. Ct. at 1197.

[27] *Id.* at 1202.

hundreds of pages of legal briefs and tens of pages of court opinions over a decade, as well as a substantial portion of oral argument before the Court.

Second, Justice Breyer conceded the issue of the copyrightability of the declaring code for argument's sake about halfway through his opinion for the Court, which left scant time for him to address the other two issues. Yet, after detailing the nature of APIs as computer software programs, reviewing the facts, summarizing copyright policy and doctrine, and restating the two issues posed by Google in its cert petition, one thing is clear: all of the Court's legal work would be in a fair use analysis, constituting about half of the Court's entire opinion. Justice Breyer spent a surprisingly small portion of his opinion on the substantive legal analysis that produced the heart and core of the Court's decision, in much the same way that Google, in Justice Breyer's view, had copied only a relatively small portion of the Java program when viewed in the context of Java's millions of lines of code.

Finally, this conditional assumption on the copyrightability of the declaring code was surprising because, as Justice Thomas stated in his dissent, the majority "opinion . . . makes it difficult to imagine any circumstance in which declaring code will remain protected by copyright."[28] It may seem easy to dismiss Justice Thomas's statement as the standard hyperbole of dissenting opinions, in which justices are wont to identify a parade of horribles that will follow from majority opinions. But in *Google*, this statement was not hyperbole: an API program is not protectible by copyright after this decision. In the prophetic words used by Justice Antonin Scalia in one of his dissents, "this wolf comes as a wolf."[29] The fair use defense enunciated by Justice Breyer is so expansive, and the protections offered by copyright for an API program are conversely so minimal, that it is virtually impossible to think of a scenario in which an unauthorized use of an API program would not be deemed justifiable as fair use.

Indeed, Justice Thomas was not alone in reaching this conclusion when the decision came down.[30] A month later, an expert

---

[28] *Id.* at 1214 (Thomas, J., dissenting).

[29] Morrison v. Olson, 487 U.S. 654, 699 (1988) (Scalia, J., dissenting).

[30] See IP Watchdog, "Stakeholders Speak Out on Google v. Oracle," IPWatchdog. com, Apr. 7, 2021, https://bit.ly/3epUcwV (quoting Bob Zeidman that the "decision effectively made software uncopyrightable").

testified in the trial for Epic's antitrust lawsuit against Apple; when pressed under cross examination on the copyrightability of Apple's APIs used in its App Store, he acknowledged that "based on [*Google v. Oracle*], not all software code is protected under the IP laws."[31] How and why an API program is no longer effectively protectible under copyright is the subject of the next section.

Transforming Fair Use into a Copyrightability Doctrine[32]

Fair use doctrine did all of the heavy lifting for the Court to reach its decision in *Google*, and Justice Breyer's opinion for the Court was novel and groundbreaking in copyright law. For the first time, the Court held that a company was immune from liability when it deliberately copied without authorization a copyrighted work for a commercial purpose, not because it was engaged in parody or commentary, but because it made and sold a competing product in the marketplace. That's definitely a "whoa!" moment in copyright law.

Although constituting about half of the entire opinion, Justice Breyer packed a lot into this fair use analysis. As with my review of the background of the case and the API program at issue, I can't possibly explore here all of the nooks and crannies of this portion of the opinion. Thus, this section details some key portions of the novel structure and substantive analysis that has led to the widely recognized result that API programs are effectively no longer protectible under copyright law.

What Is Fair Use?

Fair use doctrine is a multifactor legal doctrine that commentators and scholars have long complained is rife with indeterminacy and unpredictability. Fair use doctrine is often identified as "equitable,"

---

[31] Dorothy Atkins, "Google v. Oracle Hangs Over Apple's IP Defense in Epic Trial," Law360, May 20, 2021, https://bit.ly/3hG7xTz (reporting on testimony by John Malackowski, chief executive and cofounder of Ocean Tomo).

[32] With apologies to Laura G. Lape, Transforming Fair Use: The Productive Use Factor in Fair Use Doctrine, 58 Albany L. Rev. 677 (1994–1995).

which Justice Breyer detailed a bit in *Google*,[33] given that its roots are found in court cases, not in legislation. The foundational case for fair use doctrine was the 1841 decision in *Folsom v. Marsh* by Justice Joseph Story, riding circuit.[34] The doctrine remained a judicial gloss on the copyright statutes until Congress codified fair use in § 107 of the 1976 Copyright Act.[35] Even so, it continues to be largely defined in substance by judicial decisions.

Section 107 lists four factors for courts to assess in determining when unauthorized copying or use is immunized from liability:

(1) the purpose and character of the use, including whether such use is of a commercial nature or is for nonprofit educational purposes;

(2) the nature of the copyrighted work;

(3) the amount and substantiality of the portion used in relation to the copyrighted work as a whole; and

(4) the effect of the use upon the potential market for or value of the copyrighted work.

Although § 107 states that these factors are nonexclusive, courts have proven that codification often means ossification. Judges have generally applied only these four factors and usually in lockstep fashion in resolving defendants' claims that they are engaging in fair use.[36]

The overarching theme of the four factors, which are taken primarily from Justice Story's analysis in *Folsom*, is that the unauthorized copying and use of the work should not interfere with the commercial exploitation of the work by the copyright owner. Conversely, users of copyrighted works should be free to engage in activities or speech that are distinct from the primary markets in which

---

[33] Google, 141 S. Ct. at 1196 (quoting Stewart v. Abend, 495 U.S. 207, 236 (1990) that the fair use doctrine arose as an "equitable rule of reason"). See also Weissmann v. Freeman, 868 F.2d 1313, 1323 (2d Cir. 1989) ("Analysis begins not by elevating the statutory guides into inflexible rules, but with a review of the underlying equities.").

[34] See Folsom v. Marsh, 9 F. Cas. 342 (C.C.D. Mass. 1841) (No. 4,901) (Story, Circuit Justice).

[35] See Pub. L. No. 94-553, 90 Stat. 2541, 2546 (1976).

[36] Barton Beebe, An Empirical Study of U.S. Copyright Fair Use Opinions, 1978–2005, 156 U. Pa. L. Rev. 549, 561–62 (2008).

a copyrighted work is sold. Thus, for instance, a news article may report on a famous book, such as one of the Harry Potter novels, or a scholar may quote the book in an academic article or discuss its characters in teaching a class. These are all express fair uses of a copyrighted work.[37] Again, these are activities that do not produce market substitutes for the copyrighted work in the relevant market in which the work is sold and used.

Unsurprisingly, factor one and factor four have been mostly front and center in judicial analyses of fair use claims with heavy emphases on the nature of the allegedly infringing use and the impact on the current or potential market for the copyrighted work. This is also reflected in the now-dominant judicial standard for assessing factor one, which asks whether the use by the defendant is *transformative*.[38] Again, this standard makes sense from a commercialization perspective. A transformative use of a work neither serves as a market substitute nor forecloses potential commercial uses within a relevant market.

The Nature of Computer Code as an Expressive Work

As noted, courts typically begin their fair use analysis with factor one—the purpose and character of the use and whether it is commercial or not—and this is where courts address the question of whether the unauthorized use is transformative or not. But Justice Breyer began his fair use analysis with factor two—the nature of the work—and not with factor one. Although skipping over factor one is not completely unheard of in copyright law, it is very uncommon among lower courts, and the Supreme Court had not done so before in any of its prior fair use cases under § 107.

Justice Breyer invoked the "equitable," context-specific nature of fair use doctrine to justify starting with the second factor (nature of the work), and this is significant for two reasons. First, Justice Breyer argued that computer code is different from literary works like Harry Potter because computer programs "always serve

---

[37] In addition to the four factors, § 107 expressly states that "criticism, comment, news reporting, teaching (including multiple copies for classroom use), scholarship, or research, is not an infringement of copyright." 17 U.S.C. § 107.

[38] See Pierre N. Leval, Toward a Fair Use Standard, 103 Harv. L. Rev. 1105 (1990).

functional purposes."[39] He identified the Java API as a "user interface" that is ultimately "inextricably bound together with a general system, the division of computer tasks, that no one claims is a proper subject of copyright."[40] If you are feeling a bit of déjà vu at this moment, you are right. This was Google's method of operation/merger doctrine argument for why the declaring code was not copyrightable, which had surprised and confused both Justice Kagan and Justice Gorsuch during oral argument.[41]

For lawyers and commentators knowledgeable about these legal and technical issues, Justice Breyer confirmed this sense of déjà vu with a classic poker "tell": he cited in his factor two analysis the 1995 decision in *Lotus Development Corp. v. Borland International* by the U.S. Court of Appeals for the First Circuit.[42] In fact, he quoted from or cited *Lotus* four times in *Google*, and three of these four citations were to the concurring opinion by Judge Michael Boudin. This is odd, if only because *Lotus* was not a fair use decision.

The *Lotus* court famously held that Lotus could not copyright the pull-down (or drop-down) menu with a list of commands to select in its then-famous Lotus 1-2-3 spreadsheet program, as this was a graphical user interface that was a purely functional "method of operation" under § 102(b). In *Lotus*, Borland had replicated the pull-down menu *without* copying the computer code; it used entirely different computer code. The *Lotus* court ruled that Lotus could not extend its copyright protection over its computer code to the functional pull-down menu as a graphical interface for end users. In other words, *Lotus* is a *copyrightability decision*. Of course, this was the first issue in *Google* that the Court skipped for the sake of argument—whether Java (and APIs more generally) was uncopyrightable because the declaring code inherently merged with its programming function.[43]

---

[39] Google, 141 S. Ct. at 1198.

[40] *Id.* at 1201. See also *id.* at 1202 (stating that with declaring code, "unlike many other programs, its use is inherently bound together with uncopyrightable ideas (general task division and organization) and new creative expression (Android's implementing code)").

[41] See *supra* notes 17–24 and accompanying text.

[42] 49 F.3d 807 (1st Cir. 1995), aff'd by an equally divided Court, 516 U.S. 233 (1996).

[43] See *supra* notes 17–24 and accompanying text.

In referencing *Lotus*, Justice Breyer's statement that an API is a "user interface" is both telling and also a bit odd. The declaring code copied by Google, which was specifically at issue in this case, is not a user interface in the normal sense of this term. An API is not something an end user interfaces with in the way an end user interfaces with Outlook to write and send an email; rather, an API is an under-the-hood program in the guts of an operating system or app. In *Lotus* the company tried to copyright the "method of operation" in a user interface—the pull-down menu in a spreadsheet program—and it seems there was an important equivocation occurring in *Google* under factor two of the fair use doctrine between written code and user interface. This equivocation motivated the conclusion under factor two that an API is inherently bound up with its functionality such that the declaring code should receive very little copyright protection, or effectively none.

Second, Justice Breyer downplayed the creativity exercised by the programmers in selecting the declaring code when designing the Java API. He emphasized instead the inherently functional or mechanical nature of the declaring code in computer operations as an "interface." Here, Justice Breyer referenced his earlier, vivid description of an API program at the start of his opinion. Breyer had used numerous metaphors to characterize what an API program is and how it functions as a digital mechanism, allowing a person using an app on a digital device to work with that device and other devices to achieve the goals of the end-user app. He compared an API to an automobile gas pedal, the QWERTY keyboard, the Dewey Decimal system for categorizing books in a library, office file cabinets, and a programmable cooking robot.[44]

The combination of these two arguments—that an API is inherently functional and that, as a user interface, its functionality is necessarily intertwined with its unprotectible features—naturally led Justice Breyer to the conclusion that "the declaring code [in the Java API] is, if copyrightable at all, further than are most computer programs (such as the implementing code) from the core of copyright."[45] By reanimating the method of operation/merger doctrine argument

---

[44] Google, 141 S. Ct. at 1192–93.
[45] *Id.* at 1202.

from the copyrightability issue nominally skipped over by the Court, Justice Breyer was able to achieve under the second factor of the fair use doctrine what the Computer Software Copyright Act expressly disallowed: narrowing the scope of copyright protection for declaring code by distinguishing between types of computer programs and giving declaring code a more "thin" protection[46] than other types of computer code or expressive works deemed to be "closer to the core of copyright."[47]

This reading is a disservice to programmers and the companies that employ them to produce the innovative products and services that have driven the high-tech industry and the U.S. innovation economy for the past several decades. In each context of creative expression, whether a novel, an engraving, a map, or a computer program, the protectible creative elements are always intertwined with unprotectible facts, ideas, or functions. As Justice Thomas pointed out, even books are "inherently bound with uncopyrightable ideas—the use of chapters, having a plot, or including dialogue or footnotes. This does not place books far 'from the core of copyright.'"[48]

Programmers engage in creative labors in producing code that is often characterized as "elegant" or even "beautiful." Bad code is "cludgy." Beyond its technical sense, "cludgy" clearly conveys an artistic connotation. All engineers always aspire to find the "elegant solution" to a problem.

In denying this creativity, Justice Breyer was reaffirming a position he held 50 years ago—coding is not really a creative endeavor. In *The Uneasy Case for Copyright*, he stated that computer programs were not even as creative as the architectural drawings, photographs, or code words that were eventually brought within the protections of the copyright laws. Computer programs, he argued, "are neither of literary or artistic intent nor are they intended to convey information to another person."[49]

---

[46] *Id.* at 1197–98.

[47] *Id.* at 1202.

[48] *Id.* at 1215 (Thomas, J., dissenting).

[49] Breyer, *supra* note 1, at 340 n.233.

In fact, one of the reasons for the success of Java was precisely because of the selection of the declaring code by its programmers. That's what made it appealing for programmers, just as the selection of names of characters and even the descriptions of objects in a book can make it more appealing for readers—think Harry Potter. This creativity in selecting the declaring code used by programmers who would use it to create an API contributed in part to Java becoming massively popular as the internet itself began to grow at an even more explosive rate.

Java was so valuable that Google did not want to launch its Android smartphone platform without it, just like Harry Potter became so popular that its readers wanted more—movies, games, costumes, and other derivative works. This value is what copyright promotes and secures for its owners. It ensures they may profit from their productive labors by exclusively controlling the use of the work and derivative uses as well. Contrary to Justice Breyer's claim that the declaring code was far from the "core of copyright," the declaring code in Java seems exactly the type of valuable expressive work that is—and ought to be—protected by copyright. This is confirmed by the Software Copyright Protection Act, and by Google's desire to use the valuable declaring code for its own products.

The Purpose and Character of Google's Use of the Declaring Code

Google's unauthorized use of the declaring code leads to the first fair use factor—the purpose and character of the use. Given the equitable nature of fair use doctrine, Justice Breyer had the discretion to address the first factor second. Indeed, the equitable nature of fair use doctrine proved to be a lynchpin in *Google*. The equitable nature of the doctrine is what Justice Breyer invoked to give him the discretion to ultimately conclude under the second factor (analyzed first) that there was very *narrow* copyright protection for the declaring code, as opposed to other copyrighted works. Now, under the first factor, this same discretion worked in the other direction: Justice Breyer *expansively* construed the "transformative" nature of Google's copying of the Java declaring code for use in the Android smartphone platform.

Justice Breyer noted that Google's copying of the Java declaring code for use in its Android smartphone platform was clearly transformative. Notably, Justice Breyer continued to refer to the

Java declaring code as an "interface."[50] He explained, in the high-tech industry, programmers often "reimplement" a computer program interface by adopting it for "a distinct and different computing environment."[51] This is certainly correct if one is speaking about interfaces, such as the pull-down menus now ubiquitous in end-user apps using graphical user interfaces such as word processors, spreadsheets, and email clients. Justice Breyer extended this reimplementation theory to the copying of the declaring code in the Java API. He argued that, in copying the declaring code for the new smartphone platform in Android, Google was simply engaging in its own reimplementation of a computer interface, transforming it for a new computing environment (smartphones) in an innovative and creative way.

Apparently, Justice Breyer wanted to have his equity cake and eat it too. First, he invoked the equitable nature of fair use doctrine to give him the discretion to apply fair use in novel and unusual ways—both formally and substantively. Then he shunted to the side the important inquiries courts typically make when a defendant invokes an equitable doctrine to shield itself from legal liability. One such inquiry is whether the defendant acted with bad faith, or, in the case of copyright infringement, engaged in explicit piracy in deliberately copying a work for commercial gain. Here, Justice Breyer addressed these issues in just two paragraphs and deemed them to be either "not dispositive" or "not determinative" in this case.[52]

Google did not dispute that it deliberately copied 11,500 lines of Oracle's Java declaring code after a breakdown in lengthy negotiations for a license. It couldn't deny this inescapable fact. As one revealing internal email to Andy Rubin, head of the Android team at Google, stated: "What we've actually been asked to do (by Larry [Page] and Sergey [Brin]) is to investigate what technical alternatives exist to Java for Android and Chrome. We've been over a bunch of these, and think they all suck. We conclude that we need

---

[50] Google, 141 S. Ct. at 1203–04. Again, this is, at best, loose and confusing terminology, or, at worst, simply incorrect, as code is not the same thing as the appearance or function of a computer program.

[51] *Id.* at 1203.

[52] *Id.* at 1204.

to negotiate a license for Java under the terms we need."[53] Another email to Rubin stated: "With talks with Sun broken off where does that leave us regarding Java class libraries? Ours are half-ass at best. We need another half of an ass."[54] Desiring a better half of an ass, Google deliberately made the business decision to pirate the 11,500 lines of valuable declaring code. This was the easiest solution, given that Google could not square the circle of making Android immediately appealing to programmers while rejecting the interoperability requirement in Oracle's three license options, including even in its free, open-source GPL.

Contrary to Justice Breyer's claim that "it would have been difficult, perhaps prohibitively so, to attract programmers to build its Android smartphone system without" the Java declaring code, Google could have written its own API program without copying the Java declaring code. As noted earlier, Apple did exactly this. So did Microsoft. Alternatively, Google could have simply rethought its business model for Android as an open source, proprietary smartphone platform, as opposed to the open source, interoperable version that Oracle implemented through Java. Oracle had licensed the successful Java program through multiple commercial options for many years, contributing to the explosive growth of the interoperable internet and mobile devices. Instead, Google copied the declaring code because it was simply a cheaper, easier, and quicker route to its commercial goal of producing a successful smartphone platform—it engaged in what is now called predatory infringement (and what policy wonks call "efficient infringement").[55]

Justice Breyer neither acknowledged this piracy nor even disputed the evidence of the piracy in his equitable analysis of Google's fair use claim. This point bears highlighting: Google committed piracy. It deliberately copied the declaring code for its own commercial

---

[53] Exhibit C to Oracle's Opposition to Motion to Preclude Submission of Willfulness to Jury, Oracle America, Inc. v. Google Inc., Docket No. 3:10-cv-03561 (N.D. Cal., Aug. 12, 2010) (Doc. 1299-4).

[54] Exhibit L to Oracle's Opposition to Motion to Preclude Submission of Willfulness to Jury, Oracle America, Inc. v. Google Inc., Docket No. 3:10-cv-03561 (N.D. Cal., Aug. 12, 2010) (Doc. 1299-13).

[55] See Adam Mossoff & Bhamati Viswanathan, Explaining Efficient Infringement, Ctr. for Intellectual Prop. & Innovation Pol'y, May 11, 2017, https://bit.ly/3wKbhrJ.

benefit to make a commercial substitute for the original copyrighted Java computer program in its extremely successful smartphone platform. In his earlier review of the facts and procedural history of the case, Justice Breyer stated some of the facts of Google's piracy, but did not identify it as piracy. He had to acknowledge these facts, if only because they were undeniable and undisputed. "Because Google wanted millions of programmers, familiar with Java, to be able to easily work with its new Android program, it also copied roughly 11,500 lines of code from the Java SE program."[56] This decision to copy the valuable declaring code, contributing to Android's success, was immensely profitable for Google. As of 2015, Google had earned more than $42 billion from the Android smartphone platform; it has earned tens of billions more since that time.[57]

Justice Breyer addressed only obliquely and in a few sentences the longstanding recognition in fair use doctrine that the "good faith" of the defendant is a legitimate concern. In highly generalized language (declining to engage with the specific facts of the piracy, in contrast to Justice Thomas in his dissent), Justice Breyer noted that good faith was not necessarily dispositive in a fair use decision. This is certainly true as a matter of general legal doctrine; it is rare for courts to apply per se rules within an equitable doctrine.[58] Presumptions tend to be more common, and here the Court did adopt in its 1984 decision in *Sony v. Universal Studios* a presumption against fair use if the copying was done for a commercial purpose,[59] but it abandoned this presumption in its 1994 decision in *Campbell v. Acuff-Rose Music*.[60]

---

[56] Google, 141 S. Ct. at 1191.

[57] *Id.* at 1194.

[58] See Sony Corp. of Am. v. Universal City Studios, Inc., 464 U.S. 417, 448 n.31 (1984) (quoting from the House Report for § 107 that fair use is an "equitable rule of reason" and noting both the House and Senate followed the courts' jurisprudence in adopting § 107 and thus "eschewed a rigid, bright line approach to fair use").

[59] See *id.* at 451 (stating that "every commercial use of copyrighted material is presumptively an unfair exploitation of the monopoly privilege that belongs to the owner of the copyright").

[60] See Campbell v. Acuff-Rose Music, Inc., 510 U.S. 569, 584 (1994) ("The language of [§ 107] makes clear that the commercial or nonprofit educational purpose of a work is only one element of the first factor enquiry into its purpose and character.").

Justice Breyer was correct that a commercial purpose pursued with bad faith does not automatically doom a defendant's fair use defense, but it has proven to be highly dispositive in practice. This result is unsurprising for an "equitable" doctrine that naturally involves inquiries into a litigant's state of mind or willingness to engage in strategic behavior. The question reaches back to the foundation of fair use doctrine in the 1841 *Folsom v. Marsh* decision, which was cited in *Google* (as it has been in almost all major fair use decisions).[61] In *Folsom*, Circuit Justice Story stated simply as legal truth that a copyright is "private property" and that the law secures an owner, including a commercial intermediary like a publisher, against "piracy."[62] An oft-cited, rigorous empirical study of modern fair use cases found that findings of bad faith are not common, but "in the few cases where courts explicitly found that the defendant's conduct was undertaken in bad faith, courts almost invariably found no fair use."[63] Thus, despite no per se rule or presumption against fair use for commercial use undertaken with bad faith, courts routinely find that piracy is ultimately a disqualifying factor for claiming as a matter of right that one should be immune from liability for copyright infringement under an equitable doctrine.

In his dissent, Justice Thomas pointed out (under factor four) that Google's piracy of the Java declaring code destroyed Oracle's licensing business model, which was distinct from Google's ad-based business model.[64] Accordingly, Google sought to maximize as quickly as possible market adoption of the Android smartphone platform, which ultimately brought the company billions in ad-based revenue. Google was not worried about the negative commercial implications of its copying of the declaring code for Oracle, the company that actually owned this declaring code and relied on licensing as its business model to profit from its property.

The negative impact on Oracle's licensing of Java and its revenue was immediate. After the release of Android with the pirated declaring code, licensees leveraged "the cost-free availability of Android"

---

[61] Google, 141 S. Ct. at 1197.

[62] Folsom, 9 F. Cas. at 345.

[63] Beebe, *supra* note 36, at 608.

[64] Google, 141 S. Ct. at 1216–17 (Thomas, J., dissenting).

to renegotiate their licenses with Oracle. For example, Amazon reduced its royalty payments to Oracle by 97.5 percent.[65] Similarly, Samsung's license with Oracle "dropped from $40 million to about $1 million."[66] Examples like these provide substantial evidence that Google's copying of the declaring code was not "transformative"—converting the copied work into a new market context with a different function or purpose—but instead was an act of deliberate copyright infringement that struck at the core of a copyright owner's ability to reap the benefits from its property.

Justice Breyer did not address these facts in his opinion; he instead balanced an oblique reference to "good faith" against what he deemed to be the innovative technological and commercial transformation in the copied code—Google "reimplemented" the "interface" of the Java declaring code for a new smartphone device. This was important innovation that a copyright owner, argued Justice Breyer, should not be permitted to prevent. Oracle was willing to license to Google, but Google was not happy with the terms of the licensing options. Oracle, he explained, should not be able to create a "lock limiting the future creativity of new programs," as this "lock would interfere with, not further, copyright's basic creativity objectives."[67] Here, he broadly defined a use of a copied work as transformative if it somehow prevents a generalized concern about stifling of innovation and commercial activities. For support, he cited a few appellate court opinions and some amicus briefs arguing that antitrust policies—concerns about "monopolization" and "anti-competitive power"—are fundamental to a fair use analysis.[68]

Much more can be said about the nature of Google's copying and the unusual nature of Justice Breyer's fair use analysis. For instance, as Justice Thomas pointed out, the expansive definition of transformative use "wrongly conflates transformative use with derivative use." The derivative right—the extension of a copyrighted work into a new commercial context, such as taking a character from a novel and converting it into a character in a movie, video

[65] *Id.* at 1216.
[66] *Id.*
[67] *Id.* at 1208.
[68] *Id.* at 1204, 1208.

game, or even in advertisements for household products—is expressly secured to copyright owners under the Copyright Act.[69] Justice Breyer neither defined nor discussed in the Court's opinion how he would distinguish between innovative transformative uses of explicit copies for a commercial purpose that qualify as a fair use and the exclusive right of a copyright owner to decide how and under what terms a work may be copied and used in new market contexts.

As with the earlier poker "tell" of the repeated citations to *Lotus* in the fair use analysis, another "tell" confirms how unusual and expansive Justice Breyer's fair use analysis is in *Google*. In the conclusion of the Court's opinion, in which he again cited *Lotus*, Justice Breyer stated, "We do not overturn or modify our earlier cases involving fair use—cases, for example, that involve 'knockoff' products, journalistic writings, and parodies."[70] This statement would not be necessary—unless of course the Court's analysis raised the concern by diverging from earlier fair use decisions. The Court's analysis raised many questions: How intertwined does a creative work need to be with unprotectible elements before it receives merely "thin" copyright protection? Does piracy now get a free pass under fair use? Is the derivative right now a similarly "thin" copyright protection in the face of a fair use claim to a transformative use? Justice Breyer's sentence about the limits of the decision—limiting it to the copying and use of the Java API by Google—says far more than just its literal meaning.

The Court's decision may ultimately be limited to the copyright protection for an API computer program. But it is an open question whether lawyers, judges, or academics will delimit their legal and policy analyses of *Google* to merely the facts of the API computer program and Google's copying of the declaring code for its Android smartphone platform. There are early indications of lawyers and judges being as creative with *Google* as *Google* itself was with the fair use doctrine that preexisted it. Given the explicit adoption into fair use doctrine of antitrust policy concerns about promoting

---

[69] See 17 U.S.C. § 106(2) ("[T]he owner of copyright under this title has the exclusive rights . . . to prepare derivative works based upon the copyrighted work.").

[70] Google, 141 S. Ct. at 1208.

competition and preventing monopolies stifling innovation, *Google* is already making appearances in high-tech antitrust cases, such as Epic's antitrust lawsuit against Apple.[71] In another copyright case involving a fair use defense by the estate of Andy Warhol for the late artist's unauthorized use of an image of the musician Prince in one of his iconic artworks, the Second Circuit ordered the parties to submit briefs on the impact that *Google* had on its earlier decision against the Warhol estate.[72] The Warhol estate predictably argued that *Google* "comprehensively refutes" the earlier decision that the Warhol artwork was not a fair use.[73] The decision in *Google* was surprising, but it is unsurprising to see a decision by the Court—the legal institution responsible for the final say on how legal doctrines should be interpreted and applied by all courts—now being extended beyond the narrow set of facts presented in the case.

Conclusion

Google promised to be a blockbuster case and it did not disappoint—neither with its surprising decision nor with the unusual and novel analysis employed by Justice Breyer to reach this decision. As Justice Thomas pointed out in his dissent, "we have never found fair use for copying that reaches into the tens of billions of dollars and wrecks the copyright holder's market."[74] Given the deliberate, unauthorized copying of Oracle's declaring code by Google, the unusually narrow copyright protection afforded to computer programs under fair use, and the expansive definition of "transformative use" as applied to computer programs, among other issues, I cannot imagine a scenario of unauthorized copying of an API that would not qualify as a fair use. In sum, Justice Breyer's opinion for the Court implemented a creative use of fair use doctrine to reach a result expressly prohibited by the Computer Software Protection Act of 1980: that some computer code is unprotectible under the copyright laws.

---

[71] See *supra* note 31, and accompanying text.

[72] Bill Donahue, "2nd Cir. Wants to Know If Google Ruling Alters Warhol Case," Law360, Apr. 29, 2021, https://bit.ly/3iODdWq.

[73] *Id.* The court ultimately ruled in August 2021 that nothing changed, despite 60 intellectual property professors filing an amicus brief supporting the Warhol estate.

[74] Google, 141 S. Ct. at 1218 (Thomas, J., dissenting).

Looking Ahead: A Post-COVID Return— and a Shift to the Right?

*Amy Howe**

It was truly a term like no other. Forced to shut down its in-person operations in March 2020 because of the COVID-19 pandemic, the Supreme Court operated virtually for the entire October 2020 term. From October until early May, it heard a (reasonably[1]) full slate of arguments by telephone, and it issued all its orders and opinions electronically, without ever once taking the bench.

Although the Court has released its calendar for the October argument session, the Court has not yet indicated whether it will resume in-person arguments then. Assuming that it does (or when it eventually does), the Court will have changed significantly from the last time we saw the justices in action in March 2020. The most obvious change comes in the Court's composition, with Justice Amy Coney Barrett filling the vacancy left by the September 2020 death of Justice Ruth Bader Ginsburg. And as a result, Republican-appointed justices now enjoy a 6-3 supermajority.

Not surprisingly, the newly reconstituted Roberts Court moved to the right in the 2020–2021 term, even if it wasn't as far to the right as some conservatives (including some justices) might have hoped. The justices issued decisions that (among other things) made it more difficult to challenge election regulations under the federal Voting Rights Act,[2] ruled that a state regulation that gave union organizers access to agricultural businesses to speak to employees is

---

*Amy Howe is a reporter and independent contractor for SCOTUSblog and the publisher of Howe on the Court.

[1] The Court issued only 54 signed opinions in argued cases, the second-smallest total since the 1860s. Adam Liptak, "A Supreme Court Term Marked by a Conservative Majority in Flux," N.Y. Times, July 2, 2021, https://nyti.ms/3rTggFO.

[2] Brnovich v. Democratic Nat'l Comm., 141 S. Ct. 2321 (2021).

unconstitutional,[3] and held that Philadelphia violated the Constitution's Free Exercise Clause when it stopped doing business with a Catholic organization that refused to certify same-sex couples as potential foster parents.[4]

If the Court's October 2020 term was a historic one, the October 2021 term has the potential to be epic. By the time the justices left town for their summer recess,[5] their merits docket for the upcoming term already included three of the hottest of hot-button topics—abortion, guns, and religion—with the very real prospect that they could add another controversial topic, affirmative action, before the term is over. There seems to be little doubt that the Court will continue to move to the right. The real question, in the minds of many Court watchers, is by how much? Will it be a slow but steady shift, or will it be the even sharper turn to the right that conservatives have wanted for decades? Time, presumably, will tell.

I. Abortion

At a presidential debate in 2016, when asked whether he wanted *Roe v. Wade*[6] overturned, then-candidate Donald Trump said that it would "happen automatically" because he would appoint justices who were opposed to abortion.[7] During his four years in office, Trump nominated three justices to the Court: Neil Gorsuch in 2017, Brett Kavanaugh in 2018, and Amy Coney Barrett in 2020. In 2021, the Court will hear oral argument in *Dobbs v. Jackson Women's Health Organization*,[8] a case that is likely to test Trump's assurances about *Roe*.

Dobbs will be the Court's second abortion case in as many years. In 2020, in *June Medical Services L.L.C. v. Russo*,[9] a divided Court

---

[3]Cedar Point Nursery v. Hassid, 141 S. Ct. 2063 (2021).

[4]Fulton v. City of Philadelphia, 141 S. Ct. 1868 (2021).

[5]Or whatever the equivalent of "leaving town" is while we are still in a pandemic and the justices did not need to be in Washington, D.C., to issue the remaining opinions before their summer recess.

[6]410 U.S. 113 (1973).

[7]Dan Mangan, "Trump: I'll Appoint Supreme Court Justices to Overrule Roe v. Wade Abortion Case," CNBC, Oct. 19, 2016, https://cnb.cx/2WSsrHp.

[8]Jackson Women's Health Org. v. Dobbs, 945 F.3d 265 (5th Cir. 2019), cert. granted sub nom. Dobbs v. Jackson Women's Health, 209 L. Ed. 2d 748 (U.S. May 17, 2021) (No. 19-1392).

[9]140 S. Ct. 2103 (2020).

struck down a Louisiana law that would have required doctors who perform abortions to have the right to admit patients at nearby hospitals. Chief Justice John Roberts joined the Court's four liberals to provide the key vote to invalidate the law. In a separate concurring opinion, Roberts wrote that although he had disagreed with a 2016 ruling that struck down a similar law in Texas, and he continued to believe that the Texas case was "wrongly decided," he agreed with his liberal colleagues that the Louisiana law was so similar to the Texas law that, based on the doctrine of *stare decisis*, it could not stand.[10]

Dobbs comes to a Court with a very different make-up than the one that decided *June Medical* in June 2020. At issue in the case is a Mississippi law that would ban most abortions after the 15th week of pregnancy. When Jackson Women's Health, the state's only licensed abortion clinic, went to federal court to challenge the law, the district court blocked the state from implementing the law. The court reasoned that the Supreme Court's decisions in *Roe* and *Planned Parenthood v. Casey*[11] prohibit states from banning abortions before the fetus becomes viable. Because the Mississippi law bars abortions at 15 weeks, which is before viability, the district court concluded the law is unconstitutional.[12]

Mississippi went to the Supreme Court in June 2020, but the Court repeatedly rescheduled the case before finally considering the state's petition for the first time in January 2021. The justices then considered the case at 13 consecutive conferences before announcing in May 2021 that they would take up the case in the 2021–2022 term.

Although the state had told the justices in its petition for review that the questions it was asking them to resolve did "not require the Court to overturn *Roe* or *Casey*," the state's brief on the merits urged the Court to do just that.[13] *Roe* and *Casey*, the state contended, are "egregiously wrong" and "shackle States to a view of the facts that is decades out of date"—in particular, the assumption that if

[10]*Id.* at 2133 (Roberts, C.J., concurring).

[11]505 U.S. 833 (1992).

[12]Jackson Women's Health Org. v. Currier, 349 F. Supp. 3d 536, 544 (S.D. Miss. 2018), aff'd sub nom. Jackson Women's Health Org. v. Dobbs, 945 F.3d 265 (5th Cir. 2019).

[13]Petition for a Writ of Certiorari at 5, Dobbs v. Jackson Women's Health, No. 19-1392 (U.S. June 15, 2020).

abortion is not available, women would be resigned to a "distressful life and future." But in fact, the state countered, today "adoption is accessible," birth control is widely available, and women can "attain both professional success and a rich family life." Moreover, the state added, "scientific advances show that an unborn child has taken on the human form and features months before viability." But even if the Supreme Court does not overrule *Roe* and *Casey*, the state continued, it should at the very least hold that states can ban abortion before viability.

In exhorting the justices to deny review, the clinic stressed that the Mississippi law was clearly unconstitutional. *"Roe* and *Casey*, and the Court's subsequent cases, are clear that, before viability, it is for the pregnant person, and not the State," it reiterated, to "make the ultimate decision whether to continue a pregnancy."[14] And there is no need for the Court to disturb that precedent. The Supreme Court's decision in *Casey*, the clinic noted, acknowledged that "the State has legitimate interests from the outset of the pregnancy in protecting the health of the woman and the life of the fetus," but the Court concluded that the State's interests are not strong enough before viability to support a ban on abortion. Drawing a line that prohibits states from banning abortion before viability not only leaves a clear line in place, the clinic added, but also a workable one, especially when the point at which a fetus becomes viable has remained the same—at approximately 23 or 24 weeks—since 1992.

Even before the Court tackles *Dobbs*, it will hear argument in another case involving a state's efforts to restrict abortions. The question before the Court in *Cameron v. EMW Women's Surgical Center, P.S.C.*[15] is a procedural one that does not implicate the constitutionality of the law itself, but—in this era of divided government—could have implications far beyond the issue of abortion.

The case arises from a challenge to a Kentucky law, passed in March 2018, that generally prohibits doctors from using the "dilation and evacuation" method, a procedure commonly used to end

[14]Brief in Opposition at 1, Dobbs v. Jackson Women's Health, No. 19-1392 (U.S. Aug. 19, 2020).

[15]EMW Women's Surgical Ctr., P.S.C. v. Friedlander, 831 Fed. Appx. 748 (6th Cir. 2020), cert. granted sub nom. Cameron v. EMW Women's Surgical Ctr., P.S.C., 141 S. Ct. 1734 (Mar. 29, 2021) (No. 20-601).

a pregnancy during the second trimester.[16] When a Kentucky abortion clinic and two doctors who perform abortions went to court to challenge the law, the state's health secretary defended the law at trial.

A federal district court blocked Kentucky from enforcing the law, and the health secretary appealed to the U.S. Court of Appeals for the Sixth Circuit. After the briefing was completed in the court of appeals in 2019, the state's attorney general, Democrat Andy Beshear, was elected governor, defeating Republican incumbent Matt Bevin. The state's new health secretary, appointed by Beshear, continued to defend the law on appeal.

In June 2020, a divided Sixth Circuit upheld the district court's decision barring Kentucky from enforcing the law.[17] At that point, the health secretary told the state's new attorney general, Republican Daniel Cameron, that he would not seek rehearing in the Sixth Circuit or file a petition for certiorari in the Supreme Court. Two days later, Cameron filed a motion to intervene in the Sixth Circuit and, eventually, a petition for rehearing.

The Sixth Circuit rejected Cameron's request, prompting him to go to the Supreme Court to ask the justices to take up the question of whether he should have been allowed to intervene. The justices granted his petition for review in March 2021, although they declined to address the constitutionality of the law itself—specifically, whether they should send the case back to the lower courts for another look in light of the Supreme Court's 2020 decision in *June Medical Services v. Russo*.[18]

In the Supreme Court, Cameron argues that states should have the power to enforce their own laws—and to decide who represents them in defending those laws in federal court. In this case, he tells the justices, Kentucky law gives the attorney general the power "to defend state law when no other official will"; indeed, he notes, the

[16] EMW Women's Surgical Ctr., P.S.C. v. Meier, 373 F. Supp. 3d 807, 812 (W.D. Ky. 2019), aff'd sub nom. EMW Women's Surgical Ctr., P.S.C. v. Friedlander, 960 F.3d 785 (6th Cir. 2020).

[17] EMW Women's Surgical Ctr., P.S.C. v. Friedlander, 960 F.3d 785 (6th Cir. 2020).

[18] EMW Women's Surgical Ctr., P.S.C. v. Friedlander, 831 Fed. Appx. 748 (6th Cir. 2020), cert. granted sub nom. Cameron v. EMW Women's Surgical Ctr., P.S.C., 141 S. Ct. 1734 (Mar. 29, 2021) (No. 20-601).

health secretary did not oppose his motion to intervene.[19] "Federal courts," he stresses, "should have no interest in who a State designates to defend its laws."[20] It is also, he adds, "hard to imagine how the Attorney General could have moved more quickly" once he learned that the health secretary would no longer defend the law. He fully briefed his motion to intervene and filed his timely petition for rehearing within a week.[21]

Opposing Supreme Court review, the plaintiffs respond that the Sixth Circuit's denial of Cameron's motion to intervene does not have any impact on his general power to defend Kentucky's laws. Although the Sixth Circuit has allowed Cameron to intervene in other recent cases, they observe, the court of appeals "simply conclude[d] that the Attorney General's intervention in this particular case" came too late.[22]

The Sixth Circuit's decision denying Cameron's motion to intervene should only be reversed, the plaintiffs argue, if it was an abuse of discretion, but it was "plainly correct."[23] Among other things, they contend, motions like Cameron's, which come after the court of appeals has issued its decision, are "disfavored."[24] Otherwise, they posit, would-be intervenors can wait to see whether they approve of the court's decision before trying to enter the case. The Sixth Circuit also concluded that allowing the attorney general to intervene after its decision would be unfair to the plaintiffs because the main issue that Cameron sought to raise—whether the plaintiffs had a legal right to challenge the law on behalf of their patients—was an issue that Kentucky had previously waived.[25]

[19]Brief for Petitioner at 3, Cameron v. EMW Women's Surgical Ctr., P.S.C., No. 20-601 (U.S. June 14, 2021).

[20]*Id.* at 25.

[21]*Id.* at 31.

[22]Brief in Opposition at 10, Cameron v. EMW Women's Surgical Ctr., P.S.C., No. 20-601 (U.S. Feb. 5, 2021).

[23]*Id.* at 29.

[24]*Id.*

[25]EMW Women's Surgical Ctr., P.S.C. v. Friedlander, 831 Fed. Appx. 748, 752 (6th Cir. 2020).

II. Second Amendment

In April 2021, the more conservative version of the Roberts Court opted to add another controversial issue to its docket for the 2021–2022 term: gun rights. In 2008, in *District of Columbia v. Heller*,[26] the Supreme Court ruled that the Second Amendment protects an individual right to have a handgun in the home for self-defense. Two years later, in *McDonald v. City of Chicago*,[27] the Court made clear that the right also applied to the states. But, in the years that followed, the Court—to the disappointment of gun-rights supporters and some justices—declined to say anything more about the scope of the Second Amendment.

During the 2019–2020 term, gun-rights advocates hoped that the Court was poised to issue a ruling that would address the right to have a gun outside the home. In December 2019, the justices heard argument in *New York State Rifle and Pistol Association v. City of New York*, a challenge to New York City's ban on transporting licensed handguns outside the city, including to shooting ranges and vacation homes. But in April 2020, the justices sent the case back to the lower court, holding that the challenge was moot because the city had changed its rule.[28]

Justice Samuel Alito dissented from the decision in an opinion joined by Justices Gorsuch and (for the most part) Clarence Thomas.[29] In a concurring opinion, Justice Kavanaugh agreed that the challengers' claims were moot, but he also sympathized with Alito's "concern that some federal and state courts may not be properly applying *Heller* and *McDonald*."[30] Kavanaugh suggested that the Court "should address that issue soon, perhaps in one of the several Second Amendment cases with petitions for certiorari now pending before the Court."[31]

The Court further raised the hopes of gun-rights supporters when it quickly distributed 10 petitions for review that it had apparently been deferring while considering the New York City case. The justices considered the petitions at six consecutive conferences before

---

[26] 554 U.S. 570 (2008).

[27] 561 U.S. 742 (2010).

[28] N.Y. State Rifle & Pistol Ass'n v. City of New York, 140 S. Ct. 1525, 1526 (2020).

[29] *Id.* at 1527 (Alito, J., dissenting).

[30] *Id.* (Kavanaugh, J., concurring).

[31] *Id.*

denying review in June 2020. There is no way to know why the Court declined to take up the issue when four justices—the number needed to grant certiorari—had seemingly expressed a willingness to weigh in on the scope of the Second Amendment again. One theory posited that those four justices were not certain that they would have a fifth vote—presumably the chief justice—in favor of a more expansive view of gun rights.

When *New York State Rifle and Pistol Association* returned to the Supreme Court in December 2020, it found a different, and likely more receptive, audience than the Court it had faced during the previous term. Justice Ginsburg had passed away in the interim and been replaced by Justice Barrett. As a judge on the U.S. Court of Appeals for the Seventh Circuit, Barrett dissented from a challenge to federal and state laws that barred a business owner convicted of mail fraud from owning a gun. While the majority rejected the man's appeal, Barrett agreed with him that, in the absence of any evidence that he would be "dangerous if armed," the ban was unconstitutional as it applied to him.[32]

The new case, *New York State Rifle and Pistol Association v. Bruen*, is a challenge to New York's regime for issuing licenses to carry a gun outside of the home. Under state law, anyone who wants to carry a gun outside the home must demonstrate "proper cause" to do so—which the state's courts have interpreted as requiring an applicant to show a "special need for self-protection."[33] That requirement, the New York State Rifle and Pistol Association (NYSRPA) contends, basically makes it impossible for the average person to obtain a license.

The NYSRPA went to federal court, arguing that the New York scheme violates the Second Amendment, but both the district court and the Second Circuit rejected that argument.[34] The group then came to the Supreme Court, which agreed in April 2020 to weigh in.[35]

[32] Kanter v. Barr, 919 F.3d 437, 468 (7th Cir. 2019) (Barrett, J., dissenting).

[33] See, e.g., Bando v. Sullivan, 735 N.Y.S.2d 660, 693 (N.Y. App. Div. 2002) (quoting Klenosky v. N.Y.C. Police Dep't, 428 N.Y.S.2d 256, 257, aff'd, 421 N.E.2d 503 (N.Y. 1981)).

[34] N.Y. State Rifle & Pistol Ass'n, Inc. v. Beach, 354 F. Supp. 3d 143 (N.D.N.Y. 2018), aff'd, 818 Fed. Appx. 99 (2d Cir. 2020).

[35] N.Y. State Rifle & Pistol Ass'n, Inc. v. Beach, 818 Fed. Appx. 99 (2d Cir. 2020), cert. granted sub nom. N.Y. State Rifle & Pistol Ass'n, Inc. v. Bruen, 2021 WL 1602643 (U.S. Apr. 26, 2021) (No. 20-843).

The NYSRPA describes New York's regime as "upside down," arguing that the Second Amendment "makes the right to carry arms for self-defense the rule, not the exception."[36] This is reflected, the group argues, in the text of the Second Amendment, which guarantees not only the right to keep arms but also the right to bear arms—an addition that would be superfluous if you could only exercise it in the house. Moreover, the group adds, the history also "overwhelmingly confirms that the Second Amendment protects a right to carry firearms outside the home."[37] The constitutional problems with the regime are made worse, the group notes, by the "practically unreviewable" discretion that government officials enjoy in determining whether an applicant has shown proper cause.[38] Indeed, the challengers note, the law was originally passed to ensure that "newly arrived immigrants, particularly those with Italian surnames," could not obtain a carry license.[39]

In its brief opposing Supreme Court review, the state counters that its regime "descends from a long Anglo-American tradition of regulating the carrying of firearms in public."[40] New York defends its "proper cause" requirement as a "flexible standard." It notes that although state and local authorities have traditionally had "significant discretion to regulate the public carrying of" guns, "numerous" New Yorkers have received a public-carry license when they have had an "actual" need to do so for self-defense.[41] Finally, the state emphasizes, the regime promotes New York's compelling interest in public safety and preventing crime.

Amicus briefs filed on behalf of the NYSRPA came from many of its usual sources of support, including Second Amendment scholars, gun-rights advocacy groups, and members of Congress. But one brief, filed by public defenders and black legal aid lawyers, garnered more attention when it was filed in late July.[42] The lawyers

[36] Brief for Petitioners at 2, N.Y. State Rifle & Pistol Ass'n, Inc. v. Bruen, No. 20-843 (U.S. July 13, 2021).

[37] *Id.* at 23.

[38] *Id.* at 42.

[39] *Id.* at 43.

[40] Brief in Opposition at 1, N.Y. State Rifle & Pistol Ass'n, Inc. v. Bruen, No. 20-843 (U.S. Feb. 22, 2021).

[41] *Id.* at 1, 7, 20.

[42] Brief of the Black Attorneys of Legal Aid, the Bronx Defenders, Brooklyn Defender Services, et al. as Amici Curiae in Support of Petitioners, N.Y. State Rifle & Pistol Ass'n v. Bruen, No. 20-843 (U.S. July 22, 2021).

told the justices that the consequences of New York's licensing scheme are "brutal" for racial and ethnic minorities.[43] They write that they "routinely see people charged with a violent felony for simply possessing a firearm outside of the home, a crime only because they had not gotten a license beforehand."[44] The lawyers' perspective may appeal to some justices as well. In his opinion for the Court in *Americans for Prosperity Foundation v. Bonta*,[45] striking down California's requirement that charities and nonprofits in the state provide the state attorney general's office with the names and addresses of their biggest donors, Chief Justice Roberts pointed to the "full range" of amicus briefs in the case as evidence of the "gravity of the privacy concerns" at issue. Although the oral argument has not yet been scheduled in *Bruen*, look for the public defenders' brief to make a similar cameo.

III. Religion

The Court will also revisit another topic that it tackled during the 2019–2020 term: public funding for religious schools. In June 2020, in *Espinoza v. Montana Department of Revenue*,[46] a divided Court ruled that the state's exclusion of religious schools from a program that provided scholarships to attend private schools, simply because of the school's religious character, violates the Constitution's Free Exercise Clause. Just over a year later, the justices granted review in *Carson v. Makin*,[47] a case that presents a question that they left unresolved in *Espinoza*: whether a state violates the Constitution when it excludes families and schools from a tuition-assistance program when the aid would be used to attend schools that provide religious instruction.

The case comes to the Court from Maine, whose Constitution and state laws require local governments to support and maintain public schools to ensure that all school-age children can "receive the benefits of a free public education."[48] Because over half of all school

---

[43]*Id.* at 5.

[44]*Id.* at 17.

[45]Ams. for Prosperity Found. v. Bonta, 141 S. Ct. 2373, 2388 (2021).

[46]140 S. Ct. 2246 (2020).

[47]Carson v. Makin, 979 F.3d 21 (1st Cir. 2020), cert. granted sub nom. Carson v. Makin, 2021 WL 2742783 (U.S. July 2, 2021) (No. 20-1088).

[48]Me. Rev. Stat. Ann. tit. 20-A, § 2(1) (West 2021).

districts (known in Maine as "school administrative units") do not operate their own public high schools, those school districts have two options. They can make arrangements with another school (either public or private) to take their students, or they can pay tuition for a student to attend a public school or the "approved private school of the parent's choice at which the student is accepted."[49]

In 2018, a group of parents—represented by the Institute for Justice, which also represented the mothers in *Espinoza*—went to federal court. They argued that the requirement that a private school must be a "nonsectarian" school to qualify as an "approved" school and receive tuition-assistance payments violates their First Amendment right to freely exercise their religion. The district court rejected their challenge, and the First Circuit upheld that ruling.[50]

The First Circuit acknowledged the Supreme Court's recent decisions in *Espinoza* and *Trinity Lutheran Church v. Comer*,[51] holding that Missouri's exclusion of a church preschool from a grant program to resurface its playground violated the church's constitutional right. But Maine's restriction, the court of appeals concluded, "unlike the one at issue in *Espinoza*, does not bar schools from receiving funding simply based on their religious identity."[52] Rather, the First Circuit stressed, Maine's rule prohibits the private schools that the plaintiffs would like their children to attend from receiving the funding because they would use the money for religious purposes. This distinction is especially appropriate, the court of appeals suggested, because the Maine program was created to guarantee that students who cannot attend a school in their own hometown "can nonetheless get an education that is 'roughly equivalent to the education they receive in public schools.'"[53]

In urging the Court to take up the case, the parents argued that the current "state of affairs—in which a state cannot deny a benefit to a student because she wishes to attend a school that *is* religious, but can deny it because the school *does* religious things is unstable

---

[49]*Id.* § 5204(4).

[50]Carson v. Makin, 401 F. Supp. 3d 207 (D. Me. 2019), aff'd sub nom. Carson v. Makin, 979 F.3d 21 (1st Cir. 2020).

[51]137 S. Ct. 2012 (2017).

[52]Carson v. Makin, 979 F.3d 21, 40 (1st Cir. 2020).

[53]*Id.* at 42.

and untenable[.]"[54] Not only are facts malleable, so that an exclusion based on the school's religious use of funds could also be based on the school's religious status, the parents suggested, but "often-times, religious status and religious use are *inseparable*." Families believe that they are obligated to provide their children with a religious education, so excluding them from the tuition-assistance program "based on the religious use to which they would put their aid necessarily discriminates based on their religious status, as well."[55]

Opposing review, the state countered that Maine's tuition-assistance program is a "unique solution to an unusual situation."[56] Without the program, it stressed, a small group of Maine families would not have access to a public education. Therefore, the state explained, the program is intended to "engage private schools willing to deliver a specific service: an education that is substantially akin to that which a student would receive if their community operated a public school."[57] By contrast, the state contended, the schools that the plaintiffs want their children to attend admit that they discriminate against LGBTQ people and non-Christians in both hiring and admissions. Regardless of the schools' right to choose whom to admit or hire, the state stresses, the real question in the case is whether the state "must fund their educational program as the substantive equivalent of a public education"—and the answer, from the state's perspective, is clearly "no."[58]

IV. Death Penalty

In October, the justices will hear oral argument in a high-profile death-penalty case that the lower court called "one of the worst domestic terrorist attacks" since September 11, 2001.[59] Dzokhar Tsarnaev was sentenced to death for his role in the 2013 bombings near the finish line of the Boston Marathon, which killed three people and badly injured hundreds more. During the manhunt that followed, Dzokhar

---

[54] Petition for Writ of Certiorari at 29, Carson v. Makin, No. 20-1088 (U.S. Feb. 4, 2021).

[55] *Id.* at 32 (emphasis added).

[56] Brief in Opposition for Respondent at 17, Carson v. Makin, No. 20-1088 (U.S. May 21, 2021).

[57] *Id.* at 16.

[58] *Id.* at 20.

[59] United States v. Tsarnaev, 968 F.3d 24, 34 (1st Cir. 2020).

Tsarnaev and his older brother, Tamerlan, killed a fourth person, a local campus police officer. Tamerlan Tsarnaev was killed in a shootout with police, while Dzokhar Tsarneav was captured when he was found hiding in a boat in a backyard in suburban Boston.

In July 2020, the First Circuit affirmed Dzokhar Tsarnaev's convictions, but it vacated his death sentences and sent his case back to the lower court for resentencing.[60] The Trump administration came to the Supreme Court in October 2020, asking the justices to review that ruling.

By the time the Court announced in March 2021 that it would hear the case, there was a new sheriff in town. During his presidential campaign, then-candidate Joe Biden had pledged to "work to pass legislation to eliminate the death penalty at the federal level, and incentivize states to follow the federal government's example."[61] In July 2021, Attorney General Merrick Garland announced that he was imposing a moratorium on federal executions.[62] But that announcement was at odds with the brief on the merits that the Department of Justice had filed two weeks earlier, asking the justices to reinstate the death penalty for Tsarnaev and "put this case back on track toward a just conclusion."[63]

There are two issues before the Supreme Court. The first is whether the district court should have asked potential jurors what media coverage they had seen about the case. The federal government maintains that jurors can fairly decide the case even when it is "ubiquitously publicized" as long as they can "put that exposure aside" and issue a verdict based only on the evidence presented in court.[64] In this case, the government emphasizes, the district court developed a process designed to identify jurors who could provide a fair trial. By vacating Tsarnaev's death sentence because the trial judge had not asked potential jurors about their exposure to media coverage, the government contends, the First Circuit second-guessed

---

[60] *Id.* at 106.

[61] "The Biden Plan for Strengthening America's Commitment to Justice," JoeBiden.com, https://bit.ly/2TYmXK8.

[62] Michael Balsamo, Colleen Long, & Michael Tarm, "Federal Executions Halted; Garland Orders Protocols Reviewed," AP, July 1, 2021, https://bit.ly/3Cen7yc.

[63] Brief for the United States at 16, United States v. Tsarnaev, No. 20-443 (U.S. June 1, 2021).

[64] *Id.* at 17.

the trial judge and imposed a requirement inconsistent with the Supreme Court's cases.

Tsarnaev points out that the First Circuit's decision to vacate his death sentence based on the district court's failure to properly question potential jurors about their exposure to pretrial coverage of the case was consistent with a "long-established supervisory rule" designed to guarantee that "the assessment of impartiality is made by the judge, not the juror."[65] Indeed, Tsarnaev suggests, "although the government defends the district court's voir dire at great length, and touts the jurors' assurances that they could be impartial," in the case of at least two jurors, "there is every reason to doubt those assurances."[66]

The second question that the justices will consider is whether the district court properly excluded evidence that Tamerlan Tsarnaev was allegedly involved in an unrelated triple murder two years before the bombing. Here, too, the federal government describes the First Circuit's decision to vacate Tsarnaev's death sentence as an "unwarranted usurpation of the district judge's sound discretion."[67] Telling jurors about Tamerlan's alleged involvement in the crime would be more confusing and distracting than helpful, the government posits, particularly in light of all of the evidence supporting the jury's decision to sentence Dzokhar Tsarnaev to death.

Tsarnaev responds that his main strategy to defeat a death sentence was to portray him as being under the influence of (and therefore less responsible for the bombings than) his more aggressive and radicalized older brother. The district court allowed defense lawyers to introduce other evidence to make this point, Tsarnaev notes; evidence of Tamerlan's alleged involvement in the triple murder "was in the same vein—but it was far more convincing."[68] The court of appeals, Dzokhar Tsarnaev stresses, "correctly concluded that the evidence [of the triple murder] might have convinced at least one juror to vote against death"—all that would have been needed to spare Tsarnaev from the death penalty.[69]

---

[65] Brief in Opposition at 10, 28, United States v. Tsarnaev, No. 20-443 (U.S. June 1, 2021).

[66] *Id.* at 29.

[67] Brief for the United States, *supra* note 63, at 18.

[68] Brief in Opposition, *supra* note 65, at 18.

[69] *Id.* at 21.

V. Affirmative Action

Before the term is over, the Court may weigh in (or at the very least have agreed to weigh in) on yet another third-rail topic: affirmative action. Eighteen years ago, in *Grutter v. Bollinger*,[70] the Supreme Court upheld the University of Michigan Law School's consideration of race in its admissions process as part of its effort to assemble a diverse student body. But, as Justice Sandra Day O'Connor emphasized in her opinion for the majority, "[w]e expect that 25 years from now, the use of racial preferences will no longer be necessary to further the interest approved today."[71]

In 2016, the Court upheld the University of Texas at Austin's race-conscious admissions program against a challenge by a white student, Abigail Fisher, who was not admitted to the university.[72] The justices divided 4-3, with Justice Elena Kagan recused and the vacancy created by the death of Justice Antonin Scalia not yet filled. Justice Anthony Kennedy, who wrote for the majority, cautioned that the Texas program was unique, and he warned that even the University of Texas had an "ongoing obligation" to reevaluate whether the program was still necessary.[73]

Five years later, a nonprofit formed by Edward Blum, who had backed Fisher's lawsuit, came to the Court, asking the justices to weigh in on Harvard's race-conscious admissions policy for undergraduates. After the lower courts rejected the group's challenge to the policy, the group was asking the justices to rule on two issues: whether Harvard's policy violates the federal Civil Rights Act and whether the Court should overrule its 2003 decision in *Grutter*.[74]

The Court that considered the group's petition at its June 10, 2021, conference was a very different—and potentially much more sympathetic—Court than the one that decided *Fisher* just five years earlier. All three of the *Fisher* dissenters—Roberts, Thomas, and Alito—are still on the Court, but they have been joined by three more conservative justices: Gorsuch, who succeeded Scalia;

---

[70]539 U.S. 306 (2003).

[71]*Id.* at 343.

[72]Fisher v. Univ. of Tex. at Austin, 136 S. Ct. 2198 (2016).

[73]*Id.* at 2215.

[74]Petition for Writ of Certiorari at i, Students for Fair Admissions, Inc. v. President & Fellows of Harvard Coll., No. 20-1199 (U.S. Feb. 25, 2021).

Kavanaugh, who replaced Kennedy; and Barrett, who succeeded Ginsburg.

After considering the case at their conference for the first time, the justices acted quickly, calling for the views of the U.S. solicitor general on June 14. The order means that if the justices do grant review, the Court might not hear oral argument in the case until 2022. But with the 2022 midterm elections just a little over a year away, the delay may be a feature, rather than a bug, as far as some justices are concerned—particularly when, as a practical matter, a majority of the Court may not be especially interested in the Biden administration's views on affirmative action.

VI. The Breyer Retirement Watch Continues

As the Roberts Court settles into its first full term in its latest incarnation, the prospect of more change looms over One First Street, N.E. Even before President Joe Biden took the oath of office on January 20, 2021, some liberals were clamoring for the Court's oldest justice, Stephen Breyer, to step down to allow the new president to name his replacement. Justice Ginsburg had rebuffed suggestions that she should retire during the Obama administration but died before the 2020 election, allowing President Donald Trump to name her replacement. Liberals (including some Democratic lawmakers) want to avoid repeating this scenario with Breyer, who turns 83 this summer.

The end of the 2020–2021 term, often the traditional time for justices to reveal a retirement, came and went without any announcement from Breyer. In an interview in mid-July, Breyer told CNN's Joan Biskupic that he hadn't made a decision yet about when to retire. He indicated that he was enjoying his new role as the most senior member of the Court's liberal bloc, which allows him to speak third at the Court's conferences and assign dissents when the Court divides along ideological lines. His "health" and "the Court" would be, Breyer said, the primary factors in his decision about when to retire.[75]

---

[75]Joan Biskupic, "Exclusive: Stephen Breyer Says He Hasn't Decided His Retirement Plans and Is Happy as the Supreme Court's Top Liberal," CNN, July 15, 2021, https://cnn.it/37k9QWw.

If Breyer does in fact step down and Biden is able to name a replacement for him, the new justice probably would not have any real effect on the ideological balance on the Court. But with the 2022 midterm elections on the horizon, liberals fret about the prospect that Democrats could lose the Senate before a Breyer successor is confirmed, creating an opening for a Republican majority to block a Democratic nominee—perhaps indefinitely.

Conclusion

Even if the justices don't add any more blockbusters to their plate for the 2021–2022 term, Court watchers are likely to be waiting with bated breath in late spring and early summer for the Court's rulings on abortion, guns, and religion. Throw in the prospect of a Breyer retirement, and you have the recipe for an extraordinary amount of public attention on the Court and its work, in an election year. What the public will think of that work remains to be seen.

Contributors

Thomas C. Berg is the James L. Oberstar professor of law and public policy at the University of St. Thomas School of Law (Minnesota), where he teaches constitutional law, religious liberty, intellectual property, and the school's religious liberty appellate clinic. There he supervises students writing briefs in major religious-liberty cases, drawing on his experience drafting more than 50 briefs on issues of religious liberty and free speech in the Supreme Court and lower courts. Berg is among the nation's leading scholars of law and religion. He has written more than 50 book chapters and journal articles and dozens of shorter pieces on religious freedom, constitutional law, and the role of religion in law, politics, and society. His work has been cited several times by the Supreme Court and federal courts of appeals. He is the author of several books, including as co-author of the leading casebook, *Religion and the Constitution* (4th ed. 2016), and *The State and Religion in a Nutshell* (3d ed. 2016), and is at work on a new book, *Protecting Religious Liberty in a Polarized Age*. His other chief scholarly interest is the intersection of intellectual property rights, social justice, and human development. He received a B.S. in journalism from Northwestern University, an M.A. in philosophy and politics from Oxford University (as a Rhodes Scholar), and both an M.A. in religious studies and a J.D. from the University of Chicago. In law school, Berg served as executive editor of the *University of Chicago Law Review* and won two prizes for legal scholarship and writing. After clerking for Judge Alvin Rubin on the U.S. Court of Appeals for the Fifth Circuit, Berg practiced law with Mayer, Brown and Platt, doing commercial and appellate litigation.

Josh Blackman is a professor at the South Texas College of Law Houston. He specializes in constitutional law, the U.S. Supreme Court, and the intersection of law and technology. Blackman is the author of the critically acclaimed *Unprecedented: The Constitutional Challenge to Obamacare* (2013), as well as *Unraveled: Obamacare, Religious Liberty, and*

Executive Power (2016). He has also co-authored, with Randy E. Barnett, the leading casebook *Constitutional Law: Cases in Context* (3d ed. 2017). He was selected by *Forbes* for its "30 Under 30" in Law and Policy, has testified before the House Judiciary Committee on the constitutionality of executive action on immigration, and is an adjunct scholar at the Cato Institute. Blackman is the founder and president of the Harlan Institute, the founder of FantasySCOTUS, the Internet's premier Supreme Court fantasy league, and regularly blogs at JoshBlackman.com. Blackman leads the cutting edge of legal analytics as Director of Judicial Research at LexPredict. He is the author of over two dozen law review articles, including in *NYU Journal of Law & Liberty*, *Texas Law Review*, and *Harvard Journal of Law & Public Policy*. His commentary has appeared in the *New York Times*, *Wall Street Journal*, *Washington Post*, *USA Today*, *Los Angeles Times*, and other national publications. Blackman clerked for the Honorable Danny J. Boggs on the U.S. Court of Appeals for the Sixth Circuit and the Honorable Kim R. Gibson on the U.S. District Court for the Western District of Pennsylvania. Blackman earned his B.S. from Pennsylvania State University and his J.D. from George Mason University School of Law.

Trevor Burrus is a research fellow in the Cato Institute's Robert A. Levy Center for Constitutional Studies and editor-in-chief of the *Cato Supreme Court Review*. His research interests include constitutional law, civil and criminal law, legal and political philosophy, legal history, and the interface between science and public policy. His academic work has appeared in journals such as the *Harvard Journal of Law & Public Policy*, *NYU Journal of Law & Liberty*, *NYU Annual Survey of American Law*, *Syracuse Law Review*, and many others. His popular writing has appeared in the *Washington Post*, *New York Times* (online), *USA Today*, *Forbes*, *Huffington Post*, and others. Burrus lectures regularly on behalf of the Federalist Society, the Institute for Humane Studies, the Foundation for Economics Education, and other organizations, and he frequently appears on major media outlets. He is the co-host of "Free Thoughts," a weekly podcast that covers topics in libertarian theory, history, and philosophy. He is the editor of *A Conspiracy against Obamacare* (2013) and *Deep Commitments: The Past, Present, and Future of Religious Liberty* (2017). Burrus holds a B.A. in philosophy from the University of Colorado at Boulder and a J.D. from the University of Denver Sturm College of Law.

Amy Howe is a contributor at *SCOTUSblog*, the nation's premier source for Supreme Court coverage, where she previously served as an editor and reporter. She primarily writes for her eponymous blog, "Howe on the Court." Before turning to full-time blogging, Howe served as counsel in over two dozen merits cases at the Supreme Court and argued two cases before the bench. From 2004 until 2011, she co-taught Supreme Court litigation at Stanford Law School; from 2005 until 2013, she co-taught a similar class at Harvard Law School. She has also served as an adjunct professor at American University Washington College of Law and Vanderbilt Law School. Amy earned her undergraduate degree from the University of North Carolina at Chapel Hill and holds an M.A. in Arab Studies and a J.D. from Georgetown University.

David L. Hudson Jr. is assistant professor at Belmont University College of Law, where he teaches courses on legal information and communication. He has authored, co-authored, or co-edited dozens of books, including *Speech Freedom on Campus* (2020) and *Let the Students Speak!: A History of the Fight for Freedom of Expression in American Schools* (2011). His scholarship has appeared in the *Seattle University Law Review, Creighton Law Review*, and *Stanford Law & Politics Review*, among others. In addition to his teaching, Hudson is a Justice Robert H. Jackson Legal Fellow at the Foundation for Individual Rights in Education and a First Amendment Fellow at the Freedom Forum Institute. Prior to this, he was an attorney and scholar at the First Amendment Center in Nashville, Tennessee. Hudson previously taught courses at Vanderbilt Law School and Nashville School of Law, were he earned its Distinguished Faculty Award. Hudson earned his undergraduate degree from Duke University and his J.D. from Vanderbilt Law School.

Douglas Laycock is the Class of 1963 Research Professor, Robert E. Scott Distinguished Professor of Law, and Professor of Religious Studies at the University of Virginia School of Law, where he has taught courses on religious liberty, torts, remedies, and restitution. Laycock is perhaps the most prominent living scholar on religious liberty, having written countless articles on the topic and argued several cases before the Supreme Court. His unparalleled scholarship on the topic is anthologized in the seminal *Religious Liberty* (vols. 1–5).

283

He has authored or co-authored casebooks include *Restatements (Third) of Torts: Remedies* (forthcoming), *Modern American Remedies: Cases and Materials* (5th ed. 2019), and *The Death of the Irreparable Injury Rule* (1991). Before joining Virginia Law, Laycock was a member of the faculties of the University of Michigan Law School, University of Texas School of Law, and University of Chicago Law School. After law school, he clerked with Judge Walter Cummings on the U.S. Court of Appeals for the Seventh Circuit. Laycock earned a B.A. from the Honors College of Michigan State University, and his J.D. from the University of Chicago Law School.

Adam Mossoff is a professor at the Antonin Scalia Law School, George Mason University, where he teaches courses on property, patent law, trade secrets, trademark law, remedies, and Internet law. Mossoff's knowledge of intellectual property law has brought him before the Senate and the House of Representatives, as an expert witness, and he is a regular speaker at congressional staff briefings. His scholarship has appeared in the *Arizona Law Review*, *Social Philosophy & Policy*, *Harvard Journal of Law & Technology*, *Cornell Law Review*, and *Boston University Law Review*, among others. He has authored chapters in a number of books, including in *Foundations of a Free Society: Reflections on Ayn Rand's Political Philosophy* (2019), *Intellectual Property and Property Rights* (2013), and *Natural Rights Individualism and Progressivism in American Political Theory* (2012). Mossoff serves on the board of directors of the Center for Intellectual Property Understanding and is a senior fellow & chair for intellectual property at the Hudson Institute. He previously served as a Heritage Foundation fellow. After law school, Mossoff clerked for Judge Jacques L. Wiener, Jr. on the U.S. Court of Appeals for the Fifth Circuit.

Derek T. Muller is a professor and Bouma Fellow of Law at the University of Iowa School of Law, where he teaches courses on election law, federal courts, civil procedure, administrative law, and evidence. Before Iowa, Muller taught at Pennsylvania State University Dickinson School of Law, University of Notre Dame Law School, and Pepperdine University Caruso School of Law. Prior to teaching, he was an associate at Kirkland & Ellis, where he practiced litigation, and clerked for Judge Raymond W. Gruender on the U.S. Court of Appeals for the Eight Circuit. His writings have appeared in the

Georgetown Journal of Law & Ethics, Fordham Law Review, Election Law Journal, and *St. Louis University Law Journal.* He is also co-author of the casebook *Federal Courts: Cases and Materials on Judicial Federalism and the Lawyering Process* (5th ed. forthcoming, 2022), and has written chapters for *The Oxford Handbook of American Election Law* (forthcoming) and *The Best Candidate: Presidential Nomination in Polarized Times* (2020). Muller earned his B.A. from Hillsdale College and his J.D. from University of Notre Dame Law School.

Aaron L. Nielson is a professor at Brigham Young University J. Reuben Clark Law School, where he teaches courses on federal courts, civil procedure, administrative law, and directs the school's seminar in Washington, D.C. His scholarship has appeared in the *Duke Law Journal, University of Chicago Law Review, Northwestern Law Review,* and *Georgetown Law Journal,* among others. In addition to teaching, Nielson is a member of the Council of the ABA's Section of Administrative Law & Regulatory Practice, where he previously chaired its Rulemaking Committee. In 2020, the Supreme Court appointed Nielson to brief and argue *Collins v. Mnuchin,* the topic of his article for this volume. Before teaching, Nielson was a litigation partner at Kirkland & Ellis, where he represented clients before several federal circuits. After law school, he clerked for Judge Jerry E. Smith on the U.S. Court of Appeals for the Fifth Circuit, Judge Janice Rogers Brown on the U.S. Court of Appeals for the D.C. Circuit, and Justice Samuel Alito on the Supreme Court. Nielson earned his B.A. from the University of Pennsylvania, his LL.M. from the University of Cambridge, and his J.D. from Harvard Law School.

Ilya Shapiro is a vice president and director of the Robert A. Levy Center for Constitutional Studies at the Cato Institute, and publisher of the *Cato Supreme Court Review.* Before joining Cato, he was a special assistant/advisor to the Multinational Force in Iraq on rule-of-law issues and practiced international, political, commercial, and antitrust litigation at Patton Boggs and Cleary Gottlieb. Shapiro is the author of *Supreme Disorder: Judicial Nominations and the Politics of America's Highest Court* (2020), coauthor of *Religious Liberties for Corporations? Hobby Lobby, the Affordable Care Act, and the Constitution* (2014), and editor-in-chief of 11 volumes of the *Cato Supreme Court Review* (2008–18). He has contributed to many academic, popular, and professional publications, regularly provides media commentary—including an appearance on *The Colbert Report*—and is a legal consultant to CBS News. Shapiro has testified before Congress and state legislatures and, as coordinator of Cato's amicus brief program, has filed more than 450 "friend of the court" briefs in the Supreme Court. He lectures regularly on behalf of the Federalist Society, was an inaugural Washington Fellow at the National Review Institute, and has been an adjunct professor at George Washington University Law School and University of Mississippi School of Law. He is also the chairman of the board of advisers of the Mississippi Justice Institute, a barrister in the Edward Coke Appellate Inn of Court, and a member of the Virginia Advisory Committee to the U.S. Commission on Civil Rights. Shapiro clerked for Judge E. Grady Jolly on the U.S. Court of Appeals for the Fifth Circuit. He holds an A.B. from Princeton, an M.Sc. from the London School of Economics, and a J.D. from the University of Chicago.

Gregory C. Sisk holds the Pio Cardinal Laghi Distinguished Chair in Law and is co-director of the Terrence J. Murphy Institute for Catholic Thought, Law, and Public Policy at the University of St. Thomas School of Law (Minnesota), where he teaches civil procedure, legal research and writing, and appellate clinic. Prior to this, Sisk served on the faculty at Drake University Law School. Before entering the academy, he was a legislative assistance to Senator Slade Gorton of Washington, clerked with Judge Robert R. Beezer on the U.S. Court of Appeals for the Ninth Circuit, was an attorney with the Department of Justice's Civil Division, and the head of the appellate practice at the Seattle firm of Karr Tuttle Campbell. Sisk has written extensively on a diversity of topics, from religious liberty to property rights, including in the *University of Chicago Law Review, Michigan Law Review, Harvard Journal of Law & Public Policy,* and *Cornell Law Review.* He has authored casebooks on professional responsibility and federal litigation, and published a legal novel, *Marital Privilege* (2014). Sisk earned his B.A. from Montana State University and his J.D. from University of Washington Law School, where he graduated first in his class.

Christopher Slobogin is the Milton R. Underwood Chair in Law and director of the Criminal Justice Program at Vanderbilt Law School and affiliate professor of psychiatry at Vanderbilt School of Medicine, where he teaches courses on criminal law, criminal procedure and investigations, and mental health law. Slobogin is among the most cited criminal law authorities in the nation, cited in almost 5,000 law review articles and more than 200 opinions, including three Supreme Court rulings. He has had a substantial influence on the role of technology in Fourth Amendment jurisprudence. Among Slobogin's books are *Just Algorithms: Using Science to Reduce Incarceration and Inform a Jurisprudence of Risk* (forthcoming 2021) and *Proving the Unproveable: The Role of Law, Science, and Speculation in Adjudicating Culpability and Dangerousness* (2007) . His academic writings have appeared in the *Georgetown Law Journal, Northwestern Law Review, Virginia Law Review,* and *Stanford Law Review.* Slobogin has been a reporter on three ABA task forces on technology and criminal law, and is an associate reporter at the American Law Institute's Principles of Police Investigation Project. His work in psychology is equally well-regarded, earning Slobogin the American Board of Forensic Psychology's Distinguished Contribution Award and the American Psychology-Law Society's Distinguished Contributions to Psychology and Law Award, both rare honors of which Slobogin is the only dual-recipient. Before joining the faculty at Vanderbilt, Slobogin taught at the University of Florida Levin College of Law, Stanford Law School, University of Frankfurt's law school in Germany and the University of Kiev, Ukraine, where he was a Fulbright Scholar. He earned his A.B. from Princeton University, and his J.D. and LL.M from the University of Virginia School of Law.

Bradley A. Smith is the Josiah H. Blackmore II/Shirley M. Nault Professor of Law at Capital University Law School in Columbus, Ohio. He is one of the nation's top experts on election law and campaign finance, co-authoring the casebook *Voting Rights & Election Law* (3d ed. 2020). Smith's scholarship has appeared in the *Yale Law Review, George Mason Law Review, Harvard Journal of Law & Public Policy, George Washington Law Review,* and an earlier volume of the *Cato Supreme Court Review.* His commentary has appeared in the *Wall Street Journal, New York Times, Los Angeles Times, Washington Post,* and *The Atlantic.* In 2000, President Bill Clinton appointed Smith to the Federal Election Commission, where he served for five years, including as chairman. In addition to Capital Law School, Smith served on the faculty of West Virginia University and George Mason University School of Law. He was also a James Madison Fellow in the

Department of Politics at Princeton University. Smith holds a B.A. from Kalamazoo College, a J.D. from Harvard Law School, and an honorary doctorate from Augustana College.

Sam Spiegelman is a legal associate at the Cato Institute's Robert A. Levy Center for Constitutional Studies, where he specializes in takings and land-use law and writes frequently on housing policy. He has co-authored amicus briefs before the Supreme Court and several federal courts of appeals. His legal and policy commentary has appeared in *Reason*, *The Hill*, and *Los Angeles Daily News*, among others. Before Cato, Spiegelman practiced securities and corporate law at an international firm in New York City and served as a judicial intern for Judge Viktor V. Pohorelsky on the U.S. District Court for the Eastern District of New York. He earned his B.A. in history and political science from the University of Michigan, graduating from the honors program with a thesis on Jewish American history, and sojourning at the University of Oxford, where he completed courses on the politics and culture of Medieval England. Spiegelman earned his J.D. from the University of Virginia School of Law, where he was a member of the Federalist Society and served on the editorial board of the *Virginia Tax Review*.

Judge Don R. Willett has served on the U.S. Court of Appeals for the Fifth Circuit since his appointment by President Donald J. Trump in 2018. Before this, he was an associate justice of the Texas Supreme Court. Prior to joining the bench, Willett served various positions in the Bush Administration and under then-Texas Attorney General Greg Abbott (now governor). Earlier, he was in private practice with Haynes & Boone in Austin, and was a fellow with the Texas Public Policy Foundation. After law school, Willett clerked for Judge Jerre Stockton Williams on the U.S. Court of Appeals for the Fifth Circuit. He earned his B.B.A. from Baylor University and his M.A. and J.D. from Duke University.